# *PRAISE FOR* FIDEL CASTRO AND BASEBALL

"Peter Bjarkman is by far the number one American authority on Cuban baseball and the Cuban government's role in it. When I want to know something about Cuban baseball, he is the first, and only person, I call. As in all his previous works about Cuban baseball, Bjarkman dispels long-held myths. Whether or not you agree with his take on Castro's role in the development of Cuban baseball, you will find this a fascinating read."—Eric Nadel, Texas Rangers radio announcer, 2014 Winner Ford C. Frick Award, National Baseball Hall of Fame

"Peter Bjarkman deserves the largest hurrah for his exceptional research, analysis, and captivating writing style in detaching myth from reality, debunking long-established political and sporting biases, and ultimately detailing the extraordinary story of *Fidel Castro and Baseball*. It would have been easy to accept past reporting follies, or to reduce diplomatic matters to good and bad guys, and even turn a complex individual like Castro into a cartoon character. Fortunately he avoids this trap by choosing the much harder route of examining motives and 'paths not taken' with a critical but often sympathetic eye. We the reader are the wiser and better served by a book in which the conflicted nature of major league baseball's interests and those of the Cuban baseball establishment operate within the larger arena of history's judgment."—William Humber, baseball historian, 2018 inductee into the Canadian Baseball Hall of Fame

"Peter Bjarkman's *Fidel Castro and Baseball* navigates the complex dynamics of Castro, baseball, and Cuban-American relations with authority and attitude. The author provides context, flavor, and history—and debunks myths—with fervor and passion."—Todd Radom, author and graphic designer for professional sports teams and events

"Misconceptions, often willful, abound about Cuba. With the recent opening to that nation, now's the time to set the record straight. Given baseball's central place in its culture, the sport provides a revealing window into the real Cuba. To understand baseball's role in post-revolutionary Cuba, few people are as qualified as Peter Bjarkman to capture the story, given his long years immersed in the sport on the island nation. In this book, he exposes the myths and illuminates the realities behind Fidel Castro's own baseball prospects, his revolutionary uses for the sport, and Cuban baseball's professional-to-amateur transition. Bjarkman provides the first, detailed account of baseball in Cuba after the revolution (and in its current status today) while also demystifying Castro and his revolutionary objectives. This is a well-written, compelling story, filled with surprising anecdotes. Highly recommended."—Robert Elias, author of *The Empire Strikes Out* and *Baseball and the American Dream*

"For nearly three decades Peter C. Bjarkman has been the preeminent English-language interpreter of the magic and mystery of Cuban baseball. Reaching beyond the romance and the rhythms of the island, he has been our guide to the passion, pride, and religious devotion to a different kind of game, one long hidden from U.S. fans just 90 miles off their own shores. In his latest effort, perhaps his most important to date, Bjarkman blends that unique knowledge in an uncompromising work that refutes some of the most durable myths about the Cuban game and its chief benefactor, Fidel Castro."— Kevin Baxter, sports writer, *Los Angeles Times*

"Like an ace hurler on the mound, Bjarkman certainly has 'great stuff!' He fires off and deliverers a masterful, precise, and thoroughly-researched chronology of the *real story* of Fidel Castro's Cuba and baseball. Dispelling decades-old misinformation, Bjarkman enlightens readers to the truth. This one bats 1.000!"—Byron Motley, author and photographer of *Embracing Cuba*

# FIDEL CASTRO AND BASEBALL

## *The Untold Story*

**Peter C. Bjarkman**

ROWMAN & LITTLEFIELD
Lanham • Boulder • New York • London

Published by Rowman & Littlefield
An imprint of The Rowman & Littlefield Publishing Group, Inc.
4501 Forbes Boulevard, Suite 200, Lanham, Maryland 20706
www.rowman.com

Unit A, Whitacre Mews, 26-34 Stannary Street, London SE11 4AB

British Library Cataloguing in Publication Information Available

**Library of Congress Cataloging-in-Publication Data**

Names: Bjarkman, Peter C., author.
Title: Fidel Castro and baseball : the untold story / Peter C. Bjarkman.
Description: Lanham, Maryland : Rowman & Littlefield, [2019] | Includes bibliographical references and index.
Identifiers: LCCN 2018025364 (print) | LCCN 2018026520 (ebook) | ISBN 9781538110317 (electronic) | ISBN 9781538110300 (cloth : alk. paper)
Subjects: LCSH: Baseball—Cuba—History. | Sports and state—Cuba—History. | Castro, Fidel, 1926–2016.
Classification: LCC GV863.25.A1 (ebook) | LCC GV863.25.A1 B53 2019 (print) | DDC 796.35709729/1—dc23
LC record available at https://lccn.loc.gov/2018025364

∞™ The paper used in this publication meets the minimum requirements of American National Standard for Information Sciences Permanence of Paper for Printed Library Materials, ANSI/NISO Z39.48-1992.

Printed in the United States of America

To Ismael Sené Alegret

*"If there is any objection to be made about the truthful-ness of this history, it can only be that its author was an [American], and it is a well-known feature of [Americans] that they are all liars; but since they are such enemies of ours, it's to be supposed that he fell short of the truth rather than exaggerating it."—adapted from Miguel de Cervantes Saavedra,* Don Quixote

# CONTENTS

Acknowledgments ix

Prologue: A Rationale xv

**PART I: THE MYTHS** 1

**1** "History Will Absolve Me" 3

**2** Baseball's Most Outrageous Myth 31

**3** The Infamous "Barbudos" Game 57

**PART II: THE TRANSFORMATION** 87

**4** Sugar Barons and Sugar Kings, and the Death of Cuba's
Professional Baseball 89

**5** The Grand Socialist Baseball Experiment 129

**6** The Other Big Red Machine and Cuba's Dominance of
International Baseball 169

**PART III: THE LEGACY** 205

**7** The Fictional Personas of Fidel Castro 207

**8** The Cuban Baseball Defectors Phenomenon 237

**9** The Ultimate Collapse of Cuban Baseball 277

Notes 319

Sources Cited and Suggested Further Readings 345

Index 355

About the Author 363

# ACKNOWLEDGMENTS

The author of a book always gets to say the last word. This is probably unfair to Castro (but fortunate for me), since his disputatious mind would surely find some plausible reply for each criticism I offer.—Lee Lockwood, *Castro's Cuba, Cuba's Castro* [1]

This book is a product (and in many ways a culmination) of more than 20 years and almost 50 trips to the Communist nation of Cuba. Like my recent volume on the Cuban baseball defectors phenomenon, *Cuba's Baseball Defectors: The Inside Story* (2016), it is an attempt to explain the past half-century of Cuba's remarkable baseball history. It is also a major amplification and, in numerous places, a much-needed correction of articles and chapters I have earlier published in print or online detailing Fidel Castro's unique relationship with the national sport of his island nation. It is my effort at having the last word, while at the same time being fully aware (as was Lee Lockwood) that the "last word in a book is not necessarily the last word on the subject."

Truth in advertising requires a revelation here that unlike many frequent travelers to the island, I never met Fidel Castro personally or even came face-to-face with the Cuban leader—only once glimpsed him in the flesh from afar during the massive December 6, 1999, Elian González protest march along the seafront Malecón. I share this distinction of never meeting the Cuban leader with his most important English-language biographer, Robert Quirk. Nonetheless, I did enjoy contact with some family members (especially Antonio Castro) and the major baseball figures from the final decades of Fidel's presence. Those baseball connections were often tenuous—quite intimate with those on the lower rungs of the political and social ladder (i.e., ballplayers, journalists, radio and television commentators, stadium security personnel, and, most importantly, fans) but sometimes rather strained with higher-ranking personnel (provincial and national INDER sports ministry officials, national team security staff, and a pair of long-serving presidents of the Cuban Baseball Federation, Cuba's equivalent of the baseball commissioner).

Carlitos Rodríguez (1997–2007) was always warm and cordial, and demonstrated his faith that I was an important friend of Cuban baseball. Higinio Vélez (2006–2017), by contrast, always seemed resentful and suspicious of my presence as an American (i.e., enemy) outsider whose motives could never be above serious suspicion. Given how many times Cuban baseball officials were burned in the end by their good-faith trust in American journalists, I always understood and even sympathized with the doubt under which I most often fell.

I have often been asked if I had met Fidel, and the fact that I did not of course remains my single greatest regret—perhaps the only one—of two decades on the ground in Cuba. But I always respond to that inquiry by replying that although I never saw the comandante up close and personal, I was nonetheless certain he had seen me, thanks to two early and groundbreaking appearances of mine on Cuban national television in 2001 and 2003. On those occasions—a pair of interviews with veteran Havana sportscaster Carlos Hernández Luján aired on Cubavisión Internacional—I was the first American allowed to extensively voice personal assessments of the Cuban pastime, its national team successes, and the qualities of domestic league play. Known for his obsessive micromanaging, Fidel had to be watching.

※ ※ ※

My Cuban sojourn and efforts at unraveling Cuban baseball for a North American audience has been a journey with many accomplices and ardent supporters along the way. Everyone cannot be mentioned here, but a full baker's dozen need to be singled out for my special indebtedness.

Ronnie Bring Wilbur, my life's partner, has remained from first to last my greatest supporter, cheerleader, and sharp-eyed critic. She has tolerated endless trips and infinite hours at my office computer with good cheer and the faith that I was doing something truly important. A world-ranking scholar in her own right, she remains my hero and biggest inspiration.

Ismael Sené was my first baseball contact in Cuba and has, for two decades, remained my greatest champion on the island. The countless hours spent watching and debating the Cuban game with Havana's leading expert have been indispensable to whatever knowledge and insights I have stumbled on throughout the years.

Ray Otero, the dynamo behind Cuban baseball's most important online presence, gave me a forum for much of my work during the past full decade. Ray has tirelessly built and maintained the leading Cuban baseball website (BaseballdeCuba.com) with no reward in mind aside from providing others with access long hidden from American fans. One of my proudest accomplishments has been assisting him in that effort.

Mark Rucker originally opened the door to Cuba with his inspired idea of traveling there in 1996, as part of a groundbreaking research venture resulting in the much-praised book *Smoke: The Romance and Lore of Cuban Baseball*. It was that book that launched my own obsessions with Cuba.

Ernest "Kit" Krieger ("El Jefe") has played his own vital role in promoting Cuban baseball for North American audiences via his "Cubaball" tours—annual visits taking hundreds of Canadian and American aficionados to the island since 2001, for the purpose of viewing Cuban baseball and Cuban ballparks firsthand. Kit has played a major role in reshaping the image of *Yanquis* within Cuba itself, and also in tearing down the thick veil of misunderstandings surrounding this safest, most beautiful, and friendliest among Caribbean nations.

Clem Axel Paredes, Kit's "Cubaball" partner in recent years, has proven to be not only a valued companion in travels around the island on a half-dozen journeys but also has shared a vital role in Krieger's mission of building bridges between two baseball-loving nations.

Antonio "Tony" Castro (Fidel's son, long-time Cuban national baseball team doctor, and an important figure in international baseball administration) has been generous with his time, his displays of friendship, and his support for an inquisitive Yanqui outsider who might easily have raised serious suspicions with such a frequent presence in Cuba and around the Cuban national team on road trips in Latin America, Europe, and Asia.

Martin Hacthoun was another valued companion and outstanding journalist who provided support and opened doors during the first decade of my Cuban travels. Unfortunately, Martin spent much of the last decade on duty with Prensa Latina in Vietnam, India, Syria, and Argentina, and he was definitely missed during recent visits to Havana.

Eddie Artiles proved for more than a decade to be an invaluable guide, an important early contact with ballplayers in Havana, and above all a trusted and irreplaceable friend. Eddie was my dependable driver on numerous visits to Pinar, Sanctí Spíritus, and Santa Clara, and always kept me well supplied with the best of Cuban street food en route to dozens of ballparks throughout the Cuban countryside.

Carlitos Rodríguez, Cuban League commissioner from 1997 to 2007, showed unusual trust in a North American interloper. It was Carlitos who first grasped and championed my mission in Cuba and opened an important early door with other Cuban baseball authorities.

Robert Weinstein facilitated my legal Cuba travel between 2001 and his unfortunate death in 2009, and for nine years shared the Cuban adventure on the ground in Havana. Bob's interests as a former minor-league ballclub owner were focused on possible future business and investment opportunities in an evolving Cuban economy, but he was also never far from the baseball scene.

Numerous Cuban ballplayers—especially slugger Freddie Cepeda, manager Victor Mesa, pitcher Yosvany Aragón (later special assistant to the baseball commissioner), pitcher Freddie Asiel Alvarez, and the late pitcher Yadier Pedroso—provided hospitality, unique insiders' views, and, most importantly, genuine friendship. Cepeda opened his home on the island and also opened the *"amistad"* of so many teammates. The charismatic Victor Mesa, Cuba's most colorful and controversial manager of the past decade, championed my repeated presence as a "friend of Cuban baseball," and his support richly enhanced my status on the island.

Christen Karniski, my editor for this book as well as my earlier Rowman & Littlefield tome on the Cuban baseball defectors phenomenon, demonstrated the support for and faith in my work, which has led to my two most important publications.

Finally, a tip of the baseball cap to numerous correspondents, readers, and faceless Facebook "friends" in the South Florida Cuban exile community—some known and others not—most of whom will likely hate this book when they see its cover, but some of whom, at least, might learn something new if they venture to turn its pages.

# PROLOGUE: A RATIONALE

There has never been a case in which a head of state has been involved so prominently and for such a long period in a nation's favored sport as Fidel Castro has been with baseball in Cuba.—
Roberto González Echevarría, *The Pride of Havana*[1]

Roberto González Echevarría's *The Pride of Havana* offers arguably the most thoroughgoing and enlightening history of Cuba's national pastime during the 10 decades preceding Fidel Castro's 1959 socialist revolution. Yet, skimpy and certainly less-than-merited attention is paid in that volume to the game's evolution after Fidel's surprising rise to power and subsequent adoption of a socialist-inspired and amateur-oriented baseball model. González Echevarría's treatment of the island nation's favored sport unaccountably gives rather short shrift to the weightiest and most intriguing chapter of Cuba's baseball story—those recent decades during which the island sport emerged from a diminished role as satellite to North America's professional game and arrived at the forefront of late-twentieth-century world amateur competitions. And yet the Yale literature professor does strike a true chord when he points to an unparalleled connection between Latin America's most important socialist revolutionary leader and the island's remarkable passion for the sport of bats and balls.[2]

González Echevarría—a Cuban American exile whose displaced family suffered the pain of a Cuban diaspora resulting from Castro's revolutionary transformation of their homeland—rather reluctantly observes that no parallels might be found for Fidel's unique intercourse with baseball. The author of *The Pride of Havana* is forced to concede that only rather ludicrous hypothetical comparisons might be imagined for such a phenomenon. One such fantastic stretch of the mind would be to envision Francisco Franco deeply committed to the fortunes of Spanish bullfighting and thus frequently donning the *"traje de luces"* for occasional ceremonial appearances. Just as easily dismissed are other possible lame comparisons, for instance, Juan Perón taking legitimate interest in Argentinian soccer, Pérez Jimenez dedicated to the fate of Venezuelan Olympic teams, or Anastasio Somoza controlling the reins of the Nicaraguan national baseball team. For one thing, none of those comparable political strongmen lasted as long as Castro; for another, "neither soccer in Argentina, Olympic sports in Venezuela, nor baseball in Nicaragua have developed in relation to a nearby political and cultural power such as the United States and an institution like Organized Baseball."[3]

In essence, the lapse might be easy enough to explain if not to dismiss. González Echevarría also rather astutely notes that "so many controversies have surrounded the Cuban Revolution that few have taken notice or given serious thought to this phenomenon."[4] Despite acknowledging that such oversight of Fidel's central role in shaping modern-era Cuban baseball is certainly no trivial matter, the Cervantes scholar—here turned baseball historian devoted to the notion that Cuban baseball largely died after 1960—unfortunately gives the subject only the briefest of inspections in his own landmark book. One of Cuban baseball's most significant stories—indeed perhaps its most significant "untold" story—therefore continues to search for a long-overdue serious treatment.

Fidel's unparalleled baseball activities are indeed a legitimate subject that has almost entirely escaped the iconic Cuban leader's multitude of serious scholarly biographers and numerous popular press portrayers. Unfortunately, however, Fidel's misconstrued baseball connection has occasionally turned up as an entertaining reference point for North American sportscasters and even lent itself to the imaginations of novelists and spinners of fictional accounts involving the late twentieth century's most illustrious communist dictator. It most often takes shape as the surprising image of a young fastball-hurling future rebel leader and U.S. Cold War nemesis tantalizing big-league scouts with his high, hard ones and yet somehow escaping a professional career on the di-

**FASTBALL OR CURVEBALL.** Fidel heaves a ceremonial first pitch to open an early 1960s youth amateur world championship tournament in Havana. *From the author's collection*

amond that might have cancelled out his future role as prickly thorn in the side of Washington politicians.

The enticing legend of "Fidel Castro, Hot Big-League Prospect" often turns up in surprising places. One of the more concise and insightful historical overviews of American efforts to first forestall the populist rebellion against Fulgencio Batista and later unseat Castro once he took power is somehow diminished in scholarly credibility when its author, Thomas Paterson, falls prey to repeating the irresistible Fidel ball-playing saga. To quote Paterson directly:

> Fidel Castro himself had earned some baseball notoriety by the late
> 1940s. North American major-league scouts noticed his considerable
> pitching talents for the University of Havana baseball team. Known
> for "a wicked *bleeping* curveball," Castro seemed a good prospect for
> professional baseball in the United States. "He could set 'em up with
> the curve, blow 'em down with the heater," recalled a scout for the

Pittsburgh Pirates. But because his fastball was not overpowering, Castro became known as a "smart" player who kept batters guessing. In a November 1948 game against a team of touring major leaguers, Castro struck out the All-Star Hank Greenberg and gave up only three hits and no runs.[5]

The misconceptions and distortions here are legion. Presumably a careful scholar on U.S.–Cuban relations, Paterson certainly didn't apply the same rigor when it came to what he must have seen as less weighty topics like baseball. He here cites the infamous article by J. David Truby published in both *Sports History II* (March 1989) and later *Harper's Magazine* as the source for his Howie Haak quote (the scout for the Pittsburgh Pirates he refers to). The absurdities of Truby's article are taken up in chapter 2 of this book. But there is also reason to doubt Paterson's text on other counts. Castro biographer Robert Quirk, reviewing the book in the *Journal of American History*, dismisses Paterson's work as a failure to access admittedly scarce Spanish-language sources and also condemns the lack of wider knowledge of Cuban events, forcing the author to weaken his assessments of Fidel's motives, intentions, and thoughts with such qualifiers as "perhaps," "probably," or "must have." He also faults Paterson for buying into the myth of Fidel as a great athlete and, in particular, underscores the error regarding pitching to Hank Greenberg.[6]

At the supposed time of the incident (November 1948), Fidel was actually honeymooning with his new bride in New York. There is also no record of any such barnstorming visit to Cuba by Greenberg that winter or fall. The one such team including big-leaguers to visit the island that offseason was a group of mostly Negro National League stars organized by Alex Pompez, and current and future big-leaguers included on that tour were black stars Jackie Robinson, Roy Campanella, Monte Irvin, George Crowe, and Pat Scantlebury. To boot, Greenberg's final season as a big-leaguer was 1947.

Paterson's highly unreliable sources for such dubious reporting thus appear to be the same small handful frequently cited by others prone to shoddy fact-checking of the kind that might be surprising enough from novice baseball scribes but far less acceptable in the work of serious political historians. Ironically, Paterson is one of the few Fidel specialists to report on any baseball connections whatsoever, but he bungles the job by relying on spurious accounts so easily dismantled by actual fact (as demonstrated in chapter 2). One is the historically unfounded popular *Sports* magazine tale penned by former big-leaguer Don Hoak. The second is a short *Harper's* piece offered by an apparently gullible interviewer of then-septuagenarian Pirates scout Howie Haak who had whipped up a fantastic tale as mind-bending as the one dreamed up by Hoak.

❖ ❖ ❖

It is perhaps needless to stress that Cuba's indomitable leader for more than six Cold War decades is one of the most important and controversial political and historical figures of the modern era. Such claims seem redundant after such a mountainous literature debating the legacy of the controversial Cuban revolutionary leader. As a rare Fidel champion in the North American press, Herbert Matthews correctly contends as early as the first decade of Castro's remarkably long reign—one whose grip has not yet been loosened in his native land more than a decade after declining health and eventual death transferred leadership to younger brother Raúl—that the Cuban leader was without doubt the most important single figure of Latin American political history.[7] Even less-than-sympathetic biographer Georgie Anne Geyer would much later note (writing two full decades after Matthews) that on the 30th anniversary of the Cuban Revolution's initial triumph, Fidel still remained the most prominent "romantic revolutionary hero of the twentieth century."[8]

Matthews also struck a resounding chord in arguing in the immediate aftermath of Fidel's miraculous rise to power, that the Cuban leader's personal aura and makeup was indeed so complicated and shrouded in self-created mystery that no one could adequately capture the entire Fidel, and such a cogent observation has proven true in a subsequent half-century of scholarly attention to the Cuban Revolution and its extraordinary leader. Opinions on Fidel are, to a large degree, biased, as Matthews so long ago stressed. They depend entirely on the orientation of the viewer.[9] As the first Latin American figure in any field to achieve worldwide fame during his lifetime, he remains one of the most worshipped yet vilified figures of his century.

There is no middle ground on Fidel, just as there is no middle ground on the highly disruptive social revolution he brought to his island nation. For many, especially in Latin America and throughout long-exploited Third World nations, Fidel Castro is an unmatched hero. Such also remains true in Cuba itself, even if the luster and enthusiasm of the promised revolutionary dream has faded in the aftermath of collapsing Soviet economic aid, decades of public and personal sacrifice, and the eventual social and economic attrition caused, in large part, by a half-century-long U.S. economic embargo. Still, for millions of Cubans who stayed at home after the revolutionary upheaval there was much to be thankful for.

Fidel overthrew the most vicious dictatorship in the history of a country that had largely known nothing but oppressive and corrupt regimes. He and his July 26th Movement brought substantial lifestyle upgrades for lower-class Cuban peasants and laborers who previously had little or nothing to enrich their desperate existence. And perhaps most important of all to so many Cubans long suffering from a lengthy history of abuse at the hands of Spanish and North American colonial overlords, Fidel, almost overnight, made his small island nation a significant and highly unexpected "player" on a U.S.–Soviet-dominated Cold War stage.

Throughout the years, Fidel would not only emerge as an ingenious tactician and dedicated author of change in his homeland, but also prove remarkably durable to forces aimed at his eradication. He would survive numerous direct assassination attempts at the hands of U.S. operatives.[10] He would escape plans for a North American invasion (some only recently revealed with the 2017 release of long-sealed Kennedy administration documents). He would repel a direct invasion at the Bay of Pigs that cemented support at home and represented one of the largest blunders of U.S. foreign policy during the modern era. He would survive direct conflicts with his adopted Soviet masters and, while depending on the Russians for economic survival, never relinquish to them or the international Communist Party any control of his steadfastly Cuban-flavored nationalistic revolutionary movement. He would survive the collapse of the Soviet bloc and much of the Cold War Communist bloc, and also the Special Period of economic deprivation Soviet collapse imparted on Cuban society. He would only be felled eventually by the unavoidable forces of aging and the associated onset of physical incapacity during his ninth decade. Even then, he would successfully pass the torch to his brother and the political machinery he left behind, and his somewhat debilitated but still-standing revolutionary government would continue to limp on after his death.

The newly entrenched Cuban leader also repeatedly escaped numerous attempts to oust him from control via counterrevolutionary activities on the home front. Counterrevolutionary groups operated in the Cuban countryside in the months immediately following Batista's ouster, and acts of sabotage created tension in the capital city; such sporadic outbreaks (mostly isolated, minor explosions) would provide convenient excuse for North American professional baseball to cease its minor-league and winter-league operations on the island in 1960 (see chapter 4). While the most severe early threat to the new regime was the Washington-backed Bay of Pigs invasion attempt of April 1961, that CIA-sponsored plan was based, in large part, on a miscalculation that counterrevolutionary forces were indeed strong and could be relied upon to rally behind the exile invasion forces. Biographer Peter Bourne also reports on CIA efforts to recruit Mafia aid in "eliminating" the new and unsavory Cuban leader with increasing troublesome communist leanings. [11] But always Fidel survived and always only seemed to grow stronger in the aftermath.

For avowed opponents, ideological detractors, the bulk of American politicians devoted to anti-communism and American exceptionalism, and, above all, Cuban exile communities centered mostly in South Florida, Fidel steadfastly remained throughout the decades the ultimate personification of pure evil and the central tragic manifestation of unwavering, lifelong hatred. American policy on Cuba has continued to echo a single theme—no change in U.S.–Cuba relations can occur until the island is completely free of any leaders carrying the name Castro. [12] As I earlier stated the case in *Cuba's Baseball Defectors*, for Americans whose politics tip heavily to the right, "Castro's indefatigable if tarnished empire is the last vestige of a much-despised and brutal communist regime, long fantasized to be a serious threat to American-style democracy." [13] Even in the wake of Fidel's death and a new American administration, this obsession has hardly abated, especially in view of recent unsubstantiated Washington charges of supposed Cuban government "sonic attacks" on U.S. Embassy personnel in Havana and a stark reversal by the Trump administration of Obama's efforts at opening a new era of American–Cuban cooperation.

Of course, all revolutions create considerable upheaval, as eloquently observed by Herbert Matthews, and the Cuban Revolution destroyed
the nation's middle class, caused thousands to lose either their lives or
their personal freedoms in opposition to the new regime, and millions
more to be cast into resentful exile on foreign shores.[14] Castro's revolution brought with it one of the great diasporas of the past century. For
the U.S. government, which for the most part was motivated at the time
of Fidel's rebellion against Batista by an overriding desperation to pro-
tect North American business interests and an obsessive paranoia about
the spread of world communism, Castro and his rebellion became and
has since remained a lasting Cold War–era obsession. That obsession
quickly peaked with the 1962 Cuban Missile Crisis and, for the half-
century that followed, lived on as an anachronistic and clearly failed
effort to unseat the Cuban strongman. It would provide a misguided
U.S. foreign policy that did nothing to foster political change or return
Cuba to its prerevolutionary state. It only underscored Matthews's early
1960s observation that "Castro or no Castro," the Cuban Revolution of
1959 was an event that could never be successfully reversed.

❊ ❊ ❊

Fidel's baseball coin has been tarnished on both sides and was from the
outset. If the ball-playing prospect was pure mythology, the image of
Cuban baseball destroyer was very much the same kind of ruthless
fabrication. The former notion quickly evolved into a half-serious joke,
ideal for bringing the archenemy down to human size, while poking fun
at both the self-important dictator and those bosses of capitalism who
repeatedly bungled efforts to neutralize him. The second took on its
own life as a favored crutch for bitter enemies in the South Florida exile
community, gripped tightly alongside the other indispensable twin
mantras—that Fidel Castro had betrayed the original revolution he
promised and that he had been an avowed Marxist from the start. The
first side of the coin distorts Fidel's true underlying interests in his
country's national pastime, while the second ignores his immense contribution to Cuba's important baseball saga.

Fidel's full-scale impact on baseball in his homeland is, in fact, just
as undeniable, but also just as controversial as his more celebrated role
on a larger stage of domestic and international politics. The loss of

professional baseball on the island during the summer of 1960 (relocation of the minor-league Havana Sugar Kings franchise) and also at the
end of the subsequent winter-league season (closing of the four-team
Havana circuit after 73 seasons) brought unanticipated opportunities
for revamping the national sport within the envisioned framework of a
new revolutionary society. Fidel himself would be the clear architect of
that rather immense evolution of Cuba's sporting culture. The events
attached to the transition of the Cuban national pastime are yet another
example of how Fidel's revolution was always clearly a work in progress,
an ever-evolving flux, more the result of unexpected necessity than any
long-range planning. Each step in drastically overhauling Cuban society
after January 1959 ultimately resulted from unplanned and unanticipated opportunities suddenly arising in the aftermath of circumstances
most often attributable to a surrounding political landscape. Baseball
was hardly an exception.

The surviving and cherished view, of course, is that Fidel destroyed
baseball in Cuba in the wake of his 1959 revolution. That was a popular
theme struck once again in the North American press at the time of
Castro's long-anticipated but long-delayed death in late November
2016. The familiar theme was echoed by César Brioso in a USA Today
response to Fidel's ultimate demise.[15] This persistent stance was earlier
heavily promoted by Roberto González Echevarría (The Pride of Havana) and Milton Jamail (Full Count) in their treatments of Cuban baseball in the final year of the twentieth century, with Fidel still in power.

But Fidel's role was, at best, only an indirect one, and at least regarding the minor-league Sugar Kings franchise, there is every piece of
evidence that he actively worked to keep the beleaguered ballclub on
Cuban soil. An aversion to professional sport and an outspoken distaste
for contact with the American big leagues would emerge more as a
forced response than any originally held motive (see chapter 4). Events
surrounding his revolution and resulting immediate harsh opposition
from Washington provided an environment that appeared to threaten
vested interests of Organized Baseball, just as they threatened all
American business operations in Cuba. But, surprisingly, baseball was
one "business connection" Fidel seemed bent on maintaining, at least
until his hand was finally forced. In the end, it was the International
League and Major League Baseball that closed down existing Cuban
connections by the summer of 1960 and early winter of 1961. A new

Fidel-inspired version of Cuban national baseball was much more an unavoidable result than any premeditated cause of the disappearance of an American-sponsored professional game.

Those who take the view that Castro alone killed baseball in Havana are those who also see baseball as little more than a professional brand linked to the MLB model. No matter where responsibility lies for the demise of the Sugar Kings, or the idle dream of a possible Havana big-league franchise looming on the horizon, the unavoidable truth is that baseball as a viable enterprise did not end under Fidel's tightened grip in the early 1960s, nor did it disappear from the scene once the American-sponsored version closed up shop. It only changed its stripes or redefined its missions, becoming more a popular social institution than a profit-generating business. If anything, it expanded, strengthened, and became more closely linked to Cuban nationalism and Cuban pride than ever before.

The INDER-sponsored National Series, launched in 1962, quickly expanded (from an original four clubs to a dozen by the end of the first decade and 17 by the end of the second) to spread high-level competition throughout the island. Top-notch baseball spectacles were no longer restricted to four clubs entertaining admission-paying fans in Havana and employing as many or more foreign imports than native Cuban stars. The new league was by every measure Cuban-flavored, a reflection of the country's long-overdue, jealous control of its own resources. If the players were labelled "amateur" and played for patriotic ideals more so than lucrative salaries, they were still, of course, professionals in other senses—their professionalism measured by their full-time dedication to their craft and not the size of their paychecks. American naysayers would, in fact, repeatedly complain throughout the next several decades that the Cubans were using pros and not amateurs on their national squads, oftentimes embarrassing American teams in top-level international competitions (see chapters 6 and 9).

Cuban national squads under the new regime became stronger than ever, and Cuba's image as an international power on the world stage would soon far outstrip an already hefty reputation earned on international diamonds in earlier years (Cuba having dominated the first half-dozen Amateur World Series tournaments of the World War II era). By the time once strictly amateur international tournament baseball adopted wooden bats and welcomed pros from all nations (both events occurring in 1999), Cuban players were better than ever, and if there were more intense competitions and thus reduced dominance for the Cubans, nonetheless the powerhouse Fidel had built and sustained with his often-hands-on support was just peaking with its true golden age. Massive island television audiences for a first MLB-sponsored World Baseball Classic in 2006, and the wild celebrations throughout the country when the Cubans reached the showdown finals versus the Japanese pro-league all-stars in San Diego, far outstripped any baseball-related event in the island nation's history. These developments would hardly suggest baseball was moribund in Cuba. Fidel had done anything but kill the national sport. He had only taken it out of the hands of American corporate ownership.

That contemporary Cuban players (those who are true products of baseball on the island) are superior to those of any earlier generations has been fully demonstrated in the wake of massive player defections during the past decade. Recent island-trained Cuban big-leaguers like José Abreu, Aroldis Chapman, Yoenis Céspedes, Yulieski Gurriel, Yasiel Puig, Orlando and Liván Hernández, and a handful more have far outstripped the achievements and impact of such early and mid-twentieth century Cuban second-level stars as Miñoso, Pascual, Ramos, Versalles, or even Adolfo Luque. Later twentieth-century Cubans the likes of Tany Pérez, Miguel Cuéllar, Tony Oliva, José Canseco, or Rafael Palmeiro cannot be considered part of the equation here since although born on the island, they are products of training in the North American system and not escapees from the Cuban baseball culture.

An additional criticism of Fidel's baseball obsession cites its use for promoting advantages of Cuba's revamped Marxist society. This was the accusation that Fidel had "politicized the sport" with the creation of INDER in 1962, and his forced linkage of the game to his revolution and its radical goals. But this again is a frivolous charge on at least two counts. Baseball had been directly connected to displays of Cuban nationalism decades before the arrival of Fidel Castro. Baseball jingoism was never more blatantly on display than it was with the adamant focus on Cuban team victories over American barnstormers during the first decade of the twentieth century. Wins in the so-called "American Seasons" of those early years (which saw Cuban league teams facing American barnstorming squads, often vacationing big-leaguers), played against the backdrop of an unpopular U.S. military occupation, were heavily political in tone. And those victories were responsible for creating the island's earliest stars, for example, José de la Caridad Méndez (author of a string of scoreless innings on the mound against the visiting Cincinnati Reds) and Cristóbal Torriente (who struck three memorable homers to outperform Babe Ruth and the visiting New York Giants in 1920). Both pioneering Afro-Cubans would belatedly reach Cooperstown immortality in 2006, mostly on the strength of legendary feats authored against the visiting Americans. And Roberto González Echevarría, in *The Pride of Havana*, records that Méndez's 1908 fall heroics stand as one of the great achievements of Cuban baseball history and lore precisely "not only because he had trounced the major leaguers, proving that Cuban baseball was as good as any, but also because he had done it during the American occupation of the island."[16]

And on a second front, charges of politicizing baseball would have to be equally levied at the Americans themselves, at MLB, in particular (with its ballpark pregame military flyovers, patriotic seventh-inning-stretch hymns, and Old Glory team jersey flag patches), and at other nations devoted to the sport—especially those in Asia and most particularly Japan. Early on, baseball became directly connected with American imperialism, as demonstrated in fine detail by author Robert Elias in *The Empire Strikes Out: How Baseball Sold U.S. Foreign Policy and Promoted the American Way Abroad* (2010). The American national pastime grew up with militaristic overtones, and the story of American baseball's own foreign policy agendas and historic role in promoting U.S. diplomatic, military, and globalization policies is, as Elias rightfully emphasizes, the most overlooked corner of the sport's history.[17] The Japanese, Koreans, and Taiwanese followed this American model once they adopted their own versions of the so-called American pastime, and the theme of Asian "politicization" of the sport is also eloquently elaborated by Joseph Reaves in *Taking in a Game: A History of Baseball in Asia* (2002). Hence, baseball has a history in many nations as an instrument for spreading a country's ingrained sets of values and traditions, as well as their cherished forms of economics, politics, and government. In using baseball to spread the image of his new socialist society, Fidel was only rather ironically following the well-established American model.

And pervading this negativity is the widely popularized model of the young Fidel as a rising and self-deluded baseball prospect. It is an image usually presented with a hardy dose of skepticism and a distinct tone of sarcasm—"if he was such a baseball fanatic, then perhaps we should make him a more palatable czar, as baseball commissioner" or "he may not have owned a big-league fastball but he sure has been heaving political curveballs at us ever since" and so forth. This myth was not only very much a historical distortion of strictly North American origins, but also always used to treat the Cuban leader (and Cuban revolutionary society in general) in the most negative or demeaning possible light. It was largely a form of belittling Fidel and bringing him down to earth—it implied that his true passions were, nevertheless, tied to our own American game, and it was there (if not in larger political arenas) that we could dismiss him as a failure ("no true big-league fastball" after all). Reports of the July 1959 "Barbudos" pitching exhibition—with observations that an intimidated umpire was forced to call strikes with every limp delivery the comandante tossed at the plate—are one solid example. So is the tongue-in-cheek essay by former senator Eugene McCarthy in *Elysian Fields Quarterly* and the cartoon-style imitation baseball card cover that accompanied it (see chapter 3).

Among early commentators on the Cuban Revolution, Herbert Matthews and Lee Lockwood both observed the unfortunate and always slanted treatment of Fidel and his revolution by the North American press. Matthews goes so far as to charge that the "press coverage of the Cuban Revolution is the worst failure in the history of American journalism."[18] Lockwood laments that American press coverage of Fidel was from the outset "woefully inadequate" since "it reports only the negative aspects."[19] These were charges made decades in the past. Yet, they underscore a pattern that has continued largely unabated to the present. To speak well of Fidel or his revolution, especially in a public forum, is to invite hostility, a harsh truth learned several years back by Miami Marlins manager Ozzie Guillen.[20] The Maximum Leader's baseball connections and baseball adventures provide a special lightning rod. Justin Turner's useful 2012 doctoral dissertation, *Baseball Diplomacy, Baseball Deployment: The National Pastime in U.S.–Cuba Relations*, cites a litany of American press articles covering sham Cuban amateurism during the 1960s and MLB-backed efforts at baseball détente in the 1970s. And it is the tone in which most of these articles in either the *New York Times, Washington Post,* or *Christian Science Monitor* are crafted that is most telling.[21]

One of the most recent examples of U.S. press distortions related to Cuba lies in the treatment of Barack Obama's December 2014 announcement for a planned détente with the continuing communist regime, now fronted by Raúl Castro. There was precious little reporting on the Cuban interests in the matter or views concerning implications of such a Cold War sea change. Instead, the focus was on the long-awaited dismantling of the Castro government, which had obviously ruined Cuba in the minds of the South Florida exile community, or the flood of anticipated new opportunities for lucrative American business ventures and a much-coveted tourism explosion. For what was assumed to be a majority of Americans, the long-forbidden Caribbean nation was assumed to be little more than a soon-to-be-possessed fantasy tourist destination. Lost in the immediate hoopla of a new Havana gold mine of opportunity was any appreciation of what the Cuban Revolution was originally all about or what negatives might accrue to the Cuban people by a floodtide of sudden and exploitive American capitalism. Once again, American journalists saw only the Cuba they wanted to see.

Recent changes in U.S.–Cuba Cold War relations were also badly misreported when it came to the apparently evolving relationships between Cuban Baseball Federation officials and MLB bosses. A September 2013 announcement of INDER's expanded plans for new player exchange possibilities was viewed only through a big-league business-oriented perspective. A new-style Dominican Republic replete with unfettered MLB scouting operations and the construction of dozens of big-league team-owned training academies was hopefully emerging, with no attention paid to the disasters that such activities had actually already brought to the Dominican or Venezuela. Almost no effort was made to understand the plan actually being proposed by the Cubans, one that offered no possibilities of exchanges with MLB ballclubs or anything approaching free agency for Cuban League athletes, but instead was aimed at loaning select stars to the Japanese circuit and then recouping them for domestic winter-league play. American concerns were the same as those a half-century back—the potential flood of new Cuban talent to grace big-league ballparks. Once more, we had a failure of big-league interests—including the fans who followed MLB clubs and the journalists that covered them—to distinguish the forest from the trees.

It was decades of isolation—especially the isolation of Cuban baseball—that had continued to feed such misunderstanding and, in the end, even made it possible. Writers—journalists, travel writers, and novelists among them—residing north of the Straits of Florida could make claims about Fidel or any aspect of Cuba with no real need for accuracy and no real fear of contradiction. No one could be assumed to know the difference and so any wild claim apparently stood on relatively safe ground. Even some reputable reporters boasting actual time on the ground in Cuba could seemingly have a free pass.

One brief illustration will serve the purpose here. Patrick Symmes, committed to offering a view of Castro's Cuba as a nightmare scene of desperation and despair, paints a portrait (apparently designed to shock) of a visit to Latin American Stadium in Havana that is, at best, distorted and, at worst, bad fiction.[22] The ballpark scene is first punctuated with a near-riot among drunken and combative fans, an outbreak that requires police intervention. And then a late-night return walk to his downtown hotel from the stadium grounds is marred with a near-personal assault by a menacing pack of rowdy teens from whom Symmes has to flee in pure panic. I have attended hundreds of games in that very park and also hiked from there to the city center in the late evening hours on numerous occasions and have never witnessed such scenes of horrifying violence. Indeed, Havana is unquestionably the safest city I have ever encountered.

The downside of so many such portraits of the Cuban scene is that writers (usually short-term visitors) could always assume that few Americans would ever set foot on the island to actually check out their often bias-tainted literary portraits. Exclusivity seems the perfect entrée to literary license.

✿ ✿ ✿

American misunderstanding of Fidel and his revolution has therefore been as blatant when it comes to the shared national sport of baseball as in any of the more serious reporting and popular assessments of Cold War–era U.S.–Cuba relations. This book aims to clarify this too-often cloudy and usually distorted picture by providing a more balanced and

accurate treatise on Fidel Castro's central role in the past half-century
of Cuba's baseball evolution.

Given the centrality of baseball to Cuban culture, such an account is
hardly unimportant. Four overarching themes are central to the pages
that follow. First, a dismantling of popular legends that Fidel Castro
was once seen as a serious professional pitching prospect, that he was
recruited or offered contracts by big-league scouts, or that a lost opportunity for chasing his big-league dreams rather than his revolutionary
ones might have radically changed the course of a half-century of Western Hemisphere political and societal history. Second, disproving that
Fidel was personally and solely responsible for shutting down professional baseball operations on the island and that the loss of affiliation
with Organized Baseball in 1960 doomed the Cuban version to second-
class legitimacy at best. Third, eradicating any notion that Fidel diminished Cuban baseball and Cuban sport in general by "politicizing" it in
the service of propagandizing his Marxist/socialist/communist model
and that he was somehow an unacceptable outlier in his efforts to use
baseball in this particular fashion. And finally, in the process of achieving the above ends, to further demonstrate that the reigning myths
surrounding Fidel Castro's baseball connections are in large measure
part and parcel of the overall mythology that has strenuously hidden any
lucid portrait of the important Cuban leader and his resulting revolution from the American public's view.

Four early chapters deal with literature providing a rather outsized
mythology surrounding Fidel Castro, the man and the revolutionary
hero. Chapter 1, for example, discusses how and why Fidel emerged
during the earliest years of his revolutionary struggle as a figure based
more often on self-authored legends than any factual reality. That opening chapter chiefly focuses on the early 1960s-era debates between
American journalists and Castro intimates Theodore Draper and Herbert Matthews, touching on two reigning fictions—that Fidel was actually a closet Communist long before his triumph over Batista and his
seizure of national political power, and also that as a result of that
supposed secret Marxist agenda, Fidel abandoned and distorted the
original revolution he had initially planned—one based on democracy
and increased economic prosperity, which many of his most ardent
early supporters had hoped for.

Chapters 2 and 3, in turn, explore the origins of additional myths that rapidly grew concerning Fidel's alleged ball-playing skills. The notion of a talented pitching prospect coveted by big-league scouts is debunked through carefully analysis of false (often purposely distorted) reports like that of former big-leaguer Don Hoak, which originally planted the seeds for such fictions. And details surrounding the infamous July 1959 "Barbudos" game pitching exhibition offer further evidence for how the legend spread and how it shielded, and even obscured, Fidel's far more important later baseball interests and contributions.

Chapter 4 recounts the historical details surrounding the death of professional baseball in Cuba on the heels of the 1959 overthrow of Batista and the seizure of power by Fidel and his M-26-7 rebel movement. The thrust here is to dismantle a second major falsehood claiming that Fidel was personally and even solely responsible for killing baseball on the island. But a secondary theme is the argument that even if Fidel is assigned some responsibility for the abandonment of an American-backed professional sport in Havana—it was, after all, his revolution that created an environment quickly perceived as hostile to continued MLB business interests in Havana—the era that closed in 1960 and 1961 did not represent a golden age for the Cuban sport, as is often contended. That golden age would only dawn *after* Fidel's arrival, and, in truth, Fidel himself would be its most notable author.

Chapters 5 and 6 examine in further detail the actual role Fidel played in the construction of a new Cuban baseball culture and thus elaborate precisely how that baseball culture both reflected and served a drastically revamped Cuban society. The first of these chapters reprises the Cuban domestic league from its birth with the new Law 936 of February 1961, through its peak years at century's end, and eventually on to its diminished stature after massive ballplayer defections during the past half-dozen years. The second analyzes the emergence of a Cuban national team that would dominate the international tournament scene for decades and, in the process, write a remarkable legacy of unending victories rarely matched in any other realm of either professional or amateur team sports.

Fictional accounts of Fidel's mythical baseball career have also developed a life of their own and cannot be ignored here; therefore, chapter 7 examines how those who chronicled Fidel throughout the years in both fiction and scholarly biography treated the growing myth of Fidel the serious ballplayer. Absence of any even-limited discussion of baseball interest from the bulk of Fidel's serious biographers reveals both a central notion that baseball fandom was judged insignificant in reporting on the weightier matters of Castro's uprooting of Cuban culture and the slim evidence for the future leader's ball-playing efforts during his younger years. Again, we can return to Robert González Echevarría's explanation that "so many controversies have surrounded the Cuban Revolution that few have taken notice or given serious thought" to such trivial details as Castro's baseball passions. But novelists are not historians, and for the fiction writer it is good story material that looms largest. Singled out for special attention among the fictional treatments are several novels that not only exploit the entertainment value of a Fidel ball-playing legend, but also actually detract from an existing historical record of Fidel's altogether major accomplishments in the history of his nation's baseball heritage.

The book's final two chapters explore the collapse of Fidel's baseball dream in the aftermath of his debilitating 2006 illness and a long-delayed relinquishing of power to his brother Raúl and a younger generation of Cuban revolutionary leaders. Chapter 8 revisits the subject of massive player defections from the Cuban sport brought on by developments within Cuba after 2006—a subject already treated in my earlier book, *Cuba's Baseball Defectors*—but again it is vital here to the full understanding of Fidel's baseball empire. Revealed here is the no-longer-hidden saga of scandalous human tracking activities involved in Cuban ballplayer movements and the less-than-honest stance repeatedly taken by MLB ballclubs, player agents, and top team officials regarding these unsavory events. While player defections would signal the collapse of Fidel's dream of a nonmaterialistic baseball enterprise and mark the dismantling of his showcase model of socialist baseball, they would, at the same time, underscore many of the criticisms Fidel had originally levied at the greed-driven American professional version of the game. Also not to be denied is the degree to which those same events also exposed the ultimate fatal flaws in Cuba's own once-successful baseball operations. What had initially built Fidel's once-impressive baseball empire was the very fabric that would eventually destroy it.

A final chapter explores the slow death of the Cuban national sport during the past half-dozen years. It looks at the many failed efforts in earlier decades at achieving baseball détente between two baseball-loving nations and explains why that persistent détente dream was never actually a viable possibility. The roadblock to any accord always had everything to do with the clashing motives of the two baseball institutions, which today remain as irreconcilable as ever. This final segment of the book also explores not only how and why MLB was, in the end, destined to eventually win the baseball Cold War with Cuba, but also how that victory may prove substantially a pyrrhic one.

It is important to note that this book was written by an American and not a Cuban. Nonetheless, it was written by an American with more time spent on Castro's mysterious island than all but a handful of his own countrymen. Not having grown up on that island and experienced firsthand the earliest years within revolutionary Cuba, I can only rely for my views on reports delivered by those who actually were on the scene—the champions of the revolution, as well as its fiercest opponents. This book will, of course, cause much negative reaction among those who can never accept any positive accounts touching on the homeland they left behind. I sympathize with those whose families suffered from the upheaval of the revolution. But I also reject what are oftentimes interpretations couched more in the bitterness of personal history than recent firsthand experience.

For many, the myths will always remain more comfortable than any fact-based realities. For scribes reporting baseball or penning fiction, they will always prove far more marketable. As Bob Costas once reminded me, "The myth was always appealing—Don Hoak must have sensed that."[23] Yet, I also believe in the early wisdom of Lee Lockwood, who pointed out that, "If he is really our enemy we should know as much about him as possible."[24] That effort requires distinguishing the true reality from the grandiose mythology that has become Cuba's Fidel Castro. This book will hopefully do that at least with the shared national pastime of baseball.

# Part I

# The Myths

# I

# "HISTORY WILL ABSOLVE ME"

In time, every revolution has created its own mythology, but in this case, these foreign sympathizers, in lieu of embracing one ready-made, had to produce their own.—Theodore Draper, *Castro's Revolution: Myths and Realities* [1]

**S**ome readers will come to this book expecting unadorned baseball history and also likely carrying a strong aversion to the complexities of Cuba's political saga. But when it comes to Cuba, baseball and politics are never distinct; one can hardly be discussed without attention to the other. Those wishing the more limited baseball side of the Fidel Castro chronicle can perhaps skip this opening chapter and begin with the one that follows. They will likely do so, however, at considerable loss of understanding when it comes to the context in which Fidel's baseball adventures must inevitably be set.

The Cuban Revolution, which came to fruition in January 1959, and which its champions and current functionaries contend is still ongoing more than six decades later, traces its birthright to July 26, 1953. On that date, a young Fidel Castro executed his first bold assault aimed at bringing down the hated tyrant Batista with an ill-conceived attack on the Moncada military barracks in Santiago de Cuba. The rash plot failed at a cost of great human suffering among his most loyal followers, but it was nonetheless a springboard to one of the most surprising and unorthodox political and social upheavals of modern times. In every respect, Fidel Castro's rise to power constitutes a single man's revolution, perhaps the only one in human history that boasts such a claim. Early champion Herbert Matthews suggests that the Moncada failure had the same symbolic significance for the Cuban Revolution that the storming of the Bastille had for the French Revolution. And for another early Fidel apologist, Carlos Franqui, the desperate Moncada attack was indeed the "true mother of the revolution."[2]

Fidel alone conceived the revolutionary upheaval of Cuban society that transpired at mid-century and then almost single-handedly carried it out with a remarkable display of personal willpower. That he did so with little or no foreordained ideology, and with endless pragmatic twists and turns along the way, is perhaps, more than anything else, what has led to decades of misunderstanding about the nature of the profound mid-century Cuban social transformation and the enigmatic figure who planned, orchestrated, and implemented it. What remains most distressing after almost six decades of an ongoing Cuban Revolution, and more than a year after Castro's own death, is that a veritable mountain of books—political biographies of the supreme leader and scholarly tomes on every aspect of the revolution he personally created and maintained for more than half a century—have largely failed to unravel any of the mysteries surrounding Fidel Castro the man and Fidel Castro the myth-cloaked persona. Fidel remains the most controversial and misunderstood among significant political figures of the twentieth century. And that opinion is shared by his most ardent supporters and most vehement detractors alike. As so often claimed, with Fidel there has never been any middle ground.

This opening chapter—designed to set the stage and offer clues to Fidel's often-hidden and even more often fictionalized persona as the most crucial figure of modern Cuban baseball history—can only aim to pinpoint the controversies and certainly not hope to unravel them. It has been an all-too-common theme that Fidel almost immediately abandoned the revolution he had promised once he actually came to power. Those advocating this line of reasoning repeatedly point to a litany of statements by the budding revolutionary that seemingly promoted a constitutional democracy and thus inspired the dream of achieving Cuba's first-ever untainted democratic elections. It was that early vision, opponents claim, that had initially attracted the bulk of his dedicated followers and ardent supporters. In suggesting Fidel's apparent deception (one they contend he had secretly plotted from his earliest days as radical student leader, and led to his abandoning promised

**REBEL LEADER.** Fidel's most recognized image, the rebel leader with his troops in the Sierra Maestra after the significant early victory over Batista forces at Uvero. *The Rucker Archive*

democratic capitalism for unwanted Soviet-style communism), these opponents pay special attention to the neophyte rebel's famed 1953 speech first delivered at the Moncada trials and later extensively revised for wide distribution as a rallying cry and propagandistic weapon aimed at inciting opposition to the Batista dictatorship.

They also point to a pair of July 26th Movement manifestos released from both Mexico and the Sierra Maestra. As scholar/politician Eric Williams would observe early on, the original *Fidalista* program differed little from that of most, if not all, Caribbean nationalist movements. Fidel had claimed with his November 1956 Manifesto (Mexico) that his objectives were "democratic, nationalist, and dedicated to social justice."[3] A second July 1957 Declaration (Sierra Maestra) pledged political guarantees, civil rights, a newly formed civil service, trade union free elections, distribution of unused lands for peasant farming with proper compensation to former owners, a literacy campaign, increased industrialization, and a spike in new employment. Fidel, while still rebel leader of an armed guerrilla insurrection, was seemingly advocating (apparently even promising) what was, in Williams's view, a "humanist revolution" that would restrict consumption but also expand industrialization by building new factories and producing new machinery. It was an agenda, his opponents like to contend, he had no real intention of following once he held the reins of power.

But first and foremost, those who would later condemn Fidel for distorting a popular and widely backed revolution, and abandoning the dreams of those who supported him against the evils of a ruthless Batista regime, would point repeatedly as justification for their position to the idealistic promises of the young Fidel found in the "History Will Absolve Me" defense delivered at his formal trial in the aftermath of the Moncada assault. Some would even find Hitler parallels in the Moncada speech. Georgie Anne Geyer, writing on the 30th anniversary of the revolution, assumes the idealistic young revolutionary was envisioning a populist uprising of the poor led by a traditional-style Latin American leftist caudillo (strongman), and yet at key points in his delivery drew heavily from his recent avid readings of works by the German Führer.[4] The flaw here, seemingly, was to credit that Moncada document and other early speeches and declarations with being a formal blueprint for governing rather than a mere rallying cry of a youthful enthusiast almost completely devoid of any fixed ideology or any plan for actually manipulating the machinery of a newly inherited government.

The Moncada speech itself has a most interesting and telling history. There is no record of precisely what the original oration actually contained. What has come down to us is the version Fidel reconstructed during his incarceration, a document that gained most of its fame in the years after his rise to power. He first wrote of his idea for reconstructing the speech in a letter to fellow Moncadista Melba Hernández, who had already been released from her own short prison stint and was now working to rally support for Fidel's crusade in Havana. He initially tried to smudge out sentences in matchboxes but eventually hit on the ingenious idea of writing with lime juice, which produced an invisible ink text hidden between lines of letters sent to Melba and other forewarned friends.[5] Fidel, in his clandestine messages, instructed Melba and Haydeé Santamaría precisely how he wanted the document printed and originally demanded that 100,000 copies be produced. His sister Lidia was also involved in the ruse since, as a relative, she could visit him in prison and smuggle coded messages to his supporters on the outside. But limited time and money would eventually allow printing of only about 20,000 copies (some sources say 27,000, but biographer Peter Bourne suggests only 10,000), and the eventual distribution throughout the country was also a slow, chaotic process that took several months. Most copies were handed out by a loyal supporter named Gustavo Ameijeiras, who crisscrossed the island in his worn-out jalopy begging for gas money along the way.[6]

Parallels between the original speech and the later reconstructed pamphlet version are hard, if not impossible, to pin down. But there is some evidence of a close parallel. The original oration was, at the time, roughly transcribed by a young *Bohemia* magazine correspondent, Marta Rojas, assigned to cover Fidel's trial.[7] She would later express genuine amazement about how close the reconstructed version Fidel was able to produce from his Isle of Pines prison cell almost a year later was to the original oration she had witnessed and painstakingly recorded. In the view of Rojas, the latter version was definitely a sold replication, if not quite an exact match. Rojas's own notes on the trial were never published by *Bohemia* at the time (not surprising since Batista had ordered strict press censorship), but a decade later they served as a basis for her 1964 pro-*Fidelista* book entitled *La Generación del Centenario en la Moncada*. When she authored that later account, she ignored whatever had been in her original transcriptions and loyally stuck to what appeared to be Fidel's own heavily doctored version of the original speech.

The document as finally printed contains much youthful idealism. It advocates the establishment of political and personal freedoms absent under Batista and actually never known by Cubans during a long and abusive colonial history. It calls for a return to the rather impractical and never fully instituted Constitution of 1940, and to much more than even that latter document demanded in the way of human liberties. In retrospect, it seemed the somewhat irrational ideology of a youthful and rash political dreamer not yet tested by the rigors of actual warfare nor faced with the challenges of actual rebellion in the harsh struggle for power.

The printed pamphlet initially circulated during Fidel's imprisonment and, now a touchstone document in the history of the Cuban Revolution, contained five main points. Theodore Draper, in his book *Castro's Revolution*, lumps these into what he categorizes as Fidel's early promises.[8] Some of these were political, such as the first one calling for restoration of the Constitution of 1940. This initial demand implied that Fidel, at that early point, saw a democratic method of reversing the Batista dictatorship. This first pledge also contained the promise of free elections and further offered a guarantee of freedom of information, a free press, and individual and political rights. And there were also bold economic promises, for example, the granting of land to small farmers and peasants, and the rights of workers to share in profits from their labor. But further still, former landowners would be compensated when such a land redistribution took place.

The document was not only a program for reform, but also a reprise of Cuban colonial history emphasizing such national heroes as José Martí and other martyred nineteenth-century patriots who had earlier struggled for national independence and human justice. As biographer Peter Bourne describes the effort, "Fidel lavishly wraps himself in the folds of Cuban patriotism, elevating himself to the stature of these revered national heroes."[9] Hence, the document reflects far more idealistic fervor than any kind of true pragmatic program or recognizable political ideology. In short, it was a personal justification containing legal and historical rationale for exercising his right to overthrow an unjust dictator who now held power illegitimately. In the context of his October 1953 trial, the original speech was an argument against criminal guilt of any kind for launching the ill-fated Moncada attack. In the future, of course, this same document would be radically reshaped by

Fidel's apologists into an early version of a full-fledged program to justify his revolution.

Matthews best traces the sketchy history of the "History Will Absolve Me" document, which he describes as slow to emerge and extremely hard to confirm in its details.[10] The official government version of the document's evolution and precisely how it emerged in pamphlet form was published in the Communist Party newspaper *Hoy* on the occasion of the 10th Moncada anniversary. It is in that account that Melba Hernández pinpoints the first reference to a written form as occurring in a letter she received from Fidel (later published in Luis Conte Agüero's collection of *Cartas del Presidio*). In that missive, Fidel tells Melba that, "Mirta [his wife] will speak to you of a pamphlet of decisive importance for its ideological content and its tremendous accusations, and I would like you to give it your closest care."[11] At the time, there was not any formalized Castro-led revolutionary "movement" per se, since the M-26-7 group itself would not be constituted until the Moncada rebels were freed from confinement and in transit back to Havana in May 1955. But apparently Fidel was nonetheless already viewing the revamped speech he was busy reconstructing as an ideological tool with which to build and execute a popular island-wide rebel insurrection.

Both Fidel's later apologists and outspoken critics would eventually see the published document as an actual delineated program containing the seeds of the leader's earliest visions for a new and more just Cuban society. The difference—and it was considerable—was that the former group took it merely as a broad revolutionary game plan still in its earliest stages of evolution; the latter read it as a committed program for governing the nation with its promises of political parties and free elections, as well as expanded personal freedoms, earlier advocated in the overly idealistic and thus never actually implemented Constitution of 1940. Fidel's earliest comments suggest that for him, it was no more or no less an important piece of propaganda serving as an emotional rallying cry intended to inspire support for open warfare against what he saw as a ruthlessly unjust and archaic regime.

It is again Herbert Matthews who provides the most perceptive analysis of the printed *History Will Absolve Me* pamphlet and its role in the Cuban Revolution. "A cold, literary analysis [of the document] would be misleading," since its words represent not a pragmatic program for a future government but rather a "romantic revolutionary fervor of great spiritual and political value."[12] It was not a concrete plan for building a new society (as many Castro opponents later assumed) since Fidel had no such plan and little, if any, ideology on which to build one in 1953, or even in the final stage of his guerrilla rebellion five years later. It was an emotional appeal upon which to base a resurrection and, as such, a pure stroke of genius.

✿ ✿ ✿

Matthews and others stress that Fidel, at the time he triumphed over Batista and the forces of traditional politics in Cuba, was a man largely, if not entirely, without fixed ideology. Che Guevara was the ideological force in the July 26th Movement. Fidel, by contrast, proved a brilliant military tactician. His focus was on winning control of the country and seizing the power necessary to enforce his own idealistic reforms. There was little—perhaps no—advanced planning for what results the actual victory might bring or what would be needed next to meet largely unfathomed responsibilities of actually running the complex machinery of national government.

The early months, perhaps even years, in power would quickly prove to be a large-scale organizational disaster for the new Castro-led government. The Sierra combatants who had supported him in the mountains and now constituted the M-26-7 contingent suddenly thrust into power knew little beyond guerrilla warfare tactics and firing weapons; most were of middle-class origins and not peasants. Yet, their educations had, by and large, been in the tactics of rebellion. The rebel army was quickly disbanded, and previous political parties, with the exception of the original Communists (PSP, or Popular Socialist Party, which had once supported or at least cooperated with Batista) had also dissolved. In the vacuum that existed, power resided with Fidel, who in the earliest weeks operated a "government outside the government" since he held no official title before reluctantly accepting the prime minister post in mid-February. It was only a matter of months before a large portion of the middle-class technicians possessing the needed expertise to manage a government operation became either disillusioned with where the revolution seemed to be heading or fearful for their own once-privileged economic status; many of that group began fleeing the country. Fidel, for his own part, was preoccupied with consolidating his power in the face of counterrevolution threats, a necessary step if he was to make the type of revolution he envisioned.

There would be many mistakes and examples of gross mismanagement, leading close Castro watcher Herbert Matthews to remark that the "degree of disorganization in Cuba at the beginning of 1959 and all through that year was almost unbelievable." Fidel himself unabashedly acknowledged the fact that he and his July 26th followers (most still in their 20s), once in power, were entirely unprepared and only learning on the job. Referring to the troublesome governmental chaos of 1959 and 1960, he told Matthews,

> This comes from the fact we have had to use young, inexperienced men. We have had to improvise, to learn as we go along by trial and error. This is true of our whole revolutionary process . . . I try to do as much as I can, but I have innumerable things to do. I cannot do everything. I cannot watch everything. [13]

Numerous policy and program failures and the setbacks that inevitably resulted stretched across the entire first decade of Castro's nationalistic program for recasting his government into first a socialist and later a communist guise. Ultimately, there was the disaster of the failed 1970 harvest of 10 million tons of cane, for which Fidel first nobly took full blame but then also turned (as he did on many occasions) into a personal triumph, further cementing his hold on his people and their destiny. Committed to the idea that sugar production, rather than unlikely rapid industrialization, would have to remain a backbone of the economy (by then propped up with huge amounts of Soviet aid), Fidel staked the prestige of his regime and seemingly the entire future of his revolution on achieving a haul of 10 million tons during the 1970 *zafra* (harvest season)—the hope being to not only silence Moscow's criticisms that he was failing to meet obligations in the Soviet–Cuba economic pact, but also distract domestic attention away from numerous other economic shortcomings. The bold gamble failed, at a heavy price for the rest of Cuba's agriculture programs that had been put on hold during the ill-conceived effort. Speaking two months later at the 17th Moncada anniversary celebrations, Fidel brashly admitted full blame for this and other economic failings and made a half-hearted effort to resign. As always, his charisma won the day with the assembled crowds, and his hold on his adoring masses was only strengthened, even if the nation's economy continued to wallow in mismanagement.

But even earlier there were disasters prompted by faulty, ill-conceived, or overambitious economic programs. As Eric Williams emphasizes, a high price was paid for numerous early achievements, for instance, massive school and road building carried out with no regard to cost.[14] Such reckless plans brought criticisms from Fidel's strongest supporters, as well as his most outspoken enemies. Williams points first and foremost to what Che Guevara would label as "plan less planning," which manifested itself in misconceptions about the country's abilities to industrialize on a rapid scale. May 1961 would find Che boasting that the country would double its standard of living in four years; a year later, he was admitting, "We failed to put the proper emphasis on the utilization of our resources" by building factories without accounting for the missing raw materials necessary for planned manufacturing operations. And there were many similar failures connected with agricultural development, causing Che to further admit in 1963, that announcing a 15 percent increase in agricultural production had been simply ridiculous.

Williams quotes Herbert Matthews's terse warning from the late 1960s of what potentially would bring on the ultimate failure of the Cuban Revolution—the failure of the system would come with the failure to put the economy on a sound basis.[15] That failure—perhaps as much a result of the late 1980's Soviet collapse and ongoing American embargo as of poor domestic planning alone—would trigger a collapse in the moral strength of the people's revolutionary spirit. Fidel's unfettered idealism advocating moral incentives as replacement for material rewards as a fundamental basis of the new revolutionary society would simply not work in the end. Peter Bourne's final word on Fidel (and the final passage at the end of his Castro biography) would best underscore the revolution's final undoing. Cubans in the end would gladly sacrifice national pride and social equalities for a better living standard. And the same in the end would prove just as true with baseball as with any other corner of the revolutionary society. When star athletes began to abandon the homeland in droves after 2010 it was for the promise of a bulky paycheck and not for any fantasies about the advantages of American-style liberal democracy.

Acknowledging criticisms of the shortcomings of his new society and the failures of his early government programs, Fidel would repeatedly fall back on stressing that his revolution and all revolutions were an unending process. There could be no fixed plan and there was no controlling ideology. Much of what developed would come out of the necessities of a changing landscape. The revolution, at least in its earliest two decades, was always as much reaction to circumstances as result of careful forethought and detailed advanced planning. When queried by interviewer Lee Lockwood about his apparent abandonment of promises for democratic reforms Fidel would repeat his argument that all revolutionary movements initially propose the widest range of possible achievement that might later have to be sacrificed to pragmatic realities: those carrying out the French Revolution, Fidel would note, at first planned on maintaining the monarchy but later reversed field, and the Russian Bolsheviks first advocated plans that were not strictly socialist in nature. In Fidel's view (or perhaps his rationalization) "no revolutionary program implies the renunciation of new revolutionary stages, or new objectives."[16] In brief, revolutions are an ever-evolving process, and revolutionaries are always shifting their pragmatic programs. Hence Fidel, with absolute candor, could declare to Lockwood in 1965, "I told no lies in the Moncada speech since that was how I thought at the moment."

In the earliest months at least, it is true that most of Fidel's moves were actually reactions to changing domestic and international circumstances, and especially to policies and overt actions coming from Washington. His provocative steps in nationalizing Cuban industries and North American business interests were, on several occasions, forced by steps taken by the Eisenhower administration, for example, the cut in sugar purchases or the orders that American-owned refineries not process crude oil obtained from the Soviets. This did not mean, however, that Washington and its policies actually forced Fidel into adopting communism as a response. There is no direct and obvious link to be found between causes and results. Theodore Draper stresses the fallacy of thinking that American policies on Cuba and the actions that resulted from those policies were enough to explain Fidel's shift in the direction of the Soviets. A reliance on Soviet economic aid may have been a forced consequence. But not the abandonment of the M-26-7 movement or the rapid replacement of many of its members in key government posts in 1961 and 1962, by established Cuban Communist Party members. That had far more to do with Fidel's own plans for the revolution he wished to make once he had established full personal control. And the switch to using Communists in key government positions was also the means for maintaining control of power; only the established Communists seemingly possessed the political experience needed to stem the reigning government chaos in Havana. The merger of Fidelismo and communism is, of course, a much more complex story to which we will return here promptly.

A small, if not insignificant, example of Fidel's shifting positions that actually was clearly forced upon him by American actions can nonetheless be found in the saga that surrounds the removal of professional baseball from the island. Baseball developments may seem insignificant when set against more consequential events like the nationalization of American industries, the seizure of personal properties, or the repulsed Bay of Pigs invasion. But given the symbolic role of the sport in both Cuban and North American culture, those events surrounding the Havana Sugar Kings and the Cuban winter league were hardly minor episodes in the story. And those episodes will be elaborated on in the heart of this book.

But even with baseball—the replacement of an American-controlled professional game with a Cuban-controlled amateur sport—the events can only be partially, even if largely, laid at the feet of the Americans. Organized Baseball officials and Washington policy makers were an important cause but never a sole cause. The baseball transition was as much as anything part and parcel of Fidel's emerging plan of building a new type of nonmaterial society. The timing of those events in midsummer of 1960 and the early winter of 1961 is most telling, since they came at not only the apex of fears among North American baseball officials about player safety, but also the time of the first radical makeover of Fidel's new society. Plans launched by INDER (the new national sports ministry) for the abandonment of professionalism and the substitution of a new style of baseball operation came in 1962, designated by Fidel as the "Year of Planning" and devoted to a much larger reassessment and reshaping of the entirety of prerevolution Cuban culture.

Political tensions dividing Washington and Havana, as well as civil unrest and the ongoing counterrevolutionary activities in the Cuban capital city, plagued the Havana International League franchise

throughout the 1959 season. Those tensions peaked with events surrounding a first post-Batista July 26th celebration that same summer
(see chapter 3). Threats to the continued housing of Roberto "Bobby"
Maduro's ballclub in Havana had already become an issue the previous
summer season while rebels were still operating at what seemed a safe
distance in the Sierra Maestra mountains. International League officials
used the perceived threats to player safety as a rationale for contemplat-
ing relocation of the team. That same concern about player well-being
would eventually cause MLB commissioner Ford Frick to ban all big-
leaguers (except for Cubans) from winter-league games on the island, a
development that spelled the end of the Cuban circuit in the months
immediately following the actual relocation of the AAA minor-league
club to Jersey City.

As a baseball enthusiast himself, and a newly entrenched political
leader aware of the importance of the sport for maintaining morale on
the home front in the aftermath of the revolution-inspired government
upheaval, Fidel was vocal in support of keeping the International
League franchise in Havana. He spoke out to the media in support of
the team both at home in Havana and during his April visit to Washington and New York. He offered financial assistance to keep the cash-
poor club afloat. And he bolstered sagging attendance with his appearances to throw out ceremonial first pitches on Opening Day 1959 and
again in 1960. He was a physical presence and leading cheerleader on
the occasion of the Junior World Series triumphs in September and
October 1959, which provided the team's final hurrah.

Once Organized Baseball pulled out of Havana, Fidel was still vocal
in the months immediately following about allowing Cuban big-leaguers to travel freely and continue performing with their MLB teams.
Of course, this would change dramatically in the years immediately
following once Fidel and Cuba shifted their baseball priorities to a new
amateur version of the sport. Support for Cuban big-leaguers eventually
shifted to attacks on professionals, who were suddenly branded as trai-
torous mercenaries. By early 1962, the domestic amateurs alone were
praised as true revolutionaries who admirably played for country and
pride and not for Yankee dollars. Big-leaguers who remained too long at
home, like Edmundo Amoros, Borrego Alvarez, and Héctor Maestri,
were either blocked or delayed in their departure from the island, a
circumstance that sabotaged their professional careers.

Numerous troubling questions surrounding the final fate of the Sugar Kings still loom large. Did government officials in Washington—perhaps at the highest levels, for instance, Secretary of State Christian Herter—play a direct role or exert influence? Was the move a calculated blow against Castro and his government, or were the issues of player safety the only rationale for pulling the plug? Did Fidel actually resent the loss of the U.S. baseball operations, and did this perceived attack—this personal slight—motivate his subsequent hostilities toward professionalism in baseball? There are no fixed answers, but the likely conclusion regarding such questions seems to be that there is no strong support for any of the alternative interpretations. On the issue of Fidel's personal resentment, for example, Castro most certainly held other stronger motives for revamping Cuban baseball, and those motives will also be further explored in subsequent sections of this book, most fully in chapter 5, devoted to the story of the league that would be constructed on the ashes of a once-thriving island professional game.

On the surface at least, Fidel did not initially approve of ending professional baseball on the island. None of his statements or actions in 1959 and 1960 could lead to that conclusion. Of course, it is true that Fidel and his revolution changed from month to month and year to year; he always did what he thought would serve the needs of the moment, regardless of what he might have earlier promised or seemed to promise. Fidel also certainly did not orchestrate the change from pro to amateur status for the national sport; he only improvised once an opportunity suddenly presented itself. Only indirectly—since his revolution had indeed brought instability—could he be held responsible for the collapse of Maduro's Sugar Kings franchise. But once the scene shifted, the opportunistic revolutionary leader would seize on a plan for fitting developments into the mold of his new revolution.

In the year following the closing of pro baseball operations, Fidel was orchestrating a major overhaul of Cuban culture. A central focus was the revamping of Cuba's sporting culture as part of that change. One step was the creation of INDER (National Institute of Sports, Physical Education, and Recreation) and the transition of organized sports activities from a profit-making business and entertainment industry to a public right and instrument of public health in the newly emerging society. A new amateur nationwide baseball league was only one of the major results. Again, this was an example of the revolution being a constantly evolving affair that responded to emerging changes altering the Cuban social landscape.

It is true enough that Fidel did his own part in raising hostilities with his anti-Washington rhetoric. This might be partly explained by a life-long hatred of the controlling Americans.[17] In his 1970 analysis of "Castroism," Eric Williams asserts its distinguishing feature indeed to be Fidel's overriding anti-Americanism.[18] There was indeed plenty of justification for this anti-American stance in his knowledge of the U.S. historical interventionist role regarding his country. A passionate student of history, he was well aware of American abuses at the time of the revolt against Spain and the U.S. actions, which embarrassed Cubans by excluding them from final treaty accords with the defeated Spanish. He was incensed by the record of U.S. occupation of the newly "liberated" Cuba after the Spanish overlords were overthrown, by its Monroe Doctrine policies, subversion of the new constitution of 1901, with the Platt Amendment, and subsequent use of Cuba as a stage for rampant American commercial investment. His revered model had always been José Martí, the nation's most honored and equally myth-draped patriot, who first warned of the dangerous beast to the north ("I have lived in the monster and I know its entrails"), and he absorbed deep-set Cuban embarrassment concerning repeated North American assessments of Cubans as an inferior people. And he also bridled at the knowledge of repeated U.S. backing and personal enrichment of puppet Cuban presidents in the first half of the twentieth century. When Batista returned to power with the coup of March 1952, Fidel saw distinct American fingerprints on the event.

There were also more personal reasons for anger directed at the Americans. Fidel held Washington responsible for the repeated bombing of his rebels in the Sierra Maestra by a U.S.-financed Batista military. He also saw the hand of Washington clearly visible in the numerous exile-sponsored attacks on Cuban territory throughout 1959 and 1960, as well as counterrevolutionary efforts to unseat him, and, of course, responsiblity for the ill-fated Bay of Pigs assault. This personal vendetta might be revealing. Yet, it seems merely to support—to amplify—but not to supplant Fidel's most basic antagonism for the Americans. The real thorn in Fidel's side was the long-standing evil of U.S. military and economic imperialism, which throughout the twentieth century kept his homeland subservient to powerful foreign interests and thus never in control of its own national destiny. Whether it was ownership of sugar mills or baseball teams, an ironclad grip of American economic domination had to be removed, once and for all.

✿ ✿ ✿

Fidel's most reputable biographer, Robert Quirk, suggests that the earliest chroniclers and analysts of the revolution—those nearer to the events themselves both in time and physical proximity—came closest to the truth.[19] It was writers like Herbert Matthews and Theodore Draper, especially, whose early views may have offered the best accounts of what was actually occurring as Fidel and his movement first seized power, initially struggled to institute a functioning government, and then moved in the face of continued hostilities from Washington toward socialism and finally directly into the arms of the Soviet Union and the Communist camp. Again, it is to be emphasized that communism in Cuba's mid-century revolution was a result, not a cause, even if it is not always clear quite how and why the resulting transformation played out.

The literature surrounding the earliest years of Castro's revolution has long been clouded by revisionist historians, especially those from the Cuban exile community of South Florida, blinded by a hatred stemming from privileges and material possessions lost and longings for a homeland they see as being unjustly taken from them by an act of deception. Entrenched views of Fidel and his revolution have also been clouded by writers devoted to notions of American exceptionalism and the policies flowing from an early and ongoing U.S. governmental fear (one largely shared by the American press) of a perceived world communist movement and especially communist expansion in the Western Hemisphere nations of Latin America. It was this same controlling fear in Washington circles that lay behind the debacle in Vietnam, which saw the Americans rejecting the nationalist movement of Ho Chi Minh in favor of an early alliance with the ruthless imperialism of a French government that saw the strategic Asian nation as crucial to their own empire-building designs.

What has been created by this literature is not an accurate historical account as much as an all-pervasive mythology attached to both the motives and directions of the revolution itself, as well as to the larger-than-life figure who single-handedly overhauled his country and ended its history as a long-subservient pawn of colonial occupiers. Central to these myths are legends surrounding Fidel's intentional or unintentional communist sympathies and the degree to which he may well have, once in power, deceitfully abandoned a revolution he had originally launched. Matthews and Draper aim their early analyses directly at dismantling these growing mythologies, which were already clouding historical events in the early decades of revolutionary Cuba.[20] But they also insightfully explore the degree to which Fidel himself heavily and purposely contributed to his own growing personal mythology.

Other early historians and biographers have also addressed Fidel as a product of mythmaking. Notable here is Georgie Anne Geyer, whose 1991 portrait of the by-then long-entrenched Cuban strongman is at one and the same time both outspokenly critical and unavoidably flattering. For Geyer, Fidel remained, after decades in power, the "single modern revolutionary of epicentral consequence."[21] In an opening chapter exploring the extraordinary scope of powers wielded by Fidel both inside and outside of Cuba, Geyer also underscores the degree to which the Cuban leader's personal life remained an inexplicable mystery—one created by the machinations of Fidel Castro himself. She later stresses how the world continues to define Fidel in mysterious phantasmagoric ways and how much of the mystery has been attributed to Fidel's penchant for secretiveness and cloaking his life's most intimate details.[22]

The extensive debate between Theodore Draper and Herbert Matthews carried out in their collective four books published in the late 1960s and early 1970s may still provide the most balanced assessment of what the revolution, in essence, actually was. Their published positions also go a long way toward deciphering a pair of disquieting if central myths—first, that Fidel abandoned the revolution he had originally planned, and, second, that Castro had secretly been a dedicated communist from his earliest days and cleverly hid that reality from his naïve followers. These are, to be sure, the repeated mantras of Fidel's severest critics and especially those comprising a first-generation Cuban exile community.

Draper and Matthews agree on many central points, although each puts his personal stamp on the interpretations. First there is a belief that the Fidel Castro who fought in the Sierra Maestra alongside his small M-26-7 rebel army and came to power in the first month of 1959 was a man without a fixed ideology. Both authors make much here of the stark difference between Fidel the strict pragmatist and Che the budding idealist, or as Draper phrases it, between Fidel the mass intoxicator, demagogue, and popularizer, and Che the creative and original political thinker.[23] Second is a shared acknowledgment that Fidel turned his revolution into an unanticipated socialist and then communist movement in the third year of his reign and did so in response to a rapidly changing political landscape. Anticipating Geyer, there is also the shared assessment that Fidel was a most complex and mysterious figure from the outset, who hid his personal life and private thoughts from public view and thus contributed heavily to the building of his own mythology.

But on a pair of crucial points there is vital disagreement. One involves the timing and motives for Fidel's shift to the communist camp and his reported handing of the revolution to communist interests already established on the island. Neither sees Castro as being a "closet communist" during his student days, nor during planning for rebellion at the time of the Moncada escapade, nor while training his guerrilla force in Mexico or during the subsequent struggle in the Sierra Maestra. Both see Fidel's frequent claims between 1955 and 1960, that he definitely was not a communist or even a communist sympathizer, as being altogether genuine. Draper maintains that Fidel did, in fact, abandon his revolution in the end, but he also stresses that one must grasp which revolution it was that he betrayed. For Draper, there were two revolutions, an argument that provides the central thesis of his important *Encounter* article, which would become the opening chapter of his second book. In Draper's view, Fidel abandoned both revolutions, the radical democratic one he planned and then carried out with his military campaign to unseat Batista, and then the later undemocratic, if more radical, social revolution he began instituting by late 1959 and finally consolidated with the 1961 and 1962 incorporation of the Cuban Communist Party into his new government machinery. That is to say, he abandoned the one he seemed to have promised and that gained the support of his middle-class followers, and then by throwing in with the Cuban Communist Party he eventually even abandoned the one Draper believes he always intended to make. In the process he became "not the *Líder Maximo* of a new movement but the Pied Piper of an old one."[24]

Matthews, in turn, argues that Fidel's apparent shift in mid-1960, from his M-26-7 supporters to a reliance on and partnership with the old guard Cuban Communist Party, was pragmatic and not at all ideological, and resulted from a need to both justify and ultimately salvage his drifting revolutionary program. The second point of discord between the two analysts involves the precise nature of Fidel's relations with the Soviets after 1962. Draper believed that Fidel indeed did hand control to the Russians and that after that fateful step, no rupture with the Soviets could ever be possible. Matthews counters by again asking which revolution Fidel actually abandoned. His thesis was that those supporting Castro early on never truly understood the radical nature of the revolution he originally intended. Fidel was intent on not only sweeping Batista aside, but also sweeping away the entire governmental apparatus as it had long been maintained. For Matthews, Fidel possessed a true understanding of the nature of revolution—he grasped that, in the words of Abraham Lincoln, it was the quality of revolutions "not to go by old lines, or old laws, but to break up both, and make new ones."[25] A true revolution calls for radical change, turning an old system completely upside down, and introducing fundamental reconstruction. The issue was a severe misunderstanding of Fidel on the part of his advocates and not at all any deceitful shift in his own revolutionary thinking.

Draper, for his part, provides a reasoned but not altogether persuasive argument that Fidel's revolution was, in the end, a new variant among communist revolutions.[26] It was one that stemmed from what Draper terms a "national-revolutionary movement" that preceded any involvement of the communists and only found them later emerging to power within such a nationalist-inspired revolutionary movement once it was established. These are revolutions aimed at arousing national unity in opposing a hated common enemy. It is the common enemy (in this case Batista) that is their rationale and not any political or social program per se. These rebellions are most often led by men possessing special magnetic appeal among the masses but also men defined by intellectual fuzziness and huge impeding egos. The combination makes such leaders more inspiring and effective en route to gaining power than once they seize it. The political and social vacuums they leave in the wake of their victories is what then gives the communists an opportunity for success they could never have had in the revolutionary struggle itself. For Draper, the Castro revolution seems to fit this model perfectly.

In Draper's view, Fidel would abandon the M-26-7 because it was not capable of making the radical revolution he envisioned. He merged with the Cuban communists (PSP) because they offered him the missing means for maintaining control. They aided an agenda aimed squarely at eliminating anything that might restrict his personal power. And in Marxist-Leninism he found the ideology that was also so sorely missing and so clearly needed to guide the revolution once it transitioned from armed struggle to social restructuring. Once Fidel was in control, it was obvious that his continued power and earlier promises were not compatible. Hence, he had to seek a basis for his new regime that was at variance with the anti-Batista revolution he had started and guided to its conclusion. The revolution had not ended on January 1, 1959, but only just begun, and it would soon enough be launched in an entirely new direction.

A great irony here is that in dismantling a central reigning myth (Fidel's early closet communism), Draper would establish a separate mythology of his own making. Central to this new mythology are the twin notions that first Fidel consciously switched his revolutionary program in midcourse and, second, that this led to a fateful decision to turn over his revolution to Soviet control. There are strong arguments against both conclusions, and they are perhaps best voiced by Herbert Matthews, who in response to Draper, would argue that Fidel never held any ideology in the first place and that the Soviets never, in fact, held sway in controlling a revolution that always remained very much of Fidel's own construction. The difference—and it is a major one—is that Draper saw Fidel, in the end, as serving the Cuban Communist Party and in the long run also the Soviets and therefore the worldwide communist movement. This would lead Draper to his conclusion that Fidel was never the Maximum Leader of a new revolution, but only the Pied Piper of an old one.

It is with Draper's belief that Fidel became a pawn of the Cuban Communists and even of the Soviets that the stark difference between the two analysts emerges. Matthews, like Draper, addresses the prevalent mythologies that got in the way from the start in understanding Fidel and his revolution. But one myth is most central for Matthews, and that is the one that portrays Fidel as a secret Communist and thus a betrayer of the revolution he had originally intended. For Matthews, there were not two revolutions, but simply one, which, in part, was constantly shifting with necessity and, in part, also badly misunderstood from the onset. He would argue that Fidel's followers never grasped where he was headed or what he actually envisioned for Cuba after Batista fell and after decades of abuse at the hands of corrupt and all-too-frequently foreign-controlled domestic governments.

Matthews and Draper agree that Fidel's revolutionary intentions shifted after the early chaos of those first months in power. But for Matthews, communism was not a cause of the Cuban Revolution, but a not-so-inevitable result. His thesis, furthermore, is that an ensuing evolution in Cuban society was badly misinterpreted both inside and outside of Cuba. Matthews is succinct on that point. "More foolishness was said and written along Fidel Castro's path to Marxism-Leninism by ill-formed journalists, demagogic Congressmen, angry and myopic United States government officials, and ponderous scholars than about any other phase of the Cuban Revolution."[27]

Communism was indeed forced on the Cuban people and never would have been voted in by the populace. As Matthews points out, Cuba was the only country to become communist of its own accord after its leaders had taken power. In other countries that transitioned to Marxist-Leninism or other similar forms of totalitarian socialism the leaders were already Communists when they took power. But it also cannot be overlooked that Cuba was the first Latin American country to free itself from superpower imperialism. As much as Fidel's driving motives may have stemmed from his anti-materialism, they also stemmed from anti-imperialism. But both stances explain his eventual rejection of the American baseball model.

One most-favored argument of those wishing to establish Fidel's deceitful hiding of early communist sympathies is, of course, his own celebrated midnight television address of December 1–2, 1961, in which he declared, "I am a Marxist-Leninist and I shall be a Marxist-Leninist until the last day of my life." Matthews carefully examines Fidel's December 1961 speech and points out the immediate and most unfortunate misinterpretations in both Miami and Washington, which badly muddied the waters. Matthews labels the speech "a concoction, a composition, a political construction, engineered to fit the particular moment and Fidel's aims."[28] A stateside Cuban exile monitoring the

Havana broadcast for Miami UPI sent out an inaccurate version of certain passages that seemed to affirm what Castro opponents most wanted to hear. When the Havana newspaper *Revolución* published the full text several days later it was too late to correct an initial impression caused by the distorted and selective UPI report.

Matthews stresses that rather than admitting he had been a Marxist during university days, Fidel was actually apologizing for not having been an early convert as a student, or as a rebel in the Sierra Maestra, since he still had not seen the light and appreciated the great virtues of Marxism. Matthews also points to numerous inconsistencies in the speech that suggest Fidel was rationalizing his own evolution and merely excusing a later shift in philosophy that clearly had other motivations. If Fidel, by the end of 1961, was Marxist, he was a Marxist of a special color. In Matthews's words, "One could say of his Marxism-Leninism what Humpty-Dumpty said to Alice: 'When I use a word it means just what I choose it to mean—nothing more or less.'"[29]

Writing more than a quarter-century after Matthews and Draper held their debates in book form and personal correspondence, Castro biographer and critic Georgie Anne Geyer presented a very different reading of Fidel Castro as a communist.[30] Geyer proposes that it was pointless to debate when Fidel had, in fact, adopted communism because in truth, the Cuban leader never became a "communist" at all. Hers is an even stronger version of Matthews's original position since she argues rather persuasively that Fidel had accomplished a unique feat in modern history. In reality, he had destroyed the Cuban Communist Party (PSP) in its original Moscow-connected guise within the nation's political structure. He used the communist ideology and the early Soviet support to remold that ideology into his own brand; he also used it to boldly confront the United States, while at the same time currying support and backing from the Soviets. He replaced what had been the Communist Party in Cuba with what was, in reality, his own "Fidelista" party. Geyer believes, like Matthews, that Fidel never turned over any power to Moscow when it came to the direction and management of his revolution. Communism became a practical and necessary tool for the revolution he had in mind. The Communist Party never supplanted Fidel, but rather the reverse was true.

As biographer Peter Bourne would cogently observe at the end of Fidel's first three decades in power, it is often the chance comment that reveals the most irrefutable truths. Bourne offers a telling anecdote drawn from Lee Lockwood's extensive 1965 interviews with Fidel. At the end of one of the interview sessions, Lockwood asks Fidel to autograph a piece of souvenir currency that had been issued by the underground movement as a fund-raising device and that he had bought earlier in 1958, on the streets of Havana, for a dollar. Fidel jokingly remarks, "You better be careful and not show this to anyone when you get back to the States—they're liable to accuse you of having given money to support a Communist revolution." Lockwood responds in his defense, "But I didn't know it was going to turn out to be a Communist revolution when I bought it." Fidel laughed as he signed the bill and retorted, "You know something? Neither did I."[31]

❉ ❉ ❉

What, then, do we make of the central myths surrounding the figure of Fidel Castro? And how do those myths set the stage for unraveling and understanding the lesser, if nonetheless intriguing, myth of Fidel's role in revamping the island's national sport of baseball? The answers are not easily found, but neither are they entirely opaque.

Draper, at the crux of his own 1962 treatise, argues that in regard to any notions of Fidel betraying the revolution, what was in the end significant was his actions and not his words. For Draper, the issue of Fidel's supposed deceits was pointless to debate since the arguments of those making such contentions were always filled mostly with wild speculations; "more to the point is what he said and what he did."[32] In Draper's view, the issue was never the sincerity or the value of his idealistic 1953 Moncada "speech" or his addresses to the masses a decade later; it was the compromise with the Cuban Communists in 1961 and 1962, and the abandonment of his middle-class supporters from the M-26-7 movement. Matthews takes a somewhat similar position when he notes that such inconsistencies between what Fidel early said he would do and the methods he eventually used are actually historical commonplaces. To make that point, Matthews notes how Lyndon Johnson repeatedly made campaign pledges that he would never "send American boys to Vietnam to fight a war that Asiatics should fight."[33] History was to judge Johnson by his later actions and not his campaign promises. What Fidel did, of course, was to bring about an upheaval and overhaul of Cuban society that shook the country, its culture, and its population to the very roots. His actions brought disaster to the middle class and the remnants of a pre-Castro professional class. The quick dismissal of the Cuban professional class, in fact, may have been a direct cause of most of the difficulties his revolution faced in its earliest years.

That destruction of the middle class, which had supported the revolution in its earliest phases, would also become a central source of the hatred directed at the new Cuban leader and his communist-style government in years to come. It would stand alongside irrational American fears of worldwide communism as the source of all future antagonisms. And it would appeal again and again to the paranoia surrounding communism for its ammunition. But Fidel had never promised a liberal democracy if what that meant was merely replacing one despicable tyrant and then returning to the political and social system that tyrant had earlier usurped. What Fidel had proposed from the start was a radical overhaul of an entire social system, which would bring greater benefit and hope to the disadvantaged rural masses of peasants and laborers—many of them Afro-Cubans—who the previous system had always abused; he had never envisioned or promised rescuing the country for the continued advantages (and abuses) of landowners or middle-class business entrepreneurs and technocrats, and it was wishful thinking of the latter groups to read his promises that way.

Middle-class Cubans who became the victims of that radical social upheaval, an American press corps that misunderstood it, a Washington State Department alarmed by the sharp movement to the left of a Latin American neighbor so close to its own shores, and a North American business and financial sector (including Organized Baseball) that saw its investments suddenly going down the drain raised a loud and desperate cry that the revolution had been betrayed. But what revolution was betrayed? The one they had mistakenly envisioned perhaps, but not the one Fidel always had in mind. It was not for them that the revolution had been launched in the first place; and they were never its intended benefactors.

Those in the exiled Cuban community who would vent so much anger at Fidel's betrayal in the future and repeatedly rail about the need for a return to a "free" Cuba or true democracy on the island, which would come only with removal of the hated new "dictator" and his family and cronies, have always conveniently overlooked, denied, and all-too-easily dismissed some vital historical facts. They have ignored what brought Fidel to power in the first place, what accounted for his enormous initial and even ongoing support and adoration, and what has long justified his important niche in modern Latin American history.

First and most central, these critics ignore the overriding fact that Cuba has never had legitimate democratic government throughout its sad history. For centuries, the island was ruled by Spanish colonial overlords who raped the land for lucrative sugar and tobacco production, introduced slavery for needed labor (after wiping out the native indigenous population in an early effort at finding such cheap labor), exploited native landowners, and crushed attempts at rebellions aimed at achieving independence and self-determination. An American co-opting of a final push for independence in 1898 (the badly misnamed Spanish–American War) replaced one set of opportunistic overlords and exploiters with still another. The first half of the twentieth century witnessed sham independence and weak leadership propped up by U.S. officials and American business tycoons who usurped the country's resources for their own handsome profits. Such democracy American-style was quickly seen as a hoax that ultimately resulted in still further debasing of already sagging Cuban national self-esteem.

Equally ignored is the fact that the revolution improved life for the poorest Cubans. Cuba had become a prosperous country (at least by Latin American standards) in the first half of the past century, but it was a prosperity just as unevenly distributed under American underpinnings as it had been under the Spanish occupation. An urban middle class evolved that profited from a luxurious lifestyle that made them seemingly more American than Cuban and would eventually provoke such strong cultural identification with everything American—indeed a crisis of ambiguous cultural identity and a disillusionment with fading national pride that Louis Pérez Jr. would later emphasize as a deep motive in the Castro Revolution.[34]

In the meantime, the Cuban rural populations and those in the cities left to menial employment (largely a nonwhite population) lived in abject poverty and almost universal illiteracy. All this changed in the aftermath of the revolution, when public education was expanded, illiteracy was largely obliterated, farmers were given title to their land and a share in the profits of their labor, racial discrimination was largely suppressed (if not cancelled entirely), sweeping land reforms and nationalizations (although both perhaps misguided in method) drove out foreign control of Cuban industries and resources, and resorts and beaches and other forms of entertainment and recreation once reserved for the privileged were thrown open to all Cubans.

Lastly and more importantly, it is always overlooked by Fidel's critics that his presence provided Cubans with something far more important than American-style democratic institutions, which, for them, had long proven largely a sham. He created a government without rampant corruption, providing—at least in the earliest decades—the first honest administration Cuba had ever known, the only one where the nation's leaders no longer ignored domestic priorities and no longer worked only to enrich themselves. He expanded the influence of the once-dependent nation to unimaginable levels on the international Cold War stage, resurrecting long-suffering Cuban self-esteem. Some of what he gave to Cubans may have soon disappeared once Fidel adopted autocratic rule as his only viable means of continuing an often-threatened revolution. And some of the early gifts of the revolution may have largely lost their appeal for new generations of the approaching new millennium, increasingly attuned to capitalist materialism. But in the early years there could be little doubt that while some were suddenly left behind, Fidel's socialist revolution substantially improved the lives and hopes of the bulk of long-suffering Cubans.

The historical background that brought on and even explains the revolution is perhaps best captured in the opening chapter of Peter Bourne's biography. That chapter succinctly reprises the lengthy history of occupation by the Spanish and the tenacity with which the Spanish crown protected its last holding in the Western Hemisphere and created a monoculture based on lucrative sugar production. Bourne outlines late nineteenth-century American attitudes toward Cuba and its people, and reviews the long-standing imperialistic designs of American administrations. He explains how the Americans opportunistically took over the final stages of Cuba's lengthy independence war with Spain and ensured its own control of the island and their resources through the Platt Amendment. He capsulizes the American-owned puppet government that followed in the first half of the twentieth century, one propped up to guarantee the health of flourishing American business interests. There is no better summary of the reasons for deep-seated Cuban resentment of powerful American influence.

Bourne concludes that valuable chapter with a summary of the characteristics Cubans longed for in a leader. It is a perfect capsule portrait of what the Cubans saw with the emergence of the young Fidel Castro.

> Cuba, at the midpoint of the twentieth century, waited expectantly for a man who could produce a sense of national pride, a man who would stand up to the United States and not be corrupted by money and the flattery of powerful interests. They sought a leader who could finally give them back their self-respect by creating a truly independent nation, who was ready to rid the country of the infestation of corruption at all levels of the government, and who could eliminate the plague of political violence that had been inflicted on Cubans for generations. If such a man appeared, most Cubans were ready to accept him as a messiah.

It is true enough that there is sufficient rationale behind at least some exile-community anger. The revolution changed substantially throughout the years as political and historical realities changed. Personal freedoms (which Cubans had willingly surrendered in the earliest phases of the new society) were further and eventually almost entirely diminished. Promised elections and a promised multiparty system never emerged. Control moved increasingly to an entrenched Communist Party machinery that had only limited powers in the earliest years. Material sacrifices willingly accepted in the earliest years became more and more severe and therefore more onerous.

Some of those changes were explainable as the revolutionary government fought to survive against rather impossible economic conditions and also against continued U.S. harassment.[35] The U.S. embargo was repeatedly blamed for the ills befalling the nation and the shortcomings in government economic management. The collapse of Soviet aid brought on a bleak "Special Period in the Time of Peace," with its widespread near-starvation and resulting untold horrors in public health and public spirit. Free discussion in the press (what little there may have once been) was replaced by repetitious regime ideology and attacks on the competing capitalist system up north. Fidel would tell Barbara Walters in their groundbreaking 1977 ABC interview that his government did not have the same views of freedom of the press and that the Cuban press would never be free to criticize socialism and question the directions of the revolution. Limited efforts at a small decree of free enterprise in a restricted small business sector were rolled back. And revolutionary ideology seemed increasingly to be a hollow end in itself.

But the assaults on Fidel and his revolution never focused on the pragmatic shortcomings of the Cuban government in response to continuing crises. They mainly focused instead on the Fidel who was largely a creation of myth-making rather than the Fidel of practical politics. They focused on the myths they had never abandoned, the very myths Draper and Matthews had tackled at the outset. Those were the myths that Fidel abandoned the revolution, that he was always a secret communist (and thus the very incarnation of evil in American eyes), and that as an avowed communist leader positioned only 90 miles from the U.S. shoreline he was the largest threat to U.S. security in the Cold War era. If there were reasons for rejecting and even hating Fidel Castro, those were likely not the true reasons.

Fidel had boasted at the launch point of his revolution that history itself would absolve him. And of course, it never has, at least not in some larger cosmic sense. More importantly, it would, at least here in the Western Hemisphere, more than anything else work to demonize him. History (that is, historians) repeatedly distorted and mythologized one of the great figures of twentieth-century politics. But it has certainly not ignored him. At worst, it would create a mythical Fidel, and the largest myths had to do with the motives of his revolution and the notion that he, in fact, betrayed his movement with uncontrolled lust for personal power and supposedly deceptively hidden communist sympathies. Other aspects of his social revolution would also be mythologized beyond recognition and none more so than his role in revamping Cuba's popular culture and one of its central manifestations—baseball. The myths are not easily untangled or resolved—especially when it comes to the motives, successes, and failures of one of the great political upheavals of the past century. But one part of the Castro mythology does cry out for disambiguation and perhaps even lends itself to resolution. That is that myth that Fidel Castro destroyed Cuban baseball.

# 2

# BASEBALL'S MOST OUTRAGEOUS MYTH

In no field of American endeavor is invention more rampant than in baseball, whose whole history is a lie from beginning to end . . . all of it is bunk, tossed up with a wink and a nudge.—John Thorn, *Baseball in the Garden of Eden* [1]

**M**ost baseball fans tend to take their idle ballpark pastimes far too seriously. After momentary reflection, even a diehard rooter would have to admit that North American big-league baseball's most significant historical figures—say, Mickey Mantle, Ty Cobb, Barry Bonds, Walter Johnson, and even Babe Ruth himself—are nothing more than mere blips on the larger canvas of global events. After all, 95 percent (perhaps more) of the globe's population has little or no interest whatsoever in what transpires on North American, Caribbean, or Asian ballpark diamonds. Babe Ruth may well have been among the grandest icons of American popular culture. Yet, little in the nature of world events would have been altered in the slightest degree if the flamboyant Babe had never escaped the rustic grounds of St. Mary's School for Boys in Baltimore. [2]

And yet this is certainly not the case when it comes to Cuba's most notorious pitching legend turned Communist revolutionary leader. While Fidel Castro's reputed flaming fastball (novelist Tim Wendel suggests in *Castro's Curveball* that he lived by a tantalizingly crooked pitch [3]) never earned him a coveted spot on a big-league roster, as fantasized in so many latter-day accounts, the amateur ex-hurler, who once on a lark tested the baseball waters in a Washington Senators tryout camp, nevertheless one day emerged among the past century's most significant world figures. Few outside North America or the Caribbean nations have been exposed to the Castro baseball rumors; fewer still in other corners of the globe and with an eye turned to world events have missed mention of recent history's most renowned revolutionary icon.

Castro was destined to outlast nine U.S. presidents and survive almost five full decades at the helm of an often-troubled but nevertheless remarkably durable socialist revolution he in large part personally created. Cuba's "Maximum Leader" greeted the new millennium still entrenched as one of the most beloved (in some quarters, mostly Third World) or hated (in others, mostly North American) of the world's charismatic political figureheads. It is certain that no other ex-ballplayer has ever stepped more dramatically or impactfully from the schoolboy diamond into a role that so radically affected the lives and fortunes of so many millions throughout the Western Hemisphere and beyond.

**CEREMONIAL PITCHER.** Fidel prepares for a ceremonial first pitch at the International League season opener (April 1960) while new sports minister Felipe Guerra Matos (far left), Havana pitcher Orlando Peña, and Rochester Red Wings manager Clyde King (right) look on. *The Rucker Archive*

Neither his most outspoken detractors nor ardent champions deny that Fidel remains the most dominant self-perpetuating myth of the second half of the twentieth century, and this claim is equally valid when it comes to the Cuban leader's longtime personal association with North America's self-proclaimed national game. Rare indeed is the stateside baseball fan—or the political junkie—who has not heard some version of the well-worn Castro baseball tale: that Fidel once owned a tantalizing fastball as a teenage prospect and was once offered big-league contracts by several eager scouts and slipshod bird dogs (especially the colorful "Papa Joe" Cambria, employed by Clark Griffith's lackluster postwar Washington Senators), whose failures to ink the young Cuban prospect at least indirectly unleashed a coming half-century of Cold War political and economic intrigue.

The New York Yankees and Pittsburgh Pirates also somehow frequently make their way into the story. And in a scandalous article in the May 1989 issue of *Harper's Magazine*, journalist J. David Truby provides perhaps the most egregious elaboration of the myth by adding the New York Giants to the list of purported Castro suitors.[4] By profession, Truby was a journalism professor at Pennsylvania's Indiana University who wrote prolifically on military history, weapons, and Latin American political affairs. A Penn State graduate, he served in Combat Intelligence with the U.S. Army Reserves before launching his career in radio, television, and magazine journalism. He also worked in the fields of advertising and public relations before entering academia and eventually became known as an expert on topics ranging from the CIA to Central American political analysis and the assassination of JFK. Nevertheless, his article on Castro's baseball prowess and the history of big-league scouting interests in the future communist leader suggests he never let careful research stand in the way of a sensational and saleable popular magazine story.

Truby's fabricated account (a reprint lifted from his earlier monthly column in the short-lived journal *Sports History*) suggests Horace Stoneham was also hot on the trail of the young Castro, a "star pitcher for the Havana University baseball team," and quotes from supposedly extant Giants scouting reports—documents that no one else has apparently ever seen—as his proof. Yet, Truby is not alone in falling for (or in this case manufacturing) the delightful story. Reputable baseball scholars, general sports historians, numerous network news broadcasters, and even former U.S. senator Eugene McCarthy, in an obscure 1995 journal article, have been taken in by the myth of Castro as a genuine major-league pitching prospect.

A suspiciously charming related tale can also be found in the June 1964 pages of *Sport* magazine, where ex-big-leaguer Don Hoak, aided by journalist Myron Cope, recounts a distant Havana day (reputedly during the 1950–1951 winter season) when rebellious anti-Batista students interrupted Cuban League play while a young law student named Castro seized the hill and delivered several unscheduled pitches to Hoak himself.[5] Detailed available evidence deflates both the bogus Hoak rendition (easily proven to be historically impossible on several indisputable counts) and also numerous associated renditions of Castro's pitching prowess. It turns out that Fidel the ballplayer is even more of a marvelous propaganda creation (a too-good-to-be-scoffed-at fantasy) than Fidel the lionized or demonized revolutionary hero. But this is only a small part of the fascinating and mostly—if not entirely—fictionalized Fidel Castro baseball story.

Despite such fanciful reports—indeed, perhaps largely because of them—one thing remains ruthlessly clear about Fidel the baseball player: The oft-presented tale of his prowess as a potential big-league hurler simply isn't true as normally told. It may well be a most attractive supposition—one we can hardly resist—that baseball scouts might well have changed world history by better attending to Fidel's potent fastball. Such a yarn might provide perfect filler for Bob Costas during a tense World Series TV moment when Liván Hernández or "El Duque" Hernández manned the October mound in the late 1990s. It also makes for tantalizing fiction in sportswriter Tim Wendel's fast-paced 1999 novel *Castro's Curveball*, but fiction it nonetheless remains. As Costas once pointedly reminded this author in personal correspondence, in this case the full-blown fiction is far too delectable ever to be voluntarily abandoned by media types who wished to exploit its seductive appeal.[6]

But the story doesn't end here, for if Fidel was never a genuine pro pitching prospect, he was nonetheless destined to emerge as an undeniable influence on baseball's recent history within his own island nation (and also, perhaps at least a lesser influence on the big-league scene, once his 1959 revolution closed the escape hatches for numerous Cuban League stars and potential 1960s and 1970s-era MLB prospects like Agustín Marquetti, Antonio Muñoz, and Armando Capiró). Castro's reputed personal role in killing off Cuban professional baseball has been long overstated and much overhyped. Such Organized Baseball figures as MLB commissioner Ford Frick, Cincinnati Reds GM Gabe Paul, and International League president Frank Shaughnessy—plus a bevy of Washington politicos—seemingly played a far larger role than Fidel in dismantling the AAA league's Havana-based Cuban Sugar Kings franchise in 1960. At the same time, the Cuban prime minister's active involvement during the dozen or more years after seizing political power (he didn't officially become Cuba's president until 1976)—both in inspiring and also legislating a prosperous amateur version of the Cuban national sport—has equally been ignored by a full generation and more of stateside baseball historians.

Is Fidel Castro, in the end, a contemptible baseball villain, responsible for pulling the plug on the island's MLB-affiliated pro league, or a certified baseball hero, architect of a nobler flag-waving rather than dollar-waving version of the bat-and-ball sport? The answer, as with almost every element of the Cuban Revolution and its controversial leader, may well be a matter of one's own personal historical and political perspectives. Sadly, most of the motives for either opposing view stem in large part from gross misconception and outlandish misinformation.

It is a matter of historical record that the emergence of Castro's initially socialist and only later avowedly Communist revolution indeed ended once and for all professional winter-league baseball in Cuba. But that is far less than "only half of the story"—a small prologue to the recent hefty Cuban baseball saga. If Castro himself provides one Cuban baseball "myth" (in the negative sense of the term), it is a still larger misconception that a golden age for baseball ended on the island in late 1960 and early 1961; the larger truth is that Cuba's true baseball zenith was only reached in the second half of the twentieth century—a post-revolution and not prerevolution era.[7] During the 1960s and 1970s, Fidel Castro and his policies of amateurism in sport were ultimately responsible for rebuilding Abner Doubleday and Alexander Cartwright's American pastime on the Cuban landscape into a showcase for patriotic amateur-level competitions designed to contrast with the North American corporate baseball staged-for-profit model. The direct result throughout those two decades and three more to follow would be one of the world's most fascinating baseball circuits (tense annual National Series competitions spreading throughout the entire island and leading to a yearly selection of powerhouse Cuban national teams) and by far the most success-filled saga in the entire history of international amateur and Olympic-style baseball movements.

If modern-era professional baseball leaves a sour aftertaste for at least some older-generation North American fans fed up with out-of-control spendthrift owners and today's gold-digging (if not steroid-enhanced) big-leaguers, Cuban League action as played under Castro's Communist government has long provided a rather attractive alternative to pro baseball as a capitalist free-market enterprise. In brief, the future Maximum Leader, who was never enough of a fastballing "phenom" to turn the head or open the pocketbook of scouting legend Papa Joe Cambria, was nonetheless destined to play out a small part of his controversial legacy as the most significant off-the-field figure found anywhere in the sporting history of the world's second-ranking Western Hemisphere baseball power.

✿ ✿ ✿

Don Hoak didn't exactly create the myth of Fidel Castro the baseball pitcher. The light-hitting big-league infielder did, however, contribute rather mightily to the spread of one of the sport's most elaborate historical hoaxes. The journeyman career of the former Dodgers, Cubs, Reds, Pirates, and Phillies third baseman is, in fact, almost exclusively renowned for two disastrous wild tosses—one on the diamond and the other in the interview room. In the first instance, Hoak unleashed the wild peg from third base on May 26, 1959, sabotaging teammate Harvey Haddix's 12 innings of pitching perfection in Milwaukee's County Stadium (and in the process baseball's longest big-league "perfect game"). In the latter case, he teamed with a notoriety-seeking sportswriter to spin an elaborate false yarn about facing the future Cuban revolutionary leader in a highly improbable batter-versus-hurler confrontation laced with romance and dripping with patriotic fervor.

The fabricated story of Hoak's memorable square-off against one of the most famous political leaders of the twentieth century did little to immortalize the ex-big-leaguer himself. Yet, it was destined to become yet another piece—indeed, perhaps the most prominent piece—of the circulating printed and oral record that has since worked overtime to establish Fidel Castro's own seemingly impressive baseball credentials.

Hoak conspired with journalist Myron Cope and the editors of *Sport* magazine to craft his fictionalized tale in June 1964 (mere weeks after his career-ending release by the Philadelphia Phillies), launching one of the most widely swallowed baseball hoaxes of the modern era. Cope himself was a celebrated freelance sports journalist who earned his greatest celebrity as the broadcast voice of the National Football League Pittsburgh Steelers. It was in the latter capacity that he was reputed to have been largely responsible for inventing the "Terrible Towel," which became a fan-favored symbol of the popular football franchise. As a journalist, Cope won numerous writing awards, most notably the 1963 E. P. Dutton Prize recognizing the "Best Magazine Sports Writing in the Nation" (for an essay portrait of Cassius Clay, i.e., Muhammad Ali, published in *True*). On the occasion of the 50th Anniversary of *Sports Illustrated*, that publication selected his portrait of Howard Cosell as one of the 50 all-time best *SI* articles. Cope's connection with Hoak undoubtedly sprang from the ballplayer's long tenure in the city of Pittsburgh, but the motives behind the Castro story remain a mystery. Did Cope actually believe the big-leaguer's fanciful tale (and thus relate it with little perceived need for fact-checking), or did the journalist with an eye for a good yarn actually dream up the fanciful tale on his own account? In either case, it has added clever fiction writing to his already impressive journalistic legacy.

As Hoak (through words penned by Cope) tells the story, his unlikely and unscheduled at-bat against young Castro came during his lone campaign of Cuban winter-league play, which the ex-big-leaguer conveniently misremembers as the offseason of 1950–1951. Hoak's account involves a Cuban League game between his own Cienfuegos ballclub and the Marianao team, featuring legendary Havana outfielder Pedro Formental. The convenient backdrop was political unrest surrounding the increasingly unpopular government of military strongman and ruthless dictator Fulgencio Batista. During the fifth inning, and with American Hoak occupying the batter's box, a spontaneous anti-Batista student demonstration suddenly broke out (Hoak reported such uprisings as all-too-regular occurrences during that particular 1951 season), with horns blaring, firecrackers exploding, and anti-Batista forces streaming onto the field of play.

The ballplayer's fanciful account continues with the student lead-er—the charismatic Castro—marching to the mound, seizing the ball from an unresisting Marianao pitcher, and tossing several warm-up heaves to catcher Mike Guerra (a Washington Senators big-league vete-ran). Castro then barks orders for Hoak to assume his batting stance, the famed Cuban umpire Amado Maestri shrugs in agreement, the American fouls off several wild but hard fastballs, the batter and umpire suddenly tire of the charade, and the bold Maestri finally orders the military police ("who were lazily enjoying the fun from the grandstand") to brandish their riot clubs and drive the student rabble from the field. Castro left the scene "like an impudent boy who has been cuffed by the teacher and sent to stand in the corner."[8]

Hoak's wild tale underpinned a myth that was soon to take on a ballooning life of its own. The Hoak-narrated details are perhaps charming but also highly suspect from the opening sentence. Mis-spellings and misapprehensions of names, plus confusion of the baseball details, immediately destroy any credibility the enticing account might carry. The star Cuban outfielder is Formental (not "Formanthael" as Hoak and Cope have spelled it), and Formental was actually a Club Havana outfielder and not a member of the Marianao team during the early 1950s (he had played for Cienfuegos a decade earlier, before being traded to Havana for Gil Torres in the mid-1940s); the umpire is Maestri (not Cope's spelling of "Miastri"); backstop Fermín (as he was always known in Cuba) Guerra would have been managing the Almen-dares team at the time and not catching for the ballclub playing under the banner of Marianao.

To add to the implausibility of the account, the reported events themselves are entirely out of character with the several personalities allegedly involved, especially those details concerning umpire Maestri. Amado Maestri was reputed to be the island's best mid-century arbiter, a bastion of respectability, and a man who had once even ejected Mexi-can League mogul Jorge Pasquel from the stadium grounds in Mexico City. This was not a spineless umpire who would have tamely ceded control of the playing field for even a split instant to troublemaking grandstand refugees of any known ilk—especially rabble-rousing anti-government forces. In short, the details are so scrambled and outra-geously inaccurate as to suggest that Hoak (and literary assistant Cope) had indeed related this tale with tongue firmly planted in cheek, and also with a clear aim of tipping off any informed reader as to the elaborate literary joke.

Amateur baseball historian and Cuban native Everardo Santamarina would eventually point out the numerous and rampant inconsistencies and overall illegitimacy of the far-fetched Hoak account. And he does so largely by stressing the contradictions related to Hoak's own winter-league career: botched dates, incorrect Cuban ballplayer names, the inaccurate portrayal of umpire Maestri. The SABR historian is right on target by again emphasizing the total implausibility of the umpire's role in the fabricated tale. And Santamarina thus astutely concludes that "not even Babe Ruth's 'Called Shot' ever got such a free ride."[9]

There are also available facts from the Fidel Castro side of the ledger (facts largely unnoted by Santamarina) that are just as persuasive in putting a full lie to Hoak's trumped-up version of the events. An even looser playing with the historical details than with the baseball data is apparent to any reader even vaguely familiar with legitimate accounts of the Cuban Revolution and its heavily reported chronology. For starters, Pedro Formental was a well-known Batista supporter and thus not likely a "great pal of Castro" and Fidel's "daily companion at the ballpark," as Hoak reports. While Fidel had, in truth, just received his University of Havana law degree (Doctor of Laws, which qualified him to hang a shingle and begin practicing his new profession) in 1950, as Hoak/Cope accurately announce, Batista, for his part, was not then in power (he only reassumed the presidency via a coup d'état in March 1952); the student-inspired movement against Batista led by Castro and others was thus still several years away.

Still more damaging is the fact that Hoak himself was not even in Cuba the year he claims for these events, nor did he play for the team he cites until the winter season of 1953–1954, on the eve of his rookie National League campaign in Brooklyn. By the time Hoak did make his way onto the Cienfuegos roster, Castro was no longer in Havana, but instead spending time in jail on the Isle of Pines, serving the first months of an almost two-year lockup for his part in the Moncada Rebellion of July 1953, an incarceration from which he was not released until May (Mother's Day) 1955.

It might be noted here that there was, in truth, an actual event somewhat similar to the one Hoak would fictionalize, and this occurrence may indeed have contained the fertile seeds for the story conveniently dreamed up with ghostwriter Myron Cope. Cuban students did, in fact, interrupt a nationally televised ballgame in Havana's El Cerro Stadium—also called Gran Stadium at the time—in early winter of 1955 (December 4, leading to a swift intervention by Batista's militia and not the game's beleaguered umpire). At the time, Castro was already free from his shortened prison term on the Isle of Pines but at the moment was actually in Miami, en route to his Mexico City hideout (he left Miami on December 10) after several months of fund-raising stateside for his planned Cuban invasion expedition targeted for late 1956. Feeling his life might be in danger as a known anti-Batista agitator, Fidel had, several months earlier, on July 7, boarded a plane in Havana and headed off to his self-imposed Mexican exile.

A detailed account of this actual anti-Batista student demonstration is provided by Roberto González Echevarría in his book *The Pride of Havana* and seems to offer an obvious source for the Hoak–Cope distorted and recast version of events.[10] Professor González Echevarría reports that as a youngster he watched the memorable televised Sunday afternoon doubleheader nightcap pitting against one another league rivals Almendares and Habana from his childhood home in Sagua la Grande; the contest and on-field chaos it generated would provide the only such interruption of an island winter-league match caused by the tense political atmosphere surrounding a controversial late 1954 Batista presidential campaign.

As the Yale scholar describes the scene, a group of university students jumped from the right-field bleacher grandstand in full view of the behind-home-plate TV cameras and attempted to unfurl a long banner, which they carelessly held upside down as police dropped onto the field and began "clobbering them mercilessly with nightsticks." These student protesters were, in reality, led by Fidel's sometimes rival, José Antonio Echevarría, and represented the FEU (the *Directorio Estudiantil Universitario*, or Federation of University Students); the core of Fidel's own rival group (the "July 26th Movement") was, at the time, being organized in Mexico City. It was José Antonio Echevarría (no relation to the Yale professor) and not Fidel who appeared on the field in Havana and was not only beaten, but also arrested for his efforts, no brazen attempt to seize the pitcher's mound was ever made, and Professor González Echevarría recalls that the large stadium crowd roundly booed Bastista's gendarmes for their cowardly assaults on the student protesters.

But in this case, as in so many others, historical facts rarely stand in the way of enticingly good baseball folklore. The Hoak–Cope tale soon gained superficial legitimacy with its frequent revivals. Journalist Charles Einstein placed his own stamp of authority with an unquestioning and unaltered reprint in *The Third Fireside Book of Baseball* (1968), and then again in his *Fireside Baseball Reader* (1984). Noted baseball historian John Thorn followed suit in *The Armchair Book of Baseball* (1985), adding a clever, legitimizing header above the story, which reads, "Incredible but true. And how history might have altered if Fidel had gone on to become a New York Yanqui, or a Washington Senator, or even a Cincinnati Red."[11] A Tom Jozwik review of the Thorn anthology stresses with naïve amazement that the subject of the "autobiographical" piece is indeed Cuba's Fidel Castro and not major-league washout Bill Castro.[12]

❖ ❖ ❖

Hoak's entertaining if bogus fantasy is admittedly full of foreshadowing, even if it might be genuinely flimsy and fabricated. While neither Castro nor Hoak were simultaneously in Havana at the time the future political leader reputedly challenged the future big-league batsman (Hoak wasn't on the scene in 1950–1951, as claimed, and Castro wasn't there in either late 1953 or late 1955, the occasions for Hoak's lone actual Cuban season or the actual student-led anti-Batista ballpark protest), what is most remarkable about this now-indisputably apocryphal tale is the degree to which its all-too-easy acceptance throughout the years parallels dozens of other similar accounts concerning Fidel as a serious mound star—even a talented pitching prospect of big-league proportions. Throughout the years, legions of fans have encountered the Fidel Castro baseball story in one or another of its many all-too-familiar formats.

The legend usually paints Fidel as a promising pitching talent who was scouted in the late 1940s or early 1950s (details are always sketchy) and almost signed by a number of big-league clubs. The widely circulated version is the one that involves famed Clark Griffith "bird dog" Papa Joe Cambria and the Washington Senators. But the New York Giants,

New York Yankees, and Pittsburgh Pirates (as already noted) often get at least a passing mention. It is just too grand a story and thus has been swallowed hook, line, and fastball. The gist is as follows, with few variations. If only the scouts had been more persistent—or if only Fidel's fastball had a wee bit more pop and his curveball a bit more bend—the entire history of Western Hemisphere politics during the past half-century would likely have been drastically reshaped. Former semipro pitcher turned English professor and sportswriter Kevin Kerrane, for one, quotes Philadelphia Phillies Latin America scouting supervisor Ruben Amaro (a Mexican-raised ex-big-leaguer whose own father was Cuban League legend Santos Amaro) on this familiar theme. Amaro (asserting that Papa Joe twice rejected Castro for a contract) deduces that "Cambria could have changed history if he remembered that some pitchers mature late."[13] It is a fantasy devoutly to be wished and thus quite irresistible in the telling.

Kerrane, in reporting on the Phillies' extensive early emphasis on Latin American scouting in the 1960s and 1970s, remarks that Cuba was, for obvious reasons (the closure of the communist island to big-league operations after the Castro Revolution) not part of the Phillies' plans, but he claims that Amaro played in Cuba in the early 1950s and thus remembered "how it was when Joe Cambria, smoking a big cigar and wearing a white linen suit, would arrive at tryouts in his limousine and survey hundreds of candidates, finally deigning to offer one or two of them a new baseball in exchange for a signature on a Washington Senators' contract." If Ruben Amaro (born in Mexico in 1936) held such memories, they were formed as a young preteen who might have accompanied his native Cuban father to winter-league games. It was the father, Santos Amaro (not the future Phillies big-leaguer and later scout), who played in the Cuban winter league in the 1930s and 1940s, enjoying his final season with Almendares in 1949–1950 (when Ruben was only 13). According to Amaro (interviewed by Kerrane in the early 1980s), "All those kids (the Cuban prospects) were desperate to sign," implying that Castro must have been as well. Kerrane might be a skilled writer, but when it came to Fidel he, like others, was not much of a fact-checker.

Kerrane brushes the truth when he reports that "Cambria even turned Fidel Castro down twice."[14] The semiaccurate part of his account lies in the fact that Fidel did once show up at a Cambria mass tryout session; the unavoidable distortion is the implication that Castro ever earned a passing glance from the renowned bird dog. Others have followed suit and often with considerably less restraint. Michael and Mary Oleksak quote both Clark Griffith and again Ruben Amaro on the legend of Fidel and Papa Joe without much helpful detail but with the implication that the accounts are more fact than fiction.[15] Their Amaro quotation is, unfortunately, the same passage drawn from Kerrane; they quote Griffith as stating, "Uncle (*sic*) Joe scouted Castro and told him he didn't have a major-league arm,"[16] again fingering Kerrane as their source, although that line is not found on the page cited (or anywhere else in the Kerrane book for that matter). John Thorn and John Holway would pursue a more cautious route in citing Tampa-based Cuban baseball historian Jorge Figueredo's rebuttal that "there is no truth to the oft-repeated story that Fidel Castro was a potential big-league pitching prospect."[17]

The most unrestrained recounting of the myth nonetheless is reserved for Truby's *Harper's Magazine* reprint. Truby goes beyond merely repeating the well-worn line that a Castro baseball signing might have truly changed history. In adding Stoneham's Giants to the list of Fidel's pursuers, he first rationalizes the interest with a fabrication about Fidel's stature as a Havana University pitching ace, a claim entirely without merit. According to Stoneham (as quoted by Truby), "We had our top people evaluate him, as did several other teams . . . Castro was a real prospect." He next quotes scouting reports from Pittsburgh's Howie Haak (who, when already in his 70s, recalled Castro as a "big kid who threw a wicked *bleeping* curveball—nothing amateur about his pitches . . . a good prospect because he could throw and think at the same time"), Giants deceased Caribbean scout Alex Pompez ("he throws a good ball, not always hard, but smart . . . he has good control and should be considered seriously"), and finally again Cambria ("Castro is a big, powerful young man . . . his fastball is not great but passable . . . he uses good curve variety . . . he also uses his head and can win that way for us, too").[18] The trouble here (and it is considerable trouble indeed) is that no other known source has ever verified or even repeated any such existing or once-available scouting reports. (It might also be noted that the lines quoted hardly sound like serious assessments from legitimate scouts—seasoned talent hounds far more likely to report radar gun readings, or, in the 1950s, perhaps more impressionistic yet still more plausible measures of arm speed—than impressions of quick-wittedness or mental astuteness.)

Additional commentary, especially that coming from Castro's many biographers and from within Cuba itself, indicates that as a schoolboy pitcher, Fidel threw hard but wildly (the exact opposite of Truby's quotes). And Castro, in reality, never made the University of Havana team, let alone being the team's star performer; his schoolboy baseball playing was restricted to 1945, as a high school senior. Truby caps his account with a report, supposedly from Stoneham's lips, that Pompez was authorized to offer a $5,000 bonus for signing (a ridiculous figure in itself, since no Latin prospects were offered that kind of cash in 1950, most especially one who would have been 23 or 24 at the time), which Castro stunned Giants officials by rejecting. The biggest curveball in the *Harper's* account is quite obviously the one being tossed at readers by author J. David Truby himself.

With the explosion of interest in Latin American ball-playing talent in the past half-century (and thus also in the history of the game as it is played in Caribbean nations), the Castro baseball legend has inevitably taken on commercial overtones as well. One producer of replica Caribbean league hats and jerseys has recounted the glories of Fidel the pitcher in its catalogs and on its website and manages in the process to expand the story by trumpeting Fidel as a regular pitcher in the Cuban winter leagues. By the early 2000s, the Blue Marlin Corporation website was reporting that their promotional photo of Castro was actually a portrait of the dictator pitching for his famed military team (the "Barbudos") in the Cuban League (where no such team has ever existed, of course), whereas in reality the exhibition outing was nothing more than a staged one-time affair preceding a Havana Sugar Kings International League game (the subject of the next chapter). ESPN, a decade earlier, had already produced a handsome promotional flyer that used Fidel's baseball "history" as part of the hook to sell its own upcoming televised big-league games. The 1994 ESPN poster promoting Sunday and Wednesday night telecasts featured the same familiar 1959 photo of Fidel delivering a pitch in his Barbudos uniform, here superimposed with a bold-print headline, "The All-American Game That Once Recruited Fidel Castro."

One of the more prominent promotions of the Fidel ballplayer myth emerges with a Eugene McCarthy essay distributed in the obscure journal *Elysian Fields Quarterly* and reprinted from an earlier editorial column appearing in *USA Today* on March 14, 1994. Here the ex-senator and former presidential candidate stumps (half-seriously, one presumes) for Fidel as a much-needed replacement big-league baseball commissioner (viz., "what baseball most needs—an experienced dictator").[19] While McCarthy may deliver his proposals tongue-in-cheek when it comes to the commissioner campaign, he nonetheless apparently buys into the myth of Fidel's ball-playing background. Thus, "Another prospect eyed by the Senators was a pitcher named Fidel Castro, who was rejected because scouts reported he didn't have a major-league fastball." Equally sold were *Elysian Fields Quarterly* editors, who commissioned artist Andy Nelson to create a volume-cover fantasy 1953 Topps baseball card of a bearded Castro in Washington uniform as pitcher for the Clark Griffith–era woebegone, cellar-dwelling American League Senators.

Nelson's black-and-white rendered fantasy Topps 1953 bubble gum card inevitably features some immediate signals of historical anachronism that should alert perceptive readers. A 1953 Topps card neatly fits the artist's purpose, since in that particular year the Topps Chewing Gum Company indeed used just such artists' renderings of ballplayers (mostly consisting of head portraits only), and Nelson's pen-and-ink portrait thus has a special feeling of reality about it—but only for those with short memories when it comes to historical events transpiring at the time in Cuba. Castro, of course, early in the 1953 season, was still a nonbearded student leader (and already a licensed lawyer) devoted to politics and not baseball, and about to launch his revolutionary career (not his ball-playing one) with an ill-fated attack on the Moncada military barracks in Santiago.

❁ ❁ ❁

Despite this enthusiastic, if sometimes rather whimsical, media promotion, the entire Castro pitching saga is, in the end, just as much unsubstantiated myth as Hoak's published account of facing the revolutionary hurler back in 1950–1951 (or 1954–1955, or whatever season it might have been). Ultimately, Fidel was never a serious pitching prospect, a raw gem that might demand a $5,000 bonus or even a far less weighty contract offer. He was never pursued by big-league scouts, or specifically by the ubiquitous Joe Cambria. (Recall here that Cambria's modus operandi was always to sign up every kid in Cuba with even passing signs of promise and then let the Washington spring training camp sort them out later; if Fidel Castro had any legitimate big-league talent, one can assume Cambria could hardly have missed him.) Fidel was never on his way to the big leagues in Washington or New York, or any other points between, no matter how intriguing any later invention claiming that, but for a trick of cruel fate or a misjudgment by Papa Joe, he might well have been serving up smoking fastballs against 1950s-era Washington American League opponents, instead of launching his political curveballs against 1960s-era Washington bureaucrats.

What, then, are the true facts surrounding Fidel Castro and baseball, especially those touching on Fidel's own ball-playing endeavors? Close examination of the historical and biographical records makes a number of points indisputably clear. First and foremost, the young Fidel did indeed have a passion—or at least a passing fancy—for the popular sport of baseball, one that was apparent in his early childhood years in Cuba's eastern province of Oriente. Biographer Robert Quirk reports on the youngster's apparent fascination with the Cuban national game, and especially his attraction to its central position of pitcher (the "man always in control").[20] But it is also obvious from the widely available biographical accounts that young Fidel was mostly enamored of his own abilities to dominate in the sporting arena—as in all other schoolboy arenas, for example, academics and eventually student politics—and not with the lure of the game itself. He organized an informal team as a youngster in his hometown of Birán, when Angel Castro, his wealthy landowner father, provided the needed supplies of bats, balls, and gloves. And when he and his team didn't win games, he angrily packed up his father's equipment and trudged home.[21] Fidel, from the start, apparently was never essentially a team player or much of a true sportsman at heart.

Fidel's nascent baseball fantasies (like those of so many of us) were never to be matched by any remarkable batting or throwing talent. As a high school student in Havana, he maintained his early passion for sports and played on the basketball team at Belén, the private Havana Catholic secondary school he attended from 1942 to 1945. He also pitched on the baseball squad as a senior, as well as being a star track and field performer (middle distances and high jumping), a ping-pong champion, and leader of the hiking club (where Quirk reports "he could always take the lead"). When it came to basketball, his best sport, Quirk notes Fidel was never quite as good as he thought and was at first turned down by the coach and only selected for the squad after a full year of determined nighttime practice on his own, aided by lights he had persuaded the priests to install for his after-hours shooting sessions in the school courtyard. The relentless determination paid off, as he was eventually named team captain his senior year.

Biographer Quirk also suggests that during his senior season on the baseball squad, Fidel "had some extravagant notion of playing in the major leagues"—a momentary fantasy likely arising from a super-charged ego, but perhaps also inspired by the number of Cubans rushed to the majors by Joe Cambria and the Washington Senators due to the mid-1940s World War II player shortages Stateside.[22] Quirk doesn't hesitate to point out, however, that high school baseball compe-tition in Havana—comprised of mostly white upper-class students at elite private schools for the privileged—was of the lowest quality ("bush-league" is Quirk's term), whereas the finest athletes in Cuba were mostly Afro-Cubans emerging from the lowest rungs of the social ladder.

Later efforts of Castro's inner circle (although seemingly never of Fidel himself) to promote his well-rounded image by fanning the ru-mors of athletic prowess are already apparent in connection with schoolboy days. Professor Quirk, whose exhaustive study is one of the most scholarly in a long list of Fidel biographies published in both Spanish and English, reports on uncovering numerous unsubstantiated accounts that Fidel was selected Havana's schoolboy athlete of the year for 1945. Yet, when Quirk tirelessly poured over every single daily issue of the Havana sports pages (in *Diario de la Marina*) for that particular year, he could find not a single mention of Castro's name.[23] In a foot-note to his account of the Castro years at Belén, Quirk ironically dem-onstrates his own carelessness of historical details when he notes that the actual outstanding schoolboy star of that 1945 season was reported by *Diario* to be Conrado Marrero, an amateur pitching hero who him-self became legendary on Cuban diamonds of the 1940s and early 1950s, and who actually did make it onto the Washington Senators major-league roster. Surprisingly, what Quirk overlooks is the fact that Marrero was already 34 in 1945, and had long been established as a top star on the Cuban amateur national team since the late 1930s. In 1945, Marrero was pitching his eighth and final season with the Cienfuegos club of the popular national amateur league and not laboring on Havana high school diamonds.

Nevertheless, there does turn out to be a source after all in the Belén high school years for the essence of the Castro baseball legend. Biographer Quirk may falsely have assumed Fidel's recognition as a top schoolboy athlete to be based on his senior season, when in actuality the recognition came a year earlier, in 1943–1944. Another Fidel chronicler, Peter Bourne, does indeed acknowledge Castro's status as a top basketball (not baseball) player at Belén, and also his recognition as Havana's top schoolboy sportsman during that earlier winter.[24] Bourne also emphasizes Fidel's penchant for using athletics—as he also used academics, the debate society, and student politics—as a convenient method for proving he could excel in almost any endeavor imaginable. Fidel was so driven in this way that he once wagered a school chum he could ride his bicycle full speed into a brick wall. He succeeded, but the attempt actually landed him in the school infirmary for several weeks.

It is the Belén athletic successes that in the end contain the hidden key to the legend of Fidel the baseball prospect. By the mid-1940s, Joe Cambria was living at the exclusive American Club in Havana and had been for some time running Washington Senators scouting activities from his hotel room and part-time residence, also holding regular open tryout camps for the legions of eager Havana prospects, as well as beating the bushes around the rest of the island to seek out cheap Cuban talent. Fidel is reported to have shown up uninvited at two such camps between his junior and senior years, largely to prove to school chums that he might indeed be good enough to earn a pro contract offer.[25] Castro, in other words, sought out Cambria and the pro scouts, and not vice versa.

As a matter of record, no contract was ever offered to the hard-but-wild-throwing prospect. And as biographer Bourne stresses, any offer would almost certainly have been rejected in any case. Fidel was a privileged youth from a wealthy family and thus had better prospects looming on the horizon (a lucrative career in law and politics) far more promising than pro baseball. Professional ball-playing as an occupation would actually have seemed a step down for any prospective law student of that decade since even major leaguers of the era earned little better that a day laborer's wages. There were no big bonus deals in the 1940s, especially in Cuba, where Cambria's mission for the penny-pinching Clark Griffith was to find dirt-cheap talent among lower-class athletes desperate to sign for next to nothing. Fidel's own promising future was already assured in the lucrative fields of law and politics. His reported fascination with baseball could never have been more than the compulsive showoff's momentary diversion—an endeavor devoid of captivating dreams of escape into big-league glories or elusive promises of big-league riches. As Bourne suggests, Fidel's "reason for trying out was clearly more for the gratification of showing that he could have made it."[26]

When he next put in his time as a law student at the University of Havana (1945–1950), Fidel's athletic fantasies were apparently not entirely squelched, and he did play on the freshman basketball team and also try out—apparently unsuccessfully—for the college varsity baseball squad. But as biographer Quirk notes, ballplayers in Cuba (as well as top athletes in other sports, especially boxing) were already by the mid- and late 1940s coming mostly from poorer African descendants among the populace, not from the upper crust privileged students like Fidel. The future politician, from schoolboy and university days onward, displayed an abiding fascination for ballplaying—especially basketball and soccer, as later interviews would reveal—that remained with him in future years.

But it was unquestionably evident, even to Fidel, during college years that he had little serious talent as a baseball hurler. Furthermore, political activities preoccupied the ambitious law student from 1948 onward and left almost no available time for any serious practice on the baseball field. While his numerous biographers cover every aspect of his life in painstaking detail, none mention any further tryouts for baseball scouts, any serious playing on organized teams, or indeed any baseball activity at all until his eventual renewed passion for the game as a dedicated fan. And the latter passion became apparent only after a successful rise to political power in January 1959. Quirk and Bourne alone among Castro biographers emphasize Fidel's ballplaying, and then only to report that baseball never quite measured up to basketball or track and field as an arena for displaying athletic skill or releasing an obsessive drive for unlimited personal triumphs and personal domination of any and all rivals.

Yet, baseball was not entirely out of the picture for the student leader obsessed with political organizing and campus rowdiness. There does actually exist at least one documented example of Fidel's active baseball participation during student days in Havana. If Fidel was never a mound ace for the official varsity nine, as so often reported, he did apparently do some actual pitching in organized contests while on the university campus. *El Mundo*, for November 28, 1946, carries a game report and minimal box score for the university's intramural championship contest, played a day earlier between the faculties (schools) of commercial sciences (business) and law, in which one F. Castro hurled for the latter squad. The full box score may provide the only existing evidence containing actual statistics for Fidel Castro's rather abbreviated, unglamorous collegiate baseball career.[27] As the losing hurler (by a 5–4 count) Fidel struck out four, walked seven, yielded five hits, and hit one batter in his complete-game losing effort. Those numbers might be taken as support for the various observations that the young Fidel threw hard but lacked control of his speedy tosses.

Harvard University scholar and Latin American political historian Jonathan Hansen (author of *Guantanamo: An American History* and at work on a new book entitled *Young Castro*, aimed at recording Fidel's life before seizing power in 1959) has turned up several similar long-buried newspaper accounts of the youthful future "comandante" participating in organization ballgames.[28] These accounts come from the same time period as the box score reported in the previous paragraph. The first references a game on October 12, 1946, in the small town of Cueto, near Angel Castro's estate in Birán, between Las Estrellas Foraneas and Maracané Republicano. Pitching for the latter club, Fidel was shelled for five runs in the third frame and four more in the seventh as his club lost, 9–2. He did collect two base hits in four trips to the plate.

The other accounts obviously result from the same intramural championship series on the aforementioned University of Havana campus. In the first, played on November 6, 1946, Fidel's Law School club was an 11–8 loser to the Architecture School. Castro collected two hits in as many at-bats and, as a pitcher, struck out three, issued an equal number of free passes, and tossed one wild pitch. But he was not the losing hurler (someone named Montero is tagged with the defeat). The second match (November 12) found the Law students again losing, this time to the Agronomy School by a 7–1 score. Fidel was the starting pitcher but was pulled in the third frame (losing 5–0), after giving up six hits, committing one balk, and striking out only one opposing batter.

Perhaps the most balanced view of Fidel's sporadic ball-playing comes in a late 1960s book produced by American photojournalist Lee Lockwood, *Castro's Cuba, Cuba's Fidel*. Lockwood made three visits to Cuba in 1965 and 1966, including a three-and-a-half-month stay beginning in May and ending in August 1965. Reporting on the Cuba he witnessed during those visits, a significant portion of his book is taken up by dozens of his candid black-and-white photographs from throughout the island, including a two-page spread featuring on one page Raúl batting ("a competent second baseman, he is the better hitter") and Fidel attired in baseball jersey and army slacks pitching ("Fidel has good control but not much stuff"); the second full-page shot is of Fidel at midfield in army fatigues apparently heatedly disputing an umpire's call ("As in everything else he does, Fidel plays baseball to win and complains loudly to the umpire on losing a close call").

Lockwood's groundbreaking early portrait of Castro is drawn through hours of in-depth interviews transcribed in careful detail on such far-ranging topics as his assessment of his island nation's economic and political successes and failures, his own enigmatic personality, relations with the United States, and the world situation at large. The heart of the book's text is thus a composite of these extensive interviews with the Cuban leader, including a seven-hour marathon conversation at Fidel's retreat on the Isle of Pines (now the Isle of Youth). The specific topic of baseball is never broached in those lengthy discussions. Lockwood would, however, briefly also touch further on Fidel's sporting interests during the middle segment of his marathon interview sessions.[29] In that three-page passage, Fidel would speak mostly of fishing, hunting, and swimming, and also allude to his schoolboy feats in track and field, soccer, mountain hiking, and especially basketball. Notably, baseball is never mentioned.

But in one important noninterview passage, Lockwood makes a most interesting observation about Fidel's baseball playing, specifically his pitching, one of the few such accounts couched more in objectivity than hearsay or outworn mythology. Lockwood reports on visiting an army-camp ball field near Havana where Fidel happened to be playing in an informal pickup contest. As Lockwood relates, "There were about a hundred spectators, mainly soldiers and their wives or girlfriends, watching delightedly as Castro, in gay spirits, pitched and batted and jockeyed raucously from the bench and clowned hugely with players and audience alike."[30]

The remainder of Lockwood's rendition of this scene is worth quoting in its entirety:

> Though Fidel takes baseball seriously (like everything else), *it is not one of the sports at which he is most talented* [my italics for emphasis]. He throws sidearm, with good control, but with not very much on the ball. There isn't much difference between his fastball and his curve. Both are what the players call "fat pitches," and this time, as on every other occasion I have seen him play, he was clobbered unmercifully. Yet he stayed in there—what manager would dare yank Fidel Castro?

There is quite a contrast between the eloquent "scouting report" and those Truby credits to baseball lifers Stoneham, Haak, and Pompez. Lockwood ends his account by noting that since his team was losing, 11–2, Fidel insisted on extending the game an extra two innings. He also reports that as the contest dragged on, one of Fidel's teammates, top government army official Ramiro Valdez (whose wispy, pointed beard gave him the appearance of a large gnome) ragged the Jefe from the sidelines and begged him to let him pitch. When Castro pretended to ignore the taunts, Valdez called out, "Come on Fidel, let me play. I'm a much better pitcher than you are!"

Fidel's exhaustive chronicler, Tad Szulc, also mentions a later event, shedding considerable light on Castro's sublimated athletic interests. Szulc reports—with little accompanying detail—an interview with an unnamed American visitor in which Fidel suddenly and unexpectedly began to expound on the important symbolic values of his favored schoolboy sport, basketball. Basketball, Fidel reputedly observes, provides valuable indirect training for revolutionary activities.[31] It is a game requiring strategic and tactical planning, and overall cunning, plus speed and agility, the true elements of guerrilla warfare. Baseball, Fidel further noted, held no such promise for a future revolutionary. Most significantly, Szulc also points out that Fidel's comments on this occasion came during a candid response in which he "emphatically denied" the reported rumors that he once envisioned a career for himself as a professional pitcher in the North American major leagues.

Basketball held an obvious attraction for Fidel beyond the merely intellectual aspects of the game. Photojournalist Alex Arbuckle, writer and curator of historical photo essays for the website Mashable Retronaut (a global multiplatform media and entertainment company), posted a piece in October 2016, devoted to Fidel's basketball interests and exploits. Entitled "Fidel Castro Felt Basketball Was Perfect Training for Guerrilla Warfare," the online article carries minimal text, reporting on the Cuban leader's penchant for organizing pickup games during the 1960s and 1970s and also repeating the philosophizing noted by Szulc about basketball's potential role in training revolutionaries.[32] The bulk of the piece, however, provides nine 1970s-vintage Getty images capturing Fidel in heated play (dressed in an assortment of sweat suits and military fatigues) during state visits to Bulgaria and Poland, as well as in Havana matches versus assorted clubs comprised of students, amateur-league squads, and Cuban newsmen. There are also other occasional references to these impromptu pickup games scattered throughout the Castro literature, for example, several in the Szulc biography: viz., playing in June 1972, in Sofia, with an army team versus a civilian team (noted by Szulc as one of his happier moments during a lengthy African and Eastern European junket), and taking part in a rousing game during the 1971 stopover in Chile.[33]

It is clear from the historical record that Fidel was an accomplished and enthusiastic athlete as a precocious youngster and still maintained both impressive skills and polished competitive spirit well into early middle age. His many biographers underscore his repeated use of schoolboy athletics (especially basketball, track and field, and baseball) to excel among fellow students. But Fidel's consuming interests and latent talents were never devoted exclusively or even primarily to Cuba's acknowledged national sport. His strong identification with the native game after the success of his 1959 revolution—he followed Havana's Sugar Kings as a dedicated fan, staged showcase exhibitions before Cuban League games, and played frequent pickup matches with numerous close comrades and available ragtag amateur clubs—was perhaps, more than anything else, an inevitable acknowledgment of the country's national sport and its widespread hold on the Cuban citizenry. It was also a calculated step toward using baseball as a means of besting the hated imperialists at their own cherished game. And early on, baseball was also seen by the Maximum Leader as an instrument of revolutionary politics—a means to build revolutionary spirit at home and construct ongoing (and headline-grabbing) international propaganda triumphs abroad. Basketball may have contained the seeds of proper guerrilla preparation, but baseball formed the essence of Cuban national identity. Fidel may not have exercised much control over his fastball in long-lost school days. But he eventually proved a natural-born expert (a true "phenom") at controlling baseball (the institution) as a highly useful instrument for carefully building his revolutionary society and maintaining his propaganda leverage in worldwide Cold War politics.

Fidel and baseball remained inevitably linked throughout the near-half-century of Castro's active role in revolutionary Cuba, and the Maximum Leader would inevitably change the face and focus of the island's baseball fortunes, just as he so dramatically changed everything else that constituted Cuban society. But it was only as a political figurehead and Maximum Leader—not legitimate prodigy ballplayer—that Fidel Castro emerged as one of the most remarkable figures found anywhere in Cuban baseball history. As a pitcher, he was perhaps never more than the smoky essence of unrelenting myth. He certainly wasn't Cuba's hidden Walter Johnson or Christy Mathewson, or even its latter-day Dolf Luque or Conrado Marrero; his role was destined to be much more akin to the shadowy and insubstantial Abner Doubleday or Alexander Cartwright, or perhaps even the promotion-wise and always market-savvy A. G. Spalding.

Cooperstown Hall of Famer Monte Irvin, who played for Almendares during the 1948–1949 Havana winter-league season, supposedly quipped that if he and other players in the Cuban League during the late 1940s had known that the young student who hung around the Havana ballpark had designs on being an autocrat, they would have been well served to make him an umpire.[34] Perhaps Senator Eugene McCarthy had the more appropriate role in mind—that of baseball czar and big-league commissioner. Without ever launching a serious fastball or swinging a potent bat, Fidel was nonetheless destined—like Judge Landis north of the Straits of Florida a generation earlier—to have a far greater impact on his nation's pastime than several entire generations of leather-pounding or lumber-toting on-field diamond stars. As Eugene

McCarthy so astutely observed, an aspiring pitcher with a long memory, once spurned, can indeed be a most dangerous man.[35]

# 3

# THE INFAMOUS "BARBUDOS" GAME

His fastball has long since died. He still has a few curveballs, which he throws at us routinely.—Nicholas Burns, U.S. State Department spokesman[1]

The fabricated "Hoak Hoax" story may have planted the seed, but it was not likely the central culprit in cementing the Fidel ballplayer myth in North American versions of the Castro legacy. Herbert Matthews observes that Fidel himself was also a leading player in authoring his own mythology, that his indelible legend was largely a product of his successes in carefully hiding the personal life that might make him accessible or human—"he is a man who has permitted little of a personal nature to be known about his life."[2] If the Cuban Revolution he led was inarguably a product of his own invention, so was the role he would play as revolutionary leader. And it was most likely the newly established Cuban strongman's decision to play a starring role in what would become a most memorable pitching exhibition that supplied much of the later ammunition for those looking to spin a durable myth about the newly minted communist leader's prowess on the baseball diamond.

The infamous "Barbudos" exhibition game of July 24, 1959, would—for North Americans at least—provide the photographic images that would repeatedly reinforce the notion of Fidel as a serious baseball pitcher. It was one of only a hefty supply of such exhibition appearances in coming years, but it was the one that somehow seemed to capsulize the comandante's deep-rooted baseball connection. Unfortunately, what was lost in both North American news reports of the time and subsequent historical references to follow was the contemporary events that surrounded the memorable sporting event of late July 1959. The Barbudos exhibition appearance (so-called for the clever team name stitched across the green and white jerseys of Fidel's ragtag squad, composed entirely of bearded rebel soldiers) was but one result of a crucial moment in Fidel's efforts to cement his power and thus solidify his revolutionary movement.

On the eve of the fateful weekend games between the Sugar Kings and Rochester Red Wings, Fidel had staged a dramatic political move—the first of many to follow—intended to change the balance of power within his new revolutionary government. A 10-day span between July 17–26 would define his initial leadership crisis and thus offer a major turning point in the earliest months of the new revolutionary government. It would also bring a quick end to Fidel's initial indecision and doubts about the direction of his new government and his own future role in the fate of the nation.

The first six months of the new administration had been largely defined by considerable confusion, numerous missteps in planning, and

**BARBUDOS BATTERY.** Camilo Cienfuegos opted to catch rather than pitch, remarking "I don't oppose Fidel in anything, including baseball." *The Rucker Archive*

a general naiveté among young revolutionaries, who suddenly found themselves in control of the country without any adequate preparation or forethought about how they would actually govern. For his own part, Fidel's energies and attention had been narrowly concentrated for more than a decade entirely on the task of destroying Batista and turning the long-loathed Cuban government system of corruption and privilege squarely on its head. Fidel's own long delay in reaching Havana in the week after the News Year's Day triumph signaled his own uncertainty about the next necessary steps for remaking the country in a more socially conscious image. The immediate plan, if there was one, was only to bask briefly in the glory of personal triumph.

Fidel did not qualify technically for the Cuban presidency by stipulations found in the Constitution of 1940, since the minimum age requirement was 40, but that fact alone would not likely have stood in the way of occupying the highest office by popular demand. The widespread recognition that the revolution was his alone to direct was unquestioned, and public outcry was one-sided in support of Fidel maintaining complete control. But he was not at all sure he wanted the burden of national leadership. Manuel Urrutia, a moderate judge without political affiliation who had ruled during the Moncada trials that Fidel's rebels had acted constitutionally, had already been his choice for the presidency. And Fidel (like Che in the near future) seemed more enamored with the idea of carrying on the revolutionary process he started in other Latin American nations than with the nuts and bolts of running a country.

On the home front, he also initially faced the immediate concerns of keeping the remnants of the old military from seizing power. He began a process of playing off three groups one against the other—his hardcore M-26-7 coalition from the Sierra Maestra, fronted by Che and Raúl, the old school Cuban Communist Party, and the hordes of middle-class supporters and liberal reformers who now hoped for genuine democratic reform. His power base remained his immense personal popularity with the masses, and in the early months of 1959, he controlled the nation from outside the formal government structure. The crisis in formal leadership that this inevitably created caused the early resignation of Prime Minister Miró Cardona, who found himself devoid of any real power and thus walked away, recommending Fidel be handed the job. Castro was less than enthusiastic about the formal title and only reluctantly accepted the position at the urging of Celia Sánchez.

On the heels of accepting the official reins of power came a mid-April trip to Washington, DC, at the invitation of the American Society of Newspaper Editors. The visit included additional stops in New York, Princeton, and Houston. That trip, during which Fidel traveled with an entourage of 70, seemed successful enough on the surface, at least from a public relations perspective, but it also worked to sow seeds of discord with the Eisenhower administration (the president left town on a golfing junket to avoid the Cuban leader) and especially with Vice President Richard Nixon, who in a private meeting harangued Fidel with evidence of communist influence in his new government. A much-delayed journey home would reveal early but growing opposition to Fidel's control from several sources aimed at reversing the direction of the revolutionary agenda Fidel apparently had in mind. The recently enacted Agrarian Reform Act and the INRA mechanism designed to implement it caused much of the opposition; three bombs were set off in Havana by opposition terrorists on June 13, during a speech in which Fidel was defending his new agrarian reform policies. And in June there was also the celebrated defection to the U.S. of Cuban Air Force commander Pedro Diaz Lanz.

Moreover, President Manuel Urrutia had become a looming problem for Fidel. He was out of step with the young revolutionary generation, and worse still, his loud campaign against the Cuban Communist Party had become increasingly irksome. Fidel had continued to advocate for a democratic path for the new regime, but he had also increasingly seen the need for an all-inclusive power basis that required the Communists (the only group in the country that approximated a well-oiled political machine) as an integral element. Wanting to rid the government of Urrutia, Fidel skillfully held back and allowed the elder president to seal his own fate. A turning point came on July 17, when Fidel suddenly resigned the premiership and then took to the evening television airwaves to savagely attack Urrutia, in what biographer Peter Bourne calls a first sign of Fidel's potential for extreme ruthlessness. Since the average Cuban did not fear communism and thus showed little sympathy for Urrutia's warnings on that particular count, Fidel was able to underscore his attacks on Urrutia by emphasizing what he intimated were the president's hidden links to the United States. Fidel cleverly sold the message that Urrutia's anticommunism (a stance then associated by most Cubans with the Americans) was evidence of links to hostile groups outside Cuba and perhaps even a plan to reassert foreign domination on the island.

The resignation ploy had precisely the desired effect, as it forced Urrutia to immediately resign in humiliation. As Bourne observes, Urrutia was an honest but weak man apparently unable to grasp the reality that he no longer fit in Fidel's plans.[3] There had been no real evidence of the president colluding with groups plotting foreign intervention, and Fidel could have quietly convinced him to step aside, facts that lead Bourne to label Castro's actions here both vicious and roundly unjust. Osvaldo Dorticós was quickly named as Urrutia's replacement, although there is evidence he was not Fidel's first choice.[4] Fidel's own official position in the power structure remained shrouded in confusion for the next week. It would be resolved soon enough, however, with the employment of what would quickly become a favored and most skillful political tool.

A public holiday and mass rally was announced for the upcoming first annual post-Batista celebration of the 1953 Moncada attack (henceforth the country's main patriotic holiday), an event now only days away. That Sunday, July 26, celebration would feature an address to the masses by Fidel, at which time he promised to submit his personal political future directly to the people. Thousands, mostly peasants from the immediately surrounding countryside, flocked to the capital for the festivities, and it was that raucous crowd that would fill and surround Cerro Stadium for the Sugar Kings game on the eve of the July 26 rally. The weekend would also be kicked off with the "Barbudos" exhibition ballgame preceding the Friday Havana–Rochester International League game. The match would be officially billed as a fundraiser for the new agrarian reform programs legislated two months earlier.

The onetime pitching appearance in the uniform of the "Barbudos" military squad was thus very much a spectacle connected to political events of the previous several weeks.[5] If Fidel's staged resignation from the premiership was a thinly disguised ploy to rally public opinion in his favor, the baseball demonstration could have been nothing less; the two events were part and parcel of the same agenda. Wooing public support in the wake of his calculated resignation and on the weekend of his even more calculated appeal to his mass of supporters could perhaps find no wiser move than one connecting the popular revolutionary leader with the nation's beloved national pastime and its standard-bearing team in the American professional league. The crowds at the ballpark that Friday and Saturday were crammed with rebel supporters and sympathizers who had flocked from the countryside to be on hand for what was expected to be (and proved in the end definitely to be) a grand display of unrestrained political theater. In Havana, what better stage for such theatrics than a baseball diamond?

Nonetheless, while Fidel cleverly manipulated the moment and stoked his popular image with a staged Friday evening pitching appearance, it would also be true that events unfolding at the Cerro district ballpark within the next 24 hours would ironically unleash a chain of events certain to impact the status of island baseball in ways Fidel obviously could never have anticipated. It was the outbreak of perceived violence and unquestioned chaos in Havana's Gran Stadium the following evening that set in full motion events destined to spell the end for both an already besieged Sugar Kings franchise and the entire enterprise of North American–controlled professional baseball in Cuba.

*  *  *

True impetus for tales and legends of Fidel as serious ballplayer seems to follow as much from the Maximum Leader's postrevolution associations with the game as from bloated reports concerning his imagined role as erstwhile schoolboy prospect. Central here are oft-recounted— but rarely accurately portrayed—exhibition-game appearances at stadiums in Havana and elsewhere throughout the island during the first decade following the 1959–1960 Communist takeover. The most renowned single event, of course, was Fidel's onetime appearance on the mound in El Cerro Stadium (home of the Havana/Cuban Sugar Kings) wearing the uniform of his own pickup nine, aptly christened "*Los Barbudos*" ("The Bearded Ones"). Rarely, however, have any Stateside baseball historians or the North American press gotten the high-mileage "Barbudos" story entirely straight.

The celebrated but little-understood Barbudos game took place in Havana on July 24, 1959, in front of a healthy crowd of 25,000 "*fanáticos*" (26,532 to be precise), as showcase preliminary to a scheduled International League clash between Rochester's Red Wings and Havana's Sugar Kings. A single pithy newspaper account from the *Rochester* (New York) *Democrat and Chronicle* provides the source for most details of the evening's events and also a familiar Castro action photo—Fidel releasing a pitch as he warms up—which later accompanied most "Castro-as-phenom" pitching tales.

The boldface headline for the Rochester newspaper account is, "CASTRO SCORES SMASH HIT AS BASEBALL PLAYER," followed by the subheading, "Fidel Whiffs Two in Mound Stint as 25,000 Fanaticos Applaud." The exhibition match receives top billing, with the league-game summary relegated to two thin columns below ("Havana Defeats Red Wings, 4–2 on 'Cheap' Run"). Buried in that story, however, is a detail that now implies ominous foreshadowing: a note that the Wings and Cubans would begin play late the following evening—Saturday, at 9 p.m., which was actually 8 p.m. Havana time—with resumption of a suspended 0–0 contest held over from June 7, the result of those makeup innings thus dictating the later-than-normal start for the originally scheduled match. That delay would prove significant.

Predictably, the Havana press accounts are more enthusiastic still. Friday's edition of *Diario de la Marina* (the city's main daily) announces "Magnificent Benefit Festival Today in El Cerro" in its lead story atop page 3 of the sports section. It is revealed there that doctor Fidel Castro Ruz (Cuban lawyers were referred to as "doctor") "will recall his baseball days" as pitcher for the "Barbudos" (the team of revolutionary rebels), while Comandante (Major) Camilo Cienfuegos was scheduled to hurl for the military police squad. A crowd of 40,000 was predicted, a gross overestimation given the eventual turnout. Below is a photo of Cienfuegos in familiar military fatigues and peasant cowboy Stetson crouched in catcher's stance, with a caption indicating that for this occasion, Camilo would trade his catcher's mitt for a pitching assignment.

Saturday's edition of the same periodical features a page-two sports section game report that again gives Fidel's exhibition top billing— "Doctor Castro Pitches One Inning and Doesn't Allow a Hit; the Cubans Win." Included are three prominent photos: Fidel delivering a pitch, Fidel at bat swinging and connecting (wearing uniform number 19), and Camilo catching in pregame warmups after his decision to join Fidel's team and not the opposition as billed. Most interesting, however, is the *Diario* Sunday edition's pictorial spread (the day of the planned mass rally and Fidel's scheduled speech) carrying the banner headline *"Memorable Velada en la Historia del Base Ball Cubano"* ("Memorable Night in the History of Cuban Baseball"). There were two full pages of photos, the most interesting being one of Fidel autographing the game ball at home plate for umpire Amado Maestri, the same arbiter Hoak placed in his fictional account of batting against the young revolutionary leader. The photo caption reports that Fidel rushed to the plate after his complete inning on the mound (the second and final inning of the game) to congratulate Maestri for a called third strike earlier in the frame.

The *Diario* pictorial spread also further humanizes the Cuban leader and the festive moment by including a centrally placed close-up photo of Castro's young son, Fidelito (a few months shy of his 10th birthday at the time), laughing to see his father's harmless rollout to shortstop during his single at-bat. The introductory text on the previous page devotes the second of its two paragraphs to explaining that Fidelito's presence was his first public appearance after a horrible recent automobile accident from which he had ("thanks to God") speedily recovered. A second photo also shows Fidelito enjoying a hardy on-field laugh with Camilo Cienfuegos after the latter had struck out.

The American press coverage is more revealing, even without the picture montage. Fidel is reported by *Democrat and Chronicle* writer George Beahon to have practiced all day in his hotel room for his one-inning stint with the rebel army pickup team against the squad of military police officers. Beahon's account unavoidably fans the flames of legend by branding Fidel a onetime high-school pitcher and reporting that he had "tried out" for the college team, but no mention is made of any collegiate competition or any interest among scouts in his moderate throwing talents. Beahon merely reports, "His pitching, considering the weight he has added since he left the mountains to live in the plush Hilton, was surprisingly good—wild but fast and with good motions." He also confirms that Castro struck out the first two batters he faced— one with obvious umpire aid—and needlessly but ably covered first base on the ground ball that ended his single inning of labor. Moreover, Beahon mentions that when umpire Maestri called out one batter on a high-inside 3–2 count pitch, Fidel indeed "dashed to the plate to shake hands with the ump." Good theater, as intended, but not the mark of an aspiring professional pitcher. One final note by Beahon confirms that Fidel, batting in the first frame, "bounced out to short, and ran out the play on his trip to the plate."

Details of the memorable exhibition would quickly enough fade, but the photographic record—not only the Rochester and Havana press photos of the following day but dozens more from that evening's festivities that would appear during the following decades—soon enough took on a life of its own. The entire latter-day public impression of Fidel as talented mound ace (in the United States at least) is indeed built largely, if not exclusively, upon the existing photographic images culled from this single evening's events.

Perhaps the most memorable moment of the Friday evening festivities would be reserved for still another military hero of the revolution, Major Camilo Cienfuegos, originally scheduled to hurl for the opposing MP team but suddenly undergoing an apparent change of heart. Then again, it may have been part of a staged scheme to further enhance the image of the wildly popular Fidel. Moments before the opening toss, Camilo would proudly announce to surrounding press photographers and journalists, "I never oppose Fidel in anything, including baseball," then don catcher's gear and take up a post behind the plate for Fidel's Barbudos nine.[6] Nonetheless, if loyal trooper Camilo would not risk upstaging Comandante Castro, the activities of lesser-known henchmen soon enough would do precisely that, more by accident than by design. Friday night levity would soon enough be translated into Saturday night chaos.

A single evening later, one of the most infamous and portentous events of Cuban baseball history would surprisingly unfold—the oft-reported shooting incident in which Rochester third-base coach Frank Verdi and Havana shortstop Leo Cárdenas were apparently nicked by stray bullets launched by revolutionary zealots who had crowded into El Cerro Stadium replete with firearms in anticipation of wild celebrations about to unfold at the stroke of midnight. Sunday would mark the first July 26 Moncada anniversary under the new revolutionary regime, and it was the promise of patriotic fireworks (Latin American style) that had apparently drawn the rambunctious throng to the overflowing ballpark.

What followed that night in El Cerro Stadium was as much a comedy of errors as it was a tragedy of misunderstanding. And once more the facts surrounding the shooting incident itself, and the stadium frenzy that both preceded and followed, rarely get told correctly. Still on the scene, Rochester beat writer Beahon would provide a matter-of-fact account in the Monday edition of the *Democrat and Chronicle* that seemed tame enough given the headline banner above the actual story—"BULLETS BREAK UP WING-CUBAN GAME." By contrast, the Havana press had much bigger news to report in its Sunday editions than the interruptions at the ballpark. It was a scheduled weekend of grand political theater, and the focus was on Fidel's important upcoming speech, not on the fears of the somewhat shell-shocked visiting American ballplayers. In Havana itself, Fidel's Sunday agenda knocked the late-night ballpark events off the front page.

Leading Fidel biographer Robert Quirk recounts the scene as the Cubans themselves saw it on that historic weekend. In Quirk's phrasing, it was a "time of the *guajiros*" (simple uneducated peasants from the countryside), as thousands of peasants poured into the city for the Moncada Day celebration.[7] Dressed in their finest farmers' attire, mostly guayaberas, but with machetes strapped to their belts, they had been flooding the capital for 10 days on the heels of Fidel's invitation. The unfolding riotous scene was one of unfettered festive joy for the locals but had to be highly unsettling for American ballplayers marooned in the Hotel Nacional in the aftermath of ballpark gunplay. Newspaper accounting in the several Havana dailies carried editorial cartoons cautioning rustic visitors against overindulging. By Sunday morning, Havana's central districts were packed with revelers.

Fidel arrived on the scene in a military helicopter and playfully climbed atop a Sherman tank on the Malecón seafront drive, maneuvering its canon in a playful gesture to point at three fishing vessels cruising offshore. Church bells rang, white doves were released above rooftops, machetes flashed in the sun, and army troops marched in revue. That night, events were capped when Fidel, arriving two hours late to exploit the building anticipation, spoke in the Civic Plaza to a crowd estimated at more than a million (some sources say only half that). He would accept their public outcry as the "will of the people," signaling the country's unanimous decision that he should return to formal leadership as premier. This, he told his mass audience, was "true democracy," not the ballot box elections that in Cuba's past were so often demonstrably corrupt. And as machetes continued to flash in response to his message, the charismatic Fidel also warned that those Cuban blades were being sharpened to carry out the extensive social changes now required by his popular socialist revolution. A suspended ballgame one day earlier was perhaps the farthest thing from most Cuban minds.

For the American ballplayers, unaware of the events swirling around them, it was a very different story. Beleaguered Rochester Red Wings manager Ellis "Cot" Deal, three decades later, attempted an eyewitness rehash of the memorable events in his self-published autobiography, *Fifty Years in Baseball—or, "Cot" in the Act*, a rare firsthand version subsequently verified in interviews with the present author. Deal remembered a stadium jam-packed with *guajiros* and *barbudos* on hand for a planned midnight "July 26" celebration. He accurately recounts that the International League teams initially finished the June suspended game, then waded through the explosive atmosphere and intense tropical heat to a 3–3 tie at the end of regulation innings in the regularly scheduled affair. The preliminary contest was the completion of that scoreless seven-inning game from the Red Wings' previous trip into town almost two months earlier. He introduces his version with positive memories of late 1950s Havana as a most enjoyable stop on the league circuit—"people were amicable, shopping was reasonable, hotel accommodations were good, and there were many excellent restaurants and night clubs . . . and open gambling casinos."[8] In short, it was a veteran freewheeling ballplayer's dream. But Deal's true narrative interest in his autobiographical musings—signaled by his chapter title, "When a Thumb Might Have Saved Me"—was to recount how on that one night, the dream became a nightmare.

Manager Deal suspected early on that the night would be long and eventful, especially when the umps and rival skippers (Deal and Sugar Kings boss Preston Gómez) met at home plate to discuss, in lieu of customary ground rules, what would transpire in the highly likely case of serious fan interference. Havana scored in the bottom of the eighth to win the preliminary, and thus the festive stadium mood was further enlivened.

Veteran big-leaguer Bob Keegan had mopped up the preliminary game, since he had also been the starter of the suspended game in June and was once more on tap by accident of the pitching rotation to start the regularly scheduled affair to follow. Keegan pitched courageously despite the oppressive heat and held a 3–1 lead into the bottom of the eighth when sweltering humidity finally sapped his energy and Deal was resigned to changing hurlers. Replacement Tom Hurd closed the door in the eighth, but a walk and then a homer by Cuban slugger Borrego Alvarez in the bottom of the ninth spelled dreaded extra innings.

Next came the dramatic patriotic interruption. With the crowd—an overflow throng that topped 35,000—now at fever pitch, the regulation game was halted at the stroke of midnight; stadium lights were quickly extinguished, press box spotlights focused on a giant Cuban flag in center field, and the Cuban anthem was played slowly and reverently. As soon as stadium lighting was rekindled, however, all hell broke loose, and the air was suddenly filled with spasms of celebratory gunfire launched from both inside and outside the ballpark. An intimate and trusted Havana friend of the author, in attendance that night more than a half-century ago, recounted how a patron seated next to him near the visiting team dugout emptied several rounds from his pistol directly into the on-deck circle. Deal also vividly recalls one overzealous Cuban soldier (perhaps the selfsame individual) unloading an automatic pistol into the ground directly in front of the Red Wings dugout.

Play resumed, with further sporadic gunfire occasionally punctuating the diamond action. Infielder Billy Harrell homered in the top of the 11th to give Rochester the momentary lead, but in the bottom of the frame the home club rallied and the crowd again reached new heights of delirium. When Sugar Kings catcher Jesse Gonder (an American) led off the bottom of the frame with a hit slapped down the left-field line and raced toward second, he seemed—at least to skipper Deal—to hop over the first-base sack while rounding the bag, an event unnoticed by the rooting throng and the first base ump, who, like Gonder, was watching the blooper down the line, but one that predictably sent manager Deal racing onto the field to argue with umpires stationed at both first and home. As Deal saw it, the first-base umpire was trotting toward second to cover that sack because it was only a three-man crew, but by doing so he forgot his duty to police first base as Gonder flew past.

Naturally fearing an imminent riot if they now called anything controversial against the rallying home club, neither of the arbiters was disposed toward hearing Deal's protests, which under calmer circumstances might have seemed valid. (Deal thought first-base ump Frank Guzetta had turned too quickly to follow the runner to second, in case a play was made there, and therefore missed Gonder's sidestepping of first; he merely wanted the home plate ump to help out on the play.) Guzetta ignored Deal's pleas, and moments later the Rochester skipper was ejected for continuing his vehement protests. Gonder soon scored the lone run of the inning, and the contest continued into the 12th, once more knotted, now at four apiece. Having already been banished to the clubhouse, Deal himself would not be on hand to witness the further drama that next unfolded.

In the ensuing moments, Deal's ejection ironically proved to be a significant event. It was indeed the "thumb that may have saved him." As the chagrined former manager later recounted the circumstances of that "heave-ho" from the field of play, he had to admit that umpire Frank Guzetta had reacted more out of deep wisdom than shallow self-defense. In the heat of the argument, Deal had grabbed his own throat, giving a universal "choke" sign that instantaneously led to another universally understood gesture—the "thumb," which is Spanish for "adios" and English for "take a shower." Deal, in hindsight, would be much more sympathetic to the umps' plight and realize that any attempt to reverse the decision on Gonder's baserunning might well have further ignited an already rowdy (and heavily armed) grandstand throng with quite disastrous consequences.

Back on the field, fate and happenstance were once more about to intervene. More random shots were fired as play opened in the 12th, and stray bullets simultaneously grazed both third-base coach Frank Verdi and Sugar Kings shortstop Leo Cárdenas. By now the frightened umps and ballplayers had seen enough. The game was immediately suspended by the umpires, as Verdi, still dazed, was hastily carried by ashen teammates toward the Rochester locker room, followed closely by a wild swarm of escaping ballplayers. Apparently, a falling spent shell had struck Verdi's cap (which fortuitously contained a protective batting liner) and merely stunned him.

Deal, oblivious to on-field events, had just stepped from the shower when his panic-stricken team burst into the clubhouse carrying the barely conscious Frank Verdi. The runway outside the Red Wings dressing room was pure chaos as the umpires and ballplayers from both clubs scrambled for safety within the bowels of the ballpark. An immediately apparent irony was the fact that the wounded Verdi had, that very inning, substituted for the ejected manager Deal in the third-base coach's box, and while Verdi always wore a plastic liner in his cap, the fortune-blessed Deal never used such a protective device. Thus, Deal's ejection from the field had likely saved the fate-blessed manager's life, or at the very least prevented notable injury.

While umpires next desperately tried to phone league president Frank Shaughnessy in Montreal for a ruling on the chaotic situation, manager Deal and his general manager, George Sisler Jr., had already decided on their own immediate course of action. It was to get their team safely back to the downtown Hotel Nacional and then swiftly onto the next available plane en route to Rochester (or at least Miami). But at least some Cuban fans in attendance at the packed El Cerro Stadium that night (a few have been interviewed throughout the years by the author in Havana) today hold very different memories of the event, perhaps colored by the changing perspective or fading recollections of several passing decades. They remember few shots, little that was hostile in the crowd's festive response to both the patriotic celebration and the exciting ballgame, and hardly any sense of danger to either the ballplayers or the celebrants themselves. And Cuban baseball officials at the time also adopted a slightly different interpretation, vociferously denying that the situation was ever truly out of control and pressing the Rochester manager and general manager to continue both the suspended match and the regularly scheduled game on tap for the following afternoon.

Captain Felipe Guerra Matos, newly appointed director of the Cuban sports ministry, one week later cabled Rochester team officials with a formal and truly heartfelt apology, assuring Red Wings brass that Havana was entirely safe for baseball and that their team—and all International League ballclubs—would be guaranteed the utmost security on future trips to the island. Guerra Matos saw the events of the evening only as a spontaneous outpouring of unbridled nationalistic joy and revolutionary fervor by emotional Cuban soldiers and enthusiastic, if unruly, peasants, and thus a celebration of freedom no less unseemly or inappropriate perhaps than many Stateside Fourth of July celebrations.

But Deal and Sisler, at the time, persisted, despite the pressures and threats of Cuban officials, which continued throughout the night and subsequent morning. After a tense and seemingly endless Sunday, sequestered at the seaside Hotel Nacional amid the revolutionary revels continuing in the streets around them, the Rochester ballclub was finally able to obtain safe passage from José Martí Airport before yet another nightfall had arrived.

Deal, decades later (his book was published in 1992, and my own interview with him occurred in 2004), concluded with an entertaining account of the labored efforts of Cuban officials to get his team to complete the weekend series, including the previous night's suspended match, as well as the scheduled Sunday afternoon affair. While a World War II vintage bomber strafed an abandoned barge in Havana harbor as part of the ongoing revolutionary revelries, Deal and his general manager met with a pair of Cuban government officials in Sisler's hotel room, fortified only by strong cups of black Cuban coffee. The Cuban government spokesmen—in Deal's account—pleaded, cajoled, and finally even threatened boisterously in their efforts to convince the Americans to resume the afternoon's baseball venue. Deal and Sisler held fast in their refusals, and eventually the government bureaucrats departed in a barely controlled fit of anger. Deal sensed that the failed Sunday morning meeting would be most difficult for their hosts to explain to their government superiors (and perhaps even to Fidel himself).

What escaped Deal's account or those in the Rochester press were events that simultaneously occupied literally all Cubans in Havana on that Sunday morning and afternoon during the very hours that the Rochester team was sweating out its hasty escape from volatile Havana. This was the day of Fidel's announced speech and anticipated appeal to the masses aimed at deciding his own political destiny. The ballpark violence had indeed become a back-page story in light of the Sunday political theater gripping the nation. The Sugar Kings' fate had not yet been decided, and the team's demise would not become apparent for several more months.

Professional baseball was reeling in Havana, perhaps, but it was far from moribund, as Junior World Series matches in the city, still several months away, would soon demonstrate. Fidel's own personal hold on the nation would not be finally cemented for almost two more years and would come only with the repulsion of CIA-trained invaders at the Bay of Pigs. But on that late July weekend, Fidel's permanent rise and pro baseball's permanent fall were both set on an irrevocable course. Fidel's few wild Barbudos fastballs at Cerro Stadium, launched on that festive Friday night, would be largely relegated to the dustbin of history. But the "curveballs" he tossed at the masses in the Civic Plaza on Sunday afternoon (to employ a lame metaphor that soon enough became a favored cliché for American commentators) would be of far more lasting consequence.

* * *

The bottom-line result of the eventful weekend—which first saw Fidel take the mound and later witnessed chaos overtake the ballpark—was the beginning of the end for International League baseball on the communist-controlled island. But the death knell would be slow to peal for the Havana franchise. The International League's Governors' Cup championship playoffs—with surprising third-place finisher Havana defeating the fourth-place Richmond Vees—and a Junior World Series showdown with the Minneapolis Millers of the American Association (featuring a hot prospect named Carl Yastrzemski) would both enliven Havana later that same fall. And Fidel the dedicated baseball fan was, of course, a fixture during both events, although frequent reports of Comandante Castro and his comrades toting firearms, strolling uninvited inside and atop the dugouts, and even intimidating first Richmond and later Minneapolis ballplayers with threats of violent intervention have likely been mildly, if not wildly, exaggerated.

Revolutionary violence in the Cuban capital had already threatened the Sugar Kings in the previous calendar year, well before Fidel's ouster of Batista became a reality. Justin Turner (in his University of Alabama thesis) details how "as the island tumbled toward revolution and violence, baseball was hardly immune to the political upheaval."[9] But the evening of July 25–26, 1959, marked the first occasion when the violence plaguing Havana had a direct physical impact on North American ballplayers. Nonetheless, the Havana International League franchise, despite all the hopes invested in it by both owner Bobby Maduro and Fidel Castro himself, had for some time taken on the appearance of an endangered species.[10] Drawing less than hefty crowds in each of its first three seasons, the club experienced an even more severe drop in fan interest by 1957, once Fidel's rebels landed in the Sierra Maestra and antigovernment hostilities heated up throughout the country. An on-field slide in performance may have been as much to blame as anything, with the club finishing in sixth place two seasons running (1956 and

1957). But the franchise was only a moderate success from the opening bell, drawing an average attendance of 4,067 in a park that held 33,000 during its second season (1954) but seeing that turnout plummet to less than 1,100 after its second-straight sixth-place finish in 1957.[11]

But a weak or uninspiring roster may not have been the entire story, and there are also reasonable explanations for the dip in fan interest found in González Echevarría's classic history.[12] Among those causes were the timing of the minor-league season and, perhaps even more so, the nature of minor-league operations. Hot, humid weather inhibited fans in a way that it did not during the cooler winter-league season schedule. And since the parent club controlled the AAA roster, promising stars were often snatched away, while struggling and less productive players were not so easily replaced or even benched without authorization from the controlling Cincinnati Reds big-league brass. In short, Havana fans were understandably frustrated by the overall situation.

But it was attendance issues and especially the perception that interest in the team was sorely impacted by threats of political violence that loomed as the main culprits in the team's woes. Violence had reached Havana by early 1957, with several bomb explosions in the capital and the discovery of a bullet-riddled body near the ballpark.[13] It was this violence and the potential of worsening conditions that loomed large by the summer season of 1958, a full year before the Barbudos exhibition game. Before the 1958 season was even underway, the Montreal Royals cancelled a scheduled exhibition with the Sugar Kings, citing growing concerns for player safety in Havana. Even though Maduro had secured an April 1958 pledge from fellow owners that his club would not be moved, that same month (on the heels of Montreal's cancellation) Buffalo Bisons players also temporarily balked on their season-opening trip to Havana. With these crises threatening league stability, and with attendance at Sugar Kings games reaching its lowest point during the 1957 season, by October of that year talk of relocating the team was again already stirring in the office of Commissioner Shaughnessy. It was in that month that International League officials secured claims to Jersey City as a future site for either league expansion or perhaps even team relocations.

The Sugar Kings would initially survive the events in late July. In fact, the Havana team would enjoy its greatest glory stretch as the season progressed to an improbable climax. The Sugar Kings, in fact, engineered a remarkable turnaround season in 1959. A year earlier, the club was a disaster, languishing in the cellar for the entire campaign. With managerial duties split between Napoleon Reyes (fired at midyear) and Tony Pacheco, Havana won only 65 games, a franchise low, limping home 25 games off the pace. They were dead last in the circuit in team batting and fielding, didn't boast a single .300 hitter, and used an ineffective armada of 16 different pitchers (including future big-leaguers Miguel Cuéllar, Raúl Sánchez, and Orlando Peña).

But Bobby Maduro had quickly turned things around with several shrewd moves. The first was to hire Pedro (Preston) Gómez as his manager. He also revamped the lame pitching staff by adding Ted Wieand and Walter Craddock, and trading for reliever Luis ("Tite") Arroyo, a Puerto Rican lefty who would later make his mark in the majors with the Yankees. More significantly perhaps, he encouraged his new manager to give prominent roles to a pair of rookies destined for eventual big-league stardom. Leo Cárdenas—who would play a fateful role in the July 26 shooting events—quickly became the circuit's top infield defender at shortstop. Outfielder Tony González would prove to be the team MVP before the summer was out.

But for all the improvement, a league championship was a last-minute surprise. The team finished only third in the regular season but then caught fire in the playoffs. Buffalo had paced the circuit, with Columbus five and a half games off the pace. The third-place Cubans trailed the pacesetter by nine, four and a half games better than fourth-place Richmond. In postseason play, the upstart Sugar Kings swept past Columbus in a minimum four games, while pesky Richmond shocked league-leader Buffalo in a mere five contests. Deron Johnson was the star slugger for Richmond, socking six homers in the Buffalo series. Havana's second-round triumph over equally surprising Richmond in six games was mainly the result of stellar pitching by ace Ted Wieand (in the opener) and Arroyo (who won one and saved two in relief), as well as Raúl Sánchez, who blanked Richmond for fourteen and a half innings to earn the two additional Sugar Kings victories. With Havana headed to the Junior World Series to face American Association champion Minneapolis, the Cuban capital was suddenly electrified with a new baseball enthusiasm. In the aftermath of the opening-round clincher against Columbus at Cerro Stadium, *Revolución*, Havana's leading daily, had featured a photo of Fidel in the Havana locker room with winning pitcher Raúl Sánchez and catcher Enrique Izquierdo. Taking center stage as always, the following week Fidel again posed triumphantly, this time with not only Havana stars Arroyo, Miguel Cuéllar, and Tony González, but also Richmond's losing pitcher, Bill Short, and Vees manager Mike Souchock.

The Junior World Series opened in Minneapolis under inauspicious climatic conditions. Havana continued its streaking by capturing the opener against a Boston Red Sox farm club that boasted player-manager Gene Mauch; future big-leaguer Tracy Stallard (immortalized only two years later by yielding Roger Maris's landmark 61st homer); and a trio of promising outfielders in future manager Chuck Tanner, Lou Clinton, and Tommy Umphlett. Also featured was a crack young second baseman named Carl Yastrzemski. Wieand was the pitching hero in the opener, as he made four third-inning runs stand up in a 5–2 win. The Millers quickly tied the count with a day-two slugging outburst of four homers in a close 6–5 cliffhanger. But then the elements took charge as a third match was postponed due to unseasonably cold weather. With more freezing conditions in the offing, league officials decided not to wait out what might prove to be days of postponements and reluctantly transferred operations to balmy Havana for the remaining three, four, and maybe even five games.

The series was destined to go to the wire, and the five Havana contests proved nail-biters, with an element of political theater also thrown into the mix. The home club prevailed in the opener on October 1, when American Ray Shearer provided a 10th-inning game-winning single to offset an earlier mammoth homer by Yastrzemski. Yet another extra-inning thriller followed when an 11th-inning 4–3 Havana victory left the visiting Minneapolis team a single game from elimination. But Gene Mauch's forces were able to rebound when first a late Minneapolis rally negated a Daniel Morejón homer in Game 5, and then Stallard and Bowsfield combined to limit the Sugar Kings to three runs and deadlock the affair in Game 6.

As if there indeed were a prearranged script, the ultimate excitement was appropriately reserved for the closing scene. A dramatic home team victory in Game 7, on October 6, would provide the excuse for wild and unrestrained city-wide celebration. That single symbolic contest capped a year of revolutionary triumph over first Batista and now the visiting American baseballers. Fidel made his usual dramatic appearance from center field and strode to his box near home. Author Stew Thornley quotes Millers' pitcher Lefty Locklin as claiming that when the Maximum Leader passed the Minneapolis dugout during pregame ceremonies, he winsomely eyed the visiting players, patted the revolver on his hip, and boasted with clearly intended intimidation, "Tonight we win!"[14] Despite the perhaps apocryphal threat, the Millers would jump out ahead early thanks to solo homers by Joe Macko in the top of the fourth and Lou Clinton in the sixth. But the Fates now appeared to be squarely on the side of the Castro forces.

In the home eighth, Elio Chacón launched a desperate rally with a timely single, then moved over to third on Morejón's ground-rule double, which skimmed the right-field foul line before ricocheting over the wall. With two retired and the game on the line, American Larry Novak singled to center, plating the two equalizing runs. In the home ninth, the rally continued when Havana pitcher Raúl Sánchez reached on a careless walk from Minneapolis reliever Billy Muffett and was promptly advanced to second by Venezuelan Pompeyo Davalillo's sacrifice bunt. After Chacón went down swinging, manager Mauch made a fateful decision to put lefty batter Tony González aboard with an intentional pass, setting the stage for hero Dan Morejón again to strike a decisive blow. Morejón slammed the first pitch he saw from Muffett into center field, sending Sánchez scampering home ahead of Umphlett's desperate throw with the dramatic clincher. Fans and soldiers joyously streamed onto the field and carried Morejón, Sánchez, and several other giddy ballplayers on their shoulders toward Fidel's box, where the celebration continued for what seemed like more than an hour, as delirious fans refused to leave the ballpark grounds.

Fidel, as the nation's number-one symbolic cheerleader, was very much in evidence at those championship games, perhaps largely intent on feeding the growing view among Fidelistas that the team's late-season surge and peak performance in precisely the same year as the triumph of his revolution was no mere coincidence. One notable surviving press service photo captures the Cuban leader in full military regalia posing with Millers players before the opening contest at Cerro Stadium, and another shows him launching the ceremonial first pitch of the transplanted series. Fidel's ceremonial opening toss was a symbolic repetition of the one he had performed in April at the Sugar Kings home opener, marking the first postrevolution International League season.[15] It was also seen by the Cuban press as a likely good omen, with *Revolución* (September 30 edition) pointing out that the Sugar Kings had begun their late surge toward a pennant after Fidel tossed an earlier ceremonial first pitch on Agrarian Reform Day. Always a theatrical genius, Fidel strode onto the field for the opener, crossing from the center-field bullpen area to home plate, while the crowd chanted "¡*Que habla!*" (Speech!). But Fidel, when handed a microphone, demurred, claiming he had come only as a fan to watch a good game and was more than confident that since the revolution had earlier been victorious, the Havana team would also win a championship title. The ceremonial first pitch was, as expected, greeted by a standing ovation from the packed house of 30,000-plus partisans.

After the extra-inning victory by the home club in the Havana lidlifter, Fidel made his triumphant exit through the same center-field gate where he had entered, riding aboard the jeep used to shuffle pitchers in from the bullpen. The following game would find him viewing the festivities not from his home plate box, but rather from the Sugar Kings dugout, accompanied by sidekick Camilo Cienfuegos. In the final match, President Osvaldo Dorticós and Che Guerava sat in the reserved box seats behind home. On the day of the opener, Fidel had reportedly cancelled an important scheduled cabinet meeting so that top government officials could be seen at the ballpark. The political overtones to the series could hardly be missed.

For those wishing to emphasize the threats to public safety (particularly for visiting ballclubs) surrounding the Havana ballpark and the Sugar Kings operation, the final playoff games in October only seemed to provide further fodder. Chronicling details of the dramatic series almost four decades later, Stew Thornley devoted considerable attention to the hostile environment the Millers players seemed to face once the games where transferred to the Cuban capital. Relying on Minneapolis press accounts of the time, Thornley emphasizes that the American club was faced with constant reminders of the hyperenthusiastic and also somewhat chaotic atmosphere filling the city in the first months of the new government. "Everywhere the players went . . . they were greeted with the sight of Castro's bearded troopers . . . it was the only Junior Series in which the submachine guns outnumbered the bats."[16] As Thornley reports it, more than 3,000 soldiers were at the stadium the night of the opening game, many lining the field and others occupying corners of the team dugouts. Pitcher Ted Bowsfield recalled the perceived threat as intimidating: "Young people . . . waving guns around like toys." Minneapolis player-manager Gene Mauch is also quoted in the Thornley account as reporting that "our players were truly fearful of what might happen if we won." Mauch also recalled a direct threat, or at least a perceived one, made in the dugout to outfielder Tom Umphlett. But much of the concern may well have been drummed up by a U.S. press bent on demonizing Fidel and undercutting a revolution that boded ill for American business interests on the island.

Numerous existing photographs from those games do, in fact, confirm the heavy presence of Cuban soldiers on the field and even in the dugouts before, during, and after games. But a more reasonable interpretation of events is provided by future Boston Hall of Famer Carl Yastrzemski, who comments on those events in his autobiography, *Yaz*. He writes, "It was like a revolution in the streets, even though it wasn't violent. But with the guns and the noise it was just scary."[17] The potential for violence seemed apparent and was the bottom line preoccupation in most American accounts. Bowsfield is reported as recalling, "Nobody minded losing the game in that country under those circumstances."[18]

The Cuban press, of course, saw things quite differently. Some surviving Cubans who lived through the moment also hold a contrasting view more than a half-century later. Ismael Sené was at those games and told the author that the atmosphere was far more celebratory than hostile. Flush with the success of the revolutionary triumph only nine months earlier and the new beginning it represented, the entire city of Havana seemed to explode with nationalistic pride in the wake of the stunning baseball victory. *Revolución* carried a banner headline stretched across the front page—"CUBA CAMPEÓN." But since the Sugar Kings roster included American ballplayers, this could not be taken as any kind of genuine anti-American sentiment. The raw nationalism expressed was clearly one of unbridled joy stemming from a proud moment—perhaps the proudest moment ever—in the annals of the nation's beloved national pastime. For Fidel and the numerous still-ardent supporters of his nascent revolution, the prophecy had indeed been fulfilled—the Sugar Kings had prevailed, just as the revolution itself had prevailed. Decades later, Cuban historian Carlos Reig Romero (in his introduction to a book celebrating the Gold Anniversary of Cuba's revolutionary baseball) labeled the Sugar Kings championship the "success that glorified national sentiment" due to its strong support from major figures of the revolution.[19]

By any measure, it was a great final hurrah, although few could see the handwriting on the wall in the immediate afterglow of the Sugar Kings' surprise triumph. By mid-season 1960, Castro's expropriations, both actual and threatened, of U.S. business interests on the island, as well as violent outbursts of antigovernment political resistance ("terrorism") on the streets of Havana (with numerous reported destructive explosions spread throughout the city), finally convinced International League officials and their Washington backers to pull the plug on the half-dozen-year sojourn of the league's increasingly beleaguered Havana franchise.

On July 8, 1960, while on a road trip in Miami, the proud Sugar Kings (now managed by Tony Castaño and featuring future Cuban big-leaguers Mike Cuéllar, Orlando Peña, José Azcue, Leo Cárdenas, and Cookie Rojas) were closed down by the league's Montreal-based front office and relocated literally overnight to the northern climes of Jersey City. Details of those events are presented and debated in chapter 4, devoted to the controversial and still largely unresolved facts concerning the death knell for American-style professional baseball in Castro's soon-to-be publicly proclaimed Communist nation.

❉ ❉ ❉

If the Friday night Barbudos game played some measurable role in giving birth to the "Fidel as pitching prospect" myth, the chaos in Cerro Stadium 24 hours later would go a long way toward striking a death chord for more than a half-century of pro ball in Havana, along with its offshoot ties to Organized Baseball up north. And the Junior World Series only provided more of the same perceived threats to baseball security from a North American perspective. But what never ended was the central place of baseball in Cuban culture. Nor did the loss of professional baseball action on the island ever dim the Cuban leader's passions for his country's national game. Also unshakeable was Fidel's newly discovered talent for using the sport for enhancing his public image and soft-selling his political aims. If Fidel continued to pitch, most of that "pitching" involved hawking his ambitious and ever-evolving plans for a new form of revolutionary society.

Fidel would also continue and indeed increase his ceremonial ballpark appearances, and thus his avowed connections with the sport in coming decades. Many of the pitching or batting stints most visible to the press were those in the early seasons of the National Series, launched in January 1962. Some of these appearances are reported in chapter 5—a history of the new style baseball created under a reconstituted INDER sports ministry. And there were numerous others also, some removed from the spotlight (spontaneous arrivals for pickup games with locals or with his military officers) but some held in the full glare of the Cuban media. Most occurred in the 1960s and early 1970s, when the Cuban leader was still a fit and athletic figure in the prime of middle age. But his connections with the game and his cameo appearances at ballparks never ceased entirely throughout the decades. He regularly greeted national teams on their mostly victorious returns to Havana after international tournament appearances. One of the most notable occasions involved a ceremonial decoration of star pitcher José Antonio Huelga after an early 1970s triumph against the Americans in Colombia.

Even in his last years in power, Fidel was still a regular presence on the ballpark scene. The Cuban leader was, as expected, a center-stage presence at the historic Baltimore Orioles exhibition visit to Havana in March 1999—an event reopening hopes for a baseball détente accord that had itself undergone a varied lifespan throughout three decades (see chapter 9 for details) and been largely on hiatus since a 1996 defection of star pitcher Rolando Arrojo on the eve of the Atlanta Olympics. For the March 1999 Orioles–Team Cuba clash, Comandante Castro took the field to greet and briefly question Baltimore manager Ray Miller, then occupied his post behind home plate alongside Orioles owner Peter Angelos and MLB commissioner Bud Selig. The unreported game-long chat between this odd trio was more than likely little more than an exchange of pleasantries devoid of substance. But the two American dignitaries nonetheless would later be roundly criticized throughout the American anti-Castro community for their diplomatic photo op alongside the Cuban leader, and any hope they might have held for some kind of breakthrough in baseball diplomacy certainly did not materialize.

Two final similarly staged events celebrating Fidel as Cuba's number-one baseball promoter occurred in late 1999 and early 2002. Fidel was by then in his early-to-mid 70s and beyond the point of any actual performances in the guise of a pseudo athlete. His role would now be restricted to that of celebrity sideline manager, something he had already become throughout the years with his universally acknowledged role micromanaging his celebrated national team. Like the staged weekend pitching performance of late July 1959, these two particular events would also have very different results and very different long-term impacts than what Fidel or his handlers might have anticipated or perhaps planned out in advance.

The first, a festive and politically charged exhibition aimed at cementing friendship bonds between the Cuban and Venezuela communist regimes, occurred in late November 1999, several months after a powerhouse Cuban national squad had enjoyed one of its last hurrahs on the worldwide stage against the backdrop of substantial changes overtaking the world of Olympic-style international tournament play. On Friday, November 19, a rather bizarre match was played in front of a packed house in Latin American Stadium between veteran former diamond stars from both nations. The evening's events would serve to reveal a more playful side to the aging Fidel—now far more calculating and bridge-building diplomat than energetic rebel antagonist. At least that was the planned scenario. What actually transpired reflected more favorably on visiting Venezuelan president Hugo Chávez, who seemed to come away the biggest winner in the arena of public adulation.

Castro sympathizer and like-minded leftist leader Chávez, himself in his own 45th year, took the mound for the visitors and hurled four full innings, giving up four runs before lifting himself from the box and retreating to first base, where he played out the rest of the match. Chávez apparently was equally as proud of showing off his mound skills as Fidel had once been; in fact, the Venezuelan leader could apparently boast of somewhat greater youthful pitching accomplishments than his Cuban counterpart. He, too, had once harbored baseball dreams as a youth and told CNN interviewer Larry King in 1999, that he had joined the military as a 17-year-old primarily because he wanted to play Organized Baseball.

Chávez's actual baseball "career" or youthful pitching skill is about as murky as Fidel's. The subject is broached without much detail in an obituary written by Public Radio International reporter David Trifunov. Like Fidel, Chávez's passion for the American pastime was as strong as his acrimony directed toward American imperialist policies. The fandom of the Venezuelan leader—again paralleling Fidel's—is also recounted by Trifunov, who quotes Venezuelan national team manager Luis Soto as reporting that the president followed the ballclub religiously and phoned each morning to check on the squad and its progress during 2006 and 2009 editions of the World Baseball Classic. Soto claimed Hugo Chávez "lived for baseball" and thus echoes so many similar claims about Fidel.[20]

Like Fidel, Chávez was a pitcher by preference, but in his case the potential for symbolism was a bit better still since the leftist politician was also a southpaw hurler. Fidel, for his part, was now too frail for such displays of long-faded athletic skill and relegated himself to the role of the Cuban team manager. And here is where the fun began.

As the contest progressed, Fidel began to substitute some suspiciously agile replacements from his dugout, actual members of his recent Pan American Games squad, which had won gold in Winnipeg only months earlier. One by one, such stalwarts as Omar Linares, Pedro Luis Lazo, Germán Mesa, and a half-dozen other current Cuban all-stars took the field, thinly disguised with strapped-on fake beards and talcum-powered white hair. Fidel's pseudo veterans would only exert enough effort to turn the game in the Cubans' favor, while the grandstand throng and legitimate opposing Venezuelan old-timers appeared to equally enjoy the ruse.

The friendly match—televised live in both countries—was a rousing success in celebrating the baseball passions of two Caribbean nations lodged in what is largely a soccer-loving region. The only serious disruption of the evening performance came when an enthusiastic fan leaped from the grandstand and attempted to reach the Cuban dugout and hand Fidel some unidentified object before being quickly corralled by stadium security. Both leaders obviously enjoyed the spectacle and waxed enthusiastic to the press in the aftermath.

Chávez, who had impressed with his on-field efforts, was quick to assert, "Both countries won since this game deepened our mutual friendship." Fidel took a more humorous approach (as he had during the match itself), excusing his rule-bending: "Chávez named me manager of the Cuban team, thus there was no other option than to do what was necessary to win." But the Cuban leader, in also acknowledging the friendly spirit of the exhibition match, revealed in his postgame interview that in truth, the "objective wasn't really to win but to have a good joke on Chávez."[21] The image most viewers likely took away from the ballpark that evening was one of Fidel as aging trickster versus Chávez as still-youthful ball-playing dynamo—the nimble current champion of anti-imperialist resistance still in the prime of physical prowess versus the diminished former leader of Third World revolutionary causes now reduced to quaint tomfoolery. The charismatic Venezuelan, his career still in its ascendancy, seemed the clear-cut popular winner here.

The second exhibition, a staged impromptu all-star game of sorts, came during the spring 2002 goodwill visit of former U.S. president Jimmy Carter. In a bit of odd timing, the Carter stopover coincided with the final stages of a National Series season that had witnessed a record-breaking campaign by sensational young hurling ace Maels Rodríguez. The Sanctí Spiritus star had just obliterated league strikeout records and was leading his provincial club to its first serious postseason run in decades. But Rodríguez had also been overused in the effort at a coveted championship and was secretly suffering from a debilitating late-season shoulder injury. He would now be further taxed by also being put on display so that the comandante, in his guise as unofficial national team general manager, could score some important propaganda points with his high-profile American guest.

On the eve of the late May playoffs, Rodríguez was ordered to pitch (clearly at Fidel's mandate) in a staged exhibition hastily arranged by the Maximum Leader to tout the quality of his showcase national game for the visiting American ex-president. Billed as an all-star contest between teams representing the two league divisions and played in front of an overflow crowd of 50,000-plus in Latin American Stadium, the match was no more than a trumped-up opportunity to parade around Fidel's cherished national team front-liners. The actual All-Star Game had already been staged in Pinar del Río months earlier. Carter threw out the first pitch, and Maels took the hill against Pinar del Río's bulky right-hander, José Contreras, a favorite of Fidel until his own defection a year later. Although his own team was housed in the same Western Division (*Occidentales*) as Contreras's, Maels was nonetheless shifted to the Orientales lineup, where he could display his arsenal of unmatched "heaters" for Carter in the mano a mano tussle between Cuba's top two pitchers. Veteran *Granma* beat writer Sigfredo Barros would report that Maels threw a steady diet of 90-plus fastballs for five full frames, struck out seven, and permitted but two tame hits, ironically both to future defectors Kendrys Morales and Yobal Dueñas.

The playoffs began only four days later, and Maels, during the next several weeks, would set new standards for workhorse efforts. In the National Series championship finals, he would labor in all seven games, three as a starter and the others in relief. And there was also a hidden and rather sordid backstory to the entire affair, as earlier in the winter the star hurler had incurred a badly bruised back and shoulder when attacked by a bat-wielding disgruntled teammate; the damage didn't stop his manager from nonetheless using him in a league-top 200-plus innings (postseason included). It was this injury, never allowed to heal properly, that was the dark secret behind the rapid collapse of one of baseball's great unknown natural talents. Within a year, Maels, barely able to top 85 miles per hour with his once-legendary fastball, would be finished. He was left off the World Cup team in the fall of 2003, for games scheduled in Havana. Ironically, it was on the final night of that tournament—Cuba and Panama locked in a gold medal showdown—that Maels secretly left Cuba. A promising career had been sabotaged, first by an undisciplined teammate and then an overzealous manager. But Fidel's decision to press him into further taxing service for a match with little beyond propaganda value was also a contributing factor to the sudden flameout of the country's number-one pitcher.

Despite his various appearances on the diamond, Fidel would, in those later years, regularly downplay his baseball connections for a foreign press. If he stressed his baseball connections at home, he regularly belittled them with foreign interlocutors. In the landmark interview with Barbara Walters for ABC (1977), he would make light of any serious baseball connections. And as he approached the end of his fourth decade in power, he would (perhaps with tongue in cheek) remark to various visiting North American journalists that his most bothersome moments came with the constant requests that he sign baseballs.

The most elaborate discussion with a foreign correspondent touching on baseball would occur in July 1991, on the eve of the Havana Pan American Games, when Fidel sat down for a televised chat with ABC sports correspondent Jim McKay.[22] Much of the baseball talk came off-camera, with Fidel expounding his views on the sport to McKay, including his notion that the introduction of aluminum bats (at the time used in Cuba and for international amateur tournaments like the Pan Am Games) was a boon to younger players. Perhaps the key moment came when McKay, looking to break the ice, asked Fidel how good a player he actually was and whether he had indeed received a $5,000 offer from Cambria and the Washington Senators. Evasive as always on this topic, the Cuban leader would neither directly confirm nor deny such rumors. But he certainly leaned toward the latter position by reminiscing that he had been little more than a mediocre pitcher, dangerous perhaps only because his pitches were likely to hit someone.

Fidel's adopted role as super fan and "wannabe" pitcher seemed most often to be conveniently trucked out for political consumption on the home front—for what Justin Turner sees as a calculated and most effective means of linking baseball to the revolutionary government and its agendas.[23] But there were also some genuine displays of deep-seated interest as a legitimate baseball fan that pop up in the numerous biographical portraits. The most prominent perhaps is that scene in the final days of the anti-Batista guerrilla struggle when the rebel leader took a break from his campaign to chat with local villagers about his views that manager Fred Haney misused Milwaukee pitchers Spahn and Willey in recent World Series action against the Yankees. But even that reported incident soon took on a life of its own, and the version offered by Quirk gets recast in various guises.[24] Turner, for example, relying on a January 4, 1959, *Washington Post* column by Shirley Povich, has Fidel making (or perhaps repeating?) that inquiry, not to locals in the Oriente village of Guisa in November, but to broadcaster Buck Canel in Matanzas on his victory march to Havana the first week of January.[25]

The Cuban press never took those gestures for much more than they actually were. There were only oblique references to Fidel's ball-playing throughout the years and then usually only when the question was raised by Americans or an occasional visiting British commentator. When veteran Havana baseball broadcaster Eddy Martin was asked the question by British journalist Richard Williams in 1999, he offered an evasive and politically correct response.[26] Fidel's ball-playing stints, both real and imagined, were always more celebrated by North American writers and newspaper hacks enchanted by the legend that simply wouldn't seem to disappear. But if outsiders swallowed the legends all too regularly and all too naively, they always did so more with sarcasm and disdain than with any real reverence.

# Part II


# The Transformation

# 4

# SUGAR BARONS AND SUGAR KINGS, AND THE DEATH OF CUBA'S PROFESSIONAL BASEBALL

That man (referring to Fidel Castro) showed up and destroyed baseball in Cuba.—Andrés Fleitas, 1940s-era Cuban baseball star (quoted by César Brioso in *Havana Hardball*)[1]

**O**f the many overblown and distracting Castro myths, none is further off target than a cherished fantasy that Fidel killed professional baseball in Cuba. Nothing could be further from the truth or represent more superficial analysis. It is an inaccurate claim in at least three aspects. First and foremost, professional baseball certainly did not expire in Cuba in 1961; it merely transformed itself into a revamped version not at all consistent with the capitalist view of professionalism marketed in North America by MLB. Even the leading proponent of a pre-Castro "golden age" for Cuban baseball like Robert González Echevarría admits the folly of such an assessment when he notes, "Abolition of professionalism did not really take place, if one considers a professional someone who earns emoluments for what he does, and if the perfection of that skill is the most important task in his daily life."[2] Cuban League ballplayers, after the advent of the National Series in 1962, remained professionals by most reasonable measures—they were simply no longer professionals serving on the payrolls of North American ballclubs. What actually transpired was an end to Cuban League subservience to

North American big-league ownership and the controls of Organized
Baseball, and that is a far different matter.[3]

And there is far more to the story. For one thing, baseball was
anything but moribund in Cuba after the revolutionary makeover of the
national sporting scene. Solid arguments can be offered that with the
new domestic league (described in the following chapter), plus a major
upgrade in international tournament successes (the subject of chapter
6), the Cuban game actually reached its greatest heights, far outstrip-
ping in both talent level and island-wide fan support anything found in
the century's preceding six decades. Lastly and most importantly, even
if one claims—as I certainly would not—that the loss of affiliation to
Organized Baseball meant some kind of death knell for the sport, it was
not Fidel who was most responsible for that outcome. Indeed, the ouster of Batista and Fidel's advances toward communism made things
uncomfortable for not only Washington politicos, with their paranoia
about world communist domination, but also MLB businessmen, with
their capitalist profit motives. But in the end, it was the Americans who

**END OF AN ERA.** Fidel poses with Minneapolis players before Junior World Series
contest that marked both the acme and swan song for the Havana minor league
franchise. *The Rucker Archive*

decided to pull up stakes and not Fidel who orchestrated the departure by kicking them out. This chapter attempts a careful and much-needed reassessment of the actual facts embedded in the often-distorted saga surrounding removal of the Sugar Kings from Havana and the shutting down of that city's winter-league circuit only a few months later.

Baseball history is never far removed from political history when it comes to Cuba—an important insight as true in 2018 as it was in 1962, or for that matter in 1908 or even 1878.[4] The phenomenon predates Fidel Castro by almost a century. In a groundbreaking 1975 interview with American journalists Frank Mankiewicz and Kirby Jones (published as their book *With Fidel: A Portrait of Castro and Cuba*), Fidel was quick to point to a singular overriding cause for the rupture of U.S. Cuba diplomatic relations at the outset of the 1960s. That primary cause of Cold War tensions between the previously close-knit countries was to be found in the 1960 passage of Fidel's far-reaching Agrarian Reform Law, a relatively mild reform in Castro's view but an intolerable turn of events for the Americans. As Fidel explained it, the changes after Batista meant a major threat to U.S. business interests on the island.[5] The largest foreign enterprise on the island at the time was sugar production, and American interests owned a substantial percentage of the Cuban sugar-producing landscape.[6] It was the threats to the American sugar barons that caused the rupture, as much or perhaps more so than the deep-seated post–World War II Washington paranoia about international communism.

Of course, it was also true that North American Organized Baseball—that is, MLB and its minor-league subsidiaries—held a long-standing and recently expanded financial stake in Cuba as well. With long-overdue 1947 racial integration, dark-skinned Cuban players were suddenly on the radar for big-league clubs. MLB had also largely taken over Cuban winter-league operations via the 1947 peace accords, which ended a short-lived war with Mexican League mogul Jorge Pasquel, whose mid-1940s player raids had been aimed squarely at weakening MLB dominance. And through a potential partnership emerging with Havana's Bobby Maduro there was also first a lower-level minor-league club in Havana from 1946 to 1953, and then a top-level International League franchise whose motto was, "One more step and we arrive" (signaling a hoped-for big-league expansion team in Havana). When North American sugar barons found themselves overnight stripped of their Cuban holdings, it was the same spiking of Havana–Washington tensions that also worked to strip MLB "Baseball Barons" of their own Cuban enterprises and thus their coveted Cuban dreams. As we will discover in the following chapters, the American baseball barons would remain focused for the next half-century on reestablishing by one means or another their lost control of the lucrative Cuban baseball market.

The Cuban Sugar Kings franchise—representing Havana's early formal link with North American Organized Baseball and a promising if idle hope for eventual Havana major-league status—was ironically the first notable casualty of the U.S.–Cuba Cold War tensions escalating in the first two years of Fidel Castro's socialist-leaning administration. It is questionable how much longer the Havana franchise might have survived in light of poor summer-season ballpark attendance and already fomenting discussions about moving the ballclub—discussions in progress even before Fidel's unlikely victory over Batista's U.S.-supported forces. But the rupture between the new revolutionary government and the professional circuits to the North witnessed its first dramatic fallout with the removal of Bobby Maduro's ballclub to Jersey City. Against the backdrop of other explosive developments that same summer ripping apart the historic bonds between Cubans and Americans—nationalization of private business and private properties, for example—the Sugar Kings collapse might be viewed as something less than momentous. But for baseball historians and diaspora victims, it would come to represent a landmark step in the divorce between two baseball-loving nations.

A second casualty, less than a calendar year later, was the long-standing Havana-based Cuban winter-league circuit. That four-team league had also been tightly linked to Organized Baseball since the mid-1940s and had nonetheless been a troubled enterprise for most of the past decade. It too may have been on its last legs for reasons that had little to do with the revolutionary upheavals that surrounded it. And given the eventual slide of the Caribbean winter circuits in the Dominican Republic, Venezuela, and Puerto Rico during the next few decades, its future was not all that bright to start with. But for many, especially in an emerging South Florida Cuban exile community produced by the massive Cuban diaspora, its departure from the island was also viewed as a landmark event.

Never entirely resolved questions about these twin events have long focused on the degree to which Washington government officials directly influenced the decision of International League commissioner Frank Shaughnessy to finally pull the plug on the Havana franchise. The decisions surrounding the closing of winter-league operations seem, on the surface at least, somewhat less confusing. Tensions—mostly issues concerning control of team rosters and availability of quality big-leaguers for Cuban teams—had, for more than a decade, existed between MLB and Cuban League officials, and a split had already seemed to be almost inevitable for much of the preceding decade.

For those harboring strong resentments toward Castro and everything connected with his revolution, it has been common practice to repeatedly parrot the line echoed by 1940s-era Cuban League star Andres Fleitas: that Fidel was solely to blame and that, in brief, "That man came along and destroyed Cuban baseball." It is an attractive conclusion for many and perfectly fits the narrative that Fidel single-handedly destroyed everything that constituted the Cuba known to those on and off the island before January 1959. But if it is a comfortable theme for those who lost the Cuba of their youth, it is also something of a vast distortion and a conclusion that overlooks and even denies the bulk of incontrovertible historical evidence.

This same theme would be most recently echoed by Cuban American journalist César Brioso, first in his book *Havana Hardball* and then again with a *USA Today* article prompted by the November 2016 death of the supreme Cuban leader. Brioso's somewhat simplistic stance rehearses the old refrain: that the loss of the Sugar Kings minor-league connection, and then the winter-league shutdown that followed shortly thereafter, not only signaled the end of American-controlled baseball operations, but also meant—for all practical purposes—the loss of professional-style baseball, and thus the loss of any semblance of high-quality play.[7] González Echevarría reflects largely the same thesis in his seminal history *The Pride of Havana*, and the notion has long been a religious mantra in the North American Cuban exile community.

It is true enough that an immediate consequence of Organized Baseball's pullout was Fidel's new INDER operation and a significant game-changing law banning professional sports on the island. The new INDER law was aimed at establishing more expansive athletic activities open to all Cubans and not controlled as heretofore by elite private clubs. It was also intended to strike down the notion of sporting events being operated by private commercial interests as for-profit businesses. A secondary aim of the new legislation was Fidel's cherished idea that athletes at the higher levels of ability—those, for example, competing in top-level organized baseball leagues—should compete for rewards that were not merely material in nature. The goal should be the joys of competition and the thrill of victory as an end in its own right, not the pursuit of prize money or a lucrative paycheck.

But the new system was never intended to create amateur competitors in the North American sense of the term. Cuban sportsmen (male baseball players and boxers, but also women practicing track and field or volleyball or swimming), according to the new socialist system, would be full-time athletes who were financially supported by the government sports ministry, even if their salaries paled when measured against those of professionals in capitalist societies. The contrasting notions of amateurism would emerge as a major bone of contention for the Americans during the next decade when the two countries began heated baseball battles tinged with political significance in numerous Olympic-style venues.

The position maintained by Brioso and those of similar persuasion nonetheless conveniently ignores the vital fact that it was MLB forces and perhaps even Washington political pressures that pulled the plug on both the Sugar Kings and the winter league. Fidel's 1961 INDER law was a response to the developing situation and not its cause. Law 936 of February 23, 1961, was enacted only two weeks after the final winter-league game was played in Havana and had obviously been in the planning stage for several months. But despite the proximity of the two events, the creation of INDER did nonetheless follow and not precede the Organized Baseball pullout. With baseball, then, it must be claimed that the cause and effect order was precisely identical to that of the much larger rupture in Washington–Havana relations. If we are to buy Herbert Matthews's thesis that communism was not at all a cause but rather a surprising result of the Cuban Revolution (and there is plenty of support for taking that position), then we might be equally well served to see the baseball fallout of the Washington–Havana standoff in the same light.[8] The Castro plan to revamp Cuban baseball, to replace the business of professional baseball with the utility of revolutionary-style amateur baseball, was a result, a consequence, and not in any fashion a cause of the International League and MLB joint pullout from Cuba. Certainly, the first Cold War volley (relocating the Sugar Kings) chronologically precedes the new INDER law by the better part of a year. Yet, while Matthews's thesis has been supported by numerous scholars throughout the subsequent decades, the equally obvious cause-and-effect relationship in the case of baseball has been either largely ignored or conveniently misconstrued to cast the entire blame on the Cubans rather than the Americans.

When it came to sports and baseball, as in all other areas of the country's social and cultural overhaul, Cuba's initially inept and inexperienced revolutionary government was blindly feeling its way and, in most cases, reacting to opportunities or emerging necessities handed to it by decisions or policies emanating from Washington. Matthews has suggested that in the aftermath of ousting Batista and presented with the challenge of instituting his revolutionary plans without the aid of any well-formed program or ideology, Fidel was, more than anything, an "amateur theorist facing realities."[9] Yesterday's idealism rapidly became today's pragmatic and quite often ill-conceived solutions. Had the Eisenhower administration been less driven by fears of communist takeovers in Latin America, the situation might have played out differently. Had MLB commissioner Ford Frick and International League commissioner Frank Shaughnessy been less obsessed with rumors of player safety threats in Havana, the baseball scene might also have remained more stable. But as Fidel told Mankiewicz and Jones, the subsequent events were most likely entirely inevitable.[10]

What followed the rupture in baseball relations in 1960 and early 1961 was a long period of total darkness surrounding the entirety of Castro's domain, and an especially dark shroud would quickly cover Cuban baseball. Cuban baseballers retreated behind a "sugar cane curtain," and American fans missed out entirely on several decades of genuine stars performing completely off the radar in quaint ballparks of their own homeland. No one Stateside would hear of Antonio Muñoz, Agustin Marquetti, or José Antonio Huelga, even when the latter battled and defeated future Dodgers ace Burt Hooten in Cartagena, Colombia, in 1970, to ring up another gold medal and another propaganda triumph for the Cubans. Like all other news about Cuba reaching Americans, the Cuban baseball reports were always either in large part misinformed or purposely distorted by anticommunist rhetoric and anti-Castro propaganda. Mankiewicz and Jones, in 1975, would explain the motivation for their Cuban travels and resulting book, *With Fidel*, as springing from a view "we shared with many Americans that news about Castro and Cuba had been minimal and that what news appeared was based too often on ignorance and possibly even bias."[11] Baseball, especially, was lost to American journalists barred from traipsing island ballparks. The only two reports of substance were those found in a 1987 book by Thomas Boswell, *How Life Imitates the World Series*, and a 1977 *Sports Illustrated* cover story by Ron Fimrite (mentioned again in chapter 6), perceptive observers who had the rare opportunity to travel to Havana under relaxed Carter administration travel policies in the late-1970s.[12] Both would file reports that whetted the appetites of readers but shed little light on the actual scope and vibrancy of Cuba's newly entrenched baseball scene.

What later writers like Brioso and González Echevarría also fail to acknowledge (in the former case) or give full accounting for (in the latter case) is the resurgence in the quality of baseball that evolved rapidly under the new Cuban system of the 1970s and 1980s. This evolution in ballplayer talent of course only came into full view with an initial trickle in the 1990s (Rolando Arroyo, Liván Hernández, El Duque) and then the floodtide after 2010 (Chapman, Céspedes, Puig, Abreu) of defections by top Cuban League stars to the big leagues. It is rather ironic that while American baseball officials were quick to complain about Cuban definitions of amateurism when Castro's early 1960s teams manhandled their American counterparts at Amateur World Series and Pan American Games faceoffs, a notion simultaneously persisted that the Cubans maintained an amateur circuit and thus one of substantially lower quality than the American pro leagues. This was little more than a gross misconception from the start.

While the first few Cuban National Series seasons were indeed played on a strictly amateur level, by the end of the first decade league expansion was rapid and so was a spike in competitive level. Players became professionals by the most important definitions of the term, even if Fidel still labelled them otherwise. They earned salaries for their play, even if the Cuban salary scale could not compare to those of other leagues. They practiced and performed their sport on a full-time basis and were no longer also employed during the offseason in cushy office occupations, as was the case with prerevolution Cuban amateur circuits, when the "baseballers" only took to the diamonds for weekend recreation. Since the top Cuban stars found spots on various national squads competing in summer international events, there was no "offseason" in Cuban baseball.

The North American misconception of Cuban amateurism had to do with two troublesome preconceptions. The first was merely that Cuban ballplayers were not free agents, could not negotiate individual contracts with corporate team ownerships (since there were none), and could not sell their services to MLB teams so that their performances could be enjoyed by American fans and especially Cuban exiles in South Florida cut off from their abandoned homeland but still excessively proud of their ethnic origins. Another misconception was that island baseball stars could not be true professionals since they were state employees receiving the same miniscule wages as Cuban cane-cutters, hotel workers, or laundry maids. (It might be noted here that after the tourist industry picked up drastically in the late 1990s, employees in tourist hotels—bartenders, food servers, desk clerks, and even room-service maids—earned as much or more than ballplayers and also had access to tips in foreign currency.) If Cuban athletes truly were pros, the thinking went, they would be earning the same rock-star salaries today thrown at big-league baseball players plying their trade in North American ballparks.

In a marvelous moment of diplomacy—or rehearsed propaganda, as some might see it—Cuban team manager (and soon-to-be baseball commissioner) Higinio Vélez put the lie to false notions of Cuban amateurism in a memorable postgame press conference immediately after the dramatic 2006 World Baseball Classic semifinal victory against a Dominican Republic team crammed with such veteran MLB stars as Alberto Pujols, Alfonso Soriano, and Miguel Tejada. This author was in the room at the time, and the Vélez interview remains a highlight of my years on the Cuban baseball scene. The first question fired at the victorious Cuban manager by an American journalist (who apparently intended a tone of bitter irony) was the following, loosely translated: "How does it feel now that your team of rank amateurs has somehow upset a squad of the top professionals?" Vélez was ready with a most surprising and pointed reply:

Amateurs? I suppose you mean that our players are not paid what Pujols or Soriano earn. But by that standard I assume you are pre-pared to tell me that school teachers and college professors in your country are also amateurs. They also don't earn the same as top professional athletes or movie stars, do they? No, no. Our players are indeed also professionals. They devote their lives only to practice and preparation and performance in their occupation, which is baseball. That is how we measure professionals in Cuba, not by the size of the material rewards. [author's loose translation]

Vélez was only the latest to remind us that professional baseball never ended in Cuba after the revolution, and for that reason alone Fidel did not kill it off. It was only remolded by something other than American capitalist standards. It was only drastically redefined, and Fidel had been the one to redefine it.

* * *

There is substantial evidence that Fidel made a concerted personal effort to keep both the minor-league ballclub and the winter-league circuit alive. It was only once both enterprises had been pulled out from under him that an opportunity suddenly arose for reassessing the role of baseball in Cuban culture. Castro's early advocacy for the Sugar Kings is well documented and has already been briefly touched upon in a previous chapter. During his April 23, 1959, meeting with stadium and ballclub owner Roberto Maduro, he pledged both personal support and governmental assistance. One immediate result of that gesture was a cash donation of $20,000 from sugar industry leaders intended to keep the team viable despite the previous year's anemic attendance.

Later that same month, while in New York, Castro was asked about the Sugar Kings' status and vowed the ballclub would stay put even if he himself had to take the mound and pitch a few innings in a thinly veiled attempt to boost sagging attendance. While that was likely an idle boast, Fidel did toss out the ceremonial first pitches for league openers in both 1959 and 1960.[13] Only a few weeks after seizing control of the country, in an effort to lessen apprehensions, the new leader promised in a New York Times editorial that American visitors would always be welcomed on the island. Justin Turner, in his thesis, Baseball Diploma-cy, Baseball Deployment, even speculates that Castro's immediate support for the team was largely what saved the franchise during that first summer, ending with an unexpected Junior World Series championship.

But the road remained rocky in the face of an increasingly hostile Washington–Havana political standoff and growing reports of Fidel's communist leanings. The 1960 season's opening series had been threatened when Buffalo ownership balked on traveling to Havana. While league officials managed to forestall that particular crisis, a gala opening day, which featured the presentation of the International League Governors' Cup championship trophy and another Fidel ball-tossing appearance, did not escape unscathed. New American ambassador Philp Bonsal and his Canadian counterpart, Allan Anderson, attended the game but declined greeting Fidel and maintained an apparent icy posture, sitting a considerable distance from the Cuban leader.

Additional tension-raising developments on both the political and sporting front also separated the Sugar Kings championship in October from the Governors' Cup ceremonies in April. Appearing on American television, on *Meet the Press*, in February, Fidel blamed increased exile air strikes squarely on Washington. On March 4, the French munitions freighter *Coubre* exploded in Havana's harbor, and Fidel again pointed an accusing finger at malicious U.S. involvement. Days before the new baseball season opened, Castro once more lashed out at presumed American intervention, this time suggesting that the naval base at Guantanamo Bay was harboring counterrevolutionaries. On the baseball side, ill feelings were extended when the Cincinnati Reds (parent club of the Sugar Kings) cancelled a late March exhibition series in Havana with the Baltimore Orioles; the reason given by Baltimore team president Lee MacPhail for shifting the series to Miami was ballplayer and ownership uneasiness related to Fidel's repeated verbal attacks and anti-Washington accusations, which seemed to signal Americans were not actually welcome in Havana.

MacPhail's position sent a strong message about the stance of Organized Baseball. There is also plenty of additional evidence for a conclusion that U.S. interests were most directly to blame for dismantling the professional sport on the island. Those interests were perhaps best reflected by the paranoia of International League president Frank Shaughnessy and team owners—or even revealed by the decision-making policies of MLB boss Ford Frick—rather than being attributable to any direct actions by Washington politicians. Yet, wherever found, they inevitably played a far larger role than did the policies of the new Cuban government. Even pointing to the growing anti-Americanism rapidly evolving in Havana's government circles, or citing the nationalizing of American business interests, is something of a distortion since most notions about what was actually transpiring in the early months under Fidel were based on much misunderstanding, inadequate analysis, and shoddy or slanted reporting by Stateside media outlets.

There is, of course, the inarguable influence that the revolution itself and the social changes in Cuba in the period from late 1958 through early 1960 had on the future of professional baseball operations on the island. Counterrevolutionary violence made Havana a tense scene in the year and a half that separated the flight of Batista and the flight of the Sugar Kings. MLB officials repeatedly expressed growing concerns about player safety, even if that fear was not always based on objective reality and also continually ignored or discounted reassurances by Maduro, Fidel, and others in Havana. The Cubans reiterated that those fears were overblown and that anyone holding them could point to little real justification for such a stance. After all, the attention-grabbing, if relatively minor, ballpark disturbances of late July 1959 and during the Junior World Series games a few months later did not actually constitute any true threats to North American ballplayers.

It might also be admitted that growing tensions in Havana were most severely strained on the political and diplomatic front by the war of words then escalating between Fidel and Washington in late 1959 and early 1960. Much of the rhetoric was generated by Fidel, perhaps with good reason, since any actual aggression (in the form of counterrevolutionary bombings and sabotage orchestrated by a growing Miami exile community) was aimed mostly his way. Washington clearly had a different agenda regarding Cuba than the one held by Shaughnessy, Frick, and company once Fidel was entrenched in power. Angry and myopic U.S. government officials were driven by a desperate and perhaps even irrational fear of communism and not a genuine apprehension about the safety of ballplayers, or even the safety of other U.S. citizens still residing in Cuba. Above all else, for Washington, the dominant concern was a fear for the safety of American financial and business interests.

The issues were indeed complex, and much of the chaos paralyzing Havana during the earliest months of Fidel's presence has not yet been entirely straightened out by historians. The issues and events lend themselves to very different interpretations based on the political persuasions of those tackling the subject. Turner gives perhaps the most detailed and objective analysis of the events in his recent University of Alabama doctoral dissertation, devoted to delineating the role of a shared national pastime in unscrambling decades of U.S.–Cuba Cold War interactions. But in the end, even Turner leaves his readers with more ambiguity than conclusive evidence.

Nonetheless, a few points now seem indisputable. The first is that Fidel himself did more to maintain the professional baseball clubs in Havana than he did to oust them. If his revolution had created a difficult and perhaps even unsustainable environment, that is a different scenario than one that has Fidel kicking MLB off the island and deciding to replace the professional version with an amateur one. The decision to create INDER and revamp Cuban sports, including baseball, only arose in the aftermath of the island being stripped of both its minor-league franchise and its winter MLB-affiliated circuit. And the direct removal of both former American enterprises was carried out by U.S. officials (Organized Baseball officials, with possible support or encouragement, or even direct instructions, from an outgoing Eisenhower administration and a newly seated Kennedy administration) and not by Fidel Castro and his henchmen.

It is not hard to uncover troubling inconsistencies in Fidel's statements and therefore perhaps also in his hidden views about the status of the Sugar Kings or Organized Baseball's control of Cuba's professional league. His repeated post-1961 touting of his replacement amateur version as an example of the superiority of "free revolutionary baseball" over an imperialist-style baseball that exploited mercenary athletes appears to be entirely inconsistent with any efforts only a year or two earlier to keep the pros in town. Yet, in view of his constant avowals in 1959 or in the Sierra Maestra that he was not a communist, followed by his December 1961 announcement that he was and had always been a Marxist-Leninist, what did such radically altering stances suggest? Did they uncover earlier deceitfulness or simply demonstrate later opportunism? The shifting of his position on baseball was likely no more or no less revealing than his inconsistencies and wavering positions regarding other aspects of his revolutionary program or his hot-and-cold relationships with Washington.

Perhaps the best explanation for such wavering on issues, plans, and philosophies is found in Herbert Matthews's observations that with his December 1961 avowal that he had always been a Marxist-Leninist, Fidel was, like on so many other occasions, purposely presenting himself as deceitful, cunning, and scheming. Matthews would at the same time caution that in assessing Fidel's career and actions at any point in time, it was always necessary to grasp his capacity for self-deception— "his sincere convictions of one day that can change to equally sincere and quite different convictions another day." [14] If Matthews was on the right track, such an analysis would go a long way toward explaining how efforts at maintaining professional baseball throughout 1959 and 1960 suddenly turned into an apparent abhorrence for the "exploitive and nonrevolutionary" version of the sport only months later in 1961 and 1962.

There is yet another potential clue to Fidel's baseball ambivalence in the months immediately preceding and following the hijacking of the Sugar Kings and removal of the MLB-supported winter league. In a *Sports Illustrated* feature detailing the sad plight of outfielder Edmundo "Sandy" Amoros, Nicholas Dawidoff replays the distressing fate of the 1955 Brooklyn World Series hero, who apparently ran afoul of Fidel in the early winter of 1961, after he had returned home from what proved to be his final big-league season in Detroit. Dawidoff's story might provide a further clue to Fidel's unsettled position on professional baseball in 1961 (before the new INDER law of 1962), although there is also enough confusion and lack of detail in Amoros's recounting of events to weaken this particular piece of evidence.

As Amoros relates the story to Dawidoff, one day in 1960—the exact month is not mentioned—Fidel interrupted a pickup game at Santa Maria del Mar being played by Amoros and his friends, and demanded to take the field himself, to the embarrassment of the big-leaguer ("We were better players so [when Castro showed up] it wasn't fun anymore"). [15] Amoros next claims that "two years later," Fidel had decided to "form an entire professional summer league in Cuba" and therefore approached Amoros, who was spending his offseason at home outside Havana, requesting that the ballplayer stay on in Cuba and manage one of the new teams instead of heading to Mexico to play in that country's summer league. Amoros, who had doubts about working for the new communist government, told *el comandante* he knew nothing about managing; therefore, he didn't want to manage when he could still play and thus was simply not interested. The result of this refusal was catastrophic; the uncooperative ballplayer was not allowed to leave the island for the next five years, putting an end to his professional career, and he was also stripped of his prized ranch, luxury car, and cash. If indeed Fidel was intending to start a "professional summer league" (was this 1961 or 1962?) this would again suggest he had not entirely rejected professionalism in the aftermath of being shunned by Organized Baseball.

But there are obvious problems with the story. This event could not have occurred in 1962, since Fidel and INDER had by then turned their backs on professionalism and already launched the replacement amateur National Series that January. One only needs to recall Fidel's diatribe against imperialist baseball at the opening of that first domestic amateur-league season (reported in chapter 5) to discount any stories of his planning to launch a replacement pro summer league. (Was Amoros perhaps offered a managerial post in the amateur National Series?) Also, if the incident occurred a year earlier, say in January or February 1961, Amoros would have been preparing to return to Detroit for his final big-league season and not headed to the Mexican League. There might be two possible explanations: Either this was the tail end of the winter big-league offseason in early 1961, and Amoros was now confused about what his departure plans were back then, or this was early 1962, and Fidel was not planning a pro league at all but wanted Amoros to manage in the newly formed National Series, where ex-big-leaguer Fermín Guerra and former Sugar Kings skipper Antonio Castaño did serve as managers that first 1962 season. Whatever the actual facts, the Amoros report doesn't shed much light on when Fidel might actually have given up entirely on the professional version of the sport.

Returning to Fidel's actual role in the Sugar Kings' demise, a second inarguable fact sufficient to discredit the popular analysis—as demonstrated most fully in two succeeding chapters—is that Fidel and his government certainly did not consciously end baseball in Cuba. There is absolutely no evidence that baseball ever ceased on the island or was in any sense even diminished. The only rationale for that position is to contend that "baseball" per se is precisely equivalent to the business operations of corporate MLB. This might be a cherished belief of many provincial North Americans, but it hardly makes any sense to fans of the sport in such hotbeds of fanaticism as Japan, Korea, Taiwan, The Netherlands, or numerous other points spread throughout the Caribbean. Baseball might claim its highest performance levels in MLB, but it neither begins nor ends with that institution.

Rather than shut down baseball, their own cherished and traditional national game, the newly empowered Fidelistas simply rebranded it to fit a revised societal model fostered by the socialist revolution. Fleitas and those echoing his words might have been much better served to shout out "that man came along and *transformed* baseball." What ended in Cuba in 1960 and 1961 was not Cuba's national pastime (it was actually about to be infused with new life), but only the MLB-controlled business of corporate professional baseball designed for monetary profit. That is to say, the baseball transition of 1961, not surprisingly, was entirely compatible with the motives of a revolutionary movement aimed at removing all vestiges of a country controlled by exploitative North American financial interests. By pulling up stakes, the moguls in Organized Baseball simply made it much easier for the Fidelistas to comfortably fit baseball into their own emerging revolutionary agenda.

It is true enough—as Turner, González Echevarría, and so many others have stressed—that a new socialist baseball machinery would be heavily politicized and immediately used, among other things, for propagandistic victories on the ballfield that might not have been possible on the battlefield. The revamped national pastime overnight became a successful Cold War tool, as well as an instrument to display domestic values (nationalism and nonmaterialism) underpinning the new society. But even this, as I stress elsewhere, was not such a novel turn of events.[16] Cuba's baseball had, almost from the outset in the 1870s and 1880s, been politicized and even militarized. The sport emerged on the island against the backdrop of a first war of independence and provided an important political tool in combating the Spanish colonial rulers. When the Spanish were finally driven out, only to find the Americans ruthlessly replacing them with yet another decade-long occupation, again baseball was employed during late fall and early winter "American Seasons" preceding domestic-league action as a welcome stage for propagandistic victories against the American occupiers.

Cuba's effort to turn baseball, once adopted from their colonizers (in this case their supposed liberators from Spanish colonial control but in reality only a new set of foreign occupiers), into a tool for defeating or embarrassing visiting squads of American barnstormers (both black and white) only repeats a familiar pattern played out in Asia. Historians Robert Elias and Joseph A. Reaves both stress how the Japanese, Koreans, and Taiwanese each, in turn, found the baseball thrust upon them by aggressor nations to be a double-edged sword.[17] The Japanese not only adopted, but also rapidly adapted the game (making it something distinct from the American version), and were soon basing nationalistic fervor on victories against visiting American naval personnel. The Koreans and Taiwanese, in turn, were dominated culturally and economically by the Japanese but found their own spark of national pride in their boasts that at least they could beat their occupiers at their own game of baseball.

And the new "amateur" baseball in Cuba after 1962 would also reflect still another aspect of Cuba's proud baseball tradition too often overlooked by North American commentators. Amateur leagues had already been a showcase feature of Cuban baseball throughout the half-century existence of the rival professional winter league. By several measures—the number of participants, leagues, and games played; the overall quality of play; the island-wide venues and massive fan interest—the amateur game not only rivaled, but also often dwarfed its pro counterpart in the years between the two world wars. The winter professional league was always mostly, if not entirely, a Havana phenomenon and not an island-wide obsession. Many of the island's best players—mostly non-Afro-Cubans—never gravitated to the pro circuit, if only because there were more lucrative possibilities with the amateur clubs; performing for a team in the National Amateur League, the Quivicán Inter-Municipal, or the Pedro Betancourt League (the later two created in the 1940s to combat the racism still found in the Amateur Athletic Union circuit), star pitchers or sluggers were compensated with soft jobs (jobs to which they often didn't have to report since their paychecks were earned on the ball diamond) provided by team sponsors and also enjoyed a softer league schedule restricted exclusively to weekend competitions.

The myth of pre-Castro island baseball as an integrated *béisbol paradiso* remains another of the great misunderstandings surrounding Cuban baseball history, as so often portrayed by American observers, especially enthusiasts of North American black baseball history. The reigning notion was always that Cuba provided a much-coveted "Promised Land" where whites and blacks played side by side in racial harmony. While that may have been largely true of the Havana pro circuit during the first half of the twentieth century, it did not mean Cuban baseball escaped its own era of odious segregation. Blacks gravitated to the Havana-based pro league because that was the only promising employment available for many dark-skinned islanders given their lower-class origins and lack of formal education. Baseball, like boxing, was, for many Afro-Cuban males, the best, if not the only, ticket out of island poverty and into a "charmed life" of American professional sports— even if in baseball that "charmed life" before 1947 was restricted for most to the barnstorming blackball circuits. Amateur leagues where players could expect comfortable desk jobs and elevated salaries in exchange for weekend play were strictly segregated affairs open to light-skinned Cubans only, and those leagues drew some of the island's top players. Orestes "Minnie" Miñoso, Carlos Paula, and Luis Tiant the Elder were not welcome in the AAU circuit because of their skin tones. Nor were such preintegration big-leaguers as Roberto Estalella or Tomás de la Cruz. who passed the color test in North America but not on their home island.

While playing briefly in the pro winter league or with the Havana Cubans or Sugar Kings after signing big-league deals with Washington scout Joe Cambria, many of the island's best players (especially pitchers) were actually products of the AAU island-wide Cuban league.[18] Conrado Marrero and several additional ace pitchers are prime examples. The case of Marrero—who inked his first pro contract with the Havana Cubans at the advanced age of 35, and only after several suspensions from an illustrious amateur-league career brought on by his penchant for simultaneously playing with more than one club under assumed names—and other mid-century Cuban big leaguers, such as pitchers Julio Moreno, Rogelio Martínez, Sandalio Consuegra, and Santiago Ullrich, serve well here as illustrations.

Most World War II–era Washington Senators recruits and other Cuban big-leaguers of the period were white-skinned only, even though a handful of Afro-Cubans did slip through a nebulous MLB color line. Estalella and de la Cruz were two who "passed" in Washington and Cincinnati thanks to a reigning North American confusion about racial identity. Only a handful of those original Washington signees of the

1940s initially came from the pro winter league as opposed to the amateur circuits; Marrero, Moreno, Martinez, and Consuegra indeed played with the Cuban pros after inking deals with the Havana Cubans, but all four had earlier established their credentials in the early 1940s National Amateur League.

And the winter league, as noted, was mostly an exclusive Havana affair. The new Cuban League (the National Series and eventually its companion, the Selective Series) of 1962 and beyond would soon expand to reestablish the kind of island-wide circuit the original amateur leagues had previously provided. Early AAU leagues and games had stretched far outside the capital city, with top teams found in Matanzas, Cienfuegos, Artemisa, Regla, Cárdenas, Santiago de Las Vegas, and the sugar mill town of Hershey. This wider geographical scope was also true of the sugar mill circuits, which recruited mercenary athletes of both races for spirited tournaments during nonharvest months. The winter league did occasionally house teams outside Havana—briefly in Matanzas, Santa Clara, and Cienfuegos, for example—and periodically played scattered games in Cienfuegos and Matanzas. But in its dozen or so highest-profile and most stable seasons, this was no longer the case, and the team called Cienfuegos in the final dozen or more golden years of the circuit was based in the capital and not in the seaport town on the southern coast.

❖ ❖ ❖

American baseball has always been closely associated with American imperialism; ingrained Yankee values supposedly found at the heart of the bat-and-ball sport served as the perfect mechanism for spreading American cultural values and thus American economic and political structures to far corners of the globe. This argument is painstakingly laid out in considerable detail by Robert Elias in *The Empire Strikes Out* and doesn't need further elaboration here. Suffice it to say that baseball has been repeatedly used by more than one nation (Americans, Japanese, Koreans, Taiwanese, as well as Cubans) as a most effective tool for cultural infusion and economic imperialism. The evolution of the game in Asian ports finds its roots in Japanese military adventurism and efforts at "Japanization" of Korean, Taiwanese, and Chinese neighbors. Driven to seek refuge from the violence of a 30-year indepen-

dence struggle, expatriate nineteenth-century Cuban sugar cane grow-
ers transported their newly adopted baseball passions to neighboring
island shores in Puerto Rico and the Dominican Republic, and the
coasts of Mexico and Venezuela. Cubans and not Americans were the
true "apostles" of the inherited American game throughout the Caribbean region. The Castro government, in its earliest days of socialist
revolution, was only picking up on a very old theme.

That baseball was transported to other Caribbean outposts mainly
through the efforts of emigrating Cubans who also brought their sugar
cane production with them provides yet another link between the sport
and the dominant Caribbean agricultural and economic interests. Sugar
production and baseball fit perfectly since the game provided a cheap
and easy diversion for planters and harvesters during the six-month
dead period required for the plants to grow. A slow-paced game requiring only brief bursts of physical exertion fit nicely with the sweltering
Caribbean climate; the strength acquired by machete-wielding cane
harvesters also translated well to actions on the diamond. Amateur and
semiprofessional baseball, in both Cuba and other Caribbean outposts,
found an ideal setting in the numerous sugar mill leagues that rapidly
sprang up throughout the region.

American baseball imperialism indeed has an extensive, if not always
inspiring, history. Elias's well-argued theory contends that baseball, already designated the national game by the 1850s, fostered its deep
connections with American militarism and American imperialist adventures to safeguard its cherished position as the anointed national pastime. The military connections for the sport were well established during World War I, when the national anthem became a pregame fixture,
but in fact they stretch back to the American Revolution, more than a
half-century before the game's mythical immaculate conception in
Cooperstown, when the novel game was already a favorite campground
pastime among infantry soldiers. And if MLB fostered intimate connections with the U.S. military during its earliest decades, it also wasted
little time in launching imperialist programs of its own.

Part of that history would affect Cuba, as much at the midpoint of
the twentieth century as at the same century's outset decades earlier.
MLB could never abide serious competition or challenges to its own
expanding commercial empire and, from the close of the nineteenth
century onward, took up the gauntlet in various wars of its own de-

signed to squelch first domestic rivals like the short-lived 1890 Players League and 1914 Federal League, then the upstart Mexicans, who made inroads with Jorge Pasquel's recruiting forays, aimed at pilfering big-league talent, then the "outlaw" Stateside Negro Leagues, initially dismissed by a pious Branch Rickey as criminal enterprises underwritten by numbers-game gangsters but, after 1947, also available for full-scale talent raids, and eventually the competing winter circuits of the Caribbean and even their own minor-league affiliates Stateside once TV technology brought the big-league game into every living room throughout the nation. MLB's monopolistic motives would rise most obviously to the forefront in the immediate aftermath of World War II during the short-lived threat of possible Pasquel-led Mexican League expansion.

In the mid-1940s, on the eve of big-league integration and the resulting collapse of Negro circuits in the Midwest and the metropolises of the East Coast, Mexican business mogul Jorge Pasquel (import-export tycoon and friend of powerful politicians) entertained a vision of putting his Mexican circuit on par with the American majors. Pasquel had previously recruited top blackball stalwarts, including such notables as Americans James "Cool Papa" Bell and Josh Gibson, and Cubans Martin Dihigo, Lázaro Sálazar, and Ramón Bragaña. But his ambition soon grew into a notion of elevating his circuit on par with the vaunted big leagues up north. Historian John Virtue has suggested that Pasquel's thinly disguised attack on the American big-league empire was based on more than just national pride or economic adventurism.[19] A 1913 U.S. military invasion and occupation of his childhood home in the port city of Veracruz remained a raw and painful issue for the soon-to-be multimillionaire, who rose to prominence after taking over his father's import empire, as did instances of racial discrimination he had personally suffered as a young man on visits across the border to Texas, where racism targeted Mexicans, as well as African Americans. The crux of Pasquel's plan was to lure away big-league stars with lucrative cash offers, and he had the deep pockets to do it. He was successful in enticing journeymen like Mickey Owen, George Hausmann, Danny Gardella, Vern Stephens, Max Lanier, and Sal Maglie, but he was also reportedly rebuffed by superstars Stan Musial, Hank Greenberg, Bob Feller, and Enos Slaughter.[20]

Fallout from Pasquel's explosive ambitions would have unintended consequences when it briefly transformed at least some native Cuban stars into virtual exiles within their own country. The hostile recruiting wars between MLB clubs and Pasquel's Mexican League were perhaps most significant for their deep and unexpected negative impact on Cuba's upcoming winter baseball seasons of 1946–1947 and 1947–1948. When big-league commissioner Happy Chandler banned ballplayers who had signed on with Pasquel in Mexico, that action would quickly throw the Cuban circuit into temporary chaos. An immediate result was an unorthodox pair of rival Cuban leagues operating simultaneously and desperately vying for Havana's fan support.

The first Cuban campaign (1946–1947) in the wake of Chandler's edict found banned players (a contingent of Cubans including stalwarts Pedro Formental, Roberto Ortiz, Cocaina García, and Agapito Mayor, plus such top American imports as Max Lanier, George Hausmann, and Sal Maglie, who had also gone to Mexico the previous summer) moving into the newly constructed Cerro Stadium and drawing the largest crowds, if only because their circuit commanded most top attractions with its bevy of familiar and popular veteran local stars. Meanwhile, those signed on with Organized Baseball affiliates who feared expulsion if they performed on the same field with "outlaw" Mexican Leaguers remained in recently abandoned Tropical Stadium and played under the banner of a hastily constructed alternative league known as the National Federation League. Playing a leading role in organizing the new circuit were war-era Washington Senators Gilberto Torres and Fermin Guerra, and notable American recruits Ray Dandridge, Don Newcombe, and Bobo Holloman. Future big-leaguer Conrado Marrero would also debut with Oriente of the Federation League but soon skip over to the group in Cerro Stadium and the popular pennant-winning Almendares club when the alternative league was forced to fold before its scheduled campaign reached completion.

In the aftermath of a formal treaty between Organized Baseball and league owners signed in June 1947, the following winter saw the chaotic scene shift radically, with banned "outlaw" players now escaping to La Tropical and the Organized Baseball–sanctioned group in turn occupying the showcase venue in Cerro Stadium. The "ineligibles" rebranded themselves as the Liga Nacional, not to be confused with the Liga de la Federación Nacional (the "eligibles"), who had retreated to La Tropical the previous year. The outlaw circuit now included famed manager Adolfo Luque, who had regularly been a summer-season manager in Mexico, as well as such star players as Mayor, Ortiz, Tomás de la Cruz, Lázaro Sálazar, and Sandy Consuegra, among others. This second time around both circuits were able to complete full schedules, and parallel teams named Habana captured both competing league pennants. The MLB-sanctioned circuit now regained the spotlight despite its loss of considerable star power, although it did feature a number of top-flight American players (Sam Jethroe, Hank Thompson, Lennie Pearson) and also Cubans (Claro Duany, Lorenzo Cabrera, Pedro Pagés, Silvio García) from the Negro Leagues, plus such future major leaguers as Marrero and emerging Afro-Cuban prospect Minnie Miñoso.

When the peace accord between Cuban League owners and Organized Baseball management was finally reached, it represented anything but a perfect or even comfortable solution for the Cubans—either fans or owners. There were loud outcries in Havana that the new peace deal orchestrated by MLB was, in essence, forcing many Cubans out of their own league, only to be replaced by an excess of American players, for whom the controlling big-league clubs desired extra offseason fine tuning. In short, the once-independent Cuban circuit was now being consumed by MLB management and, in the process, had lost a large chunk of its native Cuban flavor. César Brioso contends that this absorption was only positive since the league stability gained far outweighed any other factors, for instance, shifting rosters, disappearing native stars, or any limited presence of big-leaguers.[21] Most Cuban fans, owners, and ballplayers certainly did not hold a similar view at the time. There were huge negatives for Cuba's cherished professional baseball to be sure. As winter-league play moved into the decade of the 1950s, Cuban owners effectively lost control of their league.

Brioso is essentially correct in claiming that the Cuban League, in its various shifting formats, had never known much stability before the MLB takeover. If it was improved on that single count it obviously paid an extremely heavy price in the bargain. Perhaps the circuit was more stable without the earlier threat of poorly financed franchises appearing and then rapidly disappearing again from season to season, but the Cuban winter league after 1947 was no longer entirely a Cuban-run enterprise. The loss of many popular native Cuban stars (those banned for their participation in Pasquel's league) would be exacerbated in the coming decade as revolutionary and counterrevolutionary violence in 1957, 1958, and 1959 not only created fears for player safety among MLB club owners, but also big-league clubs started keeping their better Cuban players out of the circuit for purely economic reasons.

At first big-leaguers with more than 45 days of service on parent-club rosters were withheld, but Cuban natives were exempted from that rule. Nonetheless, the restriction on service by major leaguers necessitated high turnovers on winter-league rosters from one campaign to the next. When the original agreement was tweaked to exempt native Cubans from MLB restrictions, the big-league clubs were simultaneously granted final say in player assignments. One result was that Miñoso, Consuegra, Camilo Pascual, and Mike Fornieles were subsequently held out of winter action by their MLB owners in 1957 and 1958. And by the beginning of the 1960s, big-leaguers were disappearing altogether in the wake of the growing player safety concerns. MLB boss Ford Frick finally pulled the plug altogether for 1960–1961, and sounded a virtual death knell for the circuit in the process. If the league reached anything like a high point with its dramatic down-to-the-wire pennant race of 1946–1947, between "Eternal Rivals" Habana and Almendares, a mere decade later it was largely on life support. The working agreement with Organized Baseball shared much, if not all, of the blame for that precipitous drop in league health and league stature.

\* \* \*

An important footnote, if not a central backdrop, to fading Cuban winter-league glory was provided by two minor-league franchises that occupied the 15 summers between World War II and the new Marxist-socialist regime destined to alter the Cuban landscape, as well as Cuban baseball, irrevocably at the height of the Cold War era. The Havana Cubans of the lower-level Class C/B Florida International League and the Cuban (Havana) Sugar Kings of the top-level Class AAA International League would together provide the final bittersweet chapter in the saga of North American-affiliated Cuban professional baseball.

Cuba's official links to Organized Baseball begin in 1946, with the modest debut of the Havana Cubans, initially a Class C club owned partially by popular Senators scout "Papa Joe" Cambria and therefore not surprisingly affiliated with the Washington American League club.

Launching play a year before the completion of Cerro Stadium, the team was initially housed in the pastoral setting of La Tropical Stadium and competed in a circuit that also included original teams in Tampa Bay (Smokers), Miami (Sun Sox, later renamed the Tourists), Miami Beach (Flamingos,), West Palm Beach (Indians), and Lakeland (Pilots), and later additions in St. Petersburg (Saints) and Ft. Lauderdale (Braves, but originally the Key West Conchs). Featuring a cast of former island amateur leaguers, the Cubans were at first head and shoulders above league competition and ran off three initial first-place regular-season finishes and two postseason titles; when the league was bumped up to Class B in 1949, Havana's early domination continued with another pair of first-place finishes and two additional trips to the league postseason finale (where they lost one year to Tampa and the next to Miami). Oscar Rodríguez piloted the club in its first five seasons and was followed on the bench by legendary pitcher Adolfo Luque, former Washington catcher Fermin Guerra, and big-league pioneer Armando Marsans (one season each for the latter three managers).

Top stars for the Cubans were a pair of future Washington big-league hurlers, Conrado Marrero (who, already in his mid-30s, had won 70 games in three campaigns and posted a string of sub-1.70 ERAs) and Julio "Jiquí" Moreno (1950 FIL ERA leader with a sterling 1.47). Despite sweltering summers not ideal for ball-playing or viewing, the club's on-field domination attracted more than 200,000 spectators through the turnstiles in each of the four inaugural campaigns. Although the club fortunes slid drastically after 1950, when Marrero and Moreno escaped to the big-time in Washington, and despite disillusionments resulting from the MLB takeover of the winter circuit, the minor-league club strengthened the links to professional baseball up north and kept alive the long-held dream of achieving higher status within Organized Baseball. That dream took a large leap forward when Havana was awarded a coveted slot in the top minor-league classification and the Cuban Sugar Kings replaced the B-Class Cubans for the 1954 International League season.

Behind the leap to Class AAA was Havana entrepreneur Bobby Maduro, who had bought a partial interest in the Class C Cubans after their initial season and, by 1949, had also gained a partial interest in the winter league Cienfuegos team. Maduro would not actually become the majority owner of the initial Havana minor-league franchise until he bought out Clark Griffith's stake early in the club's final year (1953). But he and several partners had already been responsible for a large step forward in building the island's baseball stature when they constructed state-of-the-art Cerro Stadium closer to the city center in time for the 1946 winter season. By the time he had gained full control of the Havana Cubans franchise, Maduro was already setting his sights on bigger and better things. He obtained rights to the struggling Springfield AAA International League franchise and quickly gained permission from league officers and owners to transfer the Massachusetts-based club to more promising environs in Havana. Also making additional efforts to promote baseball on an international level, the forward-thinking Maduro brought the Yomiuri Giants from Japan for an exhibition series and took his new Havana AAA ballclub to Venezuela for further "friendly" matches.

When the Havana Cubans were replaced by the newly renamed Sugar Kings in the spring of 1954, the transition was envisioned as a step that would hopefully lead to a home in the major leagues. The team motto (*Un paso más . . . y llegamos*—"One more step . . . and we arrive") reflected that ambition at the heart of Maduro's plans with its double meaning. Its players were one step from the majors since they were performing in the top minor-league circuit, but for Maduro and others it now seemed that the Cuban capital was also just one step away from the baseball big-time.

Unlike their forerunners, the Sugar Kings were not a powerhouse in their earliest seasons and struggled on the field for much of their first five campaigns. While the new team did play above .500 the first two years, they were not a pennant challenger in the higher classification. They slumped to sixth place in 1956 and 1957, and then limped home dead last in 1958. By year number four (1957), the team was drawing few fans, and as mentioned earlier, the falloff was brought on by more than just losing. The oppressive summer weather was not propitious for attracting stadium goers. And increasing anti-Batista violence sweeping the country was anything but helpful. But eventually the Sugar Kings peaked in 1959, due in part to Maduro's own shrewd executive moves, which included shaking up the organization by replacing his field manager and trading for improved pitching. And there might well have also been some raw luck involved. The team's late-season surge lifted them into the postseason as a distant third-place finisher. And perhaps inspired by the initial euphoria surrounding the Castro victory over Batista earlier in the year, the club raced down the stretch to a surprising Junior World Series victory against the American Association champion Minneapolis Millers.

Yet, despite these on-field successes, the team was already an endangered commodity by the time Fidel seized the reins of government and the Castro revolution moved from an unsettling disturbance in the Sierra Maestra to a full-blown societal overhaul in Havana. Player safety issues had rapidly been leading to a crippling loss of faith in the franchise among other league owners and officials. By 1959, Maduro was no longer fighting to get to the majors, but merely battling to keep his current ballclub in Havana. And with attendance severely sagging, he was also losing tons of money. With both the club's sagging ticket sales and the revolutionary ferment squarely in mind, league officials had met only weeks before the 1958 season opener to again discuss at least temporary relocation of the Havana club, spurred mainly by Buffalo owner John C. Stiglmeier's complaints about sending his club into a hostile and likely dangerous situation in Havana for their scheduled season-opening series.[22] Montreal, another league club, had already cancelled a preseason exhibition series on the island.

Maduro was therefore already operating in damage-control mode a full year before his team's surprising 1959 on-field resurgence. He had publicly labelled his fellow owners' fears as highly unwarranted and stressed that the revolution-related violence was 750 miles away in the eastern mountains and Havana disturbances were few and minor at best. His arguments brought a temporary reprieve, with the reluctant agreement of the wavering International League owners not to immediately move the franchise. On April 6, Commissioner Frank Shaughnessy announced that an ownership vote had confirmed that the season would indeed kick off in Havana as scheduled "unless conditions materially change."[23] At the same time, however, he warned that the league could always relocate Havana operations to Jersey City virtually overnight if the situation worsened.

But that vote did not provide much assurance for Maduro, and the crisis continued a mere week later when Stiglmeier, citing the nervousness of his players, again balked at the trip to Havana for the season opener. Shaughnessy was able to resolve this renewed flare-up by threatening the Buffalo owner with fines and forfeitures in the case of any games not played. Stiglmeier only came onboard when the league also agreed to take full responsibility for player safety on the ground in Cuba and when U.S. ambassador Earl E. T. Smith, a strong Batista supporter, phoned the Buffalo owner to personally assure him that the island was indeed safe for visiting teams. That April 1958 series of events provided a strong signal that the brewing revolution had already put the Sugar Kings' future in serious jeopardy nine months before Fidel would finally seize control of his country's fortunes. While Batista and his U.S.-backed government would be gone at year's end, the Sugar Kings so far had somehow managed to survive and were even about to undergo something of a short-lived revival as celebrated object of national pride. Yet, the proverbial handwriting was already clearly visible on the wall.

By the following spring of 1960, there were further undeniable tensions also attached to the MLB-controlled if still-Cuba-based winter league. The couple dozen major leaguers performing in the Havana winter circuit became a troublesome concern for MLB owners once Fidel grabbed the reins of power in January 1959. Since MLB and Organized Baseball had already established a "peril clause" in their working agreements with all four Caribbean winter circuits (Puerto Rico, Venezuela, and Panama, in addition to Cuba), Commissioner Ford Frick found the issue falling squarely in his own lap. Frick hesitated on any immediate mandate recalling big-leaguers from Havana but also announced that individual MLB clubs were entitled to do so if they wished.

While Clark Griffith (with nine of his own players in Havana) and other MLB owners decided not to pull players from the 1958–1959 winter-league season, Griffith nonetheless canceled his Washington Senators March 1959 spring training trip to Havana, losing $40,000 in guarantees in the process.[24] The Baltimore Orioles would reprise Griffith's actions and further add to the growing tensions a year later by cancelling their own scheduled March 1960 spring visit. Team president Lee MacPhail first announced in January that his club was considering the cancellation due to growing anti-American rhetoric flowing from Havana as the Castro regime entered its second year. But the actual cancellation was not announced until days before the scheduled matches, which brought strong rebukes from the local Cuban press.[25] Calling for the games versus the Cincinnati Reds (parent club to the

Sugar Kings) to be transferred to Miami, MacPhail again claimed safety concerns voiced by several of his players. An article in the Cuban journal *Revolución* countered that the real reason for the two Baltimore players (supposedly Willie Tasby and Gus Triandos) demurring on Cuban travel was actually some unpaid Havana hotel bills and "women problems" left behind during the previous winter-league campaign.[26]

Concerns about player safety by MLB and International League bosses seemed the major crisis plaguing Organized Baseball operations in Havana. But on the eve of the Sugar Kings' demise there was also a political backdrop that signaled far more threat to American business interests than any issues of ballplayer or tourist safety. Eisenhower's overt moves against Cuba were likely the largest factor working to increase tensions, but many of those moves were related to previous or simultaneous actions by the Cuban government. In January, Cuban officials would expropriate 70,000 acres of land owned by U.S. sugar companies. Throughout the first three months of that year, as a clear-cut response from Washington, there were U.S.-sponsored (if not orchestrated) bombings of Cuban sugar cane fields. Fidel, in those months, increased tension with his own hostile rhetoric condemning those U.S. air raids.[27]

On June 28, the Cuban government would also nationalize U.S. oil companies. But that move was an explicable reaction to a Washington dictum that those refineries not process oil purchased from the Soviets. On March 4, the French freighter *Coubre* was blown up in Havana harbor, another U.S.-sponsored provocation in Fidel's eyes. And then there were the rapid-fire events transpiring in the first week of July. On the fifth of that month, Cuba would move to nationalize remaining U.S. commercial and business properties. One day later, an exasperated Eisenhower administration cancelled the Cuban sugar quota for the remainder of the year. And the following day, the Havana minor league baseball franchise met its long-anticipated demise.

Despite the long buildup and perhaps assumed inevitability at the time, the end actually came quite suddenly in early July 1960. While the team was beginning a two-week road trip in Miami, Shaughnessy made the long-anticipated announcement that they would not return to Havana. Most of the Cuban players did not protest—at least not publicly—as they were driven by fears of losing their shot at making it to the Big Show. Several coaches and manager Tony Castaño did return home, and Napoleon Reyes was designated as the new team skipper. Reyes was, in turn, severely criticized in Cuba for his choice to stay with the ballclub, being labelled in the Havana press as the "Díaz Lanz of Cuban baseball" (in reference to an air force officer who had recently flown his hijacked fighter plane to Miami). Fidel lashed out in a July 11 television interview, charging that the move was part of coordinated Washington aggression that included the sugar quota cut.[28] Owner Bobby Maduro also abandoned ship since he didn't want to lose still more money, and it was by now obvious that his dream for elevating Cuban baseball was dead. The disillusioned owner had recently borrowed $100,000 to keep his team afloat and responded that if he were destined to lose his fortune he would rather do so in Cuba.[29]

Questions remain to this day concerning precisely how it all actually happened. There was a great irony of timing, since President Eisenhower had delivered his sugar quota announcement only a day earlier. That announcement was not likely in any manner connected to the week's baseball developments since the Eisenhower decision had been some time in the planning. But the juxtaposition nonetheless had to be noteworthy. In January, with Cuban nationalization of the bulk of lands held by U.S. sugar companies, the American sugar barons essentially lost their Cuban sugar profits. In July, with the actions of Organized Baseball, Cuba in turn lost its minor-league club and one of its two links to American Organized Baseball. That the colorful and highly symbolic team name had been chosen to celebrate Cuba's dominant economic interest was perhaps more than just a passing irony. No direct cause and effect relation between the two losses has ever been firmly established—one was not likely the sole factor (or even the main factor) in prompting the other. But the symbolic connections, both then and now, were entirely unavoidable.

The biggest mystery, of course, involves who actually made the final decision to pull the plug on the Havana ballclub. Was there U.S. government strong-arming of the International League bosses or were the announced player safety concerns truly the only factor? Was the decision made in the office of Commissioner Shaughnessy, acting on his own, or was there pressure from either top MLB boss Ford Frick or even higher up—that is, was there covert pressure from unnamed sources in Washington? One suspicious writer who would later make the suggestion of Washington's clear hand in the affair was Howard

Senzel, who cites a single *Sporting News* article to defend his less-than-well-documented conclusions. Senzel's book *Baseball and the Cold War* (taken up in more detail in chapter 7) was built around his personal crusade to pin down an attractive conspiracy theory. The pieces seemed to fit and made an intriguing argument, but where was the hard evidence? The very thrust of Senzel's autobiographical narrative in the end reveals that he spent weeks searching for an answer, which he has deep faith in uncovering but in the end never finds.

Turner, for one, suggests the rather obvious flaws in Senzel's line of argument or any other such attempts at uncovering hidden Washington collusion. The strongest rebuttal to a notion of government interference seems to lie in the fact that no baseball officials raised that point in their own defense, although they seem to have had every reason to cover their tracks by doing so. Shaughnessy and others such as Cincinnati GM Gabe Paul, who was directly involved in the subsequent relocation of his team's minor-league affiliate, might well have been expected to hide behind such an obvious defense because they took considerable heat at the time in both the United States and Cuba.

Senzel discovers his clues in the July 1960 *Sporting News* report (written by *New York World-Telegram* scribe Dan Daniel), but the chosen passage hardly seems to offer any rock-solid evidence for a budding conspiracy. Daniel merely mentions a spring Washington visit by Commissioner Frick to Secretary of State Christian Herter to discuss reportedly worsening Havana conditions. Yet, rather than suggest any budding plan to strip Cuba of its team, the Daniel report only concludes that the "administration was very forbearing and still hopeful that things would quiet down in Cuba" and that the "United States has done big things for baseball in Cuba and Cuba has given our major leagues many spectacular players."[30] Turner notes how later writers like Milton Jamail (*Full Count*) and Robert Elias (*The Empire Strikes Out*) were all-too-ready to adopt Senzel's sketchy claim with no more evidence than the hints offered by Senzel himself.[31]

There is still more counterevidence working against the Senzel conspiracy theory. Gabe Paul would move to a new post with the Cleveland Indians later that same year and pen a note to his Cincinnati successor stressing the need to continue support for Maduro, who had been left holding the bag in Havana. Paul's letter to the new Cincinnati GM, Bill DeWitt, in support of Maduro, stresses his own lack of any involvement in the Sugar Kings' demise and also offers that he knew nothing of U.S. government pressure for the move. According to that letter, neither the Reds nor Maduro wanted the transfer to take place, and Paul again places the blame on the sole fact that the league's hand was forced by players who feared further trips to the island.[32] If Paul knew of a Washington connection behind the move, why did he not also mention that in his letter to DeWitt, or elsewhere, to clear his own involvement? Or why didn't Shaughnessy do the same?

The coincidence of sugar quota restrictions by the Eisenhower administration overlapping with a decision to move Maduro's team out of Havana could not fail to raise speculation of a deeper backstory for such writers as Senzel, Jamail, and Elias. While Turner more recently finds little usable evidence for any direct Washington involvement, he also admits the harsh political tensions at the moment that perhaps might suggest not only a suspicious overlap of related events underpinning the decision, but also a hidden cause and effect relationship. Nonetheless, there remains only one final and obvious conclusion.

Whether it was Shaughnessy, or Frick, or Christian Herter in Washington (or some combination of the three) orchestrating the final events and deciding to move the Havana team, the action most certainly emanated from the United States. The Havana team was stolen from Cuba by the Americans; it was not kicked out by Fidel and his henchmen. Fidel's own response, seemingly far more genuine than staged, was, as noted, to attack the move as yet another piece of American aggression and make the link with the simultaneous sugar quota withdrawal.

The transfer Stateside of Bobby Maduro's Havana ballclub certainly can be taken more as an attack by the Americans on Cuban baseball than any Cuban government desire to ban MLB from the island. Such action by the Cubans themselves would come only later, as a reaction and response, and not as an initiation of the events: Cuban historian Félix Julio Alfonso López rightly sees the July 1960 events as a dual product of both heated nationalistic moves by the Castro regime and a covert war launched by the Americans.[33] It is perhaps only fitting that sugar industry nationalizations (by the Cubans) and sugar quota reductions (by the Americans) would attach to the sinking of the team since its name was so reflective of an earlier U.S.–Cuba business partnership. But sugar was also the most visible symbol of Cuban dependence on U.S. ownership. There had always been strong contrast between the two central industries of sugar and tobacco; while the latter produced a middle class and remained under local government control, the former produced a division between slaves and masters, and had always been under foreign control imposed upon the Cuban government (as eloquently recounted by Fernando Ortíz in *Contrapunto Cubano del Tabaco y el Azúcar*).[34] Sugar dependency was, in fact, one of the sharp thorns in Fidel's side since sugar production for generations remained a stark symbol of Cuban subjection to the United States and thus a painful reminder of American power over the island.[35] If the Cuban leader didn't welcome the loss of his baseball team, he most certainly welcomed loss of his country's sugar dependence on the Americans, which ironically enough was soon replaced with Soviet aid and a consequent dependency on the Soviets.

It was indeed ironic, then, that the acme for the Sugar Kings would come in the very year Fidel seized power, and then that their subsequent demise would unfold the following summer, when increasingly hostile rhetoric and tit-for-tat actions of the two governments also reached a peak. If further ironies are sought, they are found in the fact that the hostilities were, in no small part, focused on U.S.–Cuba sugar production business dealings.

The loss of a cherished minor-league franchise was the first and perhaps biggest immediate Cold War defeat for the Cubans, but it would soon be followed by a second equally important setback in slumping efforts to maintain a presence on the North American baseball scene. The subsequent attack on Cuban baseball would be levied against the now-fading Havana winter league. As already mentioned, Cuba's winter circuit had been sagging from the start under control by Organized Baseball and thus indirectly at least under direct MLB control. The loss of any role in determining player personnel aggravated club owners and disillusioned most fans in Havana. It was indeed a double-edged sword for both owners and fans. The loss of jobs for many native Cuban players robbed rooters of opportunities to cheer local heroes, but the influx of more American pros at the same time also failed to elevate interest since top big-leaguers became few and far between, and raw prospects sent to Cuba for seasoning often meant a lowered quality in league play. In the face of the civil unrest surrounding Batista's demise and Fidel's rise at decade's end, MLB management's fears for player safety, now voiced by Ford Frick, merely echoed those previously expounded by Shaughnessy and thus only further soured the mix.

The final winter season of 1960–1961 was played without any American imports and only a sprinkling of true Cuban big-league stars (Miñoso, Ramos, Pascual, Fornieles, Amoros, Tony Taylor), plus some rising local prospects (Miguel Cuéllar, Orlando Peña, Angel Scull, Luis Tiant Jr). Frick's restrictions on participation by non-Cuban big-leaguers meant that the four team rosters consisted of native players only (the only year that would be true in the past six decades). The results were devastating at the ticket windows. Despite another appearance by Fidel to toss out the season's opening pitch, the inaugural game was played to a half-empty stadium. Ticket prices were soon slashed, and players were also asked to take salary cuts; now organized into a trade association by the new government, the Cuban ballplayers, led by Miñoso, agreed to the salary reductions only because of an attached guarantee that they could return to their MLB clubs in the spring. The sad state of the league in its final season put the final lie to Brioso's recent claim that the Organized Baseball links after 1946 brought the league a large boost in stability at the small price of diminished autonomy. What might have looked like a golden age at the outset of the decade was shattered by rampant Washington fears of communism's potential impact on U.S. business interests in the wake of Fidel's recent takeover. If there was any all-too-brief golden age for the Cuban League of the late-1950s (or what perhaps appears like one from the distant perspective of a half-century), it was merely a doomed growth spurt already sprouting the seeds of its own destined destruction.

Tensions were further ramped up between the two countries when diplomatic ties were cut by Washington in January 1961, smack in the middle of the final sagging and almost moribund winter-league season. Despite expanding hostilities, Fidel continued to promise that Cuban MLB players would be allowed to pursue their careers uninterrupted. Of course, it would not quite turn out that way. The break in diplomatic relations meant complications for Cuban big-leaguers in obtaining necessary exit (from Cuba) and entry (to the United States) visas required for their springtime returns Stateside. While both governments agreed in January 1961 to cooperate on the visa issue—a temporary relief for MLB clubs—nevertheless the process had become more arduous since the shutdown of embassies at both ends meant a need for Cuban ball-players to obtain third-country visas for U.S. entry.

Fearing a garnishment of their big-league salaries back home, some Cuban ballplayers, like Miñoso, Pascual, and Ramos, relocated perma-nently to the United States. Others who didn't would soon find them-selves in limbo or worse. Borrego Alvarez and Sandy Amoros were two players of note who would be most adversely affected by the growing political divide and ultimate break in diplomatic relations. While the visa delays caused tardy spring training arrivals for some, like Héctor Maestri with the Senators and Julio Bécquer with the Angels, Alvarez, who had recently been traded from Cincinnati to Washington, was so tardy in making it to his new club that the earlier trade was annulled and his big-league career cut short in the process. And Amoros, who turned down Fidel's offer to manage back home, failed to make it off the island for several years, again also effectively ending his professional ball-playing career.

A major factor in the disastrous turn of events was the failed Wash-ington-sponsored Bay of Pigs invasion, which fell only days before the opening of the new MLB season in April 1961. Players with American contracts were forced into making difficult choices regarding their loy-alties to the homeland and families left behind. Miñoso's choice to relocate caused him to lose treasured possessions in Cuba and conse-quently remain forever bitter about the Castro regime. Amoros, who waited too long to abandon his Cuban home and properties—although the delays were not entirely of his own making—lost his still-active big-league career and future financial security and was doomed to a later life of illness and poverty once he finally made it to a new home in Florida. Minnesota Twins star shortstop Zoilo Versalles, who like Miñoso and Ramos had already opted for settling in the United States, was so dismayed by homesickness and separation from his young bride, still trapped in Havana, that his emotional state severely affected his mental stability and on-field performances in Minneapolis.[36]

As 1960 raced toward its conclusion, again the spike in tensions surrounding baseball in Havana paralleled larger and even more signifi-cant breakdowns on the diplomatic front, just as had happened a few months earlier with the demise of the Sugar Kings. President Eisen-hower's announcement of a full economic trade embargo on October 19 overlapped in eerie fashion with MLB commissioner Ford Frick's similar embargo on American players traveling to Cuba. By early September, Frick had already begun suggesting his possible withholding of Americans. The Cuban Sports Commission at that time had already been working to ensure sufficient resources to meet payrolls for the Americans performing in the league, getting assurances from finance minister Che Guevara that dollars would be made available for that purpose. But in the face of Frick's threats, league officials in Havana decided to pull the plug and issue a ban on the American big-leaguers and minor leaguers. A month later, perhaps wishing the last word on the matter, Frick released his own strictures on MLB teams contracting their players to the league. That ban did not include native Cubans under contract to Organized Baseball, but the commissioner did pressure Puerto Rico's winter circuit into withdrawing from the upcoming Caribbean Series winter-league championships, scheduled that February for Havana.

If Frick's player ban weakened the Cuban circuit without entirely destroying it, Eisenhower's trade embargo almost did sabotage the league in Havana, since the policy would also affect the shipment of baseball equipment to the island. American companies had long been the main suppliers of baseball items headed to Cuba, and the league had only recently placed an order for 500 dozen baseballs for the new season with the Rawlings Sporting Goods Corporation. Blocking that order would have likely brought the Cuban season to a crashing halt before year's end. Since the Cubans had sent payment before the October Eisenhower directive, Rawlings was, however, able to petition the U.S. State Department for permission to complete the transaction. Thus, Cuban baseball—specifically the dying Cuban winter league— would feel the first effects and almost become the first victim of the more than half-century-long U.S. trade embargo. Those Rawlings baseballs were one of the last American consumer items to reach Cuba before the trade stoppage took effect, and in light of the development the league instituted a new rule requiring fans to return balls hit into the grandstands to forestall any immediate shortage. The Eisenhower-initiated and long-maintained economic embargo never achieved its desired aim of ousting the Castro regime, of course. But it was a main culprit in dismantling U.S.–Cuba relations on the baseball field.

Largely stripped of big-league players, the Cuban League limped through its final season, plagued by waning fan interest and resulting empty grandstands in Cerro Stadium. A surge in emigration of middle-class Cubans already disillusioned with Fidel's restrictions on personal freedoms and emerging policies of nationalizing private properties also cut into league support; more than 60,000 upper- and middle-class Cubans left the island in 1960 alone, and a sagging economy left those who stayed with little spare cash for luxuries like baseball tickets. In the first week of February 1961, the half-century-old Cuban professional league—one of the proud emblems, if not the top showcase, for the sport played in the "offseason" throughout the Caribbean region—finally came to a sad end. Ironically, Tinti Molina, one of the early pillars of the sport in Cuba, would also die at precisely the same moment in Havana. Molina, who began his playing career in his native Key West against the backdrop of the War of Independence and who had been a key manager and entrepreneur both on the island and in the United States, succumbed a mere two days after a final league game rang down the curtain on island professionalism. There were ironic parallels here, and Roberto González Echevarría would point them out as a fitting epitaph for the reign of Organized Baseball in Cuba. In commenting on Molina's passing, González Echevarría lamented, "It was as if the Cuban League was buried with him."[37]

As tensions increased, Fidel (perhaps somewhat embittered by the turn of events) did more than merely revamp the sport on the home front in the aftermath of the pullout by Organized Baseball. Escalating the Cold War propaganda battle with Washington, he reportedly claimed a Cuban origin for the sport, as somewhat sarcastically reported in the pages of the *New York Times* and the *Christian Science Monitor*.[38] These same articles, however, also exemplified the often-distorted and usually damming tone taken by the American press regarding everything that had to do with Cuba and the increasingly demonized Cuban leader. What better excuse to ridicule Fidel than to satirize his claims about the treasured American national pastime. Of course, Cuba did not invent the sport we now know as baseball. But serious baseball scholars have long been busy also stressing that the Americans did not invent it either.

What had expired in Cuba was not the sport of baseball, nor in the long run was it even a professional version of the game, since that would slowly reemerge, although admittedly in a quite different form. What was now dead—and would remain so for at least the next six decades—

was any form of MLB-sponsored American baseball imperialism. The stage was set for a new brand of Cuban baseball that would meet the needs of the government in Havana and not the needs of big-league club owners in New York, Chicago, or Los Angeles, or the ballpark fanatics in Cleveland, Detroit, or Kansas City. And the timing here was perfect given Fidel's simultaneous plans to revamp Cuba's cultural activities—film, literature, sporting events, theater, or any other form of art and entertainment that could be construed as part of an earlier nonsocialist nation's popular culture.

A first inroads came with the formation of INDER as a replacement for the old sports ministry—the DGD, which had existed since the 1930s. The earliest steps had actually already been taken when Fidel placed Sierra Maestra veteran Felipe Guerra Matos at the head of the old ministry as one of his initial acts after the government takeover. Now the plan would be a much more ambitious overhaul of sports culture more fully aligned with the goals of the socialist revolution, and this revamped institution would control the nation's sports activity for the future life of the Cuban Revolution. It would become one of the most powerful arms of the communist government under Fidel's micromanagement. This was not surprising in light of the huge political value sports would assume in the revolutionary program, especially the branch focused far more on the development of showcase athletes and teams to carry the national banner than any use of sporting activity to promote a healthier citizenry. INDER would also evolve throughout the years, and that history is quite fully related by Paula Pettavino and Geralyn Pye's 1999 study *Sport in Cuba*.[39]

The new role and structure for sports began with the enactment of Law 936, reshaping Cuba's sporting motives and designs. But the only significant alteration on the island scene was the cutting of a linkage to the professional game up north and thus the removal of the control of the national sport from the hands of American Organized Baseball. In this respect, the nationalization of Cuban baseball bore a strong resemblance to the nationalization of Cuban sugar production. The manipulation of national teams for stoking national pride and building national stature on the ball field was itself not at all new, nor was the focus on amateurism at the root of the game's popularity. There were several only loosely related aspects to the new design for a strong nationwide sports enterprise, of course. And one of the most significant impacts—

perhaps the most significant—was its focus on baseball. Cuba's sporting national pastime, after all, had long been the heart, soul, and face of Cuban culture.

# 5

# THE GRAND SOCIALIST BASEBALL EXPERIMENT

The most significant step, which, if it were taken, would make baseball—a game which knows no barriers—possibly return to a free
enterprise economy, and would eliminate the last and only communist country in the Western Hemisphere; [it] would also give to baseball, if not a czar in the mode of Judge Landis of happy memory,
something many people think the game needs right now, namely a
real dictator. That is to say, Fidel Castro—as commissioner of baseball.—Eugene McCarthy, "Diamond Diplomacy"[1]

In his brief and perhaps only half-serious 1995 essay touting the possibilities of "Diamond Diplomacy" and penned for the short-lived fan-
zine *Elysian Fields Quarterly*, former senator and onetime presidential
candidate Eugene McCarthy of Minnesota would humorously suggest
that the entire Cold War U.S.–Cuba mess might be solved simply by
offering Fidel Castro the post of MLB commissioner.[2] It was a popular
jest that had appeared earlier in several forms perhaps different in
thrust but quite similar in spirit and playing upon distorted views of the
comandante's celebrated baseball fanaticism. What McCarthy missed
here, of course, was an inescapable irony that, in point of fact, Fidel
already held such a position—since Fidel ran everything in Cuba—in
this case for a very different style baseball found in his own homeland.

A far more serious academic treatise on U.S.–Cuba baseball-related
Cold War policies, Justin Turner's University of Alabama doctoral dissertation, *Baseball Diplomacy, Baseball Development*, maintains that

after 1961, Fidel and his subordinates recast island baseball to fit their bold new revolutionary model. In Turner's succinct phrasing, "Transformed by the Revolution, baseball could now serve the Revolution."[3]

This second observation is essentially accurate as far as it goes, but what precisely does it mean? For Turner, it could be explained in rather stark outline. The plan was multifold. First, by building stadiums, constructing a competitive league, and offering free admission to games, the regime could not only reinforce the sport as the national craze it had always been, but also exploit it as a "popular symbol of the Revolution that it could point to when extolling its own virtues." On a second level, the 1961 creation of a new sports ministry called INDER (acronym for National Institute of Sports, Physical Education, and Recreation) was, in large part, a plan to promote all sport as a method of guaranteeing a healthy population capable of military defense of the revolution in case of feared U.S. intervention. Replacement of commercial advertising with communist slogans on ballpark walls, plus Fidel's own constant presence on the scene throwing out ceremonial first pitches at league games or joining sandlot pickup games, all now worked to make the popular national pastime a political platform and symbolized its firm linkage to the Cuban state. But the devil is also in the details, and few of the details emerge from Turner's treatment of the subject.

For one thing, these efforts were, of course, not much different from American MLB practices, especially in the wake of the 9/11 terrorist attacks. Big-league clubs don American flag patches; patriotic hymns are now incorporated into the traditional seventh-inning break; military veterans are honored as heroes by tossing pregame pitches; military jet flyovers mark such occasions as Opening Day, July Fourth, and World Series or All-Star games; and some teams (most notably the San Diego Padres) occasionally don military-camouflage-style uniforms.

Fidel's plan to "politicize" and even "militarize" baseball was not an original idea, then, but an adopted one—borrowed from none other than the Americans themselves. Washington politicians, military commanders, and even MLB executives had long used the sport to disperse sacred American values throughout occupied or subservient foreign outposts in Asia and Latin America, seeing it as a positive tool in fostering American dominance throughout the world.[4] The Japanese, Koreans, and Taiwanese quickly followed suit, both in their own expansionist

**NATIONAL SERIES MAINSTAY.** Donning a jersey of the Oriente league team, Fidel poses with National Series players before the 1968 all-star game. *From the author's collection*

plans and turning the tables on their foreign occupiers.[5] Of course, Fidel was not aiming his message of baseball superiority solely at the colossus to the north; it was potentially more useful in convincing Third World nations that might perhaps best be impressed by victories for the new socialist-style Cuban athletic machine. Nor did he have only baseball in mind—there was boxing (heavyweight champions Teofilo Stevenson and Félix Savón), track and field (middle-distance ace Alberto Juantorena and female sprinter Ana Fidela Quirot), and celebrated men's and women's volleyball squads (with numerous championship medals to their credit) where Cuban victories in Olympic events could be showcased. But undeniably, baseball was the national jewel; baseball aroused the greatest boasting points at home; and tweaking the nose of the American baseballers could also not be quickly dismissed.

The conversion of the island's long-favored sport from professional profit-making enterprise to amateur community entertainment, and also to utilitarian instrument of a government propaganda machine, came in the immediate aftermath of the summer 1960 transfer of Havana's Sugar Kings to Jersey City—ending Cuba's brief 15-year association with North American minor league baseball; it also followed even more closely (by weeks only) the subsequent death of a MLB-affiliated Cuban winter league the following spring. Details of those developments are reviewed at some length in the previous chapter.

An official launching point came with the foundation of INDER in late winter of 1961, with Law 936 enacted on February 23, 1961, a mere 15 days after the final game of the professional Cuban winter-league season. One result was the incorporation of baseball within the newly formed island-wide amateur sports system, in which the national pastime would be a central showpiece, although not the lone emphasis. Baseball's new role and new embodiment would not, of course, become fully apparent until the inauguration of the first National Series championship season the following January. But a more limited and experimental national amateur championship tournament had already been launched under newly appointed sports minister Felipe Guerra Matos in mid-1960 and would later be labelled by Cuban baseball historian Carlos E. Reig Romero as a true, if now largely overlooked, "first inning of revolutionary baseball."[6]

In the early weeks of the new revolutionary government, Guerra Matos, a veteran of the Sierra Maestra campaign, had been handed the reins of the DGD (Dirección General de Deportes), the governmental branch in charge of sports administration, dating back to the late 1930s and Batista's earliest era of political control. The DGD, which would soon give way to INDER, had been advancing island-wide amateur baseball throughout the last two pre-Castro decades with its youth championship (launched in 1949), Pedro Betancourt League (started in 1944), Workers League (1940–1947), and Quivicán Inter-Municipal (beginning in 1953), among other similar efforts.

To continue this tradition under the new government, the DGD organized its first—and only—Campeonato de Béisbol Amateur de la DGD. This event would constitute Reig Romero's "first inning" of baseball under control of the revolutionary government and anticipate the National Series structure, unveiled a year later. The onetime tournament involved 5,000 athletes and 240 teams, and included a series of regional elimination rounds. The island-wide event would be won by a racially integrated team (something prerevolution amateur baseball on the island lacked) from Oriente Province, Mulos de Nicaro (Nicaro Mules), who defeated the University of Havana Caribs in a pair of final contests played first in Santiago and then at the new Havana Sports City Stadium in early December. By the following May, the championship, played but once, would give way to the early regional rounds determining the four ballclubs qualifying for the first formal National Series of January–February 1962.

A final step in eliminating any vestige of commercial baseball came with National Law 546 of 1967, which removed admission fees for sporting events (not only baseball), except in the case of those events— for example, baseball's Amateur World Series, under the direction of the International Amateur Baseball Federation (IBAF)—sponsored by international sports federations to which Cuba belonged. The rationale for such a decision was the belief (largely Fidel's original belief) that rewards should never be financial for either promoters or especially athletes.[7] But this transition from baseball based on material profits for club owners and athletes themselves to a sport advocating a new social ethic, one of moral rather than material incentives, was not an isolated event. It was an essential part of a far larger remaking of a Castro-inspired revolutionary society that began with the 1962 "Year of Planning" and focused on Fidel's initial efforts at the total overhaul of Cuban culture—the replacement of classical notions of highbrow cultural activity with the Maximum Leader's conceptions of a novel form of "popular culture."

The impetus for the overhaul was the landmark speech of December 1–2, 1961, in which Fidel announced to a national television audience his transformation to Marxism-Leninism. Implicit in that late-night rambling discourse, which extended into the early hours of the morning, was Fidel's apparent intention to transform Cuban society along the lines of an explicitly Marxist-Leninist framework. What soon became apparent, however, was that Castro was, in truth, bent on transforming Cuba in his own image and not that of either Marx or Lenin. And he would begin his radical reconstruction project by attacking what he saw as an entrenched cultural landscape needing drastic overhaul. A first step was the takeover and dismantling of the nation's film industry, and the second would be the closing of Havana's most popular literary magazine.

Fidel's longtime Communist friend from university days, Alfredo Guevara, was handed control of the Cuban Institute of Cinematic Art and Industry (ICAIC). Next followed the closure of *Lunes de la Revolución*, the popular literary supplement produced by Carlos Franqui. Following these moves, Fidel summoned a group of the country's top intellectuals to a trio of sessions at the José Martí National Library to discuss the future of culture in Cuba. It was in his address to artists and intellectuals at the final session on June 30, 1961, that the comandante issued his famous creed: "Within the Revolution, everything goes; outside the Revolution, nothing."[8] The 1961 and 1962 transformations of sports, in general, and baseball, in particular, then, overlapped with (and were a cornerstone of) this more widespread mandated cultural overhaul. In short, it wasn't just baseball that would be reenvisioned as a tool of the new regime.

There is an obvious connection here with Fidel's longstanding contempt for money, a personal idiosyncrasy that led him, on more than one occasion, to publicly quote the biblical passage that, "Man does not live by bread alone." Matthews traces the early roots of this obsession to a childhood where the young Fidel was kept on strict allowances by his moderately wealthy landowner father, but also an adulthood where he would live entirely outside a money economy.[9] After coming to power in Havana (and even before that as a charismatic rebel leader), Castro never carried any cash since he was surrounded by a phalanx of supporters who would take care of his every need. That contempt for money caused him to complain loudly, once entrenched in power, that banks should not charge interest on their loans, a view not only reflecting a throwback to medieval Catholic doctrines about the sins of usury, but also an entrenched belief that frequently led him to parrot Che Guevara's communist notions that rewards for labor should be moral and not materialistic.

It is not hard, then, to see why Fidel was so vehemently opposed to a baseball played for monetary rewards, especially if that baseball was a capitalist version where teams were for-profit companies and owners abused athletes who were nothing more than cheap labor in the service of company profits. He would frequently in the future speak of North American big-leaguers as "slaves" who were bought and sold by team management. Opposing a professional league affiliated after the mid-1940s with North American Organized Baseball was not just a rejection of foreign ownership of important Cuban resources (in this case baseball teams and not vital industries like sugar production or public utilities), although it was in part that. American imperialism was always a main target of loathing for Fidel. But more deeply underlying this rejection of baseball played for profit was Fidel's ingrained antimoney obsessions.

What has been missed in earlier accounts is the timing of these events unfolding in Havana during 1961 and 1962, which saw the overlap of the new baseball enterprise—and that of sports as a whole—with Fidel's massive plan to revamp most of Cuban culture (in the sense of "popular culture") in the process of constructing a newly minted social order, one that would serve his evolving revolution. It was Fidel's plan to build a society based not on materialism (the capitalist model), but rather moral incentives. Matthews assesses not only the surprising early successes, but also inherent future failures of the new system. Writing in the mid-1970s, Castro's early American champion notes that Fidel's early experiment in building a society based on moral incentives for work surpassed all such efforts anywhere in the Western world; if it was equaled or even surpassed in Maoist China or North Korea, it was only because in those places such a plan was thrust on a population that had, throughout modern history, never known anything but slave wages and subsistent living.[10] And here was the rub and the inherent danger for the future.

As a sophisticated, educated, and Western-minded people living in the shadow of the liberal thinking and high standard of living found in the neighboring United States, the Cubans would likely not for long voluntarily accept such a moral-incentive work system. As the years rolled by, that resistance in the Cuban population would slowly emerge. In the final pages of his own evaluation of Fidel and his revolution, Peter Bourne was forced to conclude, "Most Cubans would probably be willing to trade some of the international prestige Fidel has brought them for even a modest improvement in their sagging standard of living."[11] The disillusionment for most Cubans was somewhat long in coming, perhaps, but it would one day apply to the lesser world of baseball as much as to any other corner of Cuban society.

Part of the plan launched in the early 1960s would involve adopting a Soviet model, in which sport would be envisioned as a two-pronged national effort with slightly diverse motivations. First, sports would be subsequently used to develop the health of the entire nation's citizenry. Pettavino and Pye trace this development at great length. Facilities were built, equipment was distributed, and a wide variety of programs were aimed at enticing citizens of all ages to participate in health-building recreational sports. But at the same time, there was the companion goal of improved performance by more gifted athletes. If what Pettavino and Pye label the "democratization" of sports (universal participation) might generate a more healthy, active, and fit society necessary for the defense of the revolution, the stress on achieving high-level performance from a select few would embellish Cuban nationalism and feed an important sense of national pride through success in international competitions. There would, not surprisingly, eventually develop a strong and somewhat uncomfortable tension between the two disparate goals, as the latter would take increasing precedence in the coming decades—but not without a considerable degree of internal national debate, especially after the 1980s and 1990s sagging of the Cuban national economy.[12]

The second motivation, international successes, is the one Justin Turner focuses on. It was the use of a high-powered sports culture to produce quality national teams that could carry the country's banner in international competitions, stoking national pride but, more importantly, demonstrating the advantages and superiorities of the newly adopted communist system. This was the overt "politicization" of sport that

Turner latches onto. Cold War battles would now be fought in the sporting arena—particularly on the baseball field—a topic fully elaborated on in a following chapter. And baseball was the inevitable centerpiece of the effort. Cuba also would be noted for producing skilled boxers, volleyball teams (male and female), and track and field performers; however, it was the baseball teams that were the most visible emblem of national pride.

But there was an even more vital aspect to the change taking place. This was Fidel's long-held dream of abandoning an imperialistic and capitalistic world in which material rewards were what shaped human activity and motivated every social interaction. Fidel, like Che, envisioned a new type of citizen at the center of a new type of Cuba. In fact, he envisioned a society where there would be no cash-based economy at all. This was, of course, a largely idle dream that could never become reality. And yet the break with North American commercial and professional baseball could not have come at a more opportune time, even if Fidel had not at first either desired it or even directly contributed to it.

Fidel had actively worked to keep the Sugar Kings afloat and securely stationed in Havana. As stressed in the previous chapter, he offered full financial support from his new government. He met with club owner Bobby Maduro during his April 1959 trip to New York, three months after seizing control in Havana, and at that meeting pledged to keep the franchise in town. During that April tour of the United States—prompted by an invitation to address the American Society of Newspaper Editors in Washington—Fidel spent four days in New York, including a stop at Yankee Stadium and a brief meeting with Jackie Robinson. Staying at the Pennsylvania Hotel, he had phoned Maduro and asked him to fly north for a meeting (accompanied by Cuban lawyer Luis Botifoll, who owned a small piece of the ballclub), and at that session Fidel not only pledged support for keeping the team, but also questioned Maduro about what it might take to get the Sugar Kings into the major leagues (hardly an indication that the new Cuban leader was ready to give up on professional baseball). But the session was brought to a sudden halt by a phone call from Raúl in Havana complaining that press coverage on the island was now speculating about some sort of deal that might be struck with U.S. authorities and that this publicity was reflecting badly on Fidel on the home front.[13]

While in New York, he also fielded U.S. press questions about the Havana ballclub and once again voiced his enthusiastic support. At a United Nations correspondents luncheon, he was again queried about the minor-league club's future and vowed that he would even pitch for the team if that could boost attendance and keep Maduro's club afloat.[14] And he voted with his own charismatic presence by throwing out a pair of ceremonial pitches for season openers in 1959 and 1960. He turned the Sugar Kings' surprising late 1959 championship run into a national celebration aimed at linking club successes to the triumphs of his revolution. He emphasized the national commitment to the team and the sport by frequently dispatching his top government dignitaries to the ballpark to cheer the home club—even though some, like Che and Raúl, had little knowledge of baseball or enthusiasm for the game. Whatever his limited interests in the sport may have been as a youth—remember that on numerous occasions in future years he would emphasize his greater schoolboy interest in track and field events, soccer, swimming, or hiking—during the first year of his leadership he transformed baseball into the very symbol of a new revolutionary society. And he did this while the game in Havana was still, at the top levels, a strictly professional enterprise.

It might easily be argued in retrospect that during the 15 months between the departure of Batista and the departure of the Sugar Kings, Fidel was still only feeling his way regarding his revolution's future course. His planned revolution was only in its infancy and was a constantly evolving process, and no one, including Fidel, seemed to have a clear vision of the direction it would need to take. And there were the emerging indications of Fidel's dream of a moneyless utopia, which certainly did not bode well for profit-oriented professional sports. Nonetheless, there was no movement in the direction of abandoning a professional baseball team until Fidel, overnight, discovered in July 1960—quite likely to his initial dismay—that the task had been all too conveniently done for him.

But if Fidel had tried to hang onto the Sugar Kings, their loss and the aftermath of the death of MLB-affiliated winter-league operations provided a perfect storm scenario for change in Cuba's sports structure. As the country's main sporting obsession, baseball would be the arena for the most thoroughgoing and controversial overhaul. No more league controlled by foreign interests, crowded with imported foreign players, and accessible only to fans in the capital city. No further motivation for the nation's crop of talented pitchers and sluggers to dream of mercenary careers in a foreign land; they would now play on home soil exclusively during winter seasons, and the best would fight for national honor by carrying the national jersey into international competitions. It was all for the revolution and, by strong implication, thus also all for Fidel and his new society. Washington and the MLB commissioner may have forced the Cuban prime minister's hand in the matter, but a door was now opened to incorporating baseball within a larger master plan for a new society and a new sporting system free of materialism and personal profit as primary motivation.

The product would be a baseball that would find players competing for local, regional, and finally national honor instead of peso or dollar salaries. At first the ballplayers would be true amateurs, part-timers holding down other employment. But as the league rapidly expanded to a nationwide operation, it would take on one vestige of "professionalism," while it eschewed others. Ballplayers would soon be dedicated full-time athletes. But there would be no franchises, no marketing or trading of ballplayers, and the rewards would remain those of the amateur. And the fans would also be provided with a sporting spectacle that was part of the right of all citizens, one with free admission to games and with teams truly representing the hometown district. If there was one thing above all others that distinguished the Cuban circuit, it was the special attachment existing between players and community. There were no foreign imports, only native Cubans in the league. Players were, with only a few exceptions, drawn from local provincial training academies and would spend an entire career with the home club. The consequence was an inevitable fan and ballplayer loyalty to the hometown uniform. Fans would not cheer for mercenaries, and pride in hometown victories would be genuine.

A capsule review of the almost 60-year history of the new national baseball league demonstrates the unique features of Cuban baseball that would slowly emerge in the decades following the 1962 transformation of Cuba's sports system. It also reveals how that league subtly evolved and was reshaped during decades of economic and social changes and challenges. Finally, such a thumbnail history will also reveal the direct hand maintained by Fidel for more than a half-century in building a successful domestic league with a primary goal of constructing elite national teams capable of dominating international tournament competitions. Together the domestic national championship seasons and almost endless string of national team successes would provide one of Cuba's most remarkable cultural achievements.

✿ ✿ ✿

The popular national sport of baseball maintained and even tightened its hold on the Caribbean nation of Cuba in the aftermath of the 1959 socialist revolution, the single event which, according to so many later revisionists, had reportedly brought its ultimate demise. In fact, the national game actually expanded in popularity and elevated in talent levels during the several decades immediately following Fidel Castro's mid-century rise to power. Once the professional four-team winter league loosely affiliated with the North American big leagues was shut down after the 1961 season, the door was finally thrown open for establishing a truly island-wide baseball circuit that would feature home-grown talent rather than imported foreign professionals. And this newly revamped version of Cuban League baseball would also launch a five-decade domination of international tournament competitions that now stands as the centerpiece of almost a century and a half of island base-ball lore. With its novel brand of postrevolutionary "amateurism," Cuba would develop in the second half of the twentieth century a genuine "alternative universe" to compete with the better-publicized profession-al circuits represented by the North American and Japanese profession-al leagues.

The political estrangement between Cuba and the United States after 1962 not only largely ended the earlier moderate flow of Cuban ballplayers to North American major- and minor-league teams, but also cast an aura of mystery (even secrecy) over baseball activities on the island. North American fans have known precious little during the past half-dozen decades about Cuban baseball developments. Island-league stars have thus played in the same virtual obscurity as did the players of the North American Negro Leagues of the first half of the twentieth century. One obvious result of this isolation from the mainstream North American sporting press is an unfortunate persistence of several wide-spread myths concerning Cuba's postrevolutionary baseball era. First and most damaging has been a notion that the level of Cuban baseball diminished dramatically once the professional winter league was scrapped for a new form of "amateur" diamond competition. A related and equally false notion is one suggesting that inferior amateur-level play for the first time replaced superior professional competitions as the central focus of the Cuban national sport.

Anyone maintaining this latter view overlooks an established historical fact that widespread pre-1950 amateur leagues throughout the island drew far more fan interest and produced more native island talent than did the Havana-based pro circuit of the pre-Castro era. Cuba's professional winter league of the earlier epoch imported a hefty proportion of its star players from the ranks of North American Negro League clubs, drew a fan following among few Cubans living outside the capital city, and produced only a handful of native big-leaguers boasting true all-star stature—namely Adolfo Luque (1920s), Orestes Miñoso (1950s), and Camilo Pascual (1960s). It is also indisputable that a half-dozen or more recent Cuban leaguers who abandoned the island during the late 1990s and early 2000s for big-league careers in the United States have, by any measure, far outstripped the achievements of the small cadre of prerevolution Cuban major leaguers.

Among the new generation of superior Cuban big-leaguers originally trained in the post-1962 Cuban circuit we might count sluggers Kendrys Morales, José Abreu, Yasiel Puig, and Yoenis Céspedes; flashy infielders Alexei Ramírez, Yunel Escobar, and Adeiny Hechavarría; and frontline pitchers Orlando "El Duque" Hernández, José Ariel Contreras, and Liván Hernández, as well as fastball phenom Aroldis Chapman. Chapman, recipient of an eye-popping $30 million contract from the Cincinnati Reds in 2010, would launch a heavy recruitment of native Cuban stars (some smuggled off the island by covert human-trafficking operations), which in the second decade of the new millennium produced megadeals for the likes of Céspedes, Puig, Abreu, outfielder Yasmani Tómas, Rusney Castillo, and touted Boston Red Sox minor-league prospect Yoan Moncada.

The current Cuban League—known familiarly as the Cuban National Series—opened a golden anniversary 50th season, with the first pitch tossed in November 2010. This yearly National Series competition slowly evolved through several distinct manifestations in five-plus decades and has undergone further drastic alteration in the past half-dozen winters. While geographically based league teams have always represented provinces (Cuba's states) or groups of provinces, these league clubs have often changed names from year to year and have only in recent seasons been consistently labeled for a home-base province, with a team nickname attached (e.g., Cienfuegos Elephants, Villa Clara Orangemen, Camagüey Potters). Recent league structure involved 14 provincial teams plus two added ballclubs—the Industriales Blue Lions and Metropolitanos Warriors—representing the capital city of Havana. There have also been several manifestations along the way of a second, often shorter, Cuban League season.

A Selective Series (usually with the 16 provincial clubs combined into eight regional all-star squads) operated in late spring and summer between 1975 and 1995. And an even shorter four or five-team Super League was staged in June from 2002 to 2005. Before the idea of the additional Selective Series competition was conceived, a single "Series of the 10 Million" was staged in the early summer of 1970, with six clubs engaged in a marathon 89-game slate. The name for the three-month event was drawn from Prime Minister Castro's proclaimed goal of reaching 10 million tons in that year's sugar cane harvest, and the series was thus promoted as special entertainment for sugar industry field laborers.

The Selective Series season, played from the mid-1970s to the mid-1990s, has never been considered a true league championship by most island fanatics—that distinction always falling to the all-province National Series. It did, however, contribute several highlight moments of Cuban League history and, on several occasions, even provided the longest stretch of the year's domestic baseball action. During its first nine campaigns, the Selective Series was actually longer than the National Series: first 54 games compared to 38 (1975–1977) and then 60 games compared to 51 (1978–1983). During its final dozen seasons, the Selective Series schedule dipped to 43 contests per team (1984–1985), ballooned to 60 games (1986–1992), and then shrank again to 45 (1993–1995). It was during this competition in 1980, that Cuba celebrated its first .400-plus hitter (Héctor Olivera, Las Villa, .459—father of the future "defector" and big-leaguer of the same name); Omar Linares did not reach that plateau in the National Series until five years later. It was also in the Selective Series where Orestes Kindelán produced the first 30-plus home run total (30 in only 63 games), with Alexei Bell not reaching that same milestone in the National Series until as late as 2008 (31 in 90 games). The Selective Series also provided seven of the island's 51 rare no-hit, no-run pitching performances.

The half-dozen even shorter "second" seasons played during the past several decades—after the Selective Series tradition was finally scrapped—proved even less successful and therefore less sustainable. Two Revolutionary Cup campaigns in the 1990s, both won by Santiago de Cuba under manager Higinio Vélez, were memorable for a handful of individual record-setting performances and little else. Both 30-game events produced .450-plus batsmen (Yobal Dueñas, 1996, and Javier Méndez, 1997), and Santiago's Ormari Romero claimed 14 pitching victories without defeat in the same stretch. The four-year Super League experiment was an even larger failure, although it did witness a playoff no-hitter tossed for Centrales by Maels Rodríguez. The idea of having provincial teams combined into a smaller number of regional squads never gained much traction with island fans. Super League games also fell during the hottest—and wettest—part of the year, and most games staged in the month of June were played to empty stadiums and disappointingly sparse television viewership.

Failure of these experimental extra seasons to garner any true fan enthusiasm is largely explained by a unique feature of island baseball, which is also the basic strength of Cuban League structure. Since league teams are government operations (government properties) over-seen by a national sports ministry (INDER) baseball commission not corporate businesses run for profit—there is no trading or transferring of Cuban League players, with athletes serving on teams representing their own native province. (There is a recent exception to this tradition, which we will come to shortly.) Like all Cuban athletes, ballplayers rise through the ranks of regional sports academies, performing for their neighborhoods on various age-group youth clubs and eventually gradu-ating to Developmental League (the Cuban minors) and National Se-ries teams. With the rarest of exceptions, a Cuban League star spends his entire playing career with a single local ballclub.

The huge plus side of this unique system is both the deep-seated loyalties between fans and players, and the rabid fanaticism attached to local clubs, which, in actual fact, not merely in name, represent a fixed geographical locale. (A big-league equivalent would be a Boston Red Sox club employing only players raised and trained in the New England region.) The downside, of course, is that the Cuban League—like the majors in the era before player free agency—is not exceptionally well balanced. Larger provinces enjoy heftier talent supplies and thus usually better teams; Havana and Santiago teams (along with occasional inroads by Pinar del Río and Villa Clara) have dominated championship play throughout league history.

Because of such hometown fan loyalties and attachments to local stars, shorter seasons with fewer teams have failed to garner support, if only because the teams playing are not the usual fan favorites. Seeing the local heroes attired in strangely colored uniforms and competing for strangely named squads like "Centrales" or "Oriente" has little appeal for rooters attached by birthright and home base to Industriales, Pinar del Río, or Sancti Spíritus. What might Boston Red Sox fans make of any two- or three-month season featuring Sox players joining forces with Yankees, Mets, and Phillies stars on a team now rebranded as the Eastern Seaboard Lions? Fanaticism based on long-held tradition—and in Cuba also on the concept of local neighborhood stars—disappears in a league featuring several months of what are widely perceived as mere all-star exhibition contests.

National Series play was inaugurated in mid-January 1962, and involved only a handful of teams during its earliest campaigns. Diminutive league size was dictated by the fact that for the first handful of years, the championship season was, in truth, only the final round of winter-long playoffs featuring surviving clubs from an earlier stretch of regional competitions (Eastern and Western zones) involving teams from throughout the island. Those provincial competitions in the fall of 1961 included a full dozen ballclubs. The Occidental, or Western, Zone was comprised of Habana (regional series winner), Industriales, Matanzas, Vegueros, Henequeneros, and Pinar del Río; teams in the Oriental Zone were the Azurareros ("Cane Cutters"—the winners), Oriente, Mineros, Granjeros, Camagüey, and Las Villas. In addition to two regional champions (Habana and Azucareros), the pair of additional clubs in the culminating National Series (Occidentals and Orientales) were, as their names suggest, actually all-star squads comprised of players drawn from 10 eliminated teams. Only with the fifth National Series (1965–1966) did the league transition to a roster of permanent teams and begin expansion toward including all provinces in a true winter-long national championship.

Players for the inaugural National Series were thus drawn from all areas of the island, but the initial clubs, known as Occidentales, Azucareros, Orientales, and Habana, played the bulk of their first-season 27-game schedule in Havana's spacious Cerro Stadium, home of the professional winter circuit after 1946, rechristened Latin American Stadium in 1971, and still in use today. The concept mandated by Fidel was to replace commercial baseball with a more altruistic-style amateur play, designed to promote public health rather than financial profit (for either athletes or ballclub owners) and thus more in line with a socialist spirit of government at the heart of his emerging, revamped societal system. In the early seasons, players were indeed true amateurs, a fact reflected by the rather inept, if spirited, level of early league play. The first few seasons were short, and ball-playing was not yet a full-time occupation for athletes who also filled other occupations in the workforce of a newly minted socialist society.

The historic initial season staged in the late winter of 1962 lasted for little more than a full month and followed by less than nine months the infamous clandestine U.S.-backed invasion attempt at the Bay of Pigs. Hence, it is not surprising that a future league ballpark in the northern coastal city of Matanzas (Victory at Girón Stadium) would eventually carry the name of the landmark 1961 invasion battle that solidified Fidel's revolutionary government and his own personal charismatic hold on the bulk of the Cuban population. The label attached to the Matanzas ballpark might seem puzzling at first glance because it sits on the island's northern coast, while the invasion site lies more than 250 kilometers to the southeast along the southern coast. But the Girón Beach and the Bahía de los Cochinos (Bay of Pigs) indeed fall within the massive province of Matanzas, which stretches from north to south coasts and occupies much of the country's west-central region.

An opening set of league games was celebrated in Cerro Stadium in front of 25,000 fans on Sunday, January 14, 1962. Anxious to boast of his new baseball experiment, Fidel was on the scene to provide a lengthy speech and then step to the plate in his traditional military garb and knock out a staged ceremonial "first hit" against Azucareros starter Jorge Santín. So closely was the new league associated with the comandante himself that it was deemed necessary for Fidel alone to achieve that first successful at-bat in the new league he had created—even if the feat might have been all-too-obviously orchestrated (likely a fat pitch over the heart of the plate offered up to the idolized inspirational leader) and thus only symbolic in nature. Fidel actually received three tosses from Santín before connecting, meekly fouling off the first and letting the second pass before tapping a roller that eluded the modest efforts of the second baseman and reached the right-field grass.[15] When the actual ballplayers took the field for the first "opening day" of January 1962, Azucareros blanked Orientales, 6–0, behind three-hit pitching from Santín. In an 11-inning nightcap, Occidentales edged Habana, 3–1, with ace Manuel Hernández striking out 17 enemy batters.

A widely circulated news service photo showing Fidel stroking a season-inaugural safety delivered by Azucareros pitcher Modesto Verdura (and not Santín) is sometimes mislabeled as the January 1962 at-bat but was actually taken in the same park on opening day of National Series II later in the same calendar year. The two occasions can be distinguished by the Maximum Leader's attire, a peaked cap facing Verdura but a French Legion-style beret against Santín. Various other photos of the two at-bats shot from behind home plate reveal the unidentified Series I Azucareos catcher wearing uniform number 3 and the catcher the following season donning number 6—a further clue to which image is which.

The four clubs that participated in the initial month-long season were managed by a former big-leaguer (Fermín Guerra, Occidentales) and a former Sugar Kings skipper (Antonio Castaño, Azucareros), as well as a pair of earlier island amateur stalwarts (José María Fernández, Habana, and Pedro "Natilla" Jiménez, Occidentales). Occidentales under Guerra captured the first short-season title, outdistancing the field with the circuit's only winning ledger, and Occidentales outfielder Edwin Walter reigned as the first league batting champion. The popular Havana-based Industriales ball club debuted in the following second season, which was the first to begin in the month of December and thus the first to overlap two calendar years. Industriales—the longest existing and most successful league team—would immediately launch its proud tradition by claiming four-straight league titles in its initial four years of league play.[16]

It was the festive inaugural Sunday twin bill launching a second league season that provides us with one of the best affirmations of Fidel's immediate plans and long-range vision for his new baseball operations. For a second festive "opening day" celebration of his new league, Fidel once again took center stage, taking the field during pre-game warmups to pose with players from the four clubs—the same group as the previous year, with the single exception of Industriales replacing Habana—enjoy numerous photo ops swinging a bat, deliver a flowery pregame speech, and again collect a staged first "official" base hit of the campaign. But it is the speech that remains most notable. A first edition of what would become an off-and-on annual INDER-published *Official Baseball Guide* for the new season dedicates it opening pages to a collage of photos featuring the role of the comandante in the day's ceremonies, including his at-bat against Verdura.[17] It also includes the text of Fidel's rousing speech, editorializing on the achievement of Cuba's recently recast baseball enterprise. Segments of the published version of the oration are worth quoting here in some detail (this author's translation) since they capsulize as well as anything Fidel's newly adopted revolutionary baseball philosophy.

Fidel's description of the new-style baseball was as follows:

> Yes, now we are celebrating a national baseball championship. We owe this to the methods by which these players were selected. The ballplayers are now townspeople, very humble that they now have the chance to play baseball. The others [professional players before the revolution—PCB] were humble also, but they were exploited under a capitalist regimen. The entire sport of baseball had been converted into a capitalist business. Now the ballplayers have the opportunity to be true sportsmen and not instruments of the exploiters. This new system of selection is great because it has permitted us to choose the best players from each losing team, that is to say, that through several rounds of selection they have arrived here at a true national championship.

Fidel explained his plans for future baseball expansion as such:

> Soon we will have to expand this stadium because it will be too small to accommodate such large crowds. There is no question that this is the triumph of free baseball over slave baseball. Now the important and valued towns of the interior of the country have the chance to enjoy a championship. Before they could only see exhibition games. Also, radio and television carry all the action of the championship into their homes. At times they broadcast from various locations and those that live in the Oriente [far eastern provinces—PCB] can now

know what is happening when their provincial team is playing and also what is happening with the other teams playing here in the capital. Now you can see the advantages that this new system of sports has. Now everyone who tunes into baseball, even in the country's interior, at some point desires to come here to Havana to see baseball.

Fidel's assessment of the accomplishments of "revolutionary baseball" was as follows:

In past times baseball was only and exclusively played for the capital city, where there wasn't any genuine national championship in which athletes might participate representing their own respective regions. With this new system baseball is going to be extraordinary, we are going to have great ballplayers.

Fidel explained his vision of the future as such:

It is the same as with the country, which once belonged to the native aborigines before the Spanish conquistadors came and took it from them, and then saw the Americans come and steal it from the Spanish, but now the country has returned to the people, just as baseball has. Someday the *Yanquis* will have to come and play against us, and then they will discover what the revolution is, since the revolution can produce such magnificent ballplayers since they can defeat the players from a system that only exploits athletes. How a truly free athlete can beat the exploited athlete, how the athlete that can't be sold in the market nor sold to a capitalist business can defeat the athlete that is subdued by those humiliating conditions without moral stimulus of any kind. [18]

These words capture the entirety of Fidel's underlying motives, his operating plan, and his perhaps overly optimistic vision for drastically converting a long-cherished national game into a new design for advancing a larger revolutionary agenda. It was one of the first public declarations of what would for Fidel become a regular mantra—under his new system Cuban players would be truly free, while North American pros were nothing but slaves bought and sold by profiteering ballclub owners. It might even have had an element of truth attached to it in the decade before big-leaguers finally demanded and achieved an era of free agency by stripping away the MLB reserve clause. And it was a message that would, for several decades, sell well with both players and fans at home who bought into the system.

Of course, the idle dream of the new Cuban leaguers competing with and even defeating the big-league pros may well have seemed a bit far-fetched even to revolutionaries on the home front who heard it in 1962. But by the time of eventual renewal of at least sporadic contact in the form of the 1999 Cuba–Orioles exhibitions or the 2006 inaugural World Baseball Classic, one could claim that Fidel's dream of competing on an even footing with North American professionals might not have been such a far stretch after all.

*  *  *

The notion of seeing his "free" athletes defeat the American "slave" ballplayers, first uttered in 1962, was more than mere flowery rhetoric for Fidel. Early successes of the Cuban national team during a first decade of Castro's evolving communist administration would soon redirect league structure and philosophy toward the larger goal of developing strong national squads talented enough to allow baseball's use as an effective governmental foreign policy tool. If the capitalist *Yanquis* could not be overthrown in the political arena, at the very least important symbolic victories could be scored at the ballpark.

A string of eight-straight Amateur World Series titles in the 1970s demonstrated that Cuban baseball squads could indeed achieve impressive propaganda victories by beating the North Americans (and also the Asians and rival Caribbean neighbors) at their own proclaimed national sport. Baseball was, after all, also the long-standing Cuban national sporting passion and therefore also very much a "national pastime" shared equally with the rival Americans. As a result of the new Cuban emphasis on victories abroad in Olympic-style events, government sports academies would soon flourish throughout the island, and Cuban athletes graduating from those institutions became full-time practitioners of their assigned sporting activities—especially baseball, boxing, track and field, and volleyball. Increasingly, Cuban athletes were financially supported—even if at a modest level by North American measures—and thus they became "professionals" in at least two different important senses of the word. Cuban ballplayers have, for decades, been paid for performing, and consequently they devote all their effort and attention to their assigned "profession" of ballplaying.

As Roberto González Echevarría puts it in *The Pride of Havana*, the conversion of a professional game to a purely amateur one never really happened.[19] The fiction might have been maintained (as it also is with American collegiate football or basketball), allowing the Cuban stars to compete in amateur events like the Pan American Games or IBAF Amateur World Series. Yet, top Cuban ballplayers do nothing year-round but practice and play their sport, and most have done so since early school days in the sports academies. They receive reasonable salaries by Cuban standards and, as national team members, obtain such added perks as travel, the right to bring personal goods home from abroad, automobiles and apartments or even ample houses, and vacation time in expensive hotels usually reserved for foreign tourists.

As baseball's status evolved as a symbol of the revolution, so did Fidel's presence as constant reminder of that link. He was always on the scene in the earliest years to toss ceremonial pitches at season openers for the new league or international tournaments held on Cuban soil. And like the staged official at-bats to launch the first two National Series campaigns, he took center stage in more intrusive ways. At the season opener in 1965, Fidel handed ceremonial "first pitch" honors to visiting Venezuelan Liberation Forces leader Germán Lairet, but then in front of 32,000-plus fans, the comandante took the mound to pitch to the first official batter of the game. He frequently remained after league games to play a few pickup innings with the teams. And in 1964, he was even reported by the journal *Cuba Internacional* to have pitched seven full innings for the provincial team in Camagüey, although that appearance was not in a National Series contest.

Like Fidel's revolution itself, the new Cuban baseball operation was, from its onset, a constantly evolving work in progress. During the course of its opening decade, the National Series expanded to first six teams (1966) and eventually an even dozen ballclubs (1968). The number of games for each club also surged to 65 by mid-decade (1966) and eventually as many as 99 (1968). The league reached its full stride once all provinces were represented, by the mid-1970s, and once postseason playoffs were introduced for the 1985–1986 season as a pressure-packed means of determining an eventual league champion. As the ever-changing league evolved in size, it also regularly changed in shape, with a division into two groups or "zones" in 1987–1988 (National Series #26), and then four groups in 1992–1993 (National Series #32). The two-division structure—with a Western League (Occidental) and an Eastern League (Oriente)—was once again adopted with the more recent 2007–2008 season (National Series #47), and a 90-game schedule has been the league standard since National Series #37 (1997–1998). But with a decision in 2012 to divide the season into two 45-game segments, the league reverted to a single 16-team operation with only eight clubs qualifying for the second-half championship round (which would later be cut to only six). Division structure was thus abandoned altogether after National Series #51 (2011–2012).

Cuba's postseason playoffs have witnessed more than a three-decade history of their own and, in many respects, mirror their counterpart in the big leagues. Until a recent 2012 split-season restructuring, for a decade-plus the postseason featured quarterfinal (five games), semifinal (best-of-seven), and final series (also seven games). But beginning in the spring of 2013, the new format eliminated one postseason round since only four clubs from the campaign's second-half "championship round" were playoff qualifiers. The one major departure from major-league postseason performance derives from the practice in the Cuban circuit of counting a player's individual statistical record as part of his cumulative career totals. Individual pitching and batting titles are determined before postseason play commences, but the record 487 lifetime homers of Orestes Kindelán and the career .368 batting standard of Omar Linares do indeed include playoff numbers.

Recent campaigns have featured a string of thrilling seven-game final-round matchups that gripped the nation's television and radio audiences in the early springtime (usually late April through early May). Just as big-league championships match American and National League rivals, the finals in Cuba traditionally included the top surviving clubs representing the Eastern and Western zones of the island. (That practice was dropped once a single league structure emerged in 2012.) The island's fan favorites, the Havana-based Industriales, squared off in the winner-take-all conclusion with one of their two Western-sector rivals—either Santiago or Villa Clara—on five different occasions in the first decade of the new millennium.

Perhaps the most significant overhaul of the league format followed the establishment of the MLB World Baseball Classic in 2006, and the return of Cuba after a four-decade absence to the annual Caribbean Series, matching winter-league champions from Mexico, Puerto Rico, Venezuela, and the Dominican Republic. Since the league was conceived as a training ground and selection mechanism for all-star squads to represent the home nation in international events, the intrusion of such external tournaments on domestic play would now have to take priority over league championships, something that rarely occurred earlier, when most overseas tournaments fell in the "dead time" of the summer months.[20] But a March 2006 World Baseball Classic required a league shutdown of nearly a month to allow for training and participation of the Cuban squad, which surprisingly reached the finals in San Diego. The same occurred for the additional Classics in 2009 (with Cuba scheduled for opening-round action in Mexico City) and 2013 (with the Cubans heading to Japan). Again, a shutdown at home became necessary when league champions Villa Clara (2014), Pinar del Río (2015), and Ciego de Avila (2015) headed to Venezuela, Puerto Rico, and finally the Dominican Republic for the first three years of the country's return to Caribbean Series matches. But the Caribbean Series presented an even greater conundrum since the tournament fell in the first week of February—little more than halfway through any current Cuban season—and therefore necessitated selection of league champions from the previous National Series to represent the island.

To overcome this interruption and solve the Caribbean Series puzzle, it was decided for National Series #56 to move the traditional opening of play in late November back to August, which allowed time for completing the Cuban season in late January and not late April. With this adjustment, a fresh league champion (Granma in each of the past two years) could represent the nation, putting the Cubans on equal footing with the four other Caribbean winter circuits.

The original National Series structure of the early 1960s not only spread organized league baseball island-wide for the first time, but also extended and expanded a tradition of popular "amateur" leagues, which had been at the center of the nation's baseball since its origins in the late nineteenth and early twentieth centuries. Amateur-level baseball had always been the island's most popular sporting tradition and thus did not suddenly take hold—as popularly misconstrued—only with the Castro-led revolutionary takeover of the early 1960s. Throughout the century's first five decades, it was not the racially integrated Havana pro circuit, but rather the more geographically diverse and all-white amateur league that drew both the largest fan followings and the island's top athletic talent. Many skilled players choose to remain amateurs since the amateur teams ironically offered greater financial rewards (lucrative jobs with such sponsoring corporations as the national electric company or telephone company) and easier playing conditions (games played only on weekends). Today's government-run Cuban baseball enterprise is admittedly more commercial in nature than the original island amateur circuits. Yet, it now draws its distinctive "amateur" flavor from the complete absence of any profit-motivated corporate team ownerships or ballplayer "free agency" of the type defining pro circuits in North America, Europe, or Asia. Its players may be paid, but not nearly as much as the Cuban "amateurs" of a bygone era.

Cuba's throwback-style ballparks remain one of the league's most charming features, with their natural grass surfaces, absence of concession stands, minimalist nonvideo scoreboards, concrete bleachers, and bulky concrete electric light stanchions. Most parks were built in the 1970s and have an almost identical appearance; construction crews were drafted from the island's population of students and field workers to erect these structures as part of the government's widespread public works projects of that era. Many stadiums are named for late 1950s revolutionary military heroes or important revolutionary battle sites, but two were christened to honor star league pitchers tragically lost in 1970s-era automobile accidents. The former include Capitan San Luis (Pinar del Río) and Nelson Fernández (San José de la Lajas); the latter are José Antonio Huelga (Sancti Spíritus) and recently abandoned Santiago "Changa" Mederos (Havana). The current 16 league teams are housed in stadiums located in the capital city of each province, but most clubs also play a small portion of their league contests in smaller ballpark venues found in outlying provincial villages.

One historic older venue is Latin American Stadium, housed in the Cerro ("hill") district of Havana. The park was constructed in 1946, and is thus a holdover from the prerevolution professional league, which operated in the capital city through 1961. The last decade of that four-team circuit found almost all league games staged in the building then known as Cerro Stadium, or Gran Stadium. The structure received a major expansion and renaming in 1971, when the country hosted one of the numerous Amateur World Series events played in the capital city.

The Havana Cubans (Class B Florida International League, 1946–1953) and the Cuban Sugar Kings (Class AAA International League, 1954–1961), two minor-league clubs affiliated with Organized Baseball in the 1940s and 1950s, also called this historic structure home. Completely enclosed during its 1971 renovation, today's Latin American Stadium boasts more than 55,000 seats in its slowly deteriorating single-deck structure of covered grandstand and open-air bleachers.

Contemporary Latin American Stadium, familiarly dubbed "Latino," features much the same appearance and aura it offered a half-century ago, although the grandstand roof and home plate area box seats have fallen into more than slight disrepair. The sprawling park has, for several decades, served as home to both capital city league clubs, the Industriales, and the now-defunct Metropolitanos (more popularly called Metros). By the 2009 season, however, the also-ran and less popular Metros team was playing exclusively at the smaller-capacity Changa Mederos Stadium, located in the Havana Sports City athletic training facilities. Renovations were again done to Latino in advance of a Baltimore Orioles exhibition game versus the Cuban national team staged in late March 1999; MLB-quality outfield wall padding was provided by Major League Baseball as part of that historic exchange. A new scoreboard using solar power and designed to cut usage of precious electricity was also imported from Vietnam and installed for the opening of an historic Golden Anniversary National Series in November 2010. Several mid-2000s seasons in Havana had featured only daylight play due to damaged light towers (at both Latino and Changa Mederos) and an island-wide effort to conserve electricity in the face of the island's growing economic crisis.

Colorful team nicknames are also a special feature of the Cuban League scene, although they were rarely used by the Cuban press until the final decade of the twentieth century, when they became a regular feature of media coverage on the island. Current teams are actually named for the provinces that host them and not for provincial capital cities, which in most cases carry the same name. This has been the norm since the mid-1980s, but earlier club designations often differed from provincial labels, occasionally indicated occupations that sometimes overlapped with current club nicknames, and sometimes changed rapidly from year to year. The 1960s featured squads called Occidentales, Orientales, Granjeros (Farmers), and Azucareros (Sugar Harvest-

**HISTORIC BASE HIT. Fidel prepares to take his ceremonial cuts to launch Cuba's second National Series championship in December 1962. El comandante smacked a single off pitcher Modesto Verdura to record "revolutionary baseball's" second official (if staged) season-opening base hit.** *The Rucker Archive*

ers); the 1970s witnessed clubs labeled Mineros (Miners), Oriente, Henequeneros, Constructores, and Serranos; the 1980s introduced Camagüeyanos, Citricultores (Citrus Workers), and Vegueros (Tobacco

Harvesters). Recent-era Cuban League team names and principal ball-parks are as follows:
Occidental (Western) Sector

- Industriales Leones (Blue Lions), Latinoamericano (Latin American) Stadium
- Pinar del Río Vegueros (Tobacco Farmers), Capitán San Luis Stadium
- Habana Province Vaqueros (Cowboys), Nelson Fernández Stadium
- Sancti Spíritus Gallos (Roosters), José Antonio Huelga Stadium
- Cienfuegos Elefantes (Elephants), Cinco de Septiembre (Fifth of September) Stadium
- Matanzas Cocodrilos (Crocodiles), Victoria de Girón Stadium
- Isla de la Juventud Piratas (Pirates), Cristóbal Labra Stadium
- Metropolitanos Guerreros (Warriors), Changa Mederos Stadium
- Artemisa Cazadores (Hunters), 26 de Julio Stadium
- Mayabeque Huricanes (Hurricanes), Nelson Fernández Stadium

Oriente (Eastern) Sector

- Santiado de Cuba Avispas (Wasps), Guillermón Moncada Stadium
- Villa Clara Naranjas (Orangemen), Augusto César Sandino Stadium
- Ciego de Avila Tigres (Tigers), José Ramón Cepero Stadium
- Las Tunas Leñadores (Woodcutters), Julio Antonio Mella Stadium
- Camagüey Tinajones (Potters), Candido González, Stadium
- Guantánamo Indios (Indians), Nguyen van Troi Stadium
- Granma Alazanes (Stallions), Martires de Barbados Stadium
- Holguín Cachoros (Cubs or Puppies), Calixto García Stadium[21]

Havana's Industriales Blue Lions remain the island's most popular club, not surprisingly since that team represents the capital city region, boasting a third of the nation's population. This team and its rabid following was the subject of the 2006 award-winning Cuban documentary *Fuera de la Liga*, which earned Havana filmmaker Ian Padrón top prize at the 2009 Cooperstown Film Festival competition. The Industriales ballclub has also enjoyed the greatest championship success: The Lions have claimed a dozen title banners, four more than the Santiago de Cuba ballclub, representing the island's second most populous region. Former New York Yankees big-league pitching star Orlando "El Duque" Hernández and 2000s California Angels, Seattle Mariners, and Kansas City Royals slugger Kendrys Morales both began their stellar careers on the Industriales roster. And Yulieski Gurriel (spelled Gourriel in Cuba), first baseman for the 2017 World Series champion Houston Astros, also wore an Industriales jersey before defecting from the Cuban system at the 2016 Caribbean Series in Santo Domingo.

Cuban baseball of the modern postrevolution era is characterized by two unique features: the league's geographical rather than corporate structure and the fact that athletes traditionally have performed for regional teams during the entire duration of their careers.[22] Ballclubs representing provinces and not private corporate businesses means intense fan loyalties, since one's local team is always comprised of strictly hometown athletes. This feature of fan loyalty is intensified by the fact that Cuban ballplayers are never sold or traded from one ballclub to another, performing their entire careers with the hometown squad. One consequence of such regional structure is the aforementioned imbalanced competition, since more populous regions enjoy far greater access to ball-playing talent. But the absence of team parity seems more than cancelled out by the promise of passionate regional competitions.

Two other special features of the Cuban League also demand emphasis. One is the fact that only native-born Cuban athletes perform in the league, making it the purest example of a homegrown sporting production. The practice is in line with INDER's goal of shaping league seasons for the express purpose of training and selecting national team ballplayers. No other top circuits can boast this type of rigidly nationalistic flavor. Another oddity of league play (at least in view of traditions in Organized Baseball) is the practice of considering career statistics for individual ballplayers to be a composite of not only National Series games, but also Selective Series, Revolutionary Cup, and Super League contests. And as noted earlier, batting and pitching stats accumulated during postseason play (in effect for the past three decades) are also counted in a ballplayer's final career numbers.

The most defining element of Cuban League baseball, however, remains the use of domestic championship seasons for the primary purpose of training and selecting national team rosters. Since the 1960s, the focus of Cuban baseball has always been on capturing international championships and thus fostering the nation's celebrated socialist-style sporting image. As a result, Cuba's national teams dominated international baseball for a half-century (from the early 1960s until the integration of major-league and minor-league pros into such international events as the Olympics and the World Baseball Classic) and have, in the process, established a winning ledger that is easily the most remarkable in the history of almost any sport at any level.

The most noteworthy feat has been Team Cuba's five-decade string of either winning or at least reaching the championship game in more than 50-straight major international tournaments (53 events in total). This unparalleled victory string finally came to an end with a second-round ouster at the 2009 World Baseball Classic. Between the 1987 Pan American Games in Indianapolis and the 1997 Intercontinental Cup matches in Barcelona, the Cuban squad also claimed victory in 159-straight individual games played during major IBAF tournaments. In five full decades, Cuban teams maintained their dominance by capturing three gold and two silver medals in the five "official" Olympic baseball tournaments, as well as walking off with 18 of the 23 championship banners contested in IBAF Baseball World Cup matches. Despite a recent dip in performance after the final IBAF World Cup event in 2011, where they dropped the gold medal match to The Netherlands and its star-studded lineup, recruited from the Dutch Caribbean, Cuba's overall individual game-winning percentage since 1962 still stands at more than 90 percent.

Cuban baseball did experience its own brief game-fixing scandal in the early 1970s, although the affair was rather minor in scope when compared to the infamous big-league Black Sox Scandal or the widespread corruption that nearly sank the Taiwanese pro league in the late 1990s. The hushed-up Cuban event received no media coverage on the home island at the time and involved a contingent of Industriales players who were suspended in the late 1970s without any public admission of guilt. Among the banned was promising star infielder Rey Anglada, whose 10-year career was cut short by the indiscretion. Another was slugger Bárbaro Garbey, a former league batting champion (Selective Series, 1976) and RBI leader (National Series, 1978). Garbey left Cuba in the celebrated 1980 Mariel Boatlift and eventually showed up in North American professional baseball, which seemed to find his alleged misdeeds acceptable since they were easily dismissed as a blow against an enemy Cuban government rather than an attack on the integrity of the game. Garbey quickly proved a big-league misfit, while Anglada quietly served out two decades of rehabilitation at home and resurfaced in the early 2000s as a remarkable Cuban League managerial success story. Anglada would eventually direct his former Industriales club to three league pennants and claim both silver (IBAF World Cup) and gold (Pan American Games) medals as the 2007 bench boss for the Cuban national team.

Modern-era Cuban action has been noteworthy for several unrivaled individual performances, a few rarely, if ever, duplicated in the world's other top professional circuits. One of the most remarkable has been the home-run hitting exploits of Santiago outfielder Alexei Bell, who blasted a record seven bases-loaded home runs in the league's short 90-game schedule during National Series #49 (2010). Bell's feat of launching the 2009–2010 season with unprecedented consecutive "grand slam" home runs in the initial inning of the season's lid-lifter may be the single most memorable moment in league annals. Another noteworthy slugging display in the new millennium has been the long-ball hitting of Granma star Alfredo Despaigne, who established a single-season mark for home runs (32) in 2009, one better than Bell a year earlier, and then repeated the feat in 2012, by upping the mark to 36. Perhaps more remarkable still were five consecutive batting titles for Las Tunas outfielder Osmani Urrutia. Between 2001 and 2005, Urrutia compiled a difficult-to-imagine five-year composite batting average above .400 (.422), a feat authored in North American major-league competition only by Hall of Famer Rogers Hornsby (.402, 1921–1925).

While many Cuban League records seem suspect to North American fans because of lesser talent, shorter seasons, and several decades of aluminum bats, there are some individual performances that have no true major-league equivalents. In addition to his single-inning grand slams, Bell holds two other distinctions, one being a pair of single-inning homers in a playoff game (April 18, 2007) and the second involving another postseason single-inning three-hit outburst (April 5, 2008). A player striking two homers in a single inning has occurred on several occasions in the majors (and 27 times in the Cuban League); three hits in an inning has been achieved but twice in the majors (Gene

Stephens and Johnny Damon). But neither rarity has ever occurred during MLB playoff games.

Still another unparalleled Cuban League event is the 14 consecutive hits by Granma's Ibrahim Fuentes (1989), which outdistanced by two the 1952 big-league mark of Walt Dropo. A third unrivaled Cuban landmark would have to be the 22-strikeout game by Faustino Corrales, two above the big-league record, posted on five occasions (twice by Roger Clemens and once each by Kerry Wood, Randy Johnson, and most recently Max Scherzer). Also, in contention for special recognition is the 63 career shutouts achieved by Braudilio Vinent, which matches the Lively Ball Era major-league standard of Warren Spahn. Yet, Vinent reached the figure in only about one-third the number of starts required by Spahn. Spahn logged 665 starts in his 21 campaigns (one shutout every 10.5 starts); Vinent reached the same total during his 20 years of combined National Series and Selective Series seasons in a mere 400 starts (one shutout every 6.3 starts). Both recorded single-season highs of seven (Vinent in the 1973 National Series, Spahn in both 1947 and 1951), but again Santiago's Vinent seems to hold the edge here since Cuban seasons are briefer and thus a pitcher's game-starting opportunities far fewer.

No-hit games are as much a cherished rarity in Cuba as they are in the majors, and by at least one measure they are a much rarer phenomenon. The league witnessed only 51 no-hitters (one per year) through December 2010, the last one thrown by Pinar's Vladimir Baños only several weeks into the historic 50th National Series season. Granted, Cuban League seasons are only slightly more than half as long as big-league campaigns, and twice as many ballclubs in the two MLB circuits also means approximately twice the number of daily games. Nonetheless, by the finish of the 2010 season, the modern major leagues produced a grand total of 269 "official" nine-inning gems, or an average of 2.5 per MLB season. And this number includes only "sanctioned" MLB no-hitters, in which a game must last a full nine innings and the pitcher authoring the gem must also be the game-winner. If we add in no-hitters tossed in losing efforts (there have been three) and weather-shortened gems of less than nine frames (there have been 23 since 1903), plus games in which no-hitters were broken up in extra innings, after the first nine frames were hitless (13 of these), the pre-2011 MLB total soars to 308 and the ratio to 2.878 MLB no-hitters per season. Of

50 Cuban National Series through 2011, only a mere three (those ending in 1968, 1969, and 2000) witnessed as many as three different no-hit
efforts. There has only ever been one perfect game (without a single
baserunner) in the Cuban League (tossed by Maels Rodríguez on December 22, 1999), again making this event even rarer on the Cuban
island than in the majors.

One no-hit-related event in Cuba stands out for special mention.
The first pair of such games was thrown in 1966, during successive
starts by otherwise unheralded right-hander Aquino Abreu. Abreu, a
lifetime sub-.500 hurler, at 63–65 in 14 seasons (1962–1975), thus became the only pitcher in any major national professional league to
match Cincinnati's Johnny Vander Meer (1938) with consecutive no-hit
masterpieces. The first Abreu whitewash came on January 16, 1966, at
Augusto César Sandino Stadium (Villa Clara) during the opener of a
four-team doubleheader. Abreu (pitching for Centrales) permitted five
baserunners, including a hit batter in the ninth, yet blanked Occidentales, 10–0, without permitting a single safety. Nine days later, the feat
was repeated with a 7–0 blanking, marred only by five free passes
against Industriales in Havana's Latin American Stadium. An added
historical irony attached to Abreu's back-to-back masterpieces is that
they were also the first two such games witnessed in Cuban League
action.

When discussing pitching and batting feats in the island nation,
Cuba's half-century-long league history might best be viewed as three
distinguishable epochs. First to unfold was Cuba's version of the Dead-
ball Era, which extended for almost two decades into the late 1970s.
Batting feats remained unimpressive and pitching marks were eye-popping, especially ERA totals. Eight league leaders in the latter department posted sub-1.00 figures in the first 15 National Series seasons,
while only one slugger (Armando Capiró, 1973) was able to top the 20-
homer plateau.

Next came the upsurge in offense brought on by the 1977 introduction of aluminum bats. This era lasted a full two decades, until 1999 and
the reintroduction of wooden batting sticks. The latter event came at
the time of the Baltimore Orioles exhibition visit in March 1999 and
was spurred by changes in equipment rules for international tournament play. During this second era, slugging exploded, paced by the
home run bashing by Kindelán and the all-around offensive prowess of

Omar Linares, who batted above .425 on three occasions. The third and final era, post-2000, has witnessed an even bigger onslaught on the batting entries in league record books. And this latter surge likely has been due to increased league-wide athletic talent as much as any changes in equipment or playing conditions. By 2010 (a decade after the change), only three sluggers—Joan Carlos Pedroso in February 2009 and Yulieski Gourriel and Frederich Cepeda in January 2010— had reached 200 or more homers playing only with MLB-caliber bats, but four more would get there in the next half-dozen years (Alfredo Despaigne, Eriel Sánchez, Alexander Malleta, and Yosvany Peraza).

North American fans at all aware of Cuban baseball are seemingly most intrigued by the issue of Cuban ballplayer "defections" to the North American pro ranks, although before 2010 this was a subject much overblown in the foreign press, while at the same time almost never discussed by Cuban media. The percentage of young prospects leaving the island began soaring near the end of the first decade of the twenty-first century as economic conditions worsened in the homeland. But the fact remained that until 2010, few recognizable stars abandoned the socialist baseball system. Thus, the impact on the level of league play was quite minimal. Cuba long evaded the fate of other Caribbean hotbeds (Venezuela, the Dominican Republic, and especially Puerto Rico), which have been essentially stripped clean of their local baseball operations by the constant transfer of homegrown talent to the higher-paying North American majors and minors. This changed after 2009, when the slow trickle became first a steady leak (Aroldis Chapman [2009], Leonys Martin [2010], Yoenis Céspedes [2011], Yasiel Puig [2012], and José Abreu [2013] among the headliners) and finally a floodtide (with almost 150 Cuban League escapees in late 2014 and 2015). Many of the hair-raising escapes, mostly from the island and not during national team overseas trips, involved most unsavory tales of human trafficking violations and life-threatening scenarios for athletes and their families, as thoroughly examined in my 2016 book *Cuba's Baseball Defectors: The Inside Story*.

But some loyalists persistently resisted the siren call of big-league riches. The three most talented and celebrated players from the Cuban League of the past half century have, by wide consensus, been Omar Linares, Orestes Kindelán, and Pedro Luis Lazo. For two decades, Linares was repeatedly labeled the top all-around third baseman per-

forming anywhere outside the major leagues. "El Niño" Linares's top
achievement may well have been a career slugging percentage of .644,
outdone only by Babe Ruth in the big-league record books. Kindelán's
home run slugging was legendary both on the island and in the realm of
international tournaments. His career highlight came with 30 homers in
only 63 games during a short Selective Series season. At the Atlanta
Olympics, the oversized DH belted the longest fly ball (a homer into
the third deck in left-center field) ever witnessed in Fulton County
Stadium, former home of the Atlanta Braves. There has never been a
Triple Crown winner in National Series play, but Kindelán came tantalizingly close on several occasions. Lazo retired in December 2010, as
Cuba's all-time most successful hurler, with a record 257 victories and
2,426 career strikeouts (only 73 short of Rogelio García on the all-time
Cuban list). On the international scene the "Cuban Skyscraper" was a
dominant closer who grabbed the attention of North American audiences during the first World Baseball Classic.

The slugging feats of Linares and Kindelán now seem somewhat
muted by their career-long use of the aluminum bats employed in Cuba
from 1977 to 1999. The aluminum "lumber" and weaker competition
have caused some to contend that more recent stars like Frederich
Cepeda, Yulieski Gourriel (now spelled Gurriel since his arrival in the
big leagues), and José Abreu have outstripped the talents of the likes of
Linares, Kindelán, and other earlier league heroes; since the members
of the latter group have excelled against big-league competition it is
hard to argue with that position. By 2010, younger sluggers the likes of
Alfredo Despaigne and José Dariel Abreu were already threatening
many cherished records of earlier aluminum-bat sluggers, Abreu missing out on a Triple Crown on the season's final day in 2011, and Despaigne setting single-season home run marks and at least temporarily
overhauling Linares's hefty career slugging numbers. Pitcher Lazo is
more likely to maintain his fame for the long haul in Cuba due as much
to his colorful image and charismatic character as his mere statistical
legacy. In the final years of his storied career, Lazo became a fixture of
televised league games, regularly captured by cameras while leaning on
the dugout or bullpen railing puffing on a huge cigar during live game
action.

Another contemporary Cuban League figure who deserves note is
veteran Isla de la Juventud hurler Carlos Yanes, one of the more re-

markable "iron men" in the long annals of the sport. Completing 28 league seasons, Yanes achieved feats unprecedented in modern-era play. The Isla de la Juventud right-hander has few parallels as both a winner and loser of more than 200 games, and at the outset of the 2010–2011 campaign, he continued to maintain hope of overtaking Pedro Lazo's career victory mark; to reach that goal (he eventually fell 18 short) the breaking-ball specialist would have had to remain active for more than 30 campaigns (also beyond the ripe age of 50). Despite the shorter Cuban seasons, the crafty junk-ball hurler (235–242 at career's end) nonetheless also fell only a shade short of the unique lifetime won–lost ledger of big-leaguer Jack Powell (245–254), the sub-.500 MLB 200-game-winner with the largest number of both wins and losses. Had Yanes only pitched for a more successful ballclub, like Villa Clara or Santiago, he would likely own all the Cuban career marks. As it is, the durable 46-year-old athlete bowed out at the top of a dozen categories, most of them attached to formidable feats of mere durability.

Like any top professional league, Cuba's has produced its own collection of memorable and talented managers. National Series play serves as a proving ground for the selection of national team managers and coaches, as well as national team ballplayers. Thus, a handful of the top skippers have eventually distinguished themselves in international tournament play. The most noteworthy in this group are Servio Borges, Higinio Vélez, and Jorge Fuentes. Borges was the most successful of an early 1970s school of coaches trained entirely in the revamped revolutionary baseball system introduced by Fidel's sweeping governmental and social reforms; he also presided over the mid-1970s transition from wooden to aluminum bats. In addition to guiding eight championship squads in Amateur World Series play in a dozen summers (1969–1980), Borges claimed two National Series crowns with Azucareros (1969, 1972).

Vélez was briefly visible to North American fans as Cuba's manager during the first two editions of the MLB-sponsored World Baseball Classic. In domestic-league action, the most successful at winning championships in the long haul has been Jorge Fuentes in Pinar del Río, a five-time championship manager. Two skippers (Vélez and Pedro Jova) have strung together back-to-back-to-back league titles, and two others (Antonio Pacheco and Rey Anglada) have claimed three titles in four campaigns. But only one bench boss—Ramón Carneado—claimed four pennants in a row. The legendary Carneado worked his magic with Havana's Industriales club at the dawn of the new league (1963–1966) when the bulk of his players were still truly part-time amateurs.

More recently, Victor Mesa—an all-star outfielder of the 1980s—proved to be the island's most colorful and also most controversial manager while serving at the helm in Villa Clara from the mid-1990s to the late 2000s, then again in Matanzas after 2012, and finally with Industriales in the 2018 campaign. Before his dismissal from Villa Clara in 2009, Mesa was known for such stunts as ejecting his entire relief corps from the bullpen to the team bus during an opposition rally, berating his bench between innings in full view of television cameras, replacing one pinch-hitter with another in mid-count of an at-bat, and substituting one pinch-runner for another after a successful steal by the first substitute. Many on the island complain that Mesa hurt his squads by always attempting to attract more attention to himself than his players (while others saw that same trait as a huge plus). He also earned considerable attention off the island as manager of the powerful Cuban entry at the 2013 edition of the World Baseball Classic preliminary rounds in Japan, where again his unorthodox managerial style was blamed by some for the team's elimination loss to The Netherlands.

Even before the arrival on the Stateside scene of recent headliners like Chapman, Puig, Abreu, and Céspedes, the Cuban League of recent decades, despite its isolation, spawned a small but noticeable number of big-leaguers—especially pitchers. These players "defected" from their homeland for various personal—and not always strictly financial—reasons. René Arocha was the first of the modern-era national team stars to escape Castro's baseball empire, doing so in the aftermath of a July 1991 exhibition series in Millington, Tennessee. Two half-brothers—Liván (with the 1997 world champion Florida Marlins) and Orlando Hernández (with the 1998 world champion New York Yankees)—made their marks on major-league postseason lore. Bulky right-handed pitcher José Contreras was a major star on the Cuban national team—posting a perfect 13–0 international record—before joining the Yankees in 2003. More recent refugee hurlers have been Chapman (Cincinnati Reds) and Yunesky Maya (Washington Nationals), both debuting with the pros in 2010. Southpaw Chapman gained much press attention with his fastball, coming in at more than 100 miles per hour, surpassed in the speed department in Cuba only by Maels Rodríguez, but Maya, the number-two starter on the national team and 2005 league ERA champion, was perhaps a far greater loss—to both domestic-league action and Team Cuba fortunes in international play.

One nonpitcher to enjoy early twenty-first-century successes in the big time was California/Anaheim Angels first baseman Kendrys Morales, whose career has stretched on with Seattle, Kansas City, and Toronto. Morales exploded on the Cuban scene in 2003, as National Series rookie of the year, but he abandoned the island only three years later. The switch-hitter finally enjoyed a true breakout season with the American League Angels in 2009 (34 HR, 108 RBIs), but only after a long trial in the North American minor leagues.

Many top Cuban stars of recent decades have ranked among the world's best ballplayers, despite never showcasing their talents in the professional North American major leagues. Pinar del Río mainstay Omar Linares—the Cuban League career batting leader, with a lifetime .368 average compiled in 20 National Series and Selective Series seasons—was, for two decades, considered the world's best "amateur" player and the "greatest third baseman never to appear in the major leagues." And the inaugural three renditions of the MLB-sponsored World Baseball Classic (2006, 2009, 2013) have demonstrated that Cuban League all-stars can indeed match major leaguers in top-level tournament competitions. Cuba surprised the professional baseball world by reaching the finals of the initial MLB event, while switch-hitting outfielder Frederich "Freddie" Cepeda was both batting leader and the only unanimous all-star selection at the 2009 second-edition MLB Classic. Moreover, Granma Province slugger Alfredo Despaigne established an all-time home run mark (11 in 15 games) while leading the Cuban national squad to the finals of the 2009 penultimate IBAF Baseball World Cup in Europe.

A drastic overhaul of Cuban League structure took place in the fall of 2012, on the eve of National Series #52, with the decision to scrap divisional structure in favor of a single 16-team league and also divide the campaign into two distinct segments of 45 games each—an initial qualification round with the traditional 16 teams, followed by a championship round featuring only eight surviving clubs. Eight top players from each of the bottom (eliminated) squads would now be awarded in a supplemental player draft at midyear to the second-round ballclubs.

The major impact here was the loss of the long-standing tradition of athletes only performing with the home province; still another more impactful result was the fact that half the provinces were suddenly left without baseball for more than 50 percent of the league calendar. There was a dual motive for the change, the first being the effort to shore up recently sagging national team fortunes by providing a more competitive league (for at least part of the year), with the island's top pitchers clustered on fewer rosters. But equally at play was the reality that the Cuban Federation was finding it increasingly difficult to shoulder the cost of transporting 16 teams throughout the island for six months and lighting stadiums for night games in every province.

Four teams have dominated the past half-dozen seasons, with long-time doormat Ciego de Avila claiming three titles (including two consecutive, in 2015 and 2016) under manager Roger Machado, more traditional power Pinar del Río also tasting victory twice (2011, 2014), and Villa Clara walking off with the first title earned under the novel split-season format (2013). More recently still, Granma has emerged with back-to-back championships (2017, 2018), its first ever in that club's 42-year existence. A second novel development on the Cuban League scene has been the return of the league champion to the February Caribbean Series after a half-century-long estrangement. But a much-heralded reentry into the showcase tournament matching top squads from the Caribbean winter circuits (Mexico, Puerto Rico, Venezuela, and the Dominican Republic) has brought only mixed results; Villa Clara was unceremoniously eliminated with only a single win in four contests during the 2014 session in Venezuela, and Ciego de Avila suffered an identical fate two years later in Santo Domingo. Pinar del Río did walk off with a Caribbean Series banner in San Juan during the intervening year but only after also claiming but one victory in the opening round robin before surging in a pair of playoff matches behind the slugging of Freddie Cepeda and Yulieski Gourriel—both drafted onto the team as allowed reinforcements for the series. The Caribbean Series visits were also the unfortunate settings for several additional crucial ballplayer defections, including those of promising pitching prospect Vladimir Gutierrez in San Juan and star slugger Gourriel in Santo Domingo.

Recent Cuban seasons have been marked by a number of memorable individual performances aside from Abreu's near-Triple Crown (losing only the RBI crown to Céspedes) in the golden anniversary 2011 season and Despaigne's record-busting 36 homers a year later. Despite only one national team appearance, durable infielder Enrique Díaz retired with the 2012 disbanding of his Metros ballclub after a 26-year career stint that left him as the all-time leader in base hits, runs scored, triples, and stolen bases. Wrapping up his Cuban career with a true bang, slugger Yulieski Gourriel amassed an unparalleled .500 batting average (49 games and 174 at-bats) before abandoning the national squad in the Dominican Republic at the season's two-thirds mark. After brief controversy among league officials, who in the past have ignored the achievements of defectors, it was at least tentatively decided to enter the lofty number in the league record books as Gourriel's first official league batting crown.

Cuban League baseball has provided, for more than a full half-century, an isolated yet entertaining baseball universe unparalleled elsewhere in the sport. Both the big-league successes of a growing contingent of defectors and Cuba's surprise victories in the MLB-sponsored World Baseball Classic have demonstrated an undeniable truth: that this league, for much of its run, ranked alongside the Japanese pro leagues and perhaps just below the U.S. majors among the trio of highest-level circuits. Cuba's self-styled brand of "revolutionary baseball" today stands out for its experiment in truly regional competitions among strictly homegrown athletes. But the greatest legacy of this league in the end has to be its production of powerhouse national teams capable of dominating international tournament competitions for decades on end.

For all its boasting points, however, the post-2010 Cuban League now seems to be living on borrowed time and struggling to keep anything of its earlier luster. Exploding player defections have killed league quality and gutted a once-proud national team system. Overtures by the Obama administration after December 2014 to end Cold War hostilities with Cuba have so far brought little in the way of détente between the Cuban Baseball Federation and an MLB brain trust still largely focused on Cuba as little more than a convenient plantation for harvesting future talent. And the Cubans' efforts to relieve defection pressures on remaining top stars by allowing some to be loaned out to the Japanese circuit and the lesser Can-Am semipro league have done precious little, if anything, to stem the obvious domestic league disintegration.

# 6

# THE OTHER BIG RED MACHINE AND CUBA'S DOMINANCE OF INTERNATIONAL BASEBALL

> By making baseball part of the Revolution, however, Cuba's government also politicized baseball.—Justin Turner, *Baseball Diplomacy, Baseball Deployment: The National Pastime in U.S.–Cuba Relations* [1]

From José Martí to Fidel and Raúl Castro, and from the American charge up San Juan Hill to the bungled exile invasion operation at the Bay of Pigs, and then on for a half-century Cold War standoff, politics and baseball have always been the coziest of bedfellows on the island nation of Cuba. The only variant has been the particular political agendas that were served; what remained constant was the degree to which those agendas always involved spirited nationalism, intense revolutionary upheaval, and the avowed aim of ousting foreign imperialist occupations of the homeland.

As offered in *Baseball Diplomacy, Baseball Deployment*, Justin Turner's view that Fidel "politicized" baseball in Cuba—first with his creation of INDER in the spring of 1961, and then with the launching of a new-style National Series the following year—is perhaps a reasonable assessment as far as it goes. It can't be denied that Fidel was quick to make baseball a showcase feature of his revolution and also a political platform for scoring points in his war of words with the Americans. But any claim that baseball became a political instrument in Cuba only after

1961 also isn't a very enlightening observation—at least not without a good deal of contextual background.

Absent from Turner's analysis is any reasonable historical perspective, both regarding baseball in Castro's Cuba and baseball as a professional sport played elsewhere in the Caribbean, North America, or Asia. The novel Cuban legislations of 1961, replacing professionalism with amateurism, indeed revamped sports to fit a newly emerging socialist society. Built on a Soviet model but remaining particularly Cuban in character, the new sports program had two overriding goals: first, mass participation to increase public health and well-being, and second, discovery and development of potential international champions. In theory, the two aims were related, although eventually the latter rose to a position of prominence—perhaps because in the end it was easier to achieve and also paid greater dividends.

The latter goal was clearly focused on winning credibility for the new Marxist-style state on the international sporting scene, where pre-Cas-

**FIDEL'S SHOWCASE CHAMPIONS.** Top stars of Cuba's national team pose in the Beijing locker room after a game at the 2008 Olympic Baseball Tournament. *From the author's collection*

tro Cuba had been notoriously weak but where battles on the athletic field might now become a far less dangerous and thus more convenient stage for waging political wars by proxy. In *Sport in Cuba*, Paula Pettavino and Geralyn Pye trace in some detail the weakness of "elitist" Cuban sport before 1959, when the "distinguishing features were race and class distinctions," where only privileged whites with access to private club facilities enjoyed opportunities to prepare for Olympic sports, where the controlling interests were private and usually professional, where the island's few distinguished athletes were Afro-Cuban baseball players and boxers seeking "a possible ticket out of poverty and into what seemed to be the 'charmed' life of American professional sports."[2]

Baseball emerged as the showcase venue for this effort for several obvious reasons. It was not only the island's defining sport at the time—just as it always had been—but also since the late nineteenth-century independence wars (1868–1898) the game had always stood as the very lifeblood of Cuban culture. And not to be overlooked, since baseball claimed its origins (at least in its modern-day form) in North America, it also provided a perfect opportunity to beat the Americans at their own game, a not-to-be-missed chance for tweaking the nose of the hated *Yanqui* imperialist enemy.

But Fidel's plan for revamping baseball in the blatant service of nationalism at the outset of the 1960s also had sufficient historical precedent in both his own country and elsewhere abroad. The INDER sports overhaul was anything but a Fidel Castro invention. Baseball had served Cuban independence efforts at the birth of the new nation during the 1880s and 1890s rebellion against odious Spanish colonial control. Numerous pioneering ballplayers in the last two decades of the nineteenth century simultaneously fought in the ongoing Independence War (1895–1898) against the Spanish regime, causing some to lose their lives and prompting the colonial occupiers to ban the sport on several occasions. (Championship tournaments, later called "seasons" by modern historians, were cancelled due to war hostilities in 1895–1896 and 1896–1897, and again at the end of the 1897–1898 tournament competition.)

The sport was initially adopted not only for its intrinsic pleasures, but also as an anti-Spanish symbol and gateway to an admired alternative American culture; Spain, with its Old World elitist notions and attractions to the violent rituals of bullfighting, was an oppressive past to be overthrown; the United States, with its democratic principles and gentlemanly sport of bats and balls, was a wave of the future to be emulated. One of the sport's earliest Cuban pioneers was also one of its first martyrs to the anti-Spanish cause: Emilio Sabourín, captain/manager of the Habana ballclub, who funneled profits from his team's games into dangerous anti-Spanish causes, was arrested for conspiracy against the ruling regime and his activities as a rebel fund-raiser, and died of malnutrition and disease in a North African Spanish prison camp. Cuban baseball was thus born mainly out of the dual politics of passionate patriotism and rebellion in the name of national independence.

The American national sport was first adopted on the island in the 1870s, after being introduced by local students returning from schooling in the United States a decade earlier. It rapidly emerged as a symbol of desired modernity and the antithesis to everything that represented Spanish colonial hegemony. The first historian of Cuban baseball, Wenceslao Gálvez y Delmonte—in his 1889 *El Base-ball en Cuba*—intones that baseball fields in Cuba would most certainly outlast the Spanish passions found in the cockfight and the bullring.[3] Gálvez y Delmonte was also a shortstop on the earliest Almendares ballclubs of the 1880s. Yet, he earned his spot in the original Cuban Baseball Hall of Fame, established in 1939, along with a number of other pioneering players of his era, as much for his role as anti-Spanish revolutionary and thus national political hero as for any on-field ball-playing skills.

Roberto González Echevarría rightly notes that the volume produced by the "literary" shortstop may well be the first serious history of the sport published in Cuba or anywhere else. In treating the contributions of the island's earliest baseball historian, González Echevarría also outlines in detail the connections between baseball (adopted as an American symbol) and the Cuban anti-Spanish independence movement. He stresses that the mere fact the origins of the sport on the island coincided so directly with independence from Spain "accounts for the depth and durability of baseball as a part of modern Cuban culture."[4] Sabourín and his colleagues had every bit as much to do with the fusion of the American sport with Cuban national identity as did Fidel Castro more than a half-century later.

When Turner claims that "Castro himself also readily used baseball as a political platform" or that "once transformed by the revolution, baseball in Cuba could now serve the revolution," he fails to note that such usage of the national game as political lever and tool of Cuban national identity can be traced not to 1962, but rather all the way back to 1895.[5] If baseball was a convenient hammer to beat off the American imperialists in the mid-twentieth century, it had also been a convenient hammer to beat off the Spanish imperialists of the late nineteenth century. Put even more forcefully, if Fidel made baseball a symbol of his new government and its revamped society in Cuba's second great revolution, one aimed at combating American control, he was only reprising precisely what the leaders of the first great revolution of the 1880s and 1890s had done in their efforts to oust the Spanish.

In the wake of what can only be termed a "false independence" resulting from the defeat of the Spanish and immediate reoccupation by a caretaker American-controlled administration in 1898, baseball had also again been used in the first decade of the new century to strike another blow at unwanted occupation—this time by the previously admired Americans. In 1898, after the capitulation of the Spanish ended what was falsely labelled as the Spanish–American War by U.S. chroniclers and historians, the McKinley administration and U.S. military forces under Theodore Roosevelt not only excluded the bitter Cubans from the Treaty of Paris peace negotiations, but also established their own virtual military occupation of the island, which lasted for much of the first decade of the new century. The Americans installed a puppet president (Tomás Estrada Palma) in 1901, and wrote the Platt Amendment into a new Cuban Constitution of 1901, which allowed U.S. intervention in the country's internal affairs whenever American national interests seemed threatened. Cubans were left deeply embittered by the unexpected ending to what had been their own long and costly three-decade independence struggle, one they finally seemed on the verge of winning before U.S. intervention simply replaced one colonial occupier with another.

The "American Seasons" staged each fall as prelude to the domestic winter championship season thus proved to be not only a setting for Cuban teams and stars to test their competency against big-leaguers and crack teams of barnstorming Negro League stars, but also a means of boosting national pride with victories against a new set of unwanted and universally despised colonizers. This scenario explains the heroic role soon to be played by the island's first widely celebrated baseball hero, Afro-Cuban pitcher José de la Caridad Méndez (*El Diamante Negro*, or "Black Diamond"), or to a lesser extent the historical prominence of another Afro-Cuban trailblazer, slugger Cristóbal Torriente, who outperformed the celebrated Babe Ruth in 1920, in what turned out to be something of a sham exhibition.[6]

José de la Caridad Méndez is today considered one of the true pitching legends spawned by the island during its earliest sporting history, another of the preintegration Afro-Cubans barred by his race from big-league stardom and thus far wider recognition in the North American sporting press. Méndez would eventually make it into the hallowed halls of Cooperstown via a mass 2006 induction of overlooked blackball stars, selected by a special committee formed specifically to right that injustice. The selection of Méndez was based not so much on his stellar domestic career in Cuba, which was limited to less than a decade by an arm injury, or his tenure in the North American Negro circuits, where he mainly managed and played shortstop after the dead arm sabotaged his pitching skills. It came mainly as a result of a series of exhibition matches against barnstorming big-league clubs that visited Cuba in 1908 and 1909, as part of the much-anticipated "American Season" kicking off winter-league domestic play during that era. Teams visiting the island during those years were the Cincinnati Reds (1908), Detroit Tigers (1909, 1910), and Philadelphia Athletics (1910), as well as several blackball clubs, including the Brooklyn Royal Giants (1908), Indianapolis ABCs (1909), and Leland Giants (1910). The touring Americans squared off in several heated contests against both Almendares and Habana, the top domestic teams. And given the ongoing U.S. occupation of the island at the time, the games, especially against the big-leaguers, were charged with a heavy dose of political overtones.

Cincinnati's visit in the fall of 1908 triggered a pair of significant results. One, now less remembered, was the eventual signing by the National League club of pioneering Cuban big-leaguers Armando Marsans and Rafael Almeida (the first modern-era Cubans to reach the big time), plus Adolfo Luque, the most accomplished preintegration Cuban pitcher to perform in the majors. But more notable still was the heroic stature earned by Méndez. In a November 13 game in front of an overflowing crowd in the original Almendares Park, the Afro-Cuban ace, hurling for his Almendares club, no-hit the visiting big-leaguers until the final frame, when a scratch single by future Yankees manager

Miller Huggins ruined the masterpiece. A week later, Méndez would finish up another game against the Reds, started by Bebé Royer, and post another seven scoreless frames, running his shutout string to 16 innings. To complete the impressive skein, on December 3, Méndez blanked the Cincinnati National League team of manager John Ganzel for the third time, with yet another complete-game five-hit gem. In three hotly contested outings, the Cuban ace had become an instant national hero thanks to whitewashing big-league bats for 25-straight innings.

Many questions might be raised about the Méndez achievement. The games were undoubtedly competitive, and such a streak is impressive given any conditions. But the games were, after all, mere exhibitions—the equivalent of spring training matches—the touring Cincinnati players were a tired group mostly bent on vacationing in the Caribbean paradise after a long National League campaign in which they had limped home in fifth place. The games meant far more to the Cubans than they did to the touring big-leaguers. Did they signal Cooperstown credentials or even big-league credentials for Méndez? That is an issue open to serious debate. What was far more important about these games and the resulting Méndez heroism was the political overtones of the backdrop setting against which they were performed.

As noted in the prologue, González Echevarría would correctly observe that the Cuban ace "became a hero, a celebrity, not only because he trounced the major leaguers, proving that Cuban baseball was as good as any, but also because he had done it during the American occupation of the island."[7] In the shadow of Cuba's first great revolution and precisely a half-century before its second and more successful effort to throw off the cloak of the imperialists, Méndez had already foreshadowed the achievements of later crack national teams during Fidel's reign that also trounced the American imperialists at their own proclaimed national pastime.

Those "American Season" victories at the outset of the twentieth century had already assured that internationally flavored competitions would always trump domestic-league play on the Cuban baseball scene—as much for flag-waving fans as for the patriotic ballplayers themselves. When a neophyte international amateur baseball movement first took wing at the outset of World War II, Cuba was, not surprisingly, at the forefront of the effort. González Echevarría suggests that a convergence of world politics (emerging fascism), intense nationalism, and linkages between national teams and the nation state itself—phenomena on the rise in the years between World War I and World War II—made the atmosphere ripe for the birth of international tournament challenges on something more than a mere exhibition barnstorming level.[8]

In Havana, the spark was first lit by Colonel Jaime Mariné and a newly formed DGD (Dirección General de Deportes) sports ministry, launched in June 1938, by Colonel Fulgencio Batista, at the time the military strongman behind a series of late 1930s puppet presidents. Mariné and the DGD, which he directed, would play a significant role in not only formalizing previous loose-knit amateur league competitions on the domestic scene, revamping earlier less-structured or less-centralized amateur-league organizations spread throughout the island, but also organizing more ambitious international tournament events, starting with a 1939 "Amateur World Series," which would at least prove a moderate success only a few years down the road. That the surge of amateur baseball to its first great heights in Cuba would coincide with strongman Batista's early assumption of political power in the late 1930s and early 1940s would prove something of an irony, of course, once the Castro government ousted the military dictator and itself took full credit for launching what would later be seen as a truer "amateur era" for the beloved Cuban national sport.

But the initial "world cup" baseball idea was not entirely a Cuban invention, even if it was soon to be recognized as largely a Cuban promotion. The first attempt at a world tournament featuring some of the globe's baseball-playing nations was, in reality, a championship event in name only. Staged in London in August 1938, this was actually a two-team five-game playoff of clubs featuring visiting U.S. college and high school students preparing for the abortive 1940 Olympics, along with a smattering of native British baseballers from an earlier experimental and short-lived British professional league that operated in the mid-1930s around Manchester. The onetime event was a brainchild of American businessman Leslie Mann, who wished to celebrate the sport's small inroads in the cricket-crazed British Isles. Mann presented the "John Moore Trophy" (honoring the founder of the English Baseball Federation) to a winning squad wearing uniforms with "England" emblazoned on their jerseys. Some diehard enthusiasts of the

"American sport" in the British Isles today still point with pride to their country's somewhat dubious distinction as the game's first amateur tournament world champion.

Buoyed by the earlier success of a Cuban Amateur League throughout the 1930s and the Central American Games competitions, staged in 1926 (Mexico City), 1930 (Havana), 1935 (San Salvador), and 1938 (Panama City), Cuban sports czar Colonel Mariné had decided, by late 1938, on a far more ambitious project in the form of a second world amateur tournament (this one hopefully more legitimate than its London predecessor) at Havana's picturesque La Tropical Stadium (built originally for the second Central American Games in 1930 and still in use today as a serviceable track and field facility and soccer pitch). Thirteen countries were invited to participate, but only the United States and Nicaragua answered the bell. The lackluster U.S. entrant could not hold its own against Cuban stars drawn from a thriving amateur circuit and dropped all six of its matches, including a trio to the questionably potent Nicaraguans. Mariné's tournament was hardly a "world series" by any stretch, although it did promise better and fuller competitions than Mann's simplistic effort in London. This time around at least some trained baseballers were involved.

If the Cubans were mainly responsible for launching this idea for a legitimate baseball "world series" in 1939, they could claim an even earlier effort in that direction. The pioneering idea for such competitions had actually been born at the middle of the previous decade with the first Central American Games of 1926, which included baseball as its showcase event. The first matches in Mexico City were limited in scope, with again only three countries competing and the Guatemalans showing up without a baseball team. Cuba routed the host Mexicans in the three baseball games played. Four years later, in 1930, Cuba would erect a new showcase stadium to house the second version of such matches from mid-March to early April 1930. That arena would be dubbed La Tropical Stadium, and it would also serve as the home for Cuban winter-league games for the next decade and a half. Moreover, it was also the park that at the end of its short life housed Havana's first team affiliated with Organized Baseball. The Havana Cubans of the Class C Florida International League played their initial two seasons in that venue.

The second Central American Games had been organized largely at the behest of strongman president Gerardo Machado (on the eve of his ouster by Batista's "Sergeants' Revolt") to divert attention from growing political unrest sweeping his island nation. Featuring Cuban big-league pioneer Rafael Almeida as manager, the Cuban squad swept to the title with a single loss to the improved Mexicans. The baseball field had been expanded to five with Panama, Guatemala, and El Salvador joining the competition. But the Central American Games were, of course, not exclusively baseball affairs since a number of other summer sports were on the agenda. They also did not encompass other top baseball nations, like the United States or Asian countries, which were also rapidly warming to the sport. The newly minted Amateur World Series, launched by Cuba's Amateur Athletic Union (a DGD offshoot) and the simultaneously organized International Baseball Federation (IBAF), and first hosted by the Cubans in 1939 and 1940, eventually provided that needed venue.

Cuba would experience its first moments of significant glory on an international stage with the half-dozen Amateur World Series tournaments housed in Havana between 1939 and 1943, and in Caracas in 1944. Again, the scope of these games was limited, and the focus was more regional than truly international. Future big-leaguer Conrado Marrero inherited the mantle of Méndez and Luque with his performances in these games, especially in the first three years of the 1940s. The field was increased to seven teams in 1940, and even included Japanese players representing Hawaii. Cuba again dominated in Tropical Stadium, but Nicaragua did provide some competition, splitting two games with the hosts and finishing only one game behind. But a year later, Venezuela would emerge as the first serious rival of note. Despite its limited field (now featuring nine entrants), the 1941 games provided one of the most hotly contested and memorable matches of international tournament history. On center stage was the personal duel between Marrero and Venezuelan ace Daniel Canónico. The two clubs tied for the lead at the end of regularly scheduled matches. Cuba demanded an extra playoff, and that proved a fatal decision when Canónico (allowed two additional days rest before the deciding extra game) surprised Marrero and the hosts in the finale. But Cuba rebounded in the next two editions of the event, again both staged on home turf in Havana.

The prominence of both the fledgling Amateur World Series and Cuba as an international champion would fade rapidly in the aftermath of the war. Political upheaval in the mid- and late 1950s during the rebellion against Batista added to this lull in baseball activity. Cuba slipped in the Central American Games after its final two triumphs in the late 1930s. Mass signings of young players by the pros in the early 1950s threw the Cuban amateur circuit into a precarious state, and the Central American Games were skipped altogether in 1954. Political turmoil following Fidel's ouster of Batista caused a second-straight Cuban absence from the same event in 1959. After a victory in the initial Pan American Games tournament of 1951, Cuba had also remained on the sidelines of that new event in 1955, as again much of its amateur talent had been funneled off to the Class B Havana Cubans pro team. A Cuban squad did go to Chicago for the Pan American Games in late August 1959, despite still-seething political tensions back home, but it fared poorly in Comiskey Park with only a bronze medal third-place performance.

The first legitimate Amateur World Series staged outside of Cuba, which took place in 1944, unfortunately turned into a nightmare of controversy due to incompetent umpiring. One incident saw Cuba leaving the field in protest after a baserunner was thrown out with an assist from a sideline photographer interfering with a ball in play. Cuba and Mexico would withdraw acrimoniously (both tied at 2–1 with the Venezuelans at the time), and the hosts would declare themselves champions by forfeit. After that debacle, both the Mexicans and Cubans remained on the sidelines the next time around when the games returned to Venezuela a year later. Cuba would also sit out the next two events in Colombia and Nicaragua since most top island players now held professional contracts and fielding a competitive team didn't seem possible. When Cuba returned to the scene in Managua in 1950, its first-place finish was again marred by controversy. The Dominicans originally left the field as champions after besting Venezuela in a tiebreaker playoff; but nine months later, IBAF officials annulled the result, forfeiting Puerto Rico's contests for using professionals, and thus awarding Cuba the title with a best record in the revised standings. Cuba would field another undistinguished team and again lose in 1951, but it would rebound on home soil a year later. Another tournament victory in 1953, in

Caracas, capped the last renewal of the event until the onset of the following decade.

Cuban dominance during these early pioneering years of international competition was therefore often inconsistent and occasionally marked mostly by heated controversy. Most of these events also went unnoticed in the north since American fans had almost no interest in baseball not played at the top professional levels. But Cuba was already well on the road to establishing its central role in world amateur competitions no matter how haphazard early efforts at an Amateur World Series might have been. The sparsity of top Cuban stars moving into the North American major leagues (especially before racial integration after 1947) meant much attention on the island remained focused on the amateur circuit and amateur national teams. This was the case despite a Havana-based focus on the pro winter circuit and a pair of moderately successful ventures into Organized Baseball's minor leagues with the Havana Cubans and Cuban Sugar Kings. Cuba was a true hotbed of amateur baseball for several decades before the arrival of Fidel Castro and his revolution.

Of course, that amateur style baseball of the prewar and immediate postwar era had another distinguishing feature not to be overlooked. It was an exclusively segregated affair, with Afro-Cubans barred from everything but the sugar mill tournaments and winter professional circuit. It was in the pro baseball circuit, along with boxing, that mostly Afro-Cuban athletes from the disadvantaged masses were drawn in the hopes of a ticket out of island poverty through a contract to either the North American pros (after 1947) or barnstorming Negro clubs (before MLB integration). Blacks were excluded from the popular amateur circuits at home (filled mostly with teams sponsored by elite and thus all-white social clubs) until 1959, an often-ignored fact that gives the lie to popular notions that Cuban baseball on the whole was a racial paradise where blacks and whites tested their skills on an equal footing. That was true only in the Havana pro circuit and the sugar mill leagues, with tournaments played in the island's interior.

Admittedly, the pioneering international championship tournaments of the World War II era were small-scale events. They captured almost no attention in the baseball hotbeds of North America and excluded emerging baseball epicenters in Asia. They had nothing of the glamour, high-level competition, or media attention focused on the World Baseball Classic events of the twenty-first century, which only arose once MLB was overrun with international talent and backed its way into efforts at baseball globalization. Those early tournaments also featured none of the political overtones and Cold War hostilities that would emerge once the Cubans became the only baseball-oriented country integrated into the Soviet communist camp. But it is nonetheless significant to stress that two full decades before Fidel Castro was a dominant presence, the Cuban sports ministry had already seized on the sport for image-building and launching its long reign as global amateur baseball powerhouse. The merger of sport and politics—or at least the melding of baseball and national image-building—was already a Cuban hallmark by the time a teenaged Fidel Castro left the Dolores Boys Academy in Santiago and entered the Jesuit Belén High School in Havana.

* * *

Cuba's first significant triumph on the international amateur baseball scene in the aftermath of Fidel's seizure of power arose from an almost eerily ironic overlapping of events. The country's hastily assembled entrant at the April 1961 renewal of the eight-year-dormant Amateur World Series, held in San José, Costa Rica, ran roughshod over five other participating teams at precisely the same moment Fidel's army was repulsing a Washington-backed military invasion on the home front at the Bay of Pigs. If one wishes to pinpoint a precise moment when baseball emerged as an indelible symbol of the new revolutionary government, or when victories in the ballpark came to stand for proxy victories on the Cold War battlefield, that moment can be found with the surprising national team triumph in San José.

Massive tryouts were held to select an exceptionally strong Cuban team for the first international competition after the installation of Fidel's revolutionary government. Those tryouts were also staged simultaneous to the enactment of INDER legislation (see chapter 5) aimed at revamping Cuban sporting culture and replacing professionalism with amateurism. Law 936 of February 23, 1961, went on the books six weeks before the first pitches were thrown on April 7, in San José. On the field, the Cuban team was led by the pitching of lanky black right-hander Alfredo Street (a holdover from the National Amateur League of the Batista era) and the heavy hitting of Pedro Chávez, one of the first stars in the new National Series league, which would debut the following January. Winning all nine of their games, the Cubans ran up scores of 18–0 (Dutch Antilles), 16–0 (Nicaragua), 25–0 (Guatemala), and 11–1 (Mexico) in the preliminary round, and continued the onslaught with similar routs of Panama (12–3), Guatemala (13–2), Mexico (13–1), Costa Rica (12–2), and Venezuela (9–3) in the championship round. The victory was as one-sided as the bloodier one Fidel's troops were scoring against the ragtag exile invasion forces at the Bay of Pigs assault, which overlapped the final four days of the tournament.

Cuba's surge to the title was the first step in Fidel's emerging dream of demonstrating Cuban dominance through baseball. It was a victory dulled only slightly by the absence of a team representing the United States. But soon enough, Cuban baseball would become a central feature of the symbolic battles staged in athletic arenas between the United States and Communist bloc nations. Those battles had already emerged between the Americans, Soviets, and East Germans during the 1956 (Melbourne) and 1960 (Tokyo) Olympic Games. Now with Cuba's regenerated baseball orientation, the self-declared American national game would also become a proxy battlefield for Cold War ideologies based exclusively in the Western Hemisphere.

Even with the one-sided victory in Costa Rica, and despite the fact that it came with the rival Americans on the sidelines, there were nonetheless already strong signals of Cold War tensions in the air. When the Cuban squad arrived in Costa Rica, local airport officials confiscated pro-Castro propaganda being carried by the ballplayers and coaches. And in the aftermath of the heady win, several Cuban players reportedly sought refuge in Costa Rica.[9] There was also further disappointment 16 months later at the 1962 Central American Games in Jamaica, when Cuba finished out of baseball medal contention for the only time in an eventual two dozen visits to that event. Made leery by the earlier troubles in Costa Rica, Cuban officials warned their athletes about opponents of the revolution trying to lure them away by encouraging defections. But the efforts were not entirely successful, as the entire four-man weight-lifting squad and its coach abandoned the delegation, claiming the new socialist system at home was causing the ruin of their country.[10] There was further tension as well when a group of Puerto Rican fans (including a contingent of Cuban exiles) fought behind the grandstands with Cuban fans and team officials after rain showers delayed one of the baseball games.

There was also a further baseball-related disruption connected to the August 1962 Jamaica games, and this one involved what amounted to a first documented ballplayer defection, although little-noted at the time, from the revamped revolutionary baseball system. Seventeen-year-old southpaw pitcher Manuel Enríque Hernández had starred for the Occidentales team in the first National Series of late winter 1962, posting a 1.64 ERA, a league-leading 94 strikeouts, and a 6–3 winning ledger, while earning most valuable pitcher honors. He was reportedly tabbed by Raúl Castro as the island's best pitcher and touted by Fidel as worth perhaps as much as $60,000 on the open market (while purportedly earning less than 170 Cuban pesos back home for his labor). In early August, on the eve of the Jamaica games, Hernández was suspended and branded a traitor in the Cuban press, which reported he had received an invitation from a scout for a tryout with the Cleveland Indians. Government sources also reported at the time that the Matanzas native was planning to claim he was a professional in an effort to have his country disqualified when the national team, for which he had already been selected, arrived in Jamaica. On the eve of the games, Hernández quit the Cuban squad and fled on a hazardous 17-hour journey across the Straits of Florida to permanent exile. Then the hot prospect disappeared entirely from the scene, as have so many later hopeful defectors, and there is no existing record of any successful tryout with the Indians or any signing with a professional team in the United States.

If there were already tensions on the sporting front, they had so far not involved direct clashes with the Americans. A first display of such politically inspired animosity with the rival *Yanquis* would not emerge until the late April 1963 Pan American Games in São Paulo, Brazil, precisely two years after the ill-starred Bay of Pigs fiasco. Even before the matches could begin there was political wrangling, as the Cuban delegation—including athletes in various sports and not just the ballplayers—was almost kept away from the games due to a reported paper snafu involving the International Olympic Committee. IOC officials claimed that the Cuban sports ministry had not filed the required paperwork confirming participation and therefore was not eligible to attend the event. The Cubans responded that they had not attempted to delay their response but were only seeking clarification of the entry procedure.[11] Fidel would quickly charge that the entire mess had resulted from a plot likely hatched by the Americans. He also met with Cuban athletes just before their departure to São Paulo and warned of further U.S. trickery inspired, he claimed, by the Americans' fears of losing to strong Cuban teams, particularly on the baseball field.[12]

The American baseball squad bound for São Paulo and directed by college coaching legend Archie Allen arrived in Brazil expecting to challenge a Cuban juggernaut that already boasted international amateur prowess, with eight Amateur World Series crowns to its credit. While Americans in general still did not place much emphasis on such international matches, U.S. teams had nonetheless captured medals in all three previous Pan American events (two silvers and a bronze in Chicago in 1959). And while this particular American roster boasted only one future big-leaguer—outfielder Archie Moore from Springfield College, who would enjoy a "cup of coffee" with the New York Yankees the next two summers—Allen's squad nevertheless held high expectations of victory.

Yet, once the baseball matches began in Brazil, the Cubans would dominate the Americans more thoroughly than in any previous encounters. In an opening match, Cuban bats blasted four American pitchers during a 13–1 romp, with outfielder Pedro Chávez stroking a pair of homers and second baseman Urbano González collecting five safeties. Cuban hurler Modesto Verdura went the distance, scattering five harmless base knocks. A rematch to open the second round was much tighter, with Cuba coming out on top, 3–1, and Verdura again tossing a complete game. Having lost a single contest, to Mexico by a 5–2 count, manager Gilberto Torres's veteran Cuban squad clinched first place in the double round-robin affair with a final 6–4 nail-biter against Venezuela. The Americans claimed the silver medal despite losing three times. The strong Cuban outfit boasted virtually the same lineup that had struggled in Jamaica a year earlier but had now coalesced behind the strong pitching of Verdura, Manuel Alarcón (the tournament MVP), and Aquino Abreu (the author of back-to-back no-hitters in Cuban League play several years later). The trio of hurlers each won a pair of games in São Paulo, and Cuban hitters, paced by Chávez, González, and Miguel Cuevas, topped every individual offensive category but one.

The pair of one-sided Cuban wins demonstrated the renewed strength of the revamped Cuban system, but it also exposed their new baseball to plenty of criticism from the American camp. There was, of course, now an expected dispute resulting from the two nations' different views of what constituted amateurism in the sport. The American coaches charged that the Cubans were indeed actually professionals: They were not only older, but also simply too good to be rank amateurs like the American collegians and armed services recruits. This argument was based mainly on the fact that the Cubans were drawing players from their new National Series league, which the Americans saw as amateur in name only since the players competed on a full-time basis and, in many cases, were older and more experienced than American collegians. These charges echoed those leveled earlier at the Soviet Union and East Germany concerning the athletes those countries were sending to Olympic competitions, for example, the Summer Games in Melbourne in 1956, and in Rome in 1960, where the Soviets dominated the gold medal counts. Not displaying the best of sportsmanship but fueled by their anger about what they took as politically tinged Cuban victories, the U.S. squad refused to attend the final ceremonies or accept their silver medals.

Unable to win on the field in Brazil, U.S. forces took the battle to the diplomatic front. Since the upcoming 1965 Amateur World Series was to be staged in Colombia—home to a right-wing government—and was not controlled by the IOC, U.S. officials again pressed the issue of banning the Cubans from the next occasion for a baseball square off. The Colombian military government, which had severed diplomatic ties with the Cubans four years earlier and was also propped up by U.S. military aid, was only too happy to go along with American wishes and simply refused to issue the necessary visas to the Cuban delegation. The Cubans were therefore forced to sit on the sidelines, unable to defend their 1961 crown, while the host Colombians won gold after defeating Mexico two straight in a best-of-three championship round. Cuban native Tony Pacheco, a scout with the Houston Astros, floated the idea of forming a "Free Cuba" exile team for the games, but that politically charged plan received little support.[13] While Cuba could not defend its title or continue the international dominance established two years earlier in Brazil, ironically the Americans also stayed home, perhaps in part due to their still-resonating anger concerning the embarrassing Pan American Games drubbings in São Paulo.

Further politically inspired troubles arose for the Cubans the following year, with the Central American Games, slated to be held in San Juan. Although the Americans were not a member of this confederation and never participated in the Central American Games or Caribbean Games, nonetheless since the event was scheduled for Puerto Rico, the U.S. State Department launched yet another effort to deny visas and keep the Cubans on the sidelines. For both sides, it was now clearly as much about political triumphs as it was about ballpark victories. Fidel and the Cubans again protested that this was an American-led "sports quarantine" and therefore part of a clear counterrevolutionary plot underwritten in Washington. It could now be argued that Castro's island was experiencing not only a disruptive U.S. economic blockade, but also a parallel sports embargo aimed at striking down any possible Cuban sports-related (and especially baseball-related) propaganda victories that could not be countered by less-talented American amateur squads on the playing field.

Cuba's only hope was to appeal to Avery Brundage and the IOC. The latter group and its chairman had consistently maintained the view that sports should remain free of politics, and Brundage had even lobbied with the International Baseball Federation (IBAF) on Cuba's behalf of the eve of the Amateur World Series in Colombia but without any success in impacting an event over which the Brundage committee did not have any say. But since the IOC technically did control both the Central American Games and the Pan American Games (these were Olympic-style events and not IBAF baseball tournaments), the effort was successful this time around. The State Department caved following an IOC threat to move the games from San Juan to another locale, perhaps even Havana. But the route to San Juan was still not an easy one for the Cuban delegation, even once visa issues were resolved. The Cuban team had to travel to Puerto Rico on a refitted cargo ship (the *Cerro Pelado*) since the United States had denied permission to fly directly from Havana to San Juan. Being forced to obtain entry visas by way of Jamaica caused further delays. And finally, the Cuban freighter carrying the Cuban athletes was held in the San Juan harbor by immigration officials long enough to miss the Opening Ceremonies.

There were also concerns about violence from a large Cuban exile community residing in Puerto Rico and perhaps totaling as many as 25,000. Some violence would indeed mar the baseball games when Cuban exiles tossed stones at Cuban players from the grandstands. Moreover, there was a small-scale riot at a basketball match when fans from the local exile community tried to pull down a Cuban flag hung in the arena. On the ball field itself, a series of dramatic close games featured Aquino Abreu's opening day win over Puerto Rico, a heart-breaking loss to Venezuela when a lone run scored on pitcher Gaspar Pérez's own fielding error, and a dramatic 1–0 blanking of the Dominicans keyed by Miguel Cuevas's clutch late-inning double. Rigoberto Betancourt, Cuba's star hurler of these games, would eventually become a celebrated defector a full third of a century later when he abandoned the Cuban delegation in Baltimore during the May 1999 exhibition match with the American League Orioles.[14]

The Americans would finally thwart the Cubans on the field in Winnipeg, Canada, in August 1967. In a breakout year for U.S. amateur baseball interests, the Americans captured their lone Pan American Games title by defeating the defending-champion Cubans in the first and third games of a showdown final series. The only two American losses in the preliminaries also came at the hands of the Cubans, meaning that the defending champs actually won the overall series three games to two. High drama marked the final contest when rain showers delayed the top of the ninth frame in a 1–1 tie, setting the stage for a clutch game-winning single by George Greer stroked off Cuban ace Manuel Alarcón (who was pitching on a single day's rest). For the first time, Team USA was the Pan American titleholder, but it would also be the last time, as during the next three decades and nine tournaments the Cubans would come home winners each and every time. This domination by the islanders was not halted until 2011 and 2015, with Canada defeating the Americans in the finals of both most recent tournaments and the now-weakened Cubans salvaging only a bronze medal on both occasions.

But the tide had not exactly shifted. Cuba gained revenge two years later in Santo Domingo during the 17th renewal of the Amateur World Series. Once again played with considerable political tension due to strong anti-American feeling spawned by a U.S. military invasion of the Dominican Republic four years earlier, the 1969 IBAF World Cup series was a landmark event for postrevolution Cuban baseball. It came on the heels of the 1965 banishment in Colombia and the unexpected 1967 setback in Winnipeg, while the United States itself was fielding a team in this event for the first time since their debacle of 1942. Both teams moved undefeated through the 11-team field and squared off in a spirited gold medal showdown. Gaspar Pérez was the hero of that finale, pitching brilliantly in relief, driving home a crucial tying run, and also scoring the eventual winning tally. The 2–1 finale was witnessed by 20,000 mostly pro-Cuban spectators, a third of whom were reported to be armed soldiers and military police on hand to control potential anti-American hostilities.

The 1970s and 1980s would witness both the growth of Cuba's domestic league and a true heyday for the Cuban baseballers on the international scene. It would also remain a shadowy period for those in North America who might have harbored any interest in events surrounding the Cuban pastime. There were 10 more Amateur World Series crowns captured, first in Cartagena in 1970—including a pair of thrilling pitching duels between Cuban ace José Antonio Huelga and future American big-leaguer Burt Hooten—and again in 1971, 1972, 1973, 1976, 1978, 1980, 1984, 1986, and 1988.[15] The two-decade streak ran the uninterrupted string of Cuban championships in that event to a total of 14, excluding the two sessions the Cubans failed to attend in Colombia in 1965 (when banned) and Korea in 1982 (while protesting a South Korean boycott of the 1980 Moscow Summer Olympics). During that stretch, there were 114 individual game wins in the 121 contests played, five undefeated World Cup tournament finishes, and a perfect 5–0 mark in head-to-head games with Team USA. The Americans, with minimal interest in international play, entered the IBAF championship series only five times during those two decades, including the 1982 Seoul Games, boycotted by the Cubans. The growing string of Cuban victories would go virtually unnoticed by a North American press still married to the notion that baseball began and ended with the professionals performing on the North American continent. But for fans back home in Castro's island empire, a dynasty was blooming.

Perhaps the biggest loss of these decades was the one suffered by Stateside baseball fans due to a continued shroud of mystery thrown over the island that obscured a full generation of great Cuban stars. I devote an entire chapter ("The World's Best Unknown Ballplayers") of my own 2007 volume, *A History of Cuban Baseball, 1864–2006*,[16] to portraits of such island greats as Omar Linares, Orestes Kindelán, Antonio Pacheco, Agustín Marquetti, Antonio Muñoz, Wilfredo Sánchez, Pedro Luis Lazo, Norge Luis Vera, Jorge Luis Valdés, Omar Ajete, and at least a dozen more Cuban League stalwarts who remained invisible to a baseball press and fan population residing outside their island home. There were a mere handful of scattered reports published by American journalists afforded the rare opportunity to catch even a brief glimpse of Cuba's "alternate baseball universe" and send back "battle-field" reports marked by as much awe and hyperbole as genuine appreciation.

In a dozen-page 1977 spread carried by *Sports Illustrated*, replete with several dozen atmosphere-capturing photographs, reporter Ron Fimrite would paint an intriguing portrait of a colorful island baseball scene featuring novel local customs, blaring grandstand salsa bands, aluminum bats, little visible electronic ballpark technology, arduous team road trips, and starkly primitive, if highly fan-friendly, ballparks. He also discusses a wealth of never-before-heard-of local heroes the likes of Miguel Cuevas (the "Cuban Joe DiMaggio"); Lourdes Gourriel (father of current Astros star Yulieski Gourriel and himself a substantial talent who, if uncovered Stateside, "would have big-league scouts weeping tears of gratitude in backwater Holiday Inns"); and Antonio Muñoz (an oversized slugging first sacker who could be only described as a "left-handed Tony Perez").[17]

A decade later, in his book *How Life Imitates the World Series*, *Washington Post* journalist Thomas Boswell drew on his own late 1980s visit to the same Cuban park in Pinar del Río that had provided the setting for much of Fimrite's earlier intriguing portrait. In a chapter cleverly entitled "How Baseball Helps the Harvest or What the Bay of Pigs Did to the Bigs," Boswell laments the isolation of the Cuban sport, underscores the loss of Cuban talent (which might have been thrilling fans on American shores), and speculates (in contrast to later American commentators obsessed with the sports "politicization" under the Castro regime) that "baseball may be the only facet of Cuban life that comes close to transcending politics."[18]

Periodically, at least by the late 1980s, Cuban stars like Linares, Kindelán, and company would finally make their presence felt, however briefly, in the outside baseball world, even on American turf. The latter occasions came with a barely noticed "Friendly Series" staged for much of the late 1980s and early 1990s in Millington, Tennessee, and more noteworthy gold medal triumphs, first at the 1987 Indianapolis Pan American Games against a touted American squad (featuring future MLB pitchers Jim Abbott, Greg Olsen, and Chris Carpenter), and a decade later at the 1996 Atlanta Summer Olympics (this time at the expense of the world's other international baseball superpower, Japan).

The latter two events in Indianapolis and Atlanta provided bookends for Cuba's greatest stretch of unrivaled dominance on the international scene. The Indianapolis games found the Cubans losing their first individual match in a Pan American venue since their surprise 1967 defeat at the hands of the Americans. In four subsequent renewals, they had run up a streak of 33-straight unblemished games and then won four more times in Indianapolis before being sunk again by the Americans in a preliminary round shootout on the strength of a Ty Griffin homer. In the rematch for the gold medal, a late rally against overworked U.S. reliever Chris Carpenter would not only continue Cuba's championship string, but also launch another even more impressive undefeated individual-game streak that would play out for more than a full decade. The Cubans (159–0 in that remarkable stretch) would not lose another single contest in a top-level international tournament event until finally being upended by Japan in the finale of the 1997 Intercontinental Cup tournament in Barcelona.

If the 1987 Indianapolis games launched the greatest era for Cuba's national team juggernaut, they also served as the springboard for perhaps the greatest individual island star of that or any other era. Omar Linares burst onto the scene two months before his 18th birthday at the 1985 Edmonton Intercontinental Cup matches. While still a teenager he continued his meteoric climb in Indianapolis with an eye-popping .520 batting mark to outstrip a field of impressive tournament sluggers that included potent future big-leaguers Ty Griffin, Ed Sprague, and Tino Martinez. By the time of the Atlanta Olympics, where he slugged three homers in the gold medal finale against Japan, Linares was acknowledged far and wide as the greatest third baseman anywhere in the world outside the major leagues.

Throughout Linares's 20-year active career, ending in a final undistinguished two-season stint in the Japanese Central League with the Chunichi Dragons, occasional stories circulated in the North American press about astronomical offers for his services from MLB and Japanese professional teams. One never-verified rumor had the New York Yankees offering the Cuban government $40 million for his services; another rumor involved $100 million pledged by the Toronto Blue Jays on the heels of the Atlanta Olympics in a package deal including teammate and all-time Cuban home run king Orestes Kindelán. But whatever the veracity of these alleged offers, "El Niño" Linares remained fiercely loyal to his homeland and consequently became the number-one "poster boy" for Fidel's communist baseball machinery. He repeatedly expressed his strong preference for the love of millions of Cuban fans over the lucre of millions of North American big-league dollars.

⁕ ⁕ ⁕

A new era of international baseball competition was launched in Winnipeg, Canada, in the late summer of the century's final year. The August 1999 Pan American Games would, for the first time, serve as the qualifying event to select two Western Hemisphere entrants for the upcoming 2000 Olympic Games baseball tournament on tap for Sydney, Australia, the following summer. The Winnipeg games, held in pristine, new Golden Eye Stadium, would also offer one of the best-played and hardest-fought international tournaments on record, in large part thanks to the fact that it was also the first such event in which teams—at least with the exception of Cuba—drew their rosters from AAA and AA minor-league players affiliated with Organized Baseball. Also, for the first time in more than two decades, wooden bats were being reintroduced in international tournament matches.

It had long been rumored that Fidel micromanaged Cuban teams every bit as carefully as he micromanaged the smallest details of his country's economy and politics, that he ordered starting lineups and pitching selections during important tournaments, that he even had veto power in selecting rosters for those events, and that he and not the INDER baseball commissioners hired and fired national team managers. These circulating reports might well have been apocryphal and yet might also have contained at least some grain of truth. Fidel obviously maintained a direct hand in most, if not all, crucial policy decisions, and baseball was never an insignificant matter. Nonetheless, it would be at the 1999 Winnipeg tournament that this author would experience firsthand the apparent degree to which Cuba's number-one fan actually maintained tabs on the national baseball team during international events, where Cuban pride was squarely on the line.

The Winnipeg games were the first international outing for Cuba's elite national team that I personally covered as a credentialed journalist. As I stood in front of the Cuban dugout during pregame warmups before the gold medal finale with Team USA, greeting players I already knew at least casually from several previous island visits and also offering best wishes for success to baseball commissioner Carlitos Rodríguez, the top INDER boss was suddenly distracted by his ringing cell phone. When he answered, his muted response of, "*Sí, Comandante*" revealed beyond any doubt the identity of the voice on the other end of the cyber connection.

Rodríguez politely excused himself and retreated to the privacy of the dugout, well out of my hearing range. I never knew the content of that brief conversation—was Fidel merely wishing the team luck, was he checking on preparedness, was he himself filling out the lineup card? All pure speculation, of course, as it might have been simply an expression of wishes for success similar to my own. But this was my one clear confirmation that the iconic Cuban leader was most definitely in direct contact with the Cuban bench only moments before one of the team's most high-profile international matches.

Winnipeg produced a dramatic victory and also something of a final hurrah for the Cubans on the doorstep of a new century. The team, managed for the first time by 1970s-era all-star infielder Alfonso Urquiola, would struggle in the early going, handicapped by the enhanced level of professional opposition and perhaps also by the transfer to wooden bats; after beating the Mexicans and Brazilians, as expected, the islanders were soundly dispatched by both the Americans (10–5) and the host Canadians (8–1) in elimination-round matches and suddenly seemed on the verge of blowing any chance of defending their Olympic crown in Sydney. But a stellar pitching performance by José Contreras lifted the struggling team past the Dominicans in the quarterfinals.

A tense and all-important semifinal Olympic qualifier with Canada was marred by an on-field disruption in the final frame—ironically orchestrated by the same anti-Castro protester who had stormed the field in Baltimore several months earlier. But Cuba survived the ill-timed political demonstration and a late Canadian rally when reliever Pedro Luis Lazo slammed the door on the host team during that bizarre and tense ninth inning. By contrast, the finals, matching the two Olympic qualifiers, was a one-sided affair thanks to Orestes Kindelán (awaking from a tournament-long slump with two round-trippers) and José Contreras (again dominating while starting on only two days rest). The result was a 5–1 Cuban victory over an American team featuring future big-leaguers Lance Berkman, Milton Bradley, Adam Kennedy, Matt LeCroy, Brad Penny, Dave Roberts, and J. C. Romero.

The 1999 Winnipeg tournament also proved something of a last hurrah for star sluggers Omar Linares (Cuba's career batting leader) and Orestes Kindelán (the island's all-time home run and RBI king), who were both in the final stages of remarkable careers stretching from the mid-1980s to the first years of the new millennium. In turn, it showcased new stellar prospects in Pinar del Río teammates Contreras and Lazo, the former eventually to prove Cuba's most effective international starter and the latter destined to become Cuba's greatest bullpen closer in tournament play. Contreras would ring up a remarkable, unblemished 13–0 international won–lost record before his 2002 defection; Lazo would play out his entire career in Cuba and emerge as one of the heroes of the remarkable stretch run of the 2006 World Baseball Classic.

The event also featured a backdrop of constant defection threats due to the presence of aggressive anti-Castro player agent Joe Cubas and numerous other talent bird dogs hungry for expected boatloads of Cuban stars trying to jump ship. At the top of the list of potential prize recruits was flame-throwing 19-year-old pitching star Maels Rodríguez. But Rodríguez remained in the Cuban camp and closed out the gold medal game with the Americans. The lone player loss was 21-year-old Pinar del Río prospect (and future big-league closer) Danys Baez, a little-used last man in the Cuban pitching rotation.[19]

The ultimate prize garnered by victory in Winnipeg was a chance to defend the valued Olympic title won first in Barcelona and then later impressively protected in Atlanta. After two Olympic Games outings, the Cubans still boasted a perfect 18–0 overall record in total games played, and the veteran team, heading to Sydney under well-seasoned manager Servio Borges—veteran of a half-dozen major tournaments at the helm—held every expectation of continuing unvanquished. But the

Sydney Olympics would quickly affirm how much things were changing on the international scene, with the presence of numerous legitimate professionals (including such notable future big-leaguers as Sean Burroughs, Adam Everett, Roy Oswalt, and Ben Sheets) and even a few former major leaguers (Dave Nilsson with host Australia and Pat Borders and Doug Mientkiewicz with Team USA) providing a much more competitive level of opposition. It was a much different world for an international tournament, and if a wake-up call or signal of the shifting landscape was needed, it came in the fourth preliminary-round match.

Having cruised past patsies South Africa and Italy, and nipped South Korea, the defending champs were rudely derailed by the unheralded Dutch; the 4–2 defeat came courtesy of a single-inning uprising against starter Norge Vera and reliever Maels Rodriguez. But Borges's team recovered quickly against the top three challengers and closed out the opening session by cruising past Australia (1–0, via a José Contreres three-hitter), Japan (6–1, behind the solid bullpen efforts of veteran Lázaro Valle and again Maels Rodríguez), and the United States (6–2, with José Ibar striking out 10 in seven innings). A whitewashing of Japan (3–0) in the semis set up the expected finale versus Tommy Lasorda's Team USA.

A disappointing defeat at the hands of the Americans in the finale could be attributed to two unexpected developments, one perhaps avoidable and the other beyond control. Manager Borges had elected to bring Contreras, still sporting an unblemished international record and the indisputable team ace, back for the semifinal clash against the Japanese, observing that you have to win in the semis to have a chance for gold. It was a judgment that would later be roundly second-guessed, since Borges bypassed not only Contreras, but also Ibar, who had handcuffed the Americans a few days earlier. The strategy backfired when starter Pedro Lazo surrendered a homer to Mike Neill in the opening frame, and Ibar and Rodríguez, in immediate relief, also yielded a trio of additional runs in the fifth. But the failures in managing the pitching rotation were, in the end, diminished by the surprising and heroic effort of future Milwaukee Brewers ace Ben Sheets. Sheets completely stymied the Cuban bats, yielding but three harmless hits (two by Linares), striking out five, and never issuing a walk in his brilliant complete-game effort for the Americans.

On the heels of the surprising Sydney setback, Cuba's baseball program was clearly in a transitional phase. In the aftermath of the an equally shocking loss at the Intercontinental Cup matches in Barcelona three years earlier, both the commissioner and national team manager had been summarily replaced. Borges would also once again be relieved of his post as national team skipper, replaced by longtime Santiago headman Higinío Vélez, who would quickly become a fixture in the nation's baseball management over the next two decades. Fading stars were also cast aside to clear room for new and promising prospects. Linares and several of his veteran teammates—Kindelán plus infielders Antonio Pacheco and Germán Mesa—were shipped off to Japan, the former to play two seasons in the Central League with Chunichi and the latter trio to coach and play in that country's Industrial League. It was billed as a reward for the veterans, who could now earn some extra cash at career's end as a belated payment for almost two decades of loyalty.

But the real motivation was to open roster slots and thus forestall any defection thoughts for top prospects like Michel Enríquez, Yulieski Gourriel, Kendrys Morales, and Eduardo Paret, who debuted during the October 2003 World Cup in Havana. It was these newcomers who would contribute heavily to a substantial rebound in Athens during the next Olympic event. But the Athens tournament again underscored how difficult the road was becoming. Newcomers like catcher Ariel Pestano (the Athens tournament batting champion), Alexci Ramírez, and Frederich Cepeda led the way. But in the end, Cuba again won mainly thanks to some highly fortuitous breaks. The most important of the latter was a truly bizarre ending to the title match versus Australia when center fielder Carlos Tabares saved the game in the ninth inning with his brilliant cover-up on a catch of a deep center-field fly ball that actually rebounded off the fence and should have spelled victory for the Aussies.

There were other peaks in the middle of the new millennium's first decade. Cuba successfully maintained its iron grip on the IBAF World Cup title, first with a seventh-straight crown in Taiwan in 2001, and then a shakier win at home in October 2003. The Taiwan triumph was a redemption of sorts since it seemed to be almost a replay of events in Sydney. The gold medal face-off again came against the Americans and again on the heels of a similar strategy of using ace José Contreras, in his last major outing in a national team jersey, for the semifinal clash with Japan. What had failed for manager Borges paid dividends for new skipper Vélez; first Contreras fanned 11 in a tight 3–1 extra-inning affair with Japan, and then surprise closer Vicyohandri Odelín provided the necessary heroics in relief of José Ibar in the 5–3 win against the Americans. Linares, Kindelán, Mesa, and veteran outfielder Luis Ulacia (the hitting star and tournament MVP) also closed out their brilliant international careers with the redemptive victory.

An eighth-straight World Cup crown captured on home soil two years later was hardly the kind of walk in the park the Cubans had long been used to. In fact, the hosts were lucky to reach the finals and avoid major embarrassment on their home field in Latin American Stadium. An epic defeat at the hands of unheralded Brazil in the quarterfinals seemed imminent when the lone Brazilian pitching talent, Kleber Tomita, took a 2–1 lead into the bottom of the ninth; the day and the tournament were both salvaged only when a pair of stellar rookies provided some instant last-minute heroics. Nineteen-year-old Yulieski Gourriel opened the final frame with a booming triple off the right-field foul pole and switch-hitting Kendrys Morales followed with a titanic game-winning homer off the exhausted Brazilian starter. Two nights later, it was yet another high-profile rookie, Frederich Cepeda, who provided the heroics with a pair of late-inning solo homers, clinching the 4–2 gold medal victory against Panama.

If the Cubans were now struggling in the face of a radically leveled playing field, they were not yet entirely diminished by any obvious standard. It fact, they might have been better than ever when it came to raw lineup talent. The remarkable story was how well they fared against the upgraded levels of the opposition. There was yet another world championship won in The Netherlands in the immediate aftermath of the Athens Olympic successes. Again, it was youngsters who paved the way. New shortstop Eduardo Paret led the onslaught until sidelined by injury before the final round, but replacement Juan Carlos Moreno adequately took up the slack in the championship matches with Panama and Korea. And in the end, the pitching hero was another newcomer, Santiago right-hander Dany Betancourt, who shut down the South Koreans in the 3–0 finale. This would be the final World Cup victory, but that was hardly known at the time. The greatest triumphs, in fact, still lay just months around the corner.

The Holland World Cup was played against the background of grow-ing anticipation for a new high-profile event earmarked to replace both the IBAF championships and the Olympic baseball competitions. MLB had announced plans for its own event to be launched in 2005, and played in subsequent post-Olympic years (2009, 2013, etc.). And there was already a brewing controversy surrounding the naming of the new event. The MLB commissioner's office had envisioned branding their tournament the Baseball World Cup, suggesting parallels with the wild-ly popular four-year renewals of international soccer mania staged by FIFA. But the IBAF had beaten them to the punch by earlier copy-righting that label in the world courts.[20] And there was much reason-able skepticism about the hidden goals of MLB when it came to the globalization or promotion of international baseball. As emphasized by Robert Elias in *The Empire Strikes Out* and in my own *Diamonds around the Globe*, the bosses at MLB never seemed to genuinely foster the goal of spreading the game per se, but rather cherished the more pragmatic and self-serving plan of developing markets for their own brand and extending their reach in harvesting on-field talent for their own ballclubs.[21]

The new MLB showcase event was finally penciled in for the spring of 2006, one year later than originally anticipated due to setbacks in the initial planning stage. While the idea might have been promoted as a plan to hold the games in immediate post-Olympic years, the real mo-tive seemed to be the sabotaging of Olympic baseball competition alto-gether. Cuba's participation in what MLB was now calling their World Baseball Classic was also at first very much in doubt. Again, there were State Department efforts to keep the Cubans on the sidelines, but those attempts met stiff opposition, mainly from MLB officials who obviously didn't want politics to sully what they hoped would provide a television bonanza, especially with the reputedly strong Cubans testing their prowess against big-leaguers—a most attractive and marketable story line.

Washington talk of keeping out the Cubans also prompted threat-ened withdrawal of cooperation from IBAF officials who had been brought on board by MLB to promote the new tournament outside U.S. borders. The Cubans in the end were assured a spot in the first MLB "Classic" only after some lengthy political maneuvering to guaran-tee smooth processing of visas for the entire Cuban delegation of ballplayers, press, and team officials.[22] When the games actually began there were still obstacles surrounding a Cuban team presence, the most pressing being strong concerns about possible violence generated by anti-Castro protesters that might erupt in or around San Juan's Hiram Bithorn Stadium, where the Cuban team was scheduled to debut.

Once in the fold, Cuba would prove the major surprise of the tournament—a turn of events even more shocking than the early elimination of an American MLB Dream Team featuring the likes of Derek Jeter, Alex Rodriguez, and Roger Clemens. The Cubans had certain advantages since there were legitimate questions about the readiness and patriotic sentiments of big-leaguers on other team rosters. And, of course, the Cuban team, like the Cuban government, was highly motivated to prove their own baseball was as good as any in the world. But if the Cubans had plenty of motivation, they also had plenty of luck. They escaped an opening extra-inning game with Panama only by a fluke (when a Panamanian batter ducked out of the way of a pitch in the home ninth with the bases loaded that would have forced in the game-winning tally). They survived the expected political protests that marred several of their games, notably a grandstand tussle between Cuban official Germán Mesa and banner-toting anti-Castro protesters. Nonetheless, chances of success still seemed slim after a 12–2 first-round final-game drubbing at the hands of the host Puerto Ricans. That loss might have quickly ended any Cuban pretensions of playing on equal footing with teams from the big time. But in the aftermath of that embarrassing lopsided setback, manager Vélez was ready with what turned out to be a prophetic observation. Heckled by Puerto Rican reporters at the post-game press conference, Vélez stoically reminded assembled press representatives that, "Today we have only lost the battle, and we have certainly not yet lost the war."

A second round in San Juan brought the "amateur" Cubans face-to-face with three powerhouse Caribbean rivals stocked with plenty of all-star big-leaguers. It was a true "Caribbean Series," dwarfing the annual winter-league playoffs of the same name. Play began with an eye-opening 7–2 upset of the talent-rich Venezuelans keyed by consecutive sixth-inning Cepeda and Pestano home runs. There was also a gallant losing effort against the even-stronger Dominicans, which ended with the tying runs stranded on base in the final frame. Next came perhaps the two greatest victories in the more than half-century of Cuba's postrevolution baseball. The first provided revenge against the hometown Borin-quen club in a rain-soaked game that turned on a dramatic late-inning defensive play in which Gourriel's relay from short right field cut down future MLB Hall of Famer Pudge Rodríguez at the plate and blocked a potential tying tally. The dramatic victory not only made a prophet of manager Vélez (who was now winning the war despite the earlier loss of a single battle), but also assured an unthinkable result by sending the Cubans to the finals against the Dominicans, Japanese, and Koreans.

The World Baseball Classic turned the entire Cuban nation into a baseball madhouse. Almost 10 million islanders remained glued to television sets and temporary oversized video screens in public squares to view the second miracle—a 4–2 win against the vaunted Dominicans in the semifinals at San Diego's Petco Park. The postgame press conference that followed brought both praise from the Dominicans (big-league slugger Albert Pujols claimed closer Pedro Lazo owned the most devastating forkball delivery he had ever seen) and yet another diplomatic gem from Higinío Vélez (recall the earlier account of this press conference in chapter 4). A final 10–6 loss to the Japanese was disappointing enough. Yet, having arrived at the finals itself constituted a considerable moral victory in the face of such a disappointing defeat.

The Cubans had proven beyond doubt that they belonged on the same field with top MLB professionals. Fidel would welcome the team home as true conquering heroes, and a massive turnout in Havana witnessed a victory parade stretching from the José Marti airport to the downtown Malecón. It was the largest spectacle of its kind in island history—matching the teeming throngs that had gathered for Fidel's mass-rally speeches decades earlier. The welcoming celebration concluded in the INDER Sports City stadium, where thousands of students and revolutionary "social workers" listened to Fidel salute the ballplayers individually and then launch into a lengthy speech that culminated with a reading from his collection of international press corps clippings praising the team's miraculous performance.

But it was indeed a last hurrah of rather large proportions. Only months after the euphoria related to the Classic performance, the Maximum Leader suffered a literal fall from the scene.[23] It was not the kind of departure anyone had expected after years of unsuccessful CIA and exile plotting to remove the Cuban leader. Within two years, Fidel would formally retire from public life and fully turn over power to his trusted brother Raúl. Although he would survive physically for another full decade, Fidel would no longer be directly controlling the reins of power. And he would also fade from the baseball scene as all but a shadowy spiritual presence. It was a great irony—one of the many that intruded on his career—that Fidel's fall from prominence would coincide so exactly with the final moments of glory for his cherished "revolutionary" baseball team.

The first major baseball setback in the aftermath of Fidel's departure from official power came in the 2007 World Cup in Taipei, where the title was, for the first time, lost to an American squad featuring a dozen big-league stars-in-waiting. A similar bitter defeat occurred at the Beijing Olympics 12 months later. This time victory over South Korea was clearly within grasp—trailing by one in the ninth with the tying and winning runs on the basepaths—but the game ended in exasperation when Yulieski Gourriel bounced into a dream-ending double play. One year down the road, a third blow was struck with another gold medal game meltdown at the World Cup finals in Italy. Once more the Americans won, and again largely because the Cubans seemed to self-destruct in the heat of battle. The usually reliable Pedro Lazo was victimized by a mid-game U.S. rally that turned on a throwing error by second baseman Héctor Olivera. Olivera had been the hero a few days earlier in the victory over Canada, launching the Cubans into the finals.

Cuban baseball prestige was clearly on the slide. An even bigger setback came in the renewal of the World Baseball Classic of March 2009. After a brilliant start in Mexico that included a knockout 10-run rule victory over the hosts, the Cubans could not get out of the second round in San Diego, falling twice to their nemesis from Japan. The twin losses to the defending champion Japanese not only sunk Cuban hopes for a second World Baseball Classic miracle, but also marked the end to one of the sport's most remarkable streaks. For the first time in a half-century, the Cubans did not at least reach the championship game of a major international tournament.

The losses in the final stages of high-profile international events provided a kind of perfect storm scenario surrounding Cuban baseball. Late-round collapses like the pair of gold medal losses to the Americans in the 2007 (Taiwan) and 2009 (Europe) IBAF World Cups, and the defeat at the hands of South Korea in the 2008 Beijing Olympics were difficult to swallow for spoiled Cuban fans who, for almost four decades had rarely witnessed, even in a single individual game, loss in such venues. It was not that the island nation was no longer producing the top-level talent for which it had become renowned. Man-for-man—on offense and in the pitching department—these Cuban teams were equal to or better than any that had preceded them. They were now playing on a very different stage, one filled with top professionals from North America, Asia, and the remainder of the Caribbean. But that was a change most Cubans neither understood nor were willing to accept.

Fidel himself would comment from his bedside in the aftermath of the most shocking setback of all, a second-straight defeat in a single week during the second round of the 2009 World Baseball Classic. The loss in Petco Park to the same Japanese who had ended their miracle run in the finale of the inaugural MLB-sponsored World Baseball Classic marked the Cubans' earliest exit from any top international competition since the September 1959 Pan American Games in Chicago—a tournament played only nine months after Fidel's seizure of power and a little more than a year and a half before his radical overhaul of the Cuban sports machinery.

In his essay entitled "We Are the Ones to Blame," released in English translation by an official government website, the ailing Cuban leader was more philosophical about the setback than most of his baseball-fanatic countrymen.[24] He began with a painful admission: "I doubt any team from the West can defeat Japan and Korea in the group of competitors who will be playing in Los Angeles in the next three days" (those other teams in the finals would be the Americans and the Venezuelans). He praised his athletes for their strong performance ("they competed with great courage, they didn't lose heart, and they aimed for victory right up until the last inning") and saluted INDER officials and coaches who had selected and trained the squad ("the lineup was good and inspired confidence"). But there was also room for criticism seemingly aimed at manager Higinío Vélez and his coaching staff, and in part explaining the charge leveled in the essay's title. In short, "The leadership of the team in San Diego was very poor . . . the old criteria of timeworn methods prevailed, against a capable adversary who constantly innovated." On this last count, the retired supreme leader was fully in tune with the ruling sentiments of 11 million civilian managers (Cuba's rabid fan population) residing in the homeland.

And there was plenty of space as well for excuses and—like so often in the past—the possibilities for envisioning a conspiracy behind the defeat handed to his cherished team. In particular, Fidel found fault with the tournament organizers (read, MLB), who elected to send the top three countries in the most recent IBAF world rankings into the same bracket in Asia—that is, "including Cuba arbitrarily in the Mexico and Asian group despite the fact that we are definitely in the Caribbean." It seemed to be a MLB plan to clear the way for Team USA to reach the final round and thus boost television ratings for an event that had yet to capture the fancy of North American fans.

Moreover, there was an even more obvious conspiracy at work in Fidel's mind: "What was important for the organizers was to eliminate Cuba, a revolutionary country that has heroically resisted and has not been able to be defeated in the battle of ideas. Nevertheless, one day we shall again be a dominant power in that sport." For the Cuban leader it was still about the battle of ideas, even, and most especially, when it came to baseball. It was a renewal of the card Fidel had frequently played in the 1960s and 1970s—that is, the imperialist power always feared losing to Cuban teams inspired by revolutionary spirit; therefore, their one recourse was to make sure the Cubans couldn't play.

Fidel's own waning life, the ebbing health of his fast-fading revolution, the myth of Cuban baseball invulnerability—these were all now collapsing side by side. Ever-increasing ballplayer defections and the resulting fan disillusionment that accompanied those growing losses would fatally combine to spell fast-approaching doom. Despite fielding perhaps its best teams ever on the eve of those mass defections, Cuba again finished a disappointing second in the final IBAF World Cup tournament of 2011, this time bested by an emerging Netherlands team featuring mainly athletes from the Caribbean Dutch Antilles.

At the Panama City finale, a last-inning rally fell painfully short (again with the winning runs stranded on base) in a rain-drenched Rod Carew Stadium. Not having been able to get past the Japanese in round two of the 2009 Classic, the still-potent Cubans suffered an almost identical fate, again at the hands of the Dutch, in the second round of the 2013 World Baseball Classic in Tokyo. Once more it went down to a final fateful inning, this time extra innings, after the Cubans surged ahead late in the contest only to squander their lead when manager

Victor Mesa appeared to mishandle his bullpen substitutions. Cuba was now losing all the hard-fought, crucial games it once so consistently and even almost effortlessly won.

The onetime juggernaut was also now losing much more than individual ballgames. The 2013 World Baseball Classic team boasted arguably the best Cuban starting lineup ever assembled, with adequate, if not dominant, pitching (despite the absence of the often-unhittable Pedro Lazo as the bullpen stopper), unparalleled slick infield defense with the likes of Yulieski Gourriel, Erisbel "Bárbaro" Arruebarruena, and José Miguel Fernández, and a power-packed corps of batsman fronted by Alfredo Despaigne, Gourriel, José Abreu, and Frederich Cepeda. But during the course of the next two-plus years, all but a pair of the starters from that team would abandon the homeland and find their way to the rosters of MLB teams.[25] Fidel's dream of baseball played without material rewards had etched a glorious history and lasted far longer than might ever have been expected.

But with the Maximum Leader fading from the scene the dream had apparently faded as well. For all that, the achievements can never be minimized. As Pettavino and Pye claim in the opening pages of their treatise on contemporary sport in Cuba, "Despite a limited pool of talent and a notorious weakness in certain sports, Cuba has proved itself a sporting powerhouse since the end of the nineteenth century."[26] But if that trend was launched a half-century before the world knew of Fidel Castro, by 1962 the Cuban leader had "pulled the stops on Cuban sports fanaticism" and for decades to follow "presided over unprecedented growth and mastery of a long list of international sports."[27]

Since baseball was entrenched as the national passion, and perhaps equally because it was the proclaimed pastime and pride of the rival great colossus to the north, the diamond sport would inevitably be the primary showcase of the Cuban socialist sports machine. On Fidel's watch, for nearly four decades Cuba never failed on even a single occasion to win each and every major national tournament in the sport, or at the very least reach the championship finals. Despite often weak amateur competition, potent Cuban national teams featured a revolving door of stellar sluggers and pitchers who, when briefly glimpsed outside their homeland, became a magnet for talent-hungry pro scouts and greedy player agents. Between 1987 and 1997, that showcase national team (with many of the same personnel in the lineup year after year) at one point captured 159 consecutive games without a single setback. And when Olympic baseball was finally launched, the Cubans captured the first two titles, contested in Barcelona and Atlanta, during the century's final decade. The record on the field was unrivalled at any level in the sports' almost two-century history. And like the Cuban Revolution itself, the puppeteer behind the scenes pulling the strings was always Fidel Castro.

# Part III


# The Legacy

# THE FICTIONAL PERSONAS OF FIDEL CASTRO

Writing someone else's autobiography can be less complicated than writing one's own. It can even be less fictional. Where nothing is wholly true, nothing need be wholly false.—John Krich, *A Totally Free Man*[1]

**W**hile journeyman big-leaguer Don Hoak's fantasy tale and its related spin-offs never offered much fodder for serious historians, Hoak did most certainly inspire efforts from imaginative spinners of literary fictions who knew a story too good to pass up when they saw it. One such opportunistic author did come close to matching Hoak and his literary interpreter, Myron Cope. The earlier-mentioned J. David Truby would, as late as 1989, fabricate a report concerning the imagined serious efforts of MLB scouts and club owners to pursue Fidel for big-league duties during his college and law school years. It was just the kind of story that would titillate the upscale consumers of a magazine like *Harper's*, the second-oldest continually published journal Stateside and a publication that billed itself as a serious purveyor of literature, politics, culture, finance, and the arts. Never had *Harper's* offered its readers a better piece of fiction.

Truby indeed provides a necessary veneer of plausibility for his yarn, with details of scouting reports claimed to be from a number of named sources. As earlier reported, former New York Giants owner Horace Stoneham and veteran Pittsburgh Caribbean-area scout Howie Haak are his primary and assumed authoritative sources. The details—for example, Haak's quoted recollections of a "big kid who threw a wicked *bleeping* curveball" or Stoneham's reports that Fidel sent a letter to Giants management rejecting an offered $5,000 signing bonus but "never mentioning politics" or "indicating anything revolutionary to us"—seem to have an air of authenticity, but also an air of pure fantasy when one considers the contemporary setting of the purported events.[2] Those reports—like Truby's contention that Alex Pompez told him Fidel deliberated several days with friends, family, and professors before stunning the Giants' front office with his rejection of their lucrative offer—have no verifiable basis.

Why would such reports never have surfaced anywhere else in the vast Castro literature? Why had Stoneham and Haak and Pompez never spoken to anyone else about this "big one that got away" until all three were nearing their death beds in the late 1980s? And if Truby, in truth, had such a remarkable scoop, why did he save it for a mere sidebar story of a single column in a popular culture journal? The only conclusion must be that these impressive details are merely imagined and belong, just like Hoak's fabulous tale, to the realm of pure imaginative fiction.

It is hardly insignificant that Richard Goldstein's *New York Times* obituary for Haak (March 1, 1999) underscores the legendary scout's stature in Latin America, recalls various top prospects he signed for the Pirates, and reports that he looked for pitchers with a good fastball. Yet, he makes no mention of efforts to ink Castro. Thomas Rogers's *New York Times* obit for Stoneham (January 9, 1990) displays the same curious omission. It is a reasonable assumption that if Stoneham had truly missed out on a signing that might have altered the course of world history rather than just the fate of his National League ballclub, that fact might have merited at least a mention. Either these two obit writers put no stock in Truby's report, or perhaps they had not heard of it—itself rather remarkable given the strong claims made in the *Harper's* article about Castro as a sterling prospect.

For their own part, the Cubans themselves—everyday fans as well as media scribes—have never celebrated Castro's presumed prowess in the national sport, even if they were well aware of his numerous appearances displaying his own rabid fandom. There are no stories to be found anywhere among Fidel's Cuban biographers or in the Cuban popular press about serious baseball skills; his biographers on the island never

**BIRTH OF A LEGEND.** Fidel warms up before, July 24, 1959, pitching exhibition, giving birth to the origins of baseball's most outrageous myth. *The Rucker Archive*

even mention the topic of baseball in their portraits of Fidel or accounts of his impact. And English-language biographers or serious Fidel portrayers—Quirk, Lockwood, Szulc, and especially Bourne—do so only in passing and then with evident care to downplay any reports of Fidel's rumored pitching talents.

It is only the Americans who raise the tale and usually American writers more interested in embellishing or perhaps debunking a mythical Fidel rather than conveying seriously researched and corroborated accounts of the Cuban leader's true exploits. Milton Jamail does report in his 2000 book *Full Count: Inside Cuban Baseball* an interview with a native island resident who was coaxed to reminisce about his own connections with a youthful, ball-playing Fidel.[3] During a chance encounter in Havana's Central Park, newspaper peddler Sigfredo Medina informed Jamail that while attending high school in Santiago de Cuba in 1943, he had played ball against Fidel's school, where Castro was a first baseman (and not a pitcher, it should be noted). But for all its charm, the tale is riddled with apparent errors and inconsistencies that should raise numerous red flags.

Fidel, of course, did not attend high school in Santiago, only presecondary classes at the Jesuit Colegio de Dolores; his secondary school was the Jesuit Colegio de Belén in Havana. As mentioned earlier, he did take part in some reported organized games in Oriente Province as a teen, the ones uncovered in news articles by Jonathan Hansen, but these were games with town or semipro clubs and not scholastic teams. Any such inaccuracies aside, Medina's account is perhaps most notable merely for its rarity. I myself was never able to locate even one such parallel report during my own two decades of conversations with fans and journalists throughout the Cuban countryside.

More importantly, when it comes to Jamail's retelling of his chat with the Havana newspaper vendor, the facts turn out to be just as contradictory as any relayed via Hoak's fabricated report. Having just devoted several paragraphs to citing reasons to doubt earlier reminiscence of young Fidel's ball-playing, Jamail somehow misses the historical hiccups in Sigfredo Medina's account. In 1943, Fidel was indeed a student athlete, but at the prestigious Belén private school in Havana, having left Santiago the previous year. Regarding his report that the future rebel leader was a first baseman, Medina explains, "Even though he played first base, Fidel was really a pitcher . . . he had great control . . . he always had great control." To stress his point, Medina draws a comparison with local Industriales star "El Duque" Hernández, who had yet to defect but recently been suspended from league play. Medina embellishes his account by stressing the young Fidel "had a great curveball on the outside corner . . . a low breaking ball that would come in at the knees."[4] This vivid memory, of course, contradicts most other accounts, which suggest that young Fidel could throw a baseball hard yet never displayed any control of his swift deliveries.

It is a curiosity worth noting here that Jamail was accompanied in Havana on that reported 1997 trip by fellow *USA Today* journalist Tim Wendel. One has to wonder if the latter took a clue for the title and theme of his 1999 novel, discussed later in this chapter, from Medina's statements. This is not likely the case since the novel was already in progress as a Johns Hopkins University MFA thesis. But Wendel does report the Medina conversation in the preface to his novel and uses that comment about Fidel's "great curve" as the concluding line of his prefatory "Author's Note" since it provides the perfect segue into his own fictional telling of the Castro pitching legend.

In furthering his own report on Fidel's earliest baseball adventures, Jamail offers an additional intriguing account of a mid-1980s interview with Fidel by Italian journalist Gianni Miná. Asked to explain Cuba's baseball passions, Fidel reportedly remarked that soccer should have been the Cuban game because of inherited Spanish traditions. Baseball only arrived, according to Fidel in this account, as a result of American influence and especially due to the popularity early in the century of the American big leagues. As Jamail points out, this version leaves out the facts of Cuba's true baseball heritage and its links with the early rejection of Spain (with all things Spanish), and with Cuba's nation-building at the turn of the century. Although he dabbled in baseball and many other sports as a youth and as a political leader appreciated and certainly exploited the important cultural status of the sport on the island, this account would suggest that Fidel knew little about—or at the very least ignored—the game's actual history in his homeland. He would tell ABC's Barbara Walters in an earlier celebrated interview that his favorite school subject was always history—but apparently not the history of the national game.

As we have seen, Fidel himself often made light of the popular idea of any youthful pitching prowess whenever the topic was raised by a prominent American journalist. In a 1977 television interview with Barbara Walters, he seemed to find the proposal rather humorous, as he also did in his casual banter with Jim McKay on the eve of the 1991 Pan American Games in Havana. But as with other myths of somewhat larger stature—especially those suggesting his long-hidden prerevolution commitments to Marxist-Leninist philosophy—Fidel would (as Herbert Matthews pointed out when writing in the immediate aftermath of the 1959 rise to power) do much himself to keep the rumors and speculations alive. His exhibitions at league games and neighborhood pickup games throughout the 1960s and early 1970s provided dozens of still-circulating photographs that underscored his role as a pitcher—if not one of remarkable skill, then at least one of considerable enthusiasm.

We have established that Fidel's serious biographers writing in English have paid rather scant attention to baseball connections even if they would occasionally mention the topic in passing. Peter Bourne and Robert Quirk offer the most specific references, although neither devotes attention to more than passing accounts. Although he reports on Fidel's Belén athletic career and mentions the reported Cambria tryout session, the word *baseball* is not found in Bourne's index.[5] Thus, the topic is largely buried for casual researchers. Quirk offers more extensive coverage, and there are 27 specific citations for the sport in his index. Quirk's focus is on not only the stories of Fidel as a schoolboy athlete at Belén, but also several later instances of interviews where Fidel's fandom and knowledge of the game came to the fore during his adult years. He also raises the theory that Fidel's reported aspirations of being a professional player while with the Belén high school team may have had much to do with the celebrity being attached to the handful of Cubans pitching in the big leagues (mainly with Washington) at the time.[6] As Roberto González Echevarría points out, there were too many far more serious topics and issues surrounding Fidel's impactful life or attached to the Cuban Revolution as a landmark event of the twentieth century to allow a seemingly less significant love of sport to enter seriously into the equation.[7]

Perhaps the final word should be given to the comandante himself. In a most useful volume entitled *Fidel Sobre el Deporte* [Fidel on Sports], republished by INDER on the 1980 occasion of the Second Communist Congress and later reissued in several additional reprints, the editors collected for consumption and education of the Cuban public an entire volume of Fidel's various comments on sports and recreation uttered or written during his first two decades as supreme Cuban leader.[8] The volume is arranged by year and contains only direct quotations and a large collection of photos; there is no annotation or explanation of Fidel's statements and only occasional references are provided to the specific speeches from which these passages are lifted. The uncaptioned photos feature either Fidel playing, delivering orations, or mingling with athletes. The earlier 1975 original edition features a larger number of baseball photos subsequently removed from the more compact 1980 reprint.

The prominence of baseball in Fidel's sports references is, in large part, reflected by a simple numerical inventory. Of the 28 photos placed at book's end, only four feature baseball: one of Fidel and Camilo Cienfuegos in uniform at the famed "Barbudos" game, a second of Fidel chatting with a dozen players while donning a jersey of the Oriente club (presumably after a pickup match), a third of Fidel delivering a trophy to honor pitcher José Antonio Huelga as the "Hero of Cartagena" after the 1970 World Cup triumph, and a final frequently reprinted image of a ceremonial season-opening at-bat by the Maximum Leader in his full military garb.

The number of quotations devoted to specific sports and topics is also revealing and can be easily totaled since an index lists each sport or topic and the corresponding numbered passages throughout the text. Baseball, for example, is the subject of 72 passages, tops among individual sports—a not surprising fact. But topics themselves contain the widest range of recreational activities, including for example, chess, sports teachers and trainers, hunting, Young Pioneers camps, sports activities of the enemy imperialists, construction of sports facilities, and so forth. The diversity of topics commented on by Fidel echoes a theme stated specifically in #470—"We can't be only baseball players." Despite the obvious prominence of baseball in Cuban culture, Fidel, and thus INDER officials following his lead, would repeatedly call for wide diversification as the core of a national sports agenda.[9]

But when it comes to Fidel's own commentary on the role of sports—specifically baseball—both in his personal life and his revolutionary agenda, nothing is perhaps more surprising nor more revealing than the response he gave to interviewer Lee Lockwood when asked specifically about his love for athletics.[10] The answer opens with a litany of the sports and recreations he most loved as a youth. Many are outdoor activities, but baseball is avoided. And then the discussion moves to scuba diving and swimming, which clearly were Fidel's favored pastimes. It appears here that baseball took on a much bigger role in his life after he came to power than it had claimed earlier. Fidel's connections to the sport of baseball and his avowed ballpark and sandlot fandom were always quite clearly part of a larger political agenda.

❈ ❈ ❈

Perhaps the single most intriguing, if not mystifying, account of Fidel's baseball connections appears in a volume that is nearly impossible to pigeonhole. Howard Senzel's 1970s cult classic *Baseball and the Cold War* seems, at least at first reading, a puzzling amalgam of novel, memoir, unabashed personal confessional, long-winded polemical essay, and soul-searching autobiography, with a hefty dose of historical reporting thrown in for good measure. A clue to its diverse content and complexities is found on the cover, with a subtitle that has to be one of the longest in modern publishing history: *Being a Soliloquy on the Necessity of Baseball in the Life of a Serious Student of Marx and Hegel from Rochester, New York*. On the surface, the book recounts the author's efforts to come to grips with a significant baseball-related event of his Rochester childhood during the late-1950s. But the true motive and overriding theme behind the work quickly reveals itself as the quest of a post-1960s radical to get to the bottom of a troubling conspiracy theory involving Cold War intrigue and the apparent efforts of a devious American scheme to quash the Castro Communist government through underhanded plots attached to the two countries' shared national pastime.[11]

The complexity of Senzel's odd memoir doesn't end there. As at least one contemporary reviewer saw it, the book is at bottom an "odyssey of the mind in search of an answer" to the perplexing issues surrounding a baseball fanatic's puzzling and lasting attachment to the appeals of the game itself.[12] Reviewer Richard Crepeau suggests that the volume doesn't seem to start out that way for its author but inevitably ends up there. What is the book truly about, Crepeau asks? His answer is that it seems to be mostly about Howard Senzel. But that doesn't tell the full story.

For a reader attuned to U.S.–Cuba Cold War antagonisms, the book is certainly about far more than a single writer's "extraordinary fantasy of baseball détente during the 1975 World Series and beyond."[13] The event implanted in the author's mind and giving rise to his unorthodox book is his memories almost two decades after the fact of the fateful Rochester Red Wings and Havana Sugar Kings International League game, reported on in an earlier chapter of this volume. Senzel was driven by the idea that there were indeed devious hidden conspiracies behind the failures of early efforts at U.S.–Cuba baseball détente and that those conspiracies will somehow provide a key to unraveling the events of that game, which now seem to take on a far different depth of meaning than when Senzel was a baseball-crazy teenager, listening on the radio and reading newspaper accounts in his hometown press.

Stuck in Rochester on an unappreciated visit home during the summer of 1975, and having shed his early childhood passions for baseball, Senzel would exile himself to the Rochester Public Library in an effort to rediscover details of the half-forgotten but now obsessively important moment of his baseball childhood. Somewhere in those cloudy baseball recollections there was a mystery waiting to be uncovered. *Baseball and the Cold War* is divided into three lengthy segments, the first focusing on Senzel's memories of the July 1959 game, which appeared to mark an end to professional baseball in Cuba—the last game played by Rochester in Havana, in which coach Frank Verdi was shot during a late-game revolutionary celebration. The "action" of this section is centered on hours spent in the library researching microfilm records of press coverage of that fateful game. But what also inserts itself is Senzel's personal recollections of the now-distasteful Rochester of his childhood, the issues of being a Jew in contemporary (late 1970s) corporate consumer America, the 1960s radicalism he had adopted and now seemingly lay at the heart of all his current disillusionments, and, most central of all, the meaning and function of baseball in his now-drifting life. Linking his disparate thoughts are those July 1959 events in faraway Havana when Castro came to power as America's great adversary and when American Cold War policy experienced a dark and radical shift of its own.

In part II, Senzel persists in his quest for meaning by taking an introspective odyssey out of the public library and directly pursuing the prominent actors in that crucial historical crossroads moment. He interviews sportswriter George Beahon, who had written on-the-scene accounts of the game for the *Rochester Democrat and Chronicle*, and also the current president of the International League, George Sisler Jr., who had been Red Wings general manager when the Havana drama had unfolded. While those interviews failed to shed much light on the Cold War conspiracies he was tracking, they do seem to provide some surprising clues to his childhood baseball obsession. Baseball is merely a business that spins webs of illusion to attract its needed loyal customers; to participate in this shared illusion is the very definition of play, and that is why children are the most susceptible to baseball obsessions. At the same time, the author also ventures on a personal journey through the forms and shapes baseball took during his boyhood years—memories of his first baseball glove, collecting and flipping bubblegum cards of his heroes, youth-league baseball, baseball board games, and the reading of novels by John Tunis. And finally, he caps his hometown visit by attending a live Bob Dylan concert in the Rochester War Memorial, which uncovers some surprising clues to the power of history and seems to unlock the missing keys to understanding the contrasting decades of the 1960s and 1970s.

The book's final section finds Senzel moving forward with his life but never quite escaping the overtones and residuals of that fateful game in Havana or that fateful childhood baseball obsession. He rediscovers baseball in the summer of 1975, but the season ironically ends with a Cincinnati–Boston World Series containing its own ringing connections to issues of real and imagined U.S.–Cuba baseball détente. There are circulating reports of a potential exhibition game in Havana that might reopen doors with MLB (the reports treated in this book's final chapter). There are also the poignant events surrounding star Boston pitcher Luis Tiant Jr., whose parents finally escape Cuba to witness their son perform at the apogee of his career. And there is Curt Gowdy rhapsodizing about Cuban baseball and taking more shots at the tyranny of Fidel Castro. The Cold War is still alive and well even if the mysteries of its origins have not been decoded. But Senzel's current life can now only raise painful questions about who he is, what constitutes reality, and what may remain of hope for his future. And in the end, there are few, if any, resolving answers to these perplexing dilemmas.

The author does muddy some of the historical waters here. The remembered game of July 1959 was not, in truth, the last one Rochester would play in Havana, nor was it the actual death knell for the island's professional sport. There is no evidence for Fidel trying, as reported by Senzel, to convert Cuba from baseball to soccer. Such conversion efforts would indeed become a reality in Cuba, but only in the first decade of a new millennium after Fidel's fall from power. It was Eisenhower and not Kennedy who suspended the Cuban sugar quota to spike U.S.–Cuba tensions on the eve of the Sugar Kings' demise. Gran Stadium was never renamed Stadium of the Heroic People of Vietnam, however neatly that idea might fit Senzel's Cold War narrative. Ty Cobb and Walter Johnson never did play in the Cuban leagues, and there is a major misconception in the book concerning Cuban baseball's pre–World War II freedom from racism, a claim that might be made about the pro winter circuit but not the island's popular amateur leagues. And there is absolutely no basis for Senzel's tale of Fidel's rebel army capturing a frightened teenaged Luis Tiant Jr. (wearing a baseball mitt) in Sierra Maestra jungles; the young Tiant grew up in the Marianao sector of Havana far from the Sierra Maestra guerrilla action. At times, Senzel dons his guise as novelist and becomes pure fiction weaver. But the author can perhaps be partially excused by the fact that today there is far more known about these then-still-obscure (in 1979) details of seemingly lost Cuban baseball history.

Senzel's book offers precious little insight into the events in Havana that it reports. But as Crepeau suggests in his spot-on review essay, it was at the time a valuable read for anyone thinking deeply about the hold of baseball on our collective youth or the basic tenets of our shared American culture.[14] The book is actually not about Cuba or the Cold War (subjects on which the author did not have an opinion based on much serious knowledge). It is mostly about the personal baseball odyssey of its highly literate author. But unlike so many baseball-focused volumes, its hefty dual values are the author's talents as a crafter of prose and his willingness to think more deeply about the philosophical underpinnings of what for most readers is merely an entertaining sporting spectacle or a diversionary form of popular commercial entertainment.

Senzel never touches on the mythical trappings of Fidel as a lost pitching prospect who might have altered history with a different career choice. But three American novelists of more recent minting have indeed chosen to take that more tantalizing image as their own subject of choice. Writing at the outset of the 1980s, John Krich bit off the hefty challenge of penning a fictional autobiography of the romanticized Cuban leader, a treatment in which baseball plays at least a minor role. Most recently, popular adventure novelist Randy Wayne White sends his crime-solving hero and part-time marine biologist Doc Ford on a mission to the Communist nation to uncover the unresolved myth of Fidel's ball-playing prowess. And most notably, baseball historian and occasional novelist Tim Wendel dives in all the way with a 1999 novel that exploits full bore the legend of a hot baseball prospect eventually turning to make his larger mark in the world of international politics. The three books display their considerable differences in approach, appeal, historical underpinning, and even literary merit. But they all share an obvious common slice of historical exploitation.

☼ ☼ ☼

Despite a virtual mountain of scholarly biographies, for most Americans and even a majority of Cubans, Fidel remains largely a fictional creation, a manufactured product resulting from shoddy journalism, political dogma, and half-baked fantasies. It is hardly a surprise, then, that weavers of commercial fiction would eventually seize on a topic so well-tuned to the reigning public perceptions.

Krich was first on the scene with his 1981 novel *A Totally Free Man*, presented in the guise of Fidel's long-awaited personal memoir. At least to his partial credit, he remains, for the most part, faithful to the known facts about Fidel's life, even if he spins easily the most ambitious efforts at fictionalizing the Castro persona as a living legend. There are elements of Fidel's actual biography here—the raid on the Moncada, the Isle of Pines imprisonment, the exile in Mexico and first meeting with Che, the Sierra Maestra campaign—that get direct play, unlike in the treatments by Wendel and White, where the baseball player image of the comandante takes center stage.[15] Krich has at least studied his subject a bit more thoroughly, or at least been more willing to rely on known biographical detail (however distorted or misconstrued) rather than fantasies already held by his potential readers.

And there is another element to Krich's book that distinguishes it from those by White and Wendel, who would eventually follow him down a similar trail. In the appended acknowledgments to his novel, he pays homage to Alexander Solzhenitsyn's *Lenin in Zurich*, a book and author "whose perspective could not be farther from my own." The richness of Krich's rhetorical prose and his at least occasional bows to the historical record certainly underscore his link to the Russian novelist. And so does both his apparent realization (mirroring Solzhenitsyn's view of Lenin) that the rhetoric of socialism and revolutionary upheaval can be easily usurped by authoritarian fanatics whose main goal seems to be the institutionalizing of their own personal power, plus his desire to paint his subject in the most favorable light. While Fidel is clearly a demon for White and perhaps merely a fascinating historical personage for Wendel, he takes on the shape of an admired hero for Krich.

If the attempt—perhaps motivated in large part by Fidel's own reluctance to ever finish a true autobiography and the acknowledged hunger for such a confessional from both Fidel's many critics and many adoring partisans—is admirable, the effort is, in the end, sadly lacking. The notion of the self-absorbed, immensely self-confident, and egotistical charismatic leader only reluctantly revealing his most introspective personal assessments while hiding behind the privacy of a nonresponsive tape recorder strikes an odd chord. The degree of self-knowledge a fictional Fidel reveals in these pages seems to undercut all plausibility. And despite the occasional brilliance of Krich's prose—ironically perfectly attuned to Castro's oratorical brilliance—the polished and shining Fidel Castro that he creates, one capable of such perfect balance in which his flaws are cancelled out by his most prominent virtues, offers a treatment that can only be called shallow and distressingly glib. As an anonymous *Kirkus Review* commentator best phrased it, the reader "can only be made uneasy by Krich's mythologizing," in which the "good/bad Fidel—never atilt, smoothly fluent, loudly amplified" comes off as Cuba's unlikely Wizard of Oz. [16]

Krich notes at the end of his book that it is far easier to write someone else's autobiography than to pen one's own. In doing so he reveals what he projects as the secrets to success with his own effort. There are known details of Fidel's political and personal life popping up here and there to be sure. But the author has already reminded us of his strategy with his caveat that nothing has to be true in any literal sense; Fidel's actions might be a matter of historical record, but how he views those actions (as projected by the author) can always border on fiction and fantasy, except, of course, for the character portrayal that emerges from the composite of those words and moments of self-reflection. Might we not expect the central character—the book's supposed narrator—to be Fidel Castro in more than name and fanciful reputation? Or is the author of this novel telling his readers in advance that the Fidel Castro represented is little more than a fictional character, that he is a creation only of the author's imagination and thus nothing in these pages should be taken as what it appears to be? That this is not only an "unauthorized" portrait, but also an entirely fictional one? That Krich's Castro is the equivalent of Shakespeare's evil Richard III or Disney's Blackbeard the Pirate in the guise of Captain Jack Sparrow?

Krich has his built-in defense here. There are elements in the work lifted from biographical sources and Fidel's own published comments on his earliest years. Those are too often more the product of popular myth than hard fact. Krich's Fidel says he held three boyhood wishes: "to head a conquering army, to be a lawyer delivering an eloquent summation, and to pitch for the Bronx Bombers in the seventh game of the World Series."[17] There is no record of any of these fantasies in Fidel's actual statements, and, in fact, he rarely discussed his childhood publicly. His own actual words indicate that a lawyer's career was a chance decision during early university days; any baseball fantasies were apparently never what they would later be made out to be. But the biographical elements are not the issue. They are the framework, the skeleton, but not the flesh and bones. What Krich attempts to capture is the supposed voice and popularly conceived attitudes of a self-centered and confident charismatic leader whose power over his adoring masses is the words and ideas that he wields. But it is also true that while Krich entertains, he clearly falls short of any insight into the man himself as he is most often perceived and assessed by his scholarly biographers.

Krich writes a breezy and surprisingly brief portrait (only 170-odd pages) aimed most clearly at popular consumption by North American readers perhaps looking more for confirmation of held beliefs than new insights into the complexities of one of the century's most profound characters. The entire treatment is based mainly on Fidel's presumed reluctance to expose details of his own personal life. He does so only in the guarded privacy of a reel-to-reel tape recorder, fulfilling a reluctant promise made to his recently deceased confident, handler, and perhaps lover, Celia Sánchez. Although Fidel indeed hid his personal life from public view, his willingness to speak openly for days on end in numerous widely published interviews with foreign press visitors like Lockwood, Walters, Mankiewicz, Jones, and others, especially Americans, seems to undercut the literary sleight of hand employed here about Fidel's shyness when it came to personal on-the-record dialogue.

In this last regard, Krich's thin volume falls particularly short when viewed against such more recent work as the detailed autobiographical account Fidel finally, if belatedly, dictated to French university professor and editor Ignacio Ramonet two decades later (between January 2003 and December 2005), and allowed to be published only in the landmark year (2006) when he would reluctantly relinquish the reins of power. In this massive 700-plus-page volume, the Maximum Leader, aware he is nearing life's end, is effusive about not only personal details of his early life and upbringing, but also his five decades of absolute power and control of his nation's destiny. Ramonet's text provides a far more believable version of the introspective Fidel Castro—the genuine Fidel with all his warts and foibles, and not merely a bombastic imaginary voice revealing the author's fictionalized agenda to be in total control. Here, the format is that of an interview, one that stretched for more than 100 hours over two full years, but it is Fidel who does almost all the talking. Perhaps because his French interlocutor had no interest in the subject, questions about any involvement with sports—especially the American and Cuban passion for baseball—are never raised and therefore never addressed.[18]

Another work offered for comparison is Norberto Fuentes's massive 2004 tome entitled *The Autobiography of Fidel Castro*.[19] Again, based by its author on long and intimate association with the Cuban leader and drawing from numerous preserved notes from personal conversations with Fidel, and also relying heavily on CIA and Cuban intelligence reports, the Fuentes volume differs greatly in approach and tone from the effort by Ramonet. Here the biographical account is unquestionably fictional, and the voice is that of Fuentes masterfully recreating Fidel and not Fidel speaking directly for himself. In short, this is a novelistic treatment, but a novel based on in-depth and firsthand knowledge of its subject not possessed or perhaps even desired by the author of *A Totally Free Man*. Krich relied on the notion that if nothing in his novel were actually true then nothing had to be wholly false either—a tricky conundrum at best. Krich, in the end, writes a fable and not an autobiography—his book is dangerously mistitled. Fuentes writes a legitimate, if somewhat negatively biased, biography, if not an actual autobiography, and there the false labeling is far less harmful or misleading.

The backgrounds of the authors reveal the legitimacy of their contributions to Fidel's literary legacy. Krich was a leftist-leaning "fellow traveler" who would later write excellent travel books and articles on his adopted Asia, but also a condescending and sensationalizing observer when it came to his interest in Latin American baseball. In his earlier book entitled *El Béisbol: Travels through the Pan American Pastime*,[20] he reports on his travels throughout Mexico, Puerto Rico, the Dominican Republic, Nicaragua, and Venezuela in search of keys to unlocking the Latino fascination for what is supposedly a native North American sporting creation. The tone is idiosyncratic and patronizing at best, the approach is novelistic, and the stories are often entertaining enough, but at every turn the emphasis is on the warts, follies, absurdities, and contradictions that seem, for Krich, to define the Hispanic baseball passions. He recounts adventures playing with a group of American over-40-league baseball tourists on a peace mission to Nicaragua, searching out lost legends among old-timers in Puerto Rico and the Dominican, and watching a league game in Caracas.

But as one anonymous reviewer astutely remarks, "The author's overwrought and highly personal reportage can most charitably be described as gonzo journalism."[21] The wordsmith here—as in his fictional Fidel autobiography—is seemingly always more interested in the presumed magic of his own flowery lingo than any focus on historical accuracy. The ultimate theme of his odyssey through the backwaters of Latin American baseball is reduced to a view that the Hispanic neighbors who have seemingly coopted our North American national game may soon be coopting our entire North American culture. And that prospect is not painted in the best light.

> They are coming. The bastard children are taking their revenge. The unwanted offspring of all the big-leaguers show up on their daddy's doorsteps, insisting on a fair share of their patrimony. The continental benchwarmers come in to pinch hit for their failing, doddering

idols. The bat boys wield the lumber they once toted submissively. The nightmare of every Texas rancher and DAR daughter and officer of *la migración* has come to fruition as all nightmares must. . . . They arrive covered in cocaine dust from out of the holds of unregistered planes. They squeeze through every pipeline and sewer line and regulation. They outnumber us, and they already know how to make the pivot at second base.[22]

Fuentes is anything but an outsider looking in on a subject for which he has faint knowledge built mainly through pure imagination. He is by heavy contrast a former member of the Cuban revolutionary movement and a onetime devoted Fidelista with deep connections to the leader's tight inner circle. But he would become a liability in the eyes of Castro and his devoted henchmen, and was eventually deemed a dangerous "man who know too much" after he became disillusioned with the 1989 execution of General Arnaldo Ochoa on what appeared to be false charges. He miraculously escaped a death sentence in Havana, took up exile residence in Mexico, and transformed his firsthand experiences into what the book's liner notes tout as a "brilliantly written and ultimately captivating 'autobiography' of Fidel Castro—in the Cuban leader's own outrageous, bombastic voice." Fuentes, like Krich, may well have had his own private, if more personal, literary motives. But as a chronicler of the comandante's life story, he was equipped to offer a far more believable, historically detailed, and ultimately enlightening account. If this work is historical fiction it is historical fiction coated with the thickest veneer of veracity.

*New York Times* reviewer Michiko Kakutani places Fuentes's master-work squarely in the genre he calls the Latin American strongman novel, which also includes Mario Vargas Llosa's *Feast of the Goat* (a depiction of Rafael Trujillo's rule in the Dominican Republic) and Gabriel García Marquez's *Autumn of the Patriarch* (a magical realism treatment of larger-than-life fictional tyrants).[23] The Fidel Fuentes portrays is "narcissistically long-winded, self-mythologizing, a Nietzschean operator believing in the force of his own will" and thus a proper reflection of his fictional counterpart.[24] Kakutani also raises the important question of the degree to which Fuentes channels his former comrade—the degree to which his treatment reflects his hatred of Castro versus the degree to which it reflects his firsthand knowledge of the inner workings of the revolution. On that issue the results seem to be mixed, and to a large extent the portrait is one of a figure Fuentes sees as "the great architect of destruction and the great provider of death."[25]

But in the end, the contrast between Fuentes's fictional autobiography and the one penned much earlier and with much less inside knowledge and insight is quite stark. Krich set out to spin an engaging tale that would tantalize his readers' own deeply held fantasies about Fidel and, in the process, turns his subject into a heroic figure of a leftist revolution that fits his own deep-rooted sympathies. While personally biased in a different direction, Fuentes (in the words of reviewer Kakutani) uses the format of fake autobiography "to try to spin history in the shape of his own beliefs, to create a facsimile of a Fidel who ratifies the author's own hard-won suspicions of the Cuban strongman."[26] If Fuentes likely does not necessarily have the final word on the truth concerning Fidel Castro, at least (unlike Krich) he aims his sights in that direction.

✿ ✿ ✿

The most recent weaver of Cuba adventure tales portraying Fidel and his empire for American consumption is popular crime novelist Randy Wayne White, author of the *New York Times* best-selling list of Doc (Marion) Ford adventure-crime novels. Doc Ford, a former navy seal and current CIA-operative-turned-charter-fishing-boat-pilot (imitating White's own profession before novel writing) and occasional private investigator, is a Hemingwayesque adventurer whose 20-odd fictional journeys take him throughout southern Florida and the Florida Keys, with occasional side trips into the Straits of Florida and the forbidden realm of Fidel Castro's island nation of Communist Cuba. The action is always fast and furious—sometimes too much so for some readers to judge by many published reviews—the plots are often painfully similar, and the focus is always on the daring adventures of White's alter ego, who repeatedly breaks away from his current cover profession of marine biologist to solve the latest criminal intrigue in the fashion of Travis McGee, the fictional hero of White's own literary role model, Florida crime writer John D. MacDonald.

The 1980 Mariel Boatlift provides the inventive spark for White's first Cuba-based work, which initially draws on historical events (both the island's history and the author's own) but quickly moves to a world of pure fantasy.[27] In what is supposedly perceived as a stunning move, Cuban dictator Fidel Castro has allowed thousands of disenchanted Cubans to board all manner of seagoing vessels to depart from the island for the United States and much-desired exile. But Castro is reportedly using the policy to export his worst criminals, undesirables, and political enemies to Miami, and White's hero, Dusky MacMorgan, has to enter the picture and discover the motives of the dastardly plot. The book—written using the pseudonym Randy Striker, as did several of White's earliest efforts—is heavily based presumably on the author's own involvement in the Mariel Boatlift as a Florida-based charter boat pilot.

The plot line here is easy to summarize. MacMorgan's CIA companion, Norm Fizer, still with the agency, calls on his former trusted and now-retired agent friend to help solve the mystery of three missing CIA agents earlier sent to Cuban shores to unravel the Mariel situation; had they been kidnapped or killed, or perhaps defected to the Cuban side? MacMorgan reluctantly takes on the task and sets sail for the island with another agent, who turns out to be a sultry female named Androsa Santarun. She is to pose as his Cuban American client heading to Mariel to rescue her father as one of the fleeing refugees. A series of action-packed adventures bring the pair to Mariel harbor, where the rescue mission concludes with several surprising plot twists and discoveries. Androsa is captured and held prisoner by a treacherous Cuban officer, General Halcón; Fidel himself shows up at the Mariel military installation where she is being held. MacMorgan attempts a rescue by setting off a series of explosions that lead the Cuban soldiers guarding their supreme leader to assume Fidel is under military siege; the hero has a chance to assassinate Castro with his crossbow through an open window, where the hated dictator is seen conferring with Halcón, but for some reason he himself can't understand he doesn't pull the trigger.

But Androsa, who has escaped her guard at a nearby cabin and stolen his rifle, does fire a fatal bullet, dispatching the general, who MacMorgan now believes was actually her father. The finale comes when the two are reunited in the underbrush and escape in the confusion that follows the fatal gunshot. A final dramatic plot twist comes when Lieutenant Santarun reveals it was Fidel who was his true father, but she also simply could not pull the trigger to end the life of the man who had abandoned her and her mother, and then pursued the personal political ambitions that ruined her country. It is a fantasy tale fit for consumption by anyone who swears by the concocted image of Fidel Castro as Cuba's arch-destroyer.

White himself is no stranger to Cuba, although in his most recent Ford novel he claims not to be an expert on the subject of the island's history or politics. He has been a frequent visitor to the nation, being especially involved in fostering the small but growing Masonic movement in Havana. His website biography claims he helped reintroduce Little League Baseball to Castro's Cuba, a rather incredible claim given that the INDER sports ministry has organized youth competitions in the sport from the earliest years of the revolution. What is clear beyond doubt is that White is no fan of the Castro regime, and his fictional accounts make that painfully obvious. His portraits of the Cuban leader and his image in the exile community, and of Castro family members, suggest a distaste stretching well beyond the obvious advantages of a negative portrayal that would feed the fantasies and thus increase the popularity of his novels among an American readership, especially in his home state of Florida.

One example of White's distaste for the Castros is found in a gratuitous portrait of Fidelito (Fidel Castro Jr.) in his second Cuba-based novel, entitled *North of Havana*, one of the earliest of the Doc Ford sagas. After raising the popular notion of Fidel's promiscuity in the novel's earliest pages, and reprising the presumption of dozens upon dozens of illegitimate offspring, White has a central character remark: "His only legitimate son is a lazy dope. Fidel tried to hide him away by appointing him head of the Cuban Atomic Energy Commission. That's like being appointed head of Ireland's space program."[28] This is a most unfair slander of a talented scientist who held a Moscow doctorate in nuclear physics and authored books on the subject in several languages, including English. But certainly it was music to the ears of everyone who loathed the Cuban regime.

*North of Havana* replays with slight variation the plot device of the earlier Dusty MacMorgan tale. White's hero journeys to Cuba to both solve a puzzle involving international intrigue and at the same time perform a rescue mission. Fidel Castro shows up in person at the end of the tale only again to escape assassination (apparently the author's own ultimate fantasy) by the narrowest of margins, and the hated Cuban leader remains to rule yet another day only because having him liquidated would be too convenient and too radical a departure from the known historical record. But in addition to the presence of the more full-drawn hero, who is now Ford rather than MacMorgan, another new element is introduced in the form of the popular Fidel ballplayer myth. As a baseball fanatic himself, White simply could not write another Cuba novel without exploiting one of the main staples of Cuban Revolutionary lore.

This time Ford is drawn to the communist island to bail out his constant companion, nemesis dropout prophet, and aging flower child, Sighurdhr Tomlinson, who has found himself held hostage by the Cuban government, and his beloved sailboat, *No Más*, impounded after accidently drifting into Cuban territorial waters. Despite himself being haunted by existing Cuban government suspicions of his own earlier involvement in plots against the Cuban leader, Ford nonetheless takes the risk of returning to Havana with female companion Dewey Nye (a sexually ambivalent former tennis pro) only to be deeply involved in a newly developing tangled web of murder, revenge, and assassination. Again, there is also a brief plot-ending face-off between Fidel and the novel's hero, who once more (like MacMorgan) bypasses an opportunity to gun down the despised revolutionary icon.

A backdrop to the current story becomes an important anchor for the unfolding plot. Before departing for Castroland with $10,000 cash to ransom Tomlinson, Ford contacts his old acquaintance, General Juan Rivera, prime minister of the banana republic of Masagua, a thinly disguised Hugo Chávez figure who fancies himself a talented baseball pitcher and abandoned his imagined big-league future for the attractions of political power. As a Central American military strongman, Rivera may have invaluable connections in Havana to bail out Ford if things turn sour. Ford reveals that years earlier (in 1973), he had visited the island, posing as a bullpen catcher for the American team at the Havana amateur world series (but actually working on a CIA covert operation), and found himself catching Fidel Castro in an exhibition match inaugurating the tournament. It is, unquestionably, a theme foreshadowing a similar role for Tim Wendel's hero in the novel *Castro's Curveball*, which would follow in two years. But unlike Wendel's former catcher, Billy Burke, White's catcher-turned-spy is quick to acknowledge that the dictator, "once drafted by the New York Giants," was hardly a prospect and that the entire tale of his pitching prowess was only a lie.

The bulk of the story involves the subsequent Havana kidnapping of both Ford and his female companion by a group of counterrevolutionaries known as Ocho-A. The name is, of course, based on a historical figure—General Arnaldo Ochoa, executed as a traitor by the Castro regime in the late 1980s—who here becomes a code word for the secret anti-Castro forces. Also soon revealed is that Tomlinson has not told Ford the entire story about his entanglement in Cuba, where he has apparently become involved in a complex Castro assassination plot masterminded by a drug-dealing Santeria priest who may also be another of Fidel's illegitimate offspring. The Santeria priest—Taino—has shielded his evil designs by becoming Fidel's confidant and spiritual advisor while, unbeknownst to the Maximum Leader, actually working with the Ocho-A group. Ford's lady friend Nye and his pal Tomlinson are eventually captured because it is believed they can lead the priest to a talisman that Fidel is desperately seeking—a medallion worn by Columbus believed buried in a hidden spot. Central to this plotting is a portrait of Fidel that hardly accords with any known facts but which has been designed to feed the cherished fantasies of his most ardent detractors in the exile community. Fidel is weak and fear-ridden, and has turned to Santeria (the island's popular Afro-Cuban religion) in his desperate delusion that only the Afro-Cuban gods and the Columbus talisman can save his life and floundering hold on power.

Fidel makes his actual appearance in the final chapters as the frenetic action draws to a rapid close. The Castro portrait, drawn ever so briefly but with a caustic eye, is one of a former revolutionary idol now isolated, deprived of his intellect, if not his senses, and desperately seeking to survive. Here, Fidel is easily manipulated by the story's hero, who temporarily kidnaps him, foils the assassination, and guns down Taino, but after firing three warning shots close to the comandante's ear, in the end permits Castro to escape to his nearby yacht. Here again, as in the early Striker novel, the American hero bypasses his chance for an easy assassination of the Cuban leader, but not before they exchange a pair of pointed verbal barbs—"You were a shitty catcher!" Fidel screams at Ford; "Well you're a shitty president and a shittier excuse for a pitcher," Ford retorts, before firing a final warning shot inches from the Cuban leader's ear.

It is in the most recent Doc Ford novel, *Cuba Straits* (2015), that the Fidel baseball myth finally takes center strange as a vital plot element. But White's treatment here differs considerably from Wendel's in *Castro's Curveball* or the treatments of others who have exploited the worn-out fiction. His intention is to neither dominate the plot of his intricately woven tale with that single fictional element alone nor advance the myth as it has been handed down through the years. Rather, his aim is to dismiss the legend altogether, but here with a special twist that assigns unsubstantiated motives for its origins to the current Cuban regime.

Bringing his tale up to date with current themes touching upon Cuba, the plot is launched on the strength of recent increased efforts to smuggle potentially valuable baseball talent off Castro's island. Ford's old friend and former Central American dictator, himself now in exile, has gone into the lucrative undercover business of smuggling Cuban ballplayers to the United States for windfall profits. Juan Rivera (the same General Rivera who cameos in *North of Havana* as a Hugo Chávez clone) is here a recast Central American version of Miami-based ballplayer agent Joe Cubas (whose story appears in the following chapter).

The former Masagua strongman has shown up on Ford's doorstep in Sanibel with his latest haul in tow—a weather-beaten 40-year-old Cuban shortstop named Figueroa Casanova. But Rivera also has another scheme going that involves HPCs ("high-profile collectibles") and has managed to obtain a stash of personal letters written by Fidel and Raúl between 1953 and 1963, to a previously unrevealed shared mistress. The backstory has now stretched beyond mere financial gain, since Rivera has stumbled onto a more dangerous smuggling activity that now seemingly endangers his life. When "Figgy" Casanova and the briefcase Rivera has placed in his care both disappear, and when Russian agents show up in pursuit of the mysterious briefcase and its hot contents (the Castro letters), the plot takes a turn for the worse.

Ford becomes involved in the intriguing and convoluted adventure when both the shortstop and the pilfered Castro love letters fall into limbo and he learns that his old sidekick, Tomlinson, has located them both and decided on his own to return the hot properties to their island of origin. Hot on the trail of Casanova, the letters, and Tomlinson— which also lead him into Cuba—Ford quickly becomes convinced the letters contain a dark secret that powerful forces in Cuba cannot allow to become public. As the plot thickens, the missing ballplayer—believed to be insane—turns out to be a close relative (the unacknowledged grandson) of the now-aged and dying former Castro mistress, who herself appears as a thinly disguised fictional version of actual early Fidel paramour Naty Revuelta.

There are enough subplots to keep the tale spinning to its blood-and-gore-spattered conclusion. The archvillain Russian spy also pursuing the missing letters is obsessed as well with recovering a trio of prized Harley-Davidson motorcycles buried somewhere near Havana by three American ballplayers the day Fidel took power. Ford is aided by a Cuban peasant (Marta Estéban) and her two young daughters residing it the same village that hides Casanova, his aged grandmother, and the prized motorcycles, as well as a metal film canister in Casanova's possession containing visible proof of Fidel's inept youthful softball performances. The latter is the final Castro putdown, of course, since it establishes that Fidel was lacking talent at not only the manly sport of baseball, but also the lesser woman's sport of softball. Further complications arise with the appearance of a second archvillain in the form of a crazed Santero priest named Vernum Quick, who preys on teenage village girls, has blamed his misdeeds and several slaughters on Casanova, attempts the murder of Marta and her daughters, and in the end is himself brutally castrated by Casanova's grandmother in her last revengeful act before a mysterious and unexplained death.

The gruesomely outlandish tale ultimately climaxes when the elderly Naty figure conveniently dies peacefully in the hideaway built for her as protection during the 1962 Missile Crisis, and the secret of the letters is finally revealed. That secret (confirmed by the film, which Casanova burns) turns out to be evidence that Fidel was not, in fact, a serious ballplayer, but rather a knockabout softball amateur of shamefully limited skill. This is itself presumably an embarrassing revelation inconsistent with a powerful legend fostered by the Cuban authorities to enhance their vaunted leader. White's spin is that the ball-playing myth is indeed a fiction, but one of Cuban rather than North American invention. He is thus just as far off the mark in his treatment of the historical Fidel Castro as those who might buy the myth hook, line, and curveball.

The most notable and detailed exploitation of the Fidel pitching legend would see the light in 1999, with the publication of Tim Wen-

del's novel *Castro's Curveball*.[29] The book was originally written as a
MFA thesis at Johns Hopkins University, where the author is now a
writer-in-residence. It appeared in a year that saw the first explosion of
interest in Cuban baseball among North American English-language
booksellers and their reading public. González Echevarría's *The Pride
of Havana* was printed that same year, as was Milton Jamail's *Full
Count* and this author's own project, *Smoke*, coauthored with Mark
Rucker. But Wendel had a unique take to offer on Cuba, Castro, and
the island's baseball passions. While Krich barely noticed the Fidel
baseball connection, and while for White it was only one of several key
elements in two of his most celebrated adventure novels, for Wendel it
is everything—the very rationale for writing about the Cuban strongman and his realm in the first place. And it is only Wendel who among
more recent writers sees the story as not only a convenient plot device,
but also perhaps an actual piece of the historical record.

To Wendel's credit, his novel is an engaging read in spots, especially
in its page-turning plot and carefully drawn central characters. These
include long-retired American ballplayer Billy Burke; Cuban secret police agent Señor Canillo (disguised as Burke's landlord throughout
much of the novel); and Burke's Cuban lover and Fidel supporter,
Malena Fonseca. The weakest character is an inconsistent Fidel, the
book's central figure in name only, offered up as a charismatic budding
student revolutionary leader but at key moments filled with paralyzing
doubts and often seemingly led into action only through the efforts of
the American ballplayer (the novel's true central figure and hero) and
beguiling revolutionary conspirator and amateur photographer Malena
Fonseca. The Castro portrayed here is especially troubling to anyone
even mildly familiar with the historical facts of the Cuban Revolution
and its dynamic creator. He appears to possess none of the charisma,
dominating presence, brazen self-confidence, or driving obsessions of
the young Fidel captured by his serious biographers.

Like White, Wendel is not entirely a stranger to Cuba. He first
visited in late 1997, with author Milton Jamail, in the aftermath of the
Atlanta Olympic baseball triumph. At the time, he was working on a
story for *USA Today Baseball Weekly*, and some sparse details of that
visit are presented in Jamail's book *Full Count*. The visit produced not
only the Central Park interchange, with an old-timer from Oriente
claiming a firsthand experience of high school ball-playing against Fi-

del, but also an entertaining anecdote about how the two writers boldly talked their way into a rare chance of actually viewing Fidel in the flesh as he presented awards to the full contingent of Cuba's numerous Atlanta Olympic medal-winners. That same event at the Victoria de Girón Medical School in Havana's Miramar suburb would also permit the two lucky journalists to obtain a rare face-to-face interview with the island's biggest athletic hero, star third baseman Omar Linares.

When it comes to the merits of Wendel's novel it must be acknowledged that any author of fiction owns great liberties and license when penning any work that might be considered to fall in the broad genre of "historical" novels. There is considerable debate about the definition of "historical fiction," and the genre has been characterized by widely differing notions—for example, the broad view that includes any work in which the plot is set in the past, to the more precise notion that such works pay careful attention to the manners, social conditions, or other details of the period portrayed, to the more rigid notion that works carrying this label must be set at least 50 years in the past. Such works are frequently open to being criticized for a lack of authenticity because readers are disappointed by a lack of accurate details. And there are also subgenres like "alternative history" and "historical fantasy," in which authors insert speculative or ahistorical elements. These are works aimed at exploring how the historical record might have played out somewhat differently if certain events are tweaked or characters reshaped as something other than what they actually were. Intended or not, Wendel's novel seems to best fit this last notion of the extremely plastic genre.

The plot here involves a former pro catcher returning to Havana in the late 1990s, shortly after the death of his wife, and with his grown daughter in tow. His visit is aimed at sorting out his past, especially his aborted love affair with Malena Fonseca; meeting the daughter he shared with his now-dead former lover but had never met; and, along the way, speculating on the strange triangular relationship that also involved the former pitcher he had discovered and nearly brought off the island in a failed scenario that would have radically changed the course of history. It is the full rendition of the popular "what might have been" scenario so often wistfully attached to the young Fidel Castro.

The clue to Wendel's approach is found in the novel's prologue. The author feels it necessary to explain precisely why he is attracted to the

Fidel legend in the first place, but he also seems to be on the fence about the veracity of the entire scenario. Was Fidel a budding prospect? Did he ever attract the attention of big-league scouts? Wendel seems to believe, as he reports, that the answer depends on who you talk to, that the legend is too persistent to be entirely discredited, that the issue of a signed baseball contract has never been resolved. Even in 1999, these were not very strong arguments for latching onto a tale Fidel himself (as well as a host of serious historians) had so frequently rejected. Or does this author simply feel that his story will only carry weight if readers are convinced going in that the legend is plausible and thus both author and reader are entitled to their necessary suspensions of disbelief?

Yet, if one were enticed to believe there was any basis for the legend, if there actually is any puzzling ambiguity in the stories about Fidel's baseball activities, there are simply too many other distortions of demonstrable historical fact to suggest much veracity for Wendel's tale. The impetus for the story is the reported student demonstrations that disrupt a ballgame in Cerro Stadium sometime in the late 1940s. It is the same event exploited by Don Hoak. But Wendel chooses to follow the Hoak script (although Hoak sets the disturbance in 1951) and not the real event, which took place in December 1955 and was launched against the Batista regime and not the Grau San Martin government (facts reported in chapter 2). As we have seen, Fidel at any rate, was never involved in any such occurrence.

The baseball settings are also all wrong. Billy Burke played in Havana in a fictional winter campaign based on the fondly remembered dramatic championship league season of 1946–1947. He is a catcher for the Habana team that overtakes and defeats rival Almendares in the final days. But it was Almendares that had emerged victorious during that memorable Cuban campaign. The teams here are both filled with a higher quotient of American players in starring roles than was the actual case. An air of authenticity is suggested by the use of some real ballplayer names, but those figures are not cast in their appropriate roles (Cuban Vicente López did not yet pitch for Almendares in 1947, Felipe Guerra was not that club's manager, Tommy Lasorda did not pitch in the league until 1951, infielder Spider Jorgenson also did not play in Cuba until the early 1950s, and Fred Martin did pitch in the season of the novel's action but for Habana and not Almendares—to cite some examples). Angel González is the Habana manager and is clearly a recreation of Miguel Angel González, the one-time big-leaguer and Cardinals coach. But the legendary Cuban coach (the longest tenured in winter-league history) does not ring true here. "Papa Joe" Cambria, the scout on the trail of Castro as a pitching prospect, is recast as Papa Joe Hanrahan and is as much involved in Burke's baseball career as Castro's.

There are other anachronisms. Papa Joe (the Papa Joe Cambria clone here recast as Hanrahan) turns out to be a Cuban government collaborator. He discovers Fidel at the student demonstration that invades the ballpark, not in a tryout camp, as expected if historical accuracy is a concern. There is no evidence in Wendel's treatment of Fidel pursuing Papa Joe, as is usually reported to have been the case by the future president's biographers. The climax to the tale turns on Fidel's bold stealing of a historical bell for symbolic use in a planned student march on the presidential palace. That event has a historical parallel, but here it is set on the day of the league finale in February 1947, when the actual occurrence was not until November of that year. And finally, an important climactic scene in the Colón Cemetery is an equally strange mixture of fact and fancy. *La Milagrosa*, where the crucial late scene takes place between Burke and his two daughters, is a real monument. But there is little plausibility for any rebellious Fidelista, reportedly shot in the airport by government security forces, actually being buried in the late 1950s in the Colón Cemetery. Would not this all have made more sense—to put it another way, wouldn't Wendel's underlying questions about what might have been rung a bit truer—if the baseball details were a bit more straightforward? Even if this is a work best labelled "alternative history" or "historical fantasy," the hallmark of that particular genre is usually that the remade central character (the Fidel of a different stripe) gains plausibility by existing in a historical framework that has heavy plausibility, if not strict historical accuracy. Here, neither Fidel nor the setting strike the reader as anything beyond pure fantasy.

Wendel might well be excused from these inconsistencies if his aim (knowing the potential of a good legend when he saw one) was merely to turn a good fiction into an even better one. But the troubling factor is that evidence remains suggesting the author actually buys the myth in one form or another, or at least cannot quite bring himself to entirely dismiss it. Writing about "Fidel Castro, Ballplayer" for a popular baseball website only weeks before Castro's surprising, if long anticipated, November 2016 death, Wendel is less than coy on the subject.

> Soon after *Castro's Curveball* came out, I began to receive letters about how my novel was truer than I realized. . . . What if Fidel Castro decided to pursue baseball instead of revolution? The world as we know it would have been remarkably different. No decades-long embargo with a nation only 90 miles from our shores. No Cuban Missile Crisis.[30]

A simple justification for a novel written? Or perhaps a myth simply too delicious to relinquish?

Despite the trumped-up scouting reports of an eye-popping Fidel fastball, his deliveries have been often labeled as devious curveballs in many popular accounts by both authors of fiction and such public figures as the U.S. government spokesman cited in the epigraph for chapter 3. This is the perfect metaphor when the intention is to refer to baseball pitches that trick rather than overpower, or more especially off-field actions based on the cleverest and most devious of behaviors. It is in this latter sense that Wendel perhaps quite unintentionally arrived at the most perfect title possible for his novel, for the biggest curveball in Wendel's rendition is not the one tossed by the rather poorly fictionalized future Cuban dictator, but rather the one heaved at the reading public by the author himself.

# 8

# THE CUBAN BASEBALL DEFECTORS PHENOMENON

> I know what everyone knows: Cuba is the worst place on the globe to
> be an athlete today. But I am sure I know something even stranger.
> It is also the best.—S. L. Price, *Pitching around Fidel*[1]

Historian Louis Pérez astutely notes that the Cuban Revolution was a
phenomenon of mixed change and continuity.[2] Much changed totally
and much remained the same. Cuban baseball would reflect this para-
dox perfectly: The deep-rooted national passion for the sport never
wavered after 1959, and it was only the trappings that were revamped.
It was at the end (early 2000s) and not the outset (early 1960s) of Fidel
Castro's long reign that the national sport would finally lose its prominence and its special rank as the foundation of Cuban identity and the
source of Cuban national pride.

*Sports Illustrated* prize-winning essayist S. L. Price was confident he
had it all figured out a decade and a half back. He had briefly peered
inside the "beast" that was Communist Cuba and now possessed a
unique insider's tale to share. It was a trap many of us have fallen into:
the notion that a handful of Havana visits—or even a longer string of
stopovers in "Castroland"—would yield Cuba's darkest secrets in lucid
form to the inquisitive or persistent outsider. If the intriguing story to
be unfolded required a bit of editorial fudging to spice it up and tailor it
to North American tastes, what was the harm in that? Few readers,
after all, would likely enjoy any chance to check it out for themselves. In

its published form, Price's neatly crafted 2000 exposé, *Pitching around Fidel*, would prove inflammatory, if nothing else. With sometimes titillating but also often just as bogus accounts of "life on the ground" for Cuban athletes living in Fidel Castro's Soviet-style sports regime, the privileged insider, in 1998 (the year of his final visits), seemed certain he was truly ringing out a death knell for Cuban baseball, if not for the entire Cuban sports machine at large.

It didn't quite turn out that way, of course; the greatest Cuban baseball era was just reaching its acme on the heels of a second-straight Olympic gold medal only two years earlier in Atlanta. Any collapse was to be quite a bit slower than anticipated, even if it was perhaps inevitable given a near-universal global movement in the direction of free-market capitalism. But Price, to his credit, did indeed strike at least one true note. Under the iron-fisted control of Fidel's regime, the island nation indeed had become in recent decades what the wide-eyed novice visitor could call a "sports purist's delight, an American ideal, no less,

**THE LOYALIST.** Frederich Cepeda was the one much-coveted Cuban star who remained loyal to Fidel's revolution and resisted the MLB siren call during an era of rampant ballplayer defections. *From the author's collection*

for Cuba is one of the last places where athletes play for little more than love of the game."[3] Long isolated from a frequently deprecated world of capitalist professional sports, top Cuban athletes—especially stars on the prized national baseball team, the nation's pride and its greatest boasting point—lived like true rock stars, overinflated heroes, true life-size idols. In a sense, it was in truth the best place on the globe to be a talented athlete; at least it seemed so to skilled ballplayers raised with the ethical standards of a community-oriented socialist society. They were still more than willing to trade any chance at millions of capitalist dollars for the certain adoration of millions of hometown fans and the exhilarating honor of defending their beloved flag and the seemingly still-robust revolutionary dream.

But nonetheless, cracks were showing in the armor, even if the machine itself had not yet quite split asunder, as Price believed. With island ports now flung open to growing tourism from Canada and Europe, plus increased reunion visits from gift-toting exiled Miami-based family members—and in the aftermath of a disastrous decade of extreme economic hardships known as the "Special Period in the Time of Peace" (Fidel's clever euphemism for the years following the collapse of the Soviet Union and a sudden 80 percent drop in Moscow financial support)—long-suffering Cubans were becoming increasingly aware of the even-minimal prosperity Fidel's unwavering revolutionary dreams were denying them. At the same time, radical changes on the international baseball scene after 1999 (see chapter 6) had exposed the island's top stars to the level of mind-bending financial rewards their talents might be earning them in Asia or North America. To make matters still worse, increased efforts by hard-line INDER national team handlers, led by team manager and soon-to-be commissioner Higinío Vélez, to isolate players from such looming temptations on international road trips, and thus forestall possible defections, only increased the chafing of a seemingly oppressive control. The scales were more and more rapidly beginning to tilt, especially after the revolution's number-one cheerleader and undying inspiration suddenly faded from the scene, ironically in the very year Cuban baseball reached its zenith at the 2006 MLB World Baseball Classic.

Fidel's dream of a society without material awards had been the cornerstone of his plans to revamp Cuban sports and especially Cuban baseball in the earliest years of the revolution. A point quite often missed in discussions of the 1961 transfer to amateurism in Cuban sports (one belabored in chapter 5) was the fact that this upheaval was only part of a much larger effort by the newly entrenched Cuban leadership to revamp Cuban culture. That process had already begun in the months preceding the official establishment of INDER and the formal overhauling of the country's sports machinery in March 1961. Fidel's fourth year in power (1962) was formally designated the "Year of Planning," and however disorganized that planning may actually have been, its focus was unmistakable.

As early as 1960, Fidel had begun restructuring education with his new EIR schools.[4] At the heart of the plan was the complete recasting of Cuba's popular culture. As Georgie Anne Geyer, among others, suggests, the December 1961 announcement by the Maximum Leader that he was and had always been a Marxist-Leninist might not have rung true among skeptics and was likely, more than anything, a product of political expediency. Clearly, Fidel would be remaking the nation in his own image and not the image of Marx or Lenin, or any of the world's other socialist ideologues. And it would all start with revamping popular culture, with old communist university sympathizers put in charge of a budding film industry, with closing down the independent arts journal *Lunes de Revolución*, and with the famous address to a gathering of the nation's leading intellectuals where Fidel would utter his famous and ambiguous dictum that, "within the revolution everything goes, outside the revolution nothing."[5]

This aspect of the social revolution would impact sports as heavily as any other quarter of Cuban society. Fidel's dream of baseball (and all sports) played without financial reward was a seemingly stronger motive for the change than the efficiency offered by a Soviet-style sports training system. The adoption of the Soviet system as part and parcel of the emergence of INDER was itself merely an aspect of a larger plan to revamp the very fabric of Cuban society. The new sports machinery put in place with the INDER ministry and the first sports-related laws of early 1962 had a double motive to be sure. That plan is elaborated in great detail in the excellent study authored almost a quarter-century ago by Paula Pettavino and Geralyn Pye.[6] A first element, often ignored off the island itself, was the desire to upgrade the health levels of the nation's largely rural population. It was aimed at doing for the physical fitness of the new revolutionary society what a literacy campaign, launched simultaneously, would do for its intellectual health. There was, of course, an obvious military component to the plan. With threatened invasions from the north, a national militia, including essentially the entire population, was a priority. Geyer notes that in the immediate aftermath of the Bay of Pigs, Fidel was obsessed with arming his vulnerable population.[7] But a fit citizenry, in addition to military hardware, was also a key component.

The better-known feature of the revamping was the search for potentially superb athletic talent able to carry the revolutionary banner on national teams. A Soviet system that had so effectively challenged and often embarrassed the Americans in recent years on international athletic fields (e.g., the Melbourne and Tokyo Summer Olympics) was the motive and the model here. There was no better or quicker way to gain the admiration of other Third World nations and demonstrate the power of the revolution than in the athletic arena or high-profile international sporting contests. Moreover, there was no better way to embarrass the *Yanqui* imperialists at their own self-styled national games in front of the watchful eyes of the world's second-class nations. There were, of course, tensions and conflicts between the two goals.

Pettavino and Pye record some of these issues, for example, the exploding sports bureaucracy within INDER and the inevitable debate about the amount of scarce economic resources devoted to training and equipment for potential specialists once admission charges were removed from sporting events and the government became the sole supporter. In the end, the goal of upgrading public participation and overall fitness within a general population was not a lasting triumph; as early as 1977, only 15 percent of the population was active in organized sports activities, and more than half were elementary and secondary school students.[8] But for decades—especially throughout the first quarter-century of the revolution—the devotion to building showcase national teams, especially in baseball, would be nothing short of a resounding success.

The plan for stressing athletic victories in Cold War struggles may have faced a limited life span even if that span turned out to be more fruitful and long-lived than Cuba's critics might have at first imagined. But its strengths would eventually ebb as the revolution itself altered and the external world evolved out of its Cold War status by the end of the century. In discussing Japan's first notable player "defection" by pitching phenom Hideo Nomo in the last decade of the past millennium, Japanese baseball historian Robert Whiting notes in *The Meaning of Ichiro* that, "Japan in 1995 was a much different place than it was in 1965"[9] (the year the last previous Japanese star turned his back on that country's domestic league). Television had brought the outside world into sharper focus, and Japanese players were increasingly aware that the gap between their pay and that of big-leaguers in the United States did not reflect the increasingly narrow gap between the demonstrated levels of the two leagues.

Paralleling Whiting, it can be said that Cuba was a much different place in 2009 and 2013 than it had been in 1965 or even 1975 and 1980. If international television feeds and other explosions in electronic media were not as quick to come to Havana as to Tokyo or Osaka, Cubans in the new millennium were nonetheless increasingly exposed to the possibilities of a wealthier and more liberalized outside world. Such factors as the drudgery of economic hardships felt throughout the "Special Period" and its aftermath, which lasted well beyond the dawn of the new century; the consequent erosion of revolutionary optimism and idealism; and the material and lifestyle possibilities of an external world revealed (in Havana, if not throughout the island's rural heartland) by rubbing shoulders with increasing hordes of free-spending and smartphone toting tourists contributed to expanding disillusionment at home. For the ballplayers who had long been willing to accept hero status on their isolated island as sufficient personal reward, the tide was also shifting thanks to the noticeable sag in national team fortunes—and thus a severe dip in their elevated status with hometown fans—and the enticements and dreams awakened by increased exposure to American big-leaguers through such events as the World Baseball Classic. The top Cuban stars were now being exposed to not only modest stadiums and slim crowds in Holland, Italy, or Panama, but also palace-like big-league ballparks, plush big-league locker rooms and hotels, and massive, adoring big-league crowds, and it all made a world of difference.

Of course, there was always some resistance to the tightly controlled INDER system, even in the earliest years still flush with revolutionary spirit, and there were also detectable holes in the system from the beginning. Cuban ballplayers occasionally spoke out about hopes to reach the apex of baseball in North America's big leagues. For example, there was perhaps a misperceived longing reportedly spoken by national team hero Lourdes Gourriel at the Barcelona Olympics (quoted in the following chapter) but likely shared by others. There were even some early reports of defections from the island, for instance, the one at the 1962 Central American Games in Jamaica, which came in the close aftermath of the revolutionary triumph (see chapter 6). But the true phenomenon of star players seeking an escape route actually began with Bárbaro Garbey and the Mariel Boatlift of 1980. And it is a tale almost as sordid as those that would cloud the mass defections that would not transpire for another third of a century.

Bárbaro Garbey was a talented outfielder, if not a genuine superstar, his career peaking in the late 1970s. He had accumulated a small collection of entries in the league record books, compiling a five-year .290 batting mark and pacing the circuit in runs batted in for Industriales the season before his sudden downfall. He had enjoyed brief service on the national squad and was a valued pinch-hitter and backup outfielder at the 1976 Amateur World Series in Cartagena. But he was also a prime contributor to one of the darkest moments in league history. At the end of the 1978 season, he was accused of participating in a ring of Havana players involved in a three-year plot to fix league games for cash rewards. Gambling had long been a staple in Cuban ballparks—before and after the revolution—and it had persisted even under the new social order spawned by Fidel's revolution, which has supposedly ousted such criminal elements from the scene. Garbey and two dozen others were given a lifetime ban from future league play, and the talented outfielder even served a brief prison term for his transgressions.[10]

The Garbey saga not only uncovered cracks in the Cuban system itself, but also provided an early example of hypocrisy on the part of MLB authorities when it came to dealing with leaks in the Cuban baseball empire. MLB, as is well known, owned a long-standing and self-righteous policy of intolerance when it came to ballpark betting and game fixing. But with the Garbey case, the chance to strike a blow on the Castro regime would quickly take precedence over any avowed moralistic stance regarding baseball's integrity. Released from the island as part of Fidel's policy of dumping undesirables on Florida shores via the Mariel exodus, Garbey would soon catch the attention of Detroit Tigers scout Orlando Peña, himself a onetime member of the Sugar Kings and an avowed enemy of Castro's revolution and everything it stood for. Spotted by Peña at a refugee "holding camp" in Pennsylvania, the 24-year-old Cuban was offered a $2,500 contract to join the Tigers' farm club in Lakeland.

But the success story almost turned sour when the ballplayer's past transgressions came to light with a May 1983 *Miami Herald* article in which the newly minted minor leaguer confessed to his past criminal transgressions. When the story broke, the scandal-tainted ballplayer was immediately summoned for an interview with National Association president John H. Johnson, a session in which Garbey explained in his defense that he never actually lost games but only kept them close. Life was hard in Cuba, he explained, and he desperately needed the money for his family. The explanation—falling on sympathetic ears perhaps conditioned by years of anti-Castro propaganda—proved sufficient to avoid everything but a temporary suspension from his American Association team in Evansville.[11]

Many would find it altogether acceptable that Garbey had only turned to consorting with gamblers on the island to survive the harsh conditions of Castro's socialist Cuba. But it might prove a bit more difficult to excuse such sins against the game's purity—supposedly an example of extreme treachery on the big-league scene since Judge Landis's banishment of the infamous Black Sox conspirators—simply because they occurred on Cuban soil. If nothing else, the Garbey case exposed an egregious double standard on the part of the MLB commissioner's office and Organized Baseball, one of many such conundrums when Cuba and Castro were involved. Pete Rose, only a decade later, would offer a similar excuse (that he had never thrown games per se), but that line of defense never worked for baseball's all-time hits leader. After all, Rose had struck a blow at the presumed integrity of the sacred American pastime and not at the despised communist sports system of Fidel Castro, where game fixing was apparently not actually such a sin in North American eyes as long as it had the proper political motive (or proper political result).

Isolation of the Cuban League from prying North American eyes would long work in Fidel's favor. For decades, Cuban ballplayers remained as ignorant of the big-league scene as Stateside fans and scouts did of the Cuban amateur circuit and its mother lode of promising talent. Most Cuban players would thoroughly buy into the notion of a purer form of antimaterialist sport. Omar Linares and such forerunners as sluggers Agustin Marquetti and Antonio Muñoz remained prototypes of Cuban ballplayer loyalty. The poster-boy image Linares represented for the world of Cuban socialist-style baseball hangs on frequent claims about his rejection of boatloads of dollars for mere fan adoration at home. Although many of the reports may well have been exaggerated, if not apocryphal, they never dimmed the notion that any big-league club would welcome the slugger who boasted Cuba's highest career batting mark and a home run ratio per 100 at-bats that bested all but a half-dozen of MLB's greatest legends. As noted, one rumor had the Yankees offering the Cuban government $40 million for the services of Linares, and another had the Blue Jays pitching an offer of $100 million for Linares and slugging teammate Orestes Kindelán after the Atlanta Olympic Games.

And if big-league teams were not making offers that could be pinned down, hungry player agents with both financial and political motives certainly were. Newly established Miami-based talent scout Joe Cubas—motivated as much by his hatred for the Castro regime as any emerging opportunities for personal profit—trailed the Cuban team on its Stateside visits and also in Japan during the early 1990s, especially shadowing star shortstop Germán Mesa and ace pitcher Orlando Hernández. But either an ingrained fear of reprisals or perhaps even lingering revolutionary loyalties on the part of Cuba's top stars meant there were still few, if any, listeners to Cubas's repeated sales pitches.

Yet, that resistance to the lure of big-league dollars gradually ebbed thanks mainly to the tireless persistence of the Fidel-hating exile entrepreneur. Cubas came up with a clever plan to simultaneously assail Fidel's realm and also make his own quick fortune. The genius of the plan involved a novel way to lure Cuban players, while at the same time skirting the ever-tightening U.S. economic embargo. That plan would strike some early blows at the heart of the Cuban system, but while it enjoyed such initial, if limited, successes as the luring of a handful of veteran pitchers—Osvaldo Fernández, Rolando Arrojo, and the prized Hernández brothers, Liván and El Duque—it never hit the pay dirt that the neophyte agent had hoped for, nor did it have the devastating impact he had envisioned for the Castro baseball empire. It was a start in the effort to dismantle Cuba's national sport, but it never delivered an expected final and fatal blow.

During the past two-plus decades, the highly lucrative Cuban ballplayer defection industry and high-stakes Cuban ballplayer smuggling have evolved through two separate and distinct stages. While these stages diverge sharply in sophistication and modus operandi, they nonetheless spring from the same perceived opportunities offered by flawed U.S. business and political practices. Their aim involves similar efforts to exploit opportunities offered up by still-existing absurdities of failed Havana and Washington Cold War policies; flaws in the existing MLB collective bargaining agreement that treat non-American and non-Puerto Rico-born athletes as unrestricted free agents (i.e., the absence of an international free-agent draft system); and, more than anything else, an ongoing lust on the part of MLB team officials and scouting departments for substantial hauls of new talent—especially if it could be obtained at bargain basement prices.

Phase 1 was appropriately dubbed the "Joe Cuba Plan," and it involved an innovative scheme Cubas hit upon in the summer of 1995, with his enticements of pitchers Osvaldo "Ozzie" Fernández and Liván Hernández. It was born out of Cubas's ingenious assessment that huge sums of money could be made simply by convincing players to abandon their Cuban homeland and then whisking them away to some foreign port (Cubas regularly used the Dominican Republic) to establish the required third-country residence demanded for their free-agent status. [12] This was a low-tech operation since Cubas employed only such tools as cell phones for secret contacts, rental vans to spirit players away from team hotels or practice fields, boatloads of cash to entice his prized prospects, and hotel stakeouts adjacent to Cuban national team lodgings in the United States, Mexico, Japan, and Europe during international tournament play.

Cubas didn't operate within Cuba itself—something he rightly deemed far too dangerous—but he did have inside help on the island from his cousin, Juan Ignacio Hernández Nodar, and future short-term partner Tom Cronin. That pair maintained regular contact with prized shortstop Germán Mesa (a master defender often compared to Ozzie Smith), who was unsuccessfully, if continuously, wooed and Liván's talented brother, El Duque (who would eventually be corralled only after his own self-arranged flight from the island). A major result of the operation on the ground in Cuba was the eventual arrest and conviction of Hernández Nodar, who earned a 13-year prison term for his troubles.

A second more sophisticated and deadly phase was known as the "Bolsa Negra," or "Black Bag," and involved a crime-syndicate-controlled and extremely high-tech human-trafficking ring first widely exposed by revelations surrounding Yasiel Puig (recounted in *Cuba's Baseball Defectors*, chapter 1) but tracing its roots back at least 15 years, when such slick operatives initially began smuggling family members of Miami exiles out of Cuba and into Mexico for a hefty price. It required specialized expertise in marine navigation, bribery, forgery, and money laundering, plus an intimate knowledge of complex immigration policies in several Caribbean Basin countries. It was also a sordid business that would result in the reported deaths of hundreds of Cuban citizens on Mexican soil when promised ransoms were not paid.

"Bolsa Negra" baseball-style, involving prized prospects, such as Puig, Céspedes, Abreu, and company, was an eventual and inevitable outgrowth of an established smuggling ring that promised to bring any Cuban off the island (usually through Mexico, but often through Haiti or the Dominican) whose family or other connections in Miami were willing to pay a going rate—usually $10,000 a head—for the service. When ballplayers began being trafficked in this manner, the buyers were not family connections living Stateside, but instead player agents hoping to parlay their prize recruits into big-league contract windfalls. This was, of course, a most dangerous enterprise involving numerous captures and imprisonments in Cuba, countless double crosses and dead bodies on the streets of Mexico, and hundreds, if not thousands, of stranded Cuban refugees in Mexican coastal cities like Cancún or Mérida. But for those wishing to flee Cuba, it was less risky, perhaps, than desperate journeys across the treacherous Straits of Florida on flimsy garage-built rafts or nonseaworthy inner tubes. The prime focus became baseball players only after the Cuban player market exploded in 2010, with the $30 million package thrown at untested speedball southpaw pitcher Aroldis Chapman by the spendthrift Cincinnati Reds.

The Cubas story (phase 1) and its earliest successes are outlined in considerable detail in my book *Cuba's Baseball Defectors*, as are the numerous specific escape sagas (the "Bolsa Negra," phase 2) of dozens of high-profile Cuban leaguers, including Puig, Céspedes, Abreu, Leonys Martin, Yasmany Tomás, and others. Those stories do not need to be repeated here, and readers wishing to revisit them are referred to that earlier volume. But a few groundbreaking escapes might bear at least a brief recap.

Réne Arocha had paved the way with his unexpected and daring bolt to "freedom" in the late summer of 1991. It was perhaps not surprising that the pioneer among modern-era defectors was one of Cuba's most celebrated pitchers of the 1980s, the height of the aluminum bat era. He had starred for one of the league's strongest-ever teams (Havana Industriales in the late 1980s), was later a mainstay on the national squad that was nearly invincible in international matches, and was a current popular favorite with the Havana Metropolitanos, and at 25 he was still relied on as an ace in top international tournament events. When Arocha decided to flee at the Miami airport in the midst of a U.S.–Cuba Friendly Series in the summer of 1991, his unexpected departure sent shockwaves through the Cuban baseball establishment. When the veteran failed to report for the team's return flight to Havana, panicked team officials scoured the airport grounds, assuming he was either lost or kidnapped. The team's charter was delayed for almost two hours and only departed once a near-revolt broke out among the remaining players, frustrated by what seemed to be a futile delay.

Nothing like this had happened before, and INDER officials were unnerved by the realization that the previous isolated universe of Cuban baseball had likely changed forever. Back on native soil, the entire contingent of players and coaches was summoned for closed-door meetings with top government sports officials, and for the first time a previously heralded Cuban ballplayer was officially branded a traitor to the revolution.[13] National team members were, for the first time, harangued on the imperative of remaining strong and loyal, and thus demonstrating that any such "defection" by a weak teammate could have no real impact on the revolutionary cause. But as authors Steve Fainaru and Ray Sánchez would later suggest, the reality was that for the bulk of those players, it was more likely that Arocha (whose own father had fled Cuba in 1980 during the Mariel Boatlift) would be viewed as something of a pioneering Jackie Robinson figure, one who overnight had changed their perceptions about a new way of thinking and potentially a new way of reacting to the harsh island conditions under which they were forced to play.[14]

Fainaru reports that free-spirited team captain and future manager Victor Mesa would even shout at team officials as the plane sat stranded on the Miami tarmac, "You don't treat us like the world champions you say we are. . . . You want us to play for two dollars a day? . . . Fine, Arocha's on his way to the major leagues, and maybe we can all play in the major leagues."[15] A true believer in Fidel's revolution, however, Mesa himself would always remain dedicated to the system.

Arocha's eventual success on the major league stage was limited, as was that of a pair of other veteran pitchers, Osvaldo Fernández and Ariel Prieto, who would soon follow Arocha's bold example. Each of the trio was on the downside of his career path and all had suffered sore arms on the island during an era in which they faced aluminum-bat-wielding sluggers while trying to throw their arsenal of breaking pitches with inferior and almost seamless domestic-made Batos baseballs. Prieto would be next to make headlines with his departure from the homeland, although this second veteran right-hander found another more inventive, if less sensational, route of escape.

Several months before the sudden departure of Osvaldo Fernández and the highly touted and much younger Liván Hernández in the summer of 1994, Prieto faked injury and was thus able to arrange a legal emigration exit two full decades before super-talented teenager Yoan Moncada would follow a similar and far more celebrated path.[16] Pitching for the Isla de la Juventud team at the time, Prieto had decided that the arduous life of the Special Period was not one he wished to continue. He thus went about plotting his own escape in a more ingenious and somewhat less risky manner. He cleverly nursed a reported but not actual arm injury that seemed to signal his pitching career might be over. He even staged a planned fall from a bicycle that left him with minor bruises and kept him out of the league all-star game. Since he appeared to have no further value as a reliable team ace, he was dismissed by the INDER Baseball Federation and allowed to apply for legal immigration to Puerto Rico. Arriving in Miami in April 1995, he entered the MLB free-agent draft and, with a sudden miraculous healing of his supposedly damaged wing, quickly found a home with the Oakland A's as the fifth overall first-round selection. Prieto, like Arocha, would enjoy only a handful of seasons in the majors, since actual earlier arm damage at home was sufficient to curtail his big-league career.[17]

In the immediate aftermath of the self-arranged escapes by Arocha and Prieto, Joe Cubas would enjoy his first actual successes by enticing a trio of top Cuban stars to abandon their teammates for the promise of big-league paydays. Ozzie Fernández followed the path opened by Arocha when he bolted from the Cuban squad in Millington, Tennessee, on the eve of the July 1995 U.S.–Cuba Friendly Series. Ace of the Holguín team and a member of the 1992 Barcelona squad that had struck gold in the first official Olympic tournament, the hefty righty was sharing a room with Holguín teammate Alberto Hernández at the time he decided to depart with the encouragement and assistance provided by Cubas and his entourage. The escape would turn out to have disastrous consequences for catcher Hernández, who was later condemned, alongside El Duque and Germán Mesa, during the Havana trial of Cubas's cousin Hernández Nodar, an event leading to the star-crossed catcher's own eventual flight alongside El Duque in December 1997.

Cubas and prime target Fernández apparently had been discussing the pitcher's escape for some time during furtive meetings at past tournament events in the United States and Japan, and there were also reports of secret meetings on Cuban soil between the dissatisfied pitcher and Cubas's silent partner, Tom Cronin. Once Fernández fled his Millington hotel, Cubas, by design, had him immediately spirited away to the Dominican Republic. Plans were already in place to have the veteran hurler enter the big-league free-agent market, where he would eventually land a lucrative (for both him and Cubas) $3.5 million pact with the San Francisco Giants.

Fernández's departure would come only days before Cubas received a surprise phone call revealing that Liván Hernández was also ready to jump while training with a Cuban squad in Mexico. The agent's well-laid plans were finally paying off after a couple years of frustrated efforts. The trickle was becoming a steady stream. A bigger loss still for the Cubans would unfold during the next U.S.–Cuba Friendly Series the following year, when another veteran ace, Rolando Arrojo, walked out of Cuban team quarters at an Albany, Georgia, Holiday Inn. Once more the scenario had been orchestrated by Cubas, and this time it included a secret smuggling operation that had also spirited the player's wife and two young sons from their homeland. Coming on the eve of the Atlanta Olympic Games, Arrojo's stunning defection had the additional impact of causing an almost two-decade-long suspension of the successful U.S.–Cuba Friendly Series, which had been celebrated annually since the mid-1980s.

Cubas was not only operating in U.S. territory, but also he had followed the Cubans to Asia, where several efforts at luring Germán Mesa and anyone else willing to bolt had so far met with failure for the manipulative agent. But Cuban players were seemingly now ripe for picking once the heyday of the 1970s and early 1980s turned into the spirit-sapping Special Period of the late 1980s and 1990s. Conditions were difficult at home, and if players received special perks, like better apartments and an occasional luxury auto, they also suffered severe belt-tightening, as did the entire population after the collapse of Soviet economic support. The main perks for athletes involved overseas travel, which meant a chance to acquire much-needed household items for deprived family members. But the harsh ideology of sports officials touting the purity of revolutionary spirit meant even this advantage brought plenty of frustration.

Liván, for one, would eventually speak out about his motives for leaving and conditions in Cuba (especially unsympathetic or unappreciative attitudes of baseball officials) that drove him away. The final straw for Liván, as reported by Fainaru, had to do with as simple a matter as frustrated attempts to replace a needed power tube for the family television set. But more than anything, there was the harsh and regimented treatment of star players on tournament trips abroad by overzealous Cuban security personnel—for example, searching their luggage and removing such small items as soaps and shampoos unavailable at home—which was further poisoning the waters.

Once smuggled out of Mexico by Cubas, Liván would enjoy overnight success in the United States. Cubas obtained a huge contract from the Miami-based Marlins, who had won the bidding to the tune of a $4.5 million salary and $2.5 million signing bonus. There were indeed initial difficulties in adjusting to unimagined American freedoms and a suddenly inherited luxury lifestyle, and a promising career was almost sabotaged before it got off the ground. As Fainaru phrases it, "The transition from socialism to high-octane capitalism was so dramatic as to be comical."[18] With the ink on his contract barely dry, the new big-leaguer scooped up a fleet of a half-dozen luxury autos, featuring a flashy Mercedes, a Porsche, and a Ferrari. Never one to train seriously like his half-brother El Duque and always willing to rely on his considerable natural talents alone, the undisciplined youngster also became addicted to American fast food and ballooned well beyond satisfactory playing weight on a diet of mainly McDonald's hamburgers.

But Liván was able quickly to right the ship with a bit of help, most of it coming not from agent Cubas (who with cash in hand was now focused on orchestrating other defections and other lucrative deals), but rather the agent's cousin and shadow partner, Juan Ignacio, who lifted the depressed ballplayer's spirits by transporting cash to his estranged mother back in Cuba. Rebounding from an early demotion to AA Portland, the promising Cuban reached the majors that first fall as a September call-up. His rookie campaign the following summer was the stuff of fairy tales and culminated with MVP performances in the National League Championship Series and World Series as the expansion Marlins raced to their first-ever franchise world title. Almost overnight, Liván became the toast of the Miami Cuban exile community and had, in the bargain, enjoyed the best-ever big-league debut by any defector plucked from Fidel Castro's increasingly besieged baseball system.

Fidel himself would play an odd role in the climactic moments of the initial Liván Hernández saga. It was a role designed to underscore a recent transition from unyielding revolutionary to opportunistic and savvy politician. To the surprise of many, the baseball-loving and now also apparently somewhat more mellow Fidel would offer a goodwill gesture by freeing Liván's mother, Miriam Carreras, for travel to Miami to attend the World Series finale. It was an act paralleling a similar one made two decades earlier when the Cuban leader had cooperated in permitting the father of Luis Tiant Jr. (a former Negro League great) to reach Boston for his son's moment of 1975 World Series glory. This time the gesture proved to have somewhat mixed results, when Liván would raise his MVP trophy high overhead in front of a national television audience and shout in heavily accented English the words that would make newsreel videos throughout the nation: "I love you, Miami!" It had to be a painful moment for any INDER official (perhaps even Fidel) who might later catch a glimpse of that Miami celebration and hear those defiant words.

The most celebrated case among those of star players abandoning their Cuban homeland attaches to Liván's half-brother Orlando (El Duque). Cuban authorities had forced El Duque's hand by reacting far too strongly to the earlier defection of Liván. The two brothers—sons of two different mothers but the same father, a quixotic former journeyman pitcher—had grown up apart and possessed very different personalities and baseball talents. Liván was the raw natural who, like his father Arnaldo, often seemed inexplicably careless with his substantial gifts. Orlando was a more self-made athlete whose skills were honed with dedicated practice and persistence. Liván's desertion nonetheless meant an eventual nightmare for Orlando, at the time a star hurler for the Havana Industriales club and still owner of the league's best lifetime winning percentage.

First, the elder brother was suspended despite his role as a top national team star and lack of any concrete evidence that he was also planning a similar escape route. Within months, Orlando was first saddled, during the celebrated Hernández Nodar trial, with charges of complicity, then banished from his baseball career, and finally assigned to menial janitorial duties at the Havana psychiatric hospital. The same trial also involved star shortstop Germán Mesa (who later earned rehabilitation) and aforementioned Holguín catcher Alberto Hernández (no relation, who also later bolted as a member of El Duque's own defection party).

El Duque would soon make a dramatic escape with several companions, including not only the Holguín catcher, but also his new girlfriend and eventual wife, Noris Bosch, risking his own life plus those of his friends. Fainaru provides a detailed account that was later elaborated on in an ESPN *30 for 30* series documentary film, "Brothers in Exile." The escape, which took place on Christmas Day 1997, was a carefully plotted affair that quickly went awry when the group was desperately marooned on a Bahamian island after a planned pickup by El Duque's great uncle in Miami failed to materialize. The escape story would be later distorted by an American press enthralled by the saga of a dramatic dash for the American Dream. More accurate details would eventually be exposed in a *Sports Illustrated* feature a year later penned by Jon Wertheim and Don Yaeger, "Fantastic Voyage."[19] Fainaru would, in turn, dismiss the *Sports Illustrated* account as a "particularly cynical assessment."[20]

Joe Cubas would yet again play a major role. At first it appeared that after the Cuban refugees were rescued and safely deposited in the Bahamas, they might be returned to Cuba, which held a repatriation treaty with the Bahamian government. Cubas quickly came to the rescue, motivated, of course, by a potential windfall profit. El Duque had stoically announced he would not depart the internment center where the group was being held unless his companions were also freed. In turn, Cubas orchestrated Costa Rican visas, which allowed the entire party to depart from Bahamian custody.

Within six months, El Duque landed a deal with the Yankees, who had earlier missed out on the bidding for Liván. Once on the scene in New York, the 32-year-old rookie would waste little time in matching his brother's debut one season earlier, including a stellar postseason performance and accompanying world championship. But this time it would be on a grander stage in baseball's anointed media capital of New York City. And the rookie-season triumph would have a similar fairytale ending that found Fidel again surprisingly playing a leading role. An emotional family reunion with two daughters and a mother left behind in Cuba provided one of the strangest twists in the El Duque saga. And reprising the scenario enacted a year earlier with Liván, Fidel would again play a lead role when, at the behest of an envoy from the New York archbishop, John Cardinal O'Connor, he granted permission for El Duque's mother and daughters to leave Cuba and join him in time for the New York World Series celebration.[21]

In retrospect, one might sympathize with or at least grasp the frustrations of INDER officials and perhaps Fidel himself when they witnessed what, from their perspective, were the illegal efforts to destroy their national sport for the mere profit of outsiders—intruders they viewed as capitalist villains. And it was not entirely unreasonable for Cuban authorities to also view the raiding of their players both on home soil and overseas as being connected to ongoing Miami and Washington efforts to bring down their entire revolution.

That Cuban officials and Fidel himself might have realized the error of their ways in earlier treatment of El Duque eventually would become rather apparent. The INDER administration was shuffled within a year, partly due to reported corruption scandals, but also, as Fainaru would later suggest, perhaps at least in part because of its mangling of the entire El Duque affair. And maybe even Fidel's gesture of releasing El Duque's family was yet another clever effort on the part of the savvy Maximum Leader to turn a major political blunder into something of a face-saving propaganda victory. There would be few such victories left in the last decade of Fidel's rule—perhaps only the Elian González standoff a mere two years later could be considered a parallel triumph.

But on the baseball front, the culmination of the El Duque affair would be Fidel's last noteworthy propaganda triumph.

* * *

It is difficult to deny the early achievements of the Castro revolution— gains in health care, social welfare, reduction in urban versus rural economic disparities, and large social gains for both women and lower- class Afro-Cubans. Yet, as the decades passed, the revolution's vaunted triumphs began to seriously erode in the face of mounting external and internal pressures. The most impactful external blow came from the late 1980s collapse of the Soviet bloc and a resulting loss of the econom- ic lifeline Soviet aid had represented. Corresponding internal stress accompanied Castro's tightening of already stringent limits on individu- al freedoms and a drastically sagging standard of living, both in turn brought on by government efforts to survive the crises of the Special Period triggered by Soviet abandonment.

It is not at all surprising that Cuba's baseball culture underwent precisely the same transition from admirable early achievements to near-total collapse. The setbacks simply took a decade or so longer to unfold on the baseball diamond than on the streets of Havana, Santiago, or Camagüey. Baseball would seemingly become the last bastion of the revolutionary dream of sacrifice in the service of national achievement.

On the baseball front, the erosion-triggering external conditions arose with the late 1990s shifts on the international baseball scene. The introduction of professionals to once-strictly amateur Olympic-style games meant an end to Cuba's easy domination in such events as the IBAF World Cup and Intercontinental Cup matches, Pan American Games, Central American Games, and Olympic baseball tournaments. As victories were no longer automatic, suddenly national team players were also no longer worshipped celebrities at home, but rather objects of increased criticism among disillusioned Cuban fans accustomed to uninterrupted gold medals. With the arrival of the new millennium, baseball players, for the first time, also began abandoning the home- land, creating the same talent drains experienced among the general population during the revolution's earliest years.

Efforts by INDER officials to ward off these defections with tight- ened security and ideological indoctrination of national team players—

internal pressures not unlike the crackdowns on freedoms within the larger population—only brought further resentment and disillusionment among the nation's elite athletes. While the general citizenry failed to take to the streets or rise up in rebellion like their Eastern European Soviet bloc counterparts, the nation's ballplayers—both dozens of elite stars and hundreds of hopeful young prospects dreaming of potential riches available to professionals plying their trade in North America—did begin to rebel in their own devastating fashion. The result was a growing "defectors phenomenon" guaranteed to sink one of Castro's proudest achievements.

It is now easy enough to conclude that Fidel did not kill baseball in Cuba in 1961, as former winter leaguer Andres Fleitas would have us believe. He didn't even end the professional game, as Brioso and others have written, only the grip of North American Organized Baseball. But in a final great irony, it might be argued that it was, in fact, Fidel who, in the end, slowly sounded the death knell for the baseball machinery he had so painstakingly built. But if he killed off his own form of the national sport, it happened not overnight in 1961, but slowly and inevitably four decades later. Fidel's baseball institutions failed for the same reason his great revolution also failed by the time a new century began. It was an unwillingness to sacrifice even the smallest parts of the utopia dream and allow greater economic freedom for either his adoring masses or his loyal ballplayers that triggered the agonizing death stroke in the end.

If there was a fixed turning point, it came with the opening of the international amateur game, governed by the IBAF for decades, to professional ballplayers and eventually only minimally concealed MLB control. That change first set the Cubans back on their heels with the 1999 Winnipeg Pan American Games and 2000 Sydney Olympics. Cuban "amateurs" held up surprisingly well at first. There was no immediate collapse of the Cuban juggernaut. There was still too much talent on the island for that to happen. In fact, perhaps the greatest triumphs for the Cubans were those in the first decade of the new century. There would be another Olympic crown earned at Athens in 2004. There were highly competitive showings in 2007, 2009, and 2011, at the final trio of IBAF World Cup events. Perhaps the greatest island stars yet produced were arguably those who emerged in this period and tested their considerable skills against proven big-leaguers rather than raw collegians.

There was Cepeda, Céspedes, Abreu, Chapman, and Lazo, and even super prospects like Yasiel Puig, Rusney Castillo, and Yoan Moncada, who never made it all the way to the top rung in Cuba but seemed the wave of the future for the short spell before their premature departures.

And the greatest triumph of all came in the World Baseball Classic, where Cuba first shocked the outside baseball world in 2006, then maintained surprising showings in the next two editions. Only bad luck perhaps prevented two more charges to the finals when heartbreaking losses to first the champion Japanese pros (2009) and then an emerging Dutch juggernaut boasting a lineup of Dutch Antillean pros (2013) threw up insurmountable roadblocks. But those events were also a signal of the end lurking just around the corner. Cuban players were no longer isolated from the realms of Organized Baseball, and this meant even more interest and more aggressive recruitment from the big-league clubs. But it also meant a change in the Cuban players themselves. Almost to a man, they now saw they could truly compete with the big-leaguers on a level playing field. They also became painfully aware of what they didn't have at home and so easily might possess by stepping off the island. They were no longer satisfied with the idealism of simply building a better socialist society.

Abreu, for one, has spoken out on how it was the 2013 MLB Classic in Tokyo that turned his head to far greater possibilities. He saw he could make the grade against the best the game had to offer and also that he could be a wealthy "rock star" on the biggest stage, not a hollow hero at home with no better life by most measures than any of his countrymen, left with only an increasingly hollow revolutionary dream. It was the defections of stars like Abreu, as well as the departures of so many others with far less hope of reaching the big time, that drove the final and fatal stake. Of Abreu's teammates in the starting lineup of the 2013 World Baseball Classic team, which may have been Cuba's strongest outfit ever, six of eight position players (all but aged catcher Eriel Sánchez and the untouchable Alfredo Despaigne, already embedded in Japan) and a half-dozen pitchers (including Odrisamer Despaigne and Raisel Iglesias) would be flashing their wares in the majors within the next three seasons.

There were already slow leaks in the first decade of the new millennium. The defections of Alexei Ramirez and Aroldis Chapman both provide interesting back stories. The departure of Ramirez would bring about the downfall of a successful 10-year veteran commissioner, Carlitos Rodríguez, who had granted the national team second baseman permission to travel to the Dominican Republic to visit his wife (a Dominican national he had married while she was a medical student in Havana) and children, a visit from which the ballplayer chose not to return. But it seemed that the Cubans were willing to let him go and might even benefit from his departure since it opened a national team roster spot for hot prospect Héctor Olivera. In the case of Chapman, there seemed to be a similar scenario at work when Cuban authorities appeared to be perhaps implicated in his all-too-easy escape in Rotterdam during the summer 2009 World Port Tournament.[22] Chapman had apparently become a burden to Cuban authorities, and it didn't appear he would ever fulfill his anticipated potential with the national team. But questions surrounding his departure from a team hotel in Rotterdam were inevitably raised when it turned out he had his Cuban passport in his possession, a situation never previously allowed by ever-watchful security handlers.

The dark dimensions of many ballplayer escapes from Cuba first became popular knowledge with the April 2014 exposés concerning the cloak-and-danger adventures underlying the arrival of new Dodgers sensation Yasiel Puig—stories simultaneously broken by Jesse Katz (*Los Angeles* magazine), Scott Eden (*ESPN the Magazine*), and this writer (*Daily Beast*). Puig had been transported to Mexico by smugglers connected with the Zeta drug cartel, and when his ransom fee was suddenly upped once he reached Mexico, he was hijacked from his original holders by a second group, this time financed through Miami crime elements, and secretly transported to Mexico City, where he eventually inked a Dodgers contract. But not before his life was threatened by handlers who warned they would cut off his hand if not paid in full for their efforts.

Similar tales would soon come to light surrounding outfielders Leonys Martin and Yoenis Céspedes. Family members of the former were held hostage for months in Miami, and Martin would eventually bring a successful lawsuit against his smugglers, who had continued attempting to extort money from the ballplayer after he signed his hefty deal with the Texas Rangers. While Céspedes was able to escape from his original Dominican agent/smuggler and make it to safety Stateside for a lucrative deal with Oakland, his mother and other relatives were held virtual prisoners for months in the Dominican Republic before eventually executing their own second desperate voyage onto North American soil.[23]

While there was a dark pall hanging over the American and hence MLB side of the equation, there were also unsavory reports emanating from Cuba itself. Several players are now known to have cooperated with Cuban authorities by fingering innocents supposedly involved in their early failed escapes, in the hope of earning their way back onto national teams. Usually the motive was simply to stage another escape route once the player had found his way back into INDER's good graces and had again secured a national team roster spot, which would mean an overseas trip and open doors on other potential flights to freedom.

Chapman is the best-known case, having been nabbed in a first attempt at abandoning Cuban shores in March 2008, when only 20, a bungled effort that put both his career and family in jeopardy. Less than a year later, he was again suiting up for the national team in time for the second World Baseball Classic, a surprise reprieve given the hard line usually taken with potential or accused defectors. But that odd scenario would eventually be clarified when Cuban American Danilo Curbelo García brought suit in Florida courts, claiming the ballplayer (at the time already a star closer with the Cincinnati Reds) had fingered him as a human trafficker who had supposedly tried to lure him into leaving the country. Chapman had apparently bought his way back onto the Cuban national team—where his services were still needed as a potential ace closer and occasional fireballing starter—by providing Cuban authorities with a much-needed scapegoat, whose punishment might deter other genuine agents operating secretly on the island. Puig would also later be fingered in an ESPN story by journalist Scott Eden, as a kind of double-agent informer aiding Cuban authorities seeking to nab human traffickers; Eden would also report that while already a Dodger in 2014, Puig might also have participated in a sting operation landing several other Cuban American island visitors in a Cuban prison for alleged ballplayer smuggling activities.[24]

A climax to the human trafficking saga seemed to come with the case of José Dariel Abreu. Abreu was a headline story when he broke in as a sensational rookie slugger with the Chicago American League club, although few details were at first available about how he had actually escaped his homeland. Such details would finally be revealed when Abreu sat down with journalist Michael Miller for a lengthy interview published by the monthly *Chicago* magazine on the eve of the slugger's second big-league season.[25] Revealed were details of a treacherous sea journey that nearly cost the lives of the ballplayer and several companions during the dangerous channel crossing between the northern Cuban coastline and sanctuary in nearby Haiti. The early 2016 Florida trial of Abreu's smuggler/agent, Bart Hernandez, on human trafficking charges further revealed more startling details, one of which was that the ballplayer had handed Hernandez and his partners $5.2 million from his initial White Sox contract for their illegal services.[26] Another was a bizarre report that the frightened ballplayer actually tore out and swallowed pages from a false Dominican passport supplied by his agents before reaching Miami immigration en route to inking his lucrative White Sox deal.

By the midpoint of the current decade, MLB appeared to be the end-game winner in the almost half-century Cold War standoff with the isolated universe that was Fidel's socialist Cuban League. The flow of more than a dozen top Cuban stars headed by the likes of Abreu, Chapman, Gurriel (the new spelling upon his MLB arrival), Céspedes, Moncada, Leonys Martin, and Aledmys Díaz—to name only the most noteworthy—has enlivened MLB rosters and depleted the Cuban domestic game. But there have also been negatives for the North American pro circuit.

The way the scenario has played out has done little to diminish the notion that MLB's concept of globalization has never moved far from thinly veiled attempts to raid and exploit foreign lands to sate its own hunger for fresh talent. Big-league owners have been caught up in an unnecessary frenzy of speculative spending on Cuban free-agent prospects who have, at the worst, failed to live up to excessive hype or, at the best, been corralled at much steeper market prices than equivalent Stateside native talent might have demanded. And any hopes for a working agreement with the Cubans expected to lead to island-based academies and open access to young Cuban prospects—paralleling either Cuba itself in the 1950s or such modern-day Caribbean outposts as the Dominican Republic—have so far failed to materialize.

And worst of all has been the distasteful and embarrassing role of MLB executives and scouting departments in the objectionable business of what can only be labelled ballplayer human trafficking. As stressed elsewhere, there is no clear evidence that MLB executives have either orchestrated or encouraged the illegal trafficking of Cuban athletes—only that they have been all too willing to enjoy its windfall benefits and all too reticent to take actions to bring it to an end.[27] The willingness of MLB clubs to gobble up players represented by league-sanctioned agents known to be involved in such schemes is as big a black eye for the sport as any previous scandals involving game-fixing (the Black Sox), betting on baseball (Pete Rose), or the use of performance-enhancing drugs (Barry Bonds and Roger Clemens). It has only been less acknowledged and less celebrated in the North America media.

✿ ✿ ✿

A turning point in the ballplayer defection phenomenon seemed to come with the departure of Aroldis Chapman and especially in the aftermath of Chapman's bank-busting major-league contract. The slender, hard-throwing lefty was not such a huge loss to the Cuban national team. His performances had been inconsistent: Perhaps unnerved by the aforementioned but still secret details of earlier defection attempts, he pitched his way off the 2008 Beijing Olympic squad with several shoddy performances at a June 2008 Havana domestic tournament being used as a final audition for Olympic hopefuls; he also was not—as assumed in U.S. press reports—a top-line pitcher in the Cuban arsenal. Moreover, the recent combination of international tournament setbacks and player losses had already created a perfect storm for the Cubans. It was a vicious cycle that fed on itself.

When more stars left the national squad and the domestic league was also further weakened as a consequence, fans quickly became disaffected and began reassessing their loyalties. This meant even less reason for players to stay at home. And the first major switch in the loyalty of domestic fans attached itself to Chapman, Cuba's first $30 million ballplayer. That huge MLB contract, whose actual numbers could hardly be fathomed by most Cubans, opened the eyes of fans in Havana and throughout the island. It seemed a loud and clear signal that Cuban players were indeed as good as any to be found elsewhere. Fans could now suddenly feed their fragile pride with images of their own stars blossoming in MLB parks, even if the long-cherished national squad was sagging. And Chapman became a primary focus of that major shift in allegiance.

It was not that Cuba was no longer producing the same top level of talent it had always produced. I argued at the time in a series of controversial articles on the North American website BaseballdeCuba.com and also in a landmark interview published by the Cuban media (in the conservative arts journal *La Calle del Medio*) that between 2003 and 2013, Cuban talent was indeed the best ever. This recent generation of players was heads above those of an aluminum bat era, players who never faced true professionals and thus never amplified their game. It was just that the international scene had shifted rather drastically. It wasn't that Cuban talent had diminished, but rather that the playing field had now been completely leveled to the Cubans' distinct disadvantage.

Spoiled Cuban fans never grasped this shift in the international landscape. They had been conditioned to believe that endless uninterrupted victories had been a signal of true eminence in the sport; they had bought into repeated celebratory coverage by state media trumpeting a false superiority. In turn, they also believed that if they were now no longer enjoying similar victories, it could only be because their own players had slipped drastically.

Cuban pride was so intimately linked to baseball that such setbacks seemed just another blow to the revolutionary spirit tied to the other dips in lifestyle quality that a new millennium brought with it. The national spirit had always been stoked by endless ballpark victories against other nations, and when those victories disappeared it seemed somehow an insufferable last straw. Of course, the losses were not such a catastrophe if taken in proper perspective.

The national squad performed amazingly well against the new competition: They shocked "doubting Thomases" in Asia and North America with their second-place finish at the inaugural World Baseball Classic; at first there were no early eliminations from any major tournaments, only second-place finishes, disappointing at home but rather impressive in other quarters. But second place to the rival Americans, now boasting big-leaguers-in-training (e.g., in the 2007 and 2009 IBAF World Cups), was hardly palatable in Havana no matter how surprising elsewhere. If Fidel's longtime use of baseball to prove Cuban worth had not convinced rivals of the Cuban socialist system, it had worked only too well to stoke pride at home and prop up belief in the merits of the still-standing revolution. When the endless winning stopped, all that was left (for the adoring fans if not the hard-line government) was alternative pride in those who had left home for successes on the sport's main stage in a once-demonized world of North American professional baseball.

Native-born Cubans had succeeded in the majors long before Aroldis Chapman. Most recently there was Ramirez, who drew plenty of attention as a crack shortstop with the White Sox. But for the locals, it was the blockbuster contract that seemed to throw Chapman into the main spotlight. Rafael Palmeiro and José Canseco had been stars during the previous decade but got little notice on the island. The Cuban fanatics were interested only in those who had played in their National Series, those who truly were products and thus genuine representatives of their own hometown game. The outsized heroes were no longer the loyalists who remained home but were no longer proving invincible on the world tournament scene, but rather the few who were leaving and demonstrating Cuban talent on a larger stage.

And there was another reason tied to the defections—aside from loss of local fan support and top on-field talent—that was also weakening Cuban national teams. With so many young players departing, many without any true prospect for success in the north, the level of league play dipped substantially. Teenaged prospects called into premature service as replacements were not talented enough or well-enough prepared. The top Cuban stars who remained, like Cepeda, Gourriel, and Pestano, among others, were no longer facing an elevated level of competition at home adequate to prepare them for international events now filled with current or future big-leaguers. Frederich Cepeda—Cuba's most consistent slugger—complained about this to me repeatedly. Facing young pitchers throwing 85 miles per hour and possessing a repertoire of one or two deliveries meant huge adjustments when Cuba's best hitters were put up against North American or Asian pros in such events as the World Cup or MLB Classic. As a consequence, Cuban teams now started slowly in such events (early round defeats were becoming more common), and Cuban batsmen often didn't adjust until later tournament rounds, if at all.

Finally, there was the constantly worsening effect of the embargo and the sagging Cuban economy. Stadiums were literally falling apart. Infields were shoddy, quality bats were in limited supply, the Mexican- or Cuban-made baseballs were inferior to those used in other leagues. Players were training in the worst of conditions. It was a small miracle that Cuban teams still did as well as they did in big-venue events.

If Chapman signaled a turning point, the severest and most damning losses came in the next couple of years. Céspedes was already a major star (a recent league home run champion) when he decided to bolt. Abreu (a league Triple Crown threat) was a bigger loss still in the aftermath of the 2013 World Baseball Classic. And some of the best young prospects, for instance, Yoan Moncada and Andy Ibáñez, would soon also leave. The slow leaks had become a torrent, and each new hometown star to make it off of the island successfully and then earn a top-dollar contact provided further incentive for flight to those left behind. Most had little chance to enjoy the successes of the most brilliant stars the likes of Abreu, Puig, Ramirez, or Chapman. But with the poor league quality, poor playing conditions, and dip in fan adoration, what, after all, was the reason for staying? Fidel's 2006 virtual departure had taken the sagging revolutionary spirit with it, although there was little reason to believe a continued presence of the Maximum Leader would have been sufficient to stem the tide in this changed environment.

A final setback for the Cuban system seemed to come—symbolically at least—with the departure of the Gourriel brothers—established veteran Yulieski and highly touted prospect Yunito (Lourdes Jr.). The Gourriels, along with an aging Freddie Cepeda and the slugging Alfredo Despaigne, had long been the final and always untouchable high-profile loyalists. Although he might not have reached the full promise displayed early on, Yulie was widely viewed as the island's best all-around player; his final shortened National Series season produced an astronomical .500 batting average in a stretch of 60-plus games. The younger brother, Lourdes Jr., was also touted as a can't- miss big-league prospect. A third brother, Yunieski was a journeyman outfielder without star quality who nonetheless filled an additional corner of the family legacy. Father Lourdes Sr. had been a major outfield star in the aluminum bat era and was still idolized for several dramatic home runs that anchored celebrated victories against the Americans. The Gourriels were the closest thing to Cuban baseball royalty.

But mystery, suspicion, and high intrigue had, as of late, surrounded the Gourriels. There was never a full explanation for the sudden transfer of Yulieski—along with his two brothers—from their home club in Sancti Spiritus to the Havana Industriales team. The explanation of their father's health condition (heart issues requiring monitoring in Havana) was never very satisfying, and word on the street was that a switch to the island's most popular club was perhaps a veiled effort at warding off possible defection. And then there were problems with a lucrative contract in Japan that was mysteriously sabotaged at the 11th hour. The defection of the brothers in Santo Domingo during the 2016 Caribbean Series was itself shrouded by a cloud of misinformation. What was clear was that by the time the two Gourriels—one the island's top performer and fan favorite, and the other a touted can't-miss prospect—finally left Cuba, their impactful loss was perhaps little more than a final resounding footnote, almost an afterthought at the end of the storm.

✿ ✿ ✿

By late 2013, Cuban authorities could no longer ignore the phenomenon of fleeing ballplayers or simply dismiss and discard those who left as unwanted traitors. It was becoming apparent even before the massive player departures in 2014 and 2015 that steps had to be taken to reverse the tide. Those initial steps ironically came precisely at the moment I had arrived in Havana with an ESPN film crew headed by reporter Paula Lavigne. The plan was to interview both Fidel's son, Antonio (Tony) Castro, and national team manager Victor Mesa, as well as star player Yulieski Gourriel, in an effort to compile a story on the current state of the island sport. (Ironically ESPN never used the bulk of Lavigne's reports, interviews, or film footage; one network executive later told Lavigne American audiences were really not interested in the island's baseball health, but only the possibility of luring more high-profile defectors to MLB ballparks.) Lavigne hoped to unravel what the recent spate of defectors signaled for the future of the sport on the island and the future of U.S.–Cuba baseball relations.

Lavigne had established solid rapport with Mesa during an earlier summer visit of the Cuban squad to the United States for the annual series with the USA Baseball Collegiate All-Stars. She had been invited to continue interviews with the Cuban manager begun in Omaha by visiting his home base in Matanzas. The visit came at the invitation of Tony Castro, who because of his excellent English and current stature as an IBAF vice president and top INDER official, plus his high profile in international baseball circles, had become a de facto spokesman for Cuban baseball operations with the foreign press.

The interviews were a surprising success and revealed the deep interest of both Tony Castro and Victor Mesa—two of the league's most high-profile personalities—in finding an avenue for Cuban players to somehow legally reach MLB. The younger Castro especially emphasized that his views were his alone and not necessarily a reflection of widespread INDER thinking. But both he and Mesa appeared to be strong advocates for change in INDER thinking. They both seemed to have a rather stilted view of the processes, while believing the only real impediment to progress was the hated economic embargo. If that could be lifted and players could freely come and go between their homeland and the majors, both sides would benefit greatly. It seemed a bit of a Pollyanna view, of course, and neither Cuban official seemed to have much appreciation for how MLB actually operated. There was little apparent understanding that once they were the property of MLB clubs, more than just embargo restrictions might prevent Cuban players from simply shuttling back and forth. MLB teams were no longer encouraging or even permitting full-scale winter-league play for high-salaried stars who might be injured or simply worn out by year-round play.

Unknown to us during our short Havana stay were several simultaneously breaking developments. Cienfuegos star slugger José Abreu had just abandoned the island, and his hot-prospect teammate, Yoan Moncada, had also left the Cienfuegos squad and was preparing his own route to legal emigration. While filming a session with Tony Castro against the backdrop of a preseason Industriales–Cienfuegos game in rickety Changa Mederos Stadium, I was puzzled by the absence of both Cienfuegos stalwarts, and when I inquired about their whereabouts Castro simply told me they were injured (although he likely knew there was a fuller explanation). Also, INDER officials were, at that very moment, preparing to publicly reveal a blockbuster plan that apparently neither Tony Castro nor Mesa were fully aware of.

That plan hit the newswires while we were in the Miami International airport en route home. My wife phoned me in Miami to excitedly relate she had heard a NPR report indicating Cuban officials were announcing they would begin releasing players for service with major-league teams, ending the long-standing Cold War with MLB and perhaps ending any need for future player defections. I was shocked and quite skeptical, and it turned out my doubts were well founded. An overenthusiastic U.S. press corps had either carelessly or purposely distorted the Cuban announcement, one that was significant enough in its import but not at all what American accounts were fantasizing it might mean.

INDER's plan was designed to hopefully head off further abandonment of star players by providing a significant, if still-slight, increase in salaries for domestic and international play. A more dramatic step would be a working arrangement with Japanese Professional Baseball that allowed selected Cubans to sign with Japanese ballclubs for summer play and pocket a much higher portion of their paychecks than ever before permitted. Those players would retain 80 percent of their contracted salaries, and INDER would retain 20 percent, an exact reversal of the earlier split for Cuban professionals (doctors, teachers, health-care workers, and technical advisors, as well as athletes and coaches), who for years were lent out to foreign countries as part of Cuba's altruistic international stance.[28]

But this plan did not mean free agency for ballplayers in the form Americans might imagine and in the form NPR and other news services seemed to be reporting. The players would not negotiate contracts; those contracts would be between Nippon Professional Baseball and INDER. Only the players selected by INDER would have such an opportunity, and those selections would be quite minimal. Japanese scouts would come to Havana to pick players they might have an interest in from a small contingent of a dozen or so who would audition in workouts at Latin American Stadium. The plan seemed designed to reward a handful of stars nearing late-career status as payment for their long loyalty. Younger prospects would see no possibility for their own selection and thus little reason to stay at home.

There was another element initially overlooked in the new Cuban plan. The players sent to Japan were on loan and not the property of the Japanese clubs beyond the single summer of their contract. They would return to play in Cuba during the winter. This last part of the deal suggested the advantages for the Cuban system and also revealed why players could never be sent to MLB via any similar arrangement. And the further perk for the Cubans was that at least a few top players would now be seasoned with better competition, a step toward strengthening the national team for future international play.

The first to benefit by the new arrangement would be Cepeda (a million-dollar deal with the Tokyo Giants), Gourriel (Yokohama Bay-Stars), and young Isla de la Juventud pitcher Héctor Mendoza (also sent to the Giants, where he pitched for the team's minor-league club). Such an arrangement was not truly novel, but only an amplification of earlier exchange efforts. Omar Linares and three other fading veterans had been sent to Japan at career's end a decade earlier. A similar arrangement had also been tried out with the Mexican League the past several summers. But the Mexican venture had unraveled when Organized Baseball stepped in and protested Alfredo Despaigne's assignment with the league's Campeche ballclub, citing Helms–Burton restrictions on direct payments to Cuban nationals. That had led to Campeche officials arranging a false Dominican passport, which in turn triggered the Cuban star's banishment from Mexico. Despaigne would subsequently follow Cepeda to Japan, where he has thrived for several summers, first with the Chiba Lotte Mariners and later with the 2017 champion Fukuoka Softbank Hawks, where he paced the Nippon Pacific League in round-trippers and RBIs.

Additional ballplayer outsourcing would involve an arrangement with the North American CanAm League and also several leagues in Europe. An entire makeshift Cuban national team would take part in the CanAm League in 2017, winning only five of 21 games and limping home seventh in an eight-team circuit. But these later efforts offered only limited benefits to those earning such assignments.[29] The salaries earned in Canada and Europe by Cuban stars were more in line with industrial league or semi-pro baseball in North America.

The exchange plan with Japan would also result in only limited success. Cepeda became the first million-dollar Cuban ballplayer, but on the field of play he proved a disappointment with Tokyo's Yomiuri Giants and spent a substantial part of his two-year tenure with the Giants' minor-league club. Language, food, and culture proved too large a hurdle to overcome. But a bigger factor was that, like Linares a decade earlier, Cepeda was already well beyond his most productive career years. He batted a mere .194 in 2014 (52 games) and failed to hit safely in 21 plate appearances during his second aborted season with the Tokyo club. Pitcher Héctor Mendoza showed some promise with the Tokyo Giants minor-league team but was released after two seasons and failed to return home, eventually inking a minor-league pact with the St. Louis Cardinals.

Young Ciego de Avila and national team outfielder José Adolis Garcia (brother of earlier defector José Adonis Garcia, who had reached the big leagues with the Atlanta Braves) proved a short-term bust after signing with Yomiuri and was quickly released, only to also defect in Europe on his return trip to Havana. Gourriel enjoyed a more successful debut season with Yokohama (hitting .305 with 11 homers in 62 games during his abbreviated 2014 season), but when he was mysteriously held back by INDER before his second season, the entire Japanese plan almost unraveled. If the INDER goal had been to scale back defections or strengthen its national squad for international contests, there is no evidence either effort had actually panned out.

Obama détente efforts also led to considerable premature and even false optimism. They also led to large misinterpretations. That was as clear with baseball as anywhere else. As the interviews with a new Cuban commissioner at the Caribbean Series in San Juan, only months after the Obama announcement, had made clear, there was no change of course in Cuba, only a retreat aimed at reinforcing former hard-line positions. The window would be closing almost as fast as it had been pried open. My trips to Cuba in late 2014 and early 2015, and discussions there with respected insiders, indicated lucidly that Havana officials had been caught completely off guard. There was little notion of how to proceed with the new reality. Had Fidel still been on the scene, there most surely would have been sharp response and quick action, which might have helped or even perhaps further hindered the situation. Fidel was always out in front of every new development and new shift in course. He was the master responder, forever quick to turn every new defeat into some form of new victory. But with the Maximum Leader gone from the scene, there was only floundering and indecision.

The only solution seemed to be one I had already suggested: a Japanese-style posting system.[30] Such a system would allow players to eventually reach MLB on a limited scale but also keep young talent home.

This option is explained in detail in *Cuba's Baseball Defectors*. It evolved in Japan in December 1998, as direct fallout from the celebrated case of former Dodgers pitcher Hideo Nomo, who had exploited a loophole in his Japanese contract to become the first NPB leaguer to relocate permanently to MLB. The Japanese had prevented further defections like Nomo's by forcing MLB into an agreement that would keep players at home until they had fulfilled their original contracts. After a period of service, they could declare free agency, which would make them eligible to depart for service with any American club that might want them. But built into the plan was another plus for NPB and its ballclubs. MLB teams would have to bid for a player's services, and the selected highest bidder would have to pay the posted amount to the departing player's former club before negotiating a deal directly with the player and his agent. In effect, the MLB team would have to pay handsomely not once, but twice; both the player and the league team owning his rights would therefore benefit.

The radical differences between Japan's capitalist baseball structure and Cuba's socialist baseball operations would, of course, provide obstacles here. Adjustments would have to be made. Cuban players do not have contracts as we know them with individual clubs, only agreements binding them to the state-run league. And as long as big-league teams could simply wait for Cubans to defect and then nab them as free agents ripe for picking, there might be little motivation for the American teams to agree to such a plan. But the defections had become an embarrassment to both sides, and some compromises seemed necessary if the Cubans wanted to salvage what was left of a domestic league and if MLB bosses wanted to end the embarrassing backdrop of human-trafficking operations sanctioned player agents had, in many cases, been involved in.

The first step would be for the Cubans to put their players under the kind of contracts that existed in the capitalist countries. With an anticipated reestablishment of normal diplomatic ties, those contracts would carry weight and could not be ignored by the Americans. MLB teams would have access to Cuban players but only on a strictly limited basis and as part of the type of business arrangement already existing with the Japanese. It would mean MLB would have to turn a page and accept normal business dealings with a rival league in a manner that might truly lead to globalization of the sport. This would be an ideal substitute for a long history of North American baseball imperialism aimed merely at exploiting rival leagues and ruthlessly consuming their talent pools by almost any route available.

The Cubans would also be winners according to such a scenario but also not without making sacrifices. They would have to enter into the world of professional baseball Fidel had so long resisted. They would have to accept a changed world, but one that would provide their only salvation. MLB posting and purchasing fees would not go to league clubs (since they were not the owners of player contracts), but to the government-run league itself, and the desperately needed cash would now be available to upgrade a sagging Cuban baseball infrastructure. Of course, such an arrangement was only possible if the Cold War embargo on doing business with Cuba was lifted. But no such plan has ever emerged. One reason was most likely the indecision plaguing Cuban government circles already alluded to—the Cubans simply did not know how to react to the changing world now confronting them.

There was also an apparent lack of understanding in Havana circles about capitalist-style contracts, which might provide a clue to the absence of any movement toward the kind of system NPB had worked out with MLB years earlier. That failure at the Cuban end became clear in 2015, with the unfolding saga of Yulieski Gourriel. Gourriel had served one partial year in the NPB with the Yokohama club (he was a late signee who played little more than a half-season). He was slated to return according to a deal that would include his super-talented younger brother. But for reasons that never completely came to light, the Gourriels were held back from reporting for the start of the 2015 Japanese season. One excuse offered by the official Cuban press was late-season injuries to both players.[31]

But there were also circulating rumors that INDER officials had worked a secret deal to send Yulieski to the Yankees, the team he often expressed a desire to someday join. This account has unnamed Havana officials telling the brothers to sit tight and all would soon be worked to their advantage. But if that was the actual plan, it quickly collapsed. The Yokohama club grew tired of the repeated stalling and sent a top official to Havana to corral the wayward Cubans. When INDER still balked, the Yokohama club promptly cancelled the contracts (reportedly a $3 million package deal) and announced that perhaps their actions would teach the Cubans what contracts actually meant.

It is hard to know what went on behind the scenes. Contacts in Havana told me there were strong rumors that a high official (perhaps even the son of Raúl Castro) was telling the Gourriel family something could be worked out with the Yankees (obviously a false notion since individual MLB clubs could not negotiate with the Cuban government). The brothers, like their father before them, had always been fiercely loyal to the system. But now not only was Yulieski's dream of reaching the majors being sabotaged, but also he and the family had lost a hefty Japanese paycheck in the bargain. Whatever the truth was, the impact proved disastrous for INDER and the Cuban League. During the coming season, Yulieski tore up depleted league pitching with a league-record .500 batting mark that almost defied belief. But then in the Caribbean Series (with the league season only two-thirds finished), the brothers sent immediate shock waves through the homeland by fleeing the delegation while the Cuban team for which they were playing was wrapping up a Caribbean Series visit to Santo Domingo.

The defection of the Gourriels was truly monumental, being seen at home and abroad as the final debacle in a collapsing Cuban system. And while it was the most celebrated of so many recent defections, it was also easily the most mysterious. The brothers' reasons for leaving were not hard to unravel: They had apparently been betrayed in the recent Japan fiasco, and Yulieski's biological time clock was now also rapidly ticking in regards to any hoped-for big-league career. But there were also rumors they had been helped from the inside during their dash for freedom, and in the aftermath, they did not receive the expected cold shoulder that usually accompanied such disloyalty. While photos of Lourdes Sr. and Yulieski immediately disappeared from their previous place of honor in the Hotel Nacional, there were now other twists that were not easily explained.

The Gourriel parents were soon traveling freely back and forth between Havana and Miami, where they purchased a second residence. The brothers themselves remained mum, unlike other defectors who were increasingly telling their stories of escape. Was their all-too-easy departure actually an arranged payoff for mistakes that had been made during the Japanese contract dispute and the false promises that might have been made to Yulieski and his family? A conspiracy theory of the highest order, perhaps. Meanwhile, Yulieski Gourriel (with a single vowel dropped from his family name and a shift in position to first base) would enjoy an instant MLB impact equal to those celebrated by Abreu, Puig, Céspedes, and Chapman. In his first full MLB season, he would play a significant role in leading the Houston Astros to the 2017 world championship.

Defections would eventually slow to a trickle and then a mere drip. A large part of the reason was the smaller number of true prospects still on Cuban soil after the floodtide of departures in 2014 and 2015. There were still a few raw talents left for the picking after the apex of ballplayer emigration, which peaked in the earliest years of the current decade with the rivals of Chapman, Puig, Céspedes, Abreu, Moncada, and a handful of other genuine prospects still toiling in the minors. Five-tool outfielder Luis Robert, from Ciego de Avila, would be scooped up by the Chicago White Sox in 2017, and he remains the next stellar Cuban prospect likely to arrive, and perhaps the last for a while. Others, like infielders Andy Ibáñez (Isla de la Juventud) and José Miguel Fernández (Matanzas), or pitchers Angel Miranda (Habana Province) and Cionel Pérez (Matanzas), have experienced a painfully slow route toward the ultimate goal of reaching big-league clubs.

The depleted Cuban League of recent seasons boasts few remaining frontline prospects that might stir excitement from a MLB scouting corps. But it has been a reassessment by MLB owners and officials that best explains the apparent end to Cuba's recent prominence as a well-spring of untapped talent. A restructuring of rules governing free-agent signings in the past two years has, more than anything else, altered the landscape. Prospects for a long-overdue international drafting system now also loom as a major game changer. But it was a bottom line cost analysis that ultimately took the edge off Cuban imports. Despite the huge success stories grabbing headlines, less-reported Cuban failures far outweighed the overnight successes.

Abreu surprisingly and quickly proved his worth with a stellar rookie campaign, as have Céspedes, Alexei Ramirez (now retired from the scene), Chapman (once his role as an incomparable closer was properly honed), and Puig (once his early erratic enthusiasms were corralled). Yulieski Gourriel (as the relabeled Yuli Gurriel) proved every bit the quality hitter in the American League that he had been for more than a decade in Cuba and provided an important cog in Houston's 2017 world championship run. But these players might well have been obtained at a far lower cash investment had the Cuban market not spun so wildly out of control for a short spell at the outset of the current decade.

Beyond their top-dollar price tags, Puig and Chapman, in particular, also brought off-field and clubhouse headaches to their MLB clubs. Puig was actually a modest investment in the modern-day market, and his five tools seemed to merit the gamble. And while he has never quite duplicated his sensational 2013 debut in the City of Angels, his troublesome wildness has been largely tamed and he has slowly proven a quality big-leaguer, if not a hoped-for superstar. Many (including this writer) thought Chapman was a poor gamble when he broke the bank in Cincinnati. Despite his headline-grabbing 100-mile-per-hour-plus fastball, he was not Cuba's top pitcher, as billed, and did not own the temperament and makeup needed for a big-league starter's role. But a series of big-league clubs would eventually figure out how to exploit his canon-like arm, and Chapman would soon enough emerge with the Cubs and Yankees as perhaps the most dominant closer of all time.

If Chapman and Puig were corralled off the field and tamed enough to allow their skills to shine through on the field, a few other high-investment Cubans proved far less manageable. Fancy-fielding shortstop Erisbel "Bárbaro" Arruebarrena proved a quick embarrassment to the Dodgers with an ugly outburst in Albuquerque that sabotaged his minor-league career before it got off the ground.[32] Héctor Olivera was another Dodgers investment that quickly turned sour. Once the best-looking young Cuban infielder in the eyes of most MLB talent scouts, Olivera would first suffer a huge personal setback when he was sidelined on the island by a rare blood disorder. When he left Cuba, the Dodgers and other clubs bid heavily despite his age (he was almost 30) and lingering health problems. With a $40 million contract in hand, Olivera was slow to progress his first summer in the Dodgers minor-league system and was dealt to Atlanta. There he showed promise until involved in an ugly domestic violence event on a Braves road trip, which ultimately ended his late-blooming career. The Braves sent him to San Diego in a deal simply designed to unload him, and he never played an inning with his third big-league outfit. Olivera proved to be little more than a $40 million headache.

There were other equally noteworthy investments gone sour. The Phillies gambled on onetime star hurler Miguel Alfredo González, and the Washington Nationals did the same earlier with right-hander Yunieski Maya. Both had been national team stars but quickly washed out as big-leaguers. González had suffered an earlier unreported arm injury that scuttled his career. Maya was rushed into the wrong role as a rarely used fill-in starter, although he did hang on for several years in AAA, the Korean League (where he threw a no-hitter), and the Dominican Winter League. But the biggest bust was Rusney Castillo with the Red Sox. Castillo was perhaps the victim of landing with the wrong team since Boston was already loaded with a talented corps of young outfield prospects blocking his route to the big time. He hit well in AAA but never had much of a legitimate shot with the parent club. The experiment might have been worthwhile if not for the price tag. Castillo had received the biggest payday of all, at $72 million, and it was money down the drain. He was certainly the biggest warning sign that set big-league GMs reassessing their insane overspeculation in the Cuban ballplayer market.

And finally, there was the increasing phenomenon of players stranded in the Dominican, Haiti, Mexico, and elsewhere. More than 135 players left Cuba between early 2013 and late 2015, the bulk of them with little or no prospect for ever reaching the Promised Land of the U.S. major leagues. Many would be marooned on foreign shores with little prospect for a better life, stuck in Haiti or the Dominican Republic, longing to reverse their earlier fatal decision to leave their homeland and families behind. That story has been eloquently told by Scott Eden, who originally also broke the Puig smuggling story.[33] More and more Cuban players were discovering the risks of flight and also realizing how they were being used by greedy agents who rarely had their best interests at heart. Some have found their way back home, and a few are even reenergizing their careers in the depleted Cuban circuit. This remains the darkest side of the story surrounding the defections that brought an inevitable end to the Cuban baseball empire.

Ironically, in the end, the United States won the long fight in every Cold War arena, even though it lost the small battles, for example, the numerous assassination attempts, the bungled Bay of Pigs invasion, and ultimately the endless aborted and misguided attempts at unseating Fidel. Those same victories would also be repeated—in truth, be precisely mirrored—in the realm of baseball after the post–2013 collapse of the Cuban League system and thus also the final culmination of Cuba's earlier international dominance in the sport.

By the start of the new millennium, the Cuban Revolution, as envisioned in its earliest years, had floundered and was seemingly on its last legs, even if still standing. It succumbed to many factors: changes on the world scene far beyond its control; the disintegration of the Soviet bloc and the international Communist bloc, which had been its lifeline; the entrenchment of centralized power that appeared necessary to forestall complete collapse; Fidel's own misjudgments; and, more than anything, Fidel's investment of all power and decision-making in his own hands. In the end, these cumulative failures left Fidel (in the words of Georgie Anne Geyer) not only a true "Communist," but also, in reality, the last Communist standing.

That slide had long been apparent. As early as 1985, Dan Rather had challenged Fidel, saying he had made Cuba "one of the most dependent nations on earth."[34] But the always-eloquent Fidel had a ready retort that while Rather might be correct in one sense, Cuba also was the *most independent* country in the world. Why? Because in Fidel's view, Cuba owned the honor of being one of the few remaining adversaries of the United States. Fidel would claim this was a great honor, if only because his small nation had made the United States "so obsessed with this little island."

By the second decade of the new millennium, Cuba's baseball empire, on both the international and domestic fronts, had finally collapsed—again via a complex combination of uncontrollable outside events, a shifting world scene with which it had not kept place, and, perhaps above all else, failures in internal management. But the Cuban baseball enterprise could also still claim a badge of honor similar to the one Fidel had cited. For decades, it had left the great imperial power of MLB obsessed with its thorny presence—with its huge, unattainable cache of talented and coveted players, its anticapitalist system advocating play for honor and pride rather than material reward, and its persistently annoying ability to repeatedly beat the Americans at their own jealously guarded national game.

# 9

# THE ULTIMATE COLLAPSE OF CUBAN BASEBALL

> It seems to me that translation from one language into another, except from those queens of languages, Greek and Latin, is like viewing Flemish tapestries from the wrong side, when, although one can make out the figures, they are covered by threads that obscure them, and one cannot appreciate the smooth finish of the right side.—Miguel de Cervantes Saavedra, *Don Quixote*, Part II, Chapter LXII

**A**t every turn it seems that efforts to unravel misunderstandings and erase follies attached to decades of bungled U.S.–Cuba relations are overlaid with thick and often impenetrable ironies. Roberto González Echevarría, author of the most elaborate treatise on Cuba's pre-1960 baseball history (published in both English- and Spanish-language versions), is widely acclaimed as a scholar of Hispanic literature, not a chronicler of the Cuban American shared national pastime. Primarily, the Yale endowed professor is celebrated in academic circles as a Cervantes expert and known to the general reading public for a scholarly introduction to a Penguin Classic edition of the Cervantes masterpiece. The irony here enters when one stumbles upon a buried passage in one of the final chapters of that world literature classic. It is a passage that González Echevarría might have better noted as a road sign warning for his own translations of Cuba's postrevolution baseball landscape.

Cervantes's narrator, musing on the act of viewing Flemish tapestries from the reverse side as a perfect metaphor for literary translation, offers a sage piece of wisdom about linguistic distance that might apply as much to the difficulties and pitfalls in deciphering other cultures as to the act of cracking diverse language codes. Castro biographer Peter Bourne rightfully argues that one cannot hope to understand the Cuban Revolution without first fully understanding the century-long history of Cuban political disillusionment that spawned it. During a historic 1977 ABC interview, Fidel himself struggled to explain to Barbara Walters the difference between Cuban and American views of a free press. When it comes to a shared national sport, baseball officials in both countries have long held far different views of the game and its potential uses after the 1961 diplomatic rupture. In short, there was never any common ground to build upon. Nor was there ever any room for accommodation or compromise when it came to the disparate views of INDER officials and the top brass at MLB.

It is an oft-repeated mantra—one heard ad nauseam during the past five or more decades—that Cuba and the United States share a common baseball heritage. Time after time we are reminded that the two neighboring countries—Cold War hostilities momentarily put aside— are quite intricately bound together by a deeply entrenched and mutually cherished love for their shared national sport. In both countries, baseball not only reigns as an officially declared national pastime, but also stirs national passions as little else can, although in recent decades that latter claim is perhaps based more on fading tradition than measurable reality when it comes to the game here in North America.

It is this notion of twin baseball passions that, for more than a half-century, has periodically given rise to the wistful belief that if there was indeed a viable path for solving the seemingly intractable hostilities between Washington and Havana, that path might well be traversed with efforts at baseball diplomacy. The idea was first raised by officials from MLB a decade after those same officials, or at least their immediate predecessors, had pulled the plug on the operations of Organized Baseball on the newly minted communist island. After a decade of increased hostilities under two Democratic administrations (Kennedy and Johnson) gave way to a Republican takeover with Richard Nixon, some, both in Washington and the baseball commissioner's office, latched onto the notion that successful efforts at ping-pong diplomacy with Communist China might provide a workable model for rapprochement with Cuba.

**THE LEGACY.** Fidel's son Antonio Castro, top INDER official and former national team doctor, poses in Latin American Stadium with a mural of his father. *From the author's collection*

Cold War apprehensions had peaked in the 1960s, first with the Bay of Pigs fiasco and Cuban Missile Crisis showdown, then with numerous not-well-hidden CIA plans to assassinate the Cuban leader, with airline hijackings that saw the Cuban government lending safe harbor to captured perpetrators, with exile-sponsored acts of terrorism on the island, with increased efforts of the Castro government to export revolution throughout Africa and Latin America, and finally with increased ties between Castro and the Kremlin that further embedded the Cubans in the Soviet camp. And there were proxy Cold War battles on the baseball diamond as well, with Fidel boasting of tournament victories against American teams and U.S. efforts to ban Cuban participation at the 1965 Amateur World Series in Colombia (successful) and the 1966 Central American Games in Puerto Rico (unsuccessful). Baseball also provided an additional touchstone for hostilities at the 1963 Pan American Games in Brazil. When Fidel's veteran ballclub pounded the undermanned American squad twice in São Paulo, U.S. coach Archie Allen and his staff accused the Cubans of gaining an unfair advantage by using professionals and then opted to boycott the awards ceremony, where they were scheduled to collect their silver medals.

But a changing political landscape brought renewed optimism at the outset of a new decade. Beginning in the early 1970s, under a newly empowered Nixon administration in Washington and the simultaneous tenure of MLB commissioner Bowie Kuhn, there were indeed efforts—some highly secret, others often well publicized—aimed precisely in the direction of finally broaching the two-decade impasse.[1] The new baseball détente plans aimed at Cuba were rather loosely related to a novel China-focused "ping-pong" diplomacy effort launched almost simultaneously.[2] But in the Cuban case, the link seemed for many to be even more logical and promising given the lofty status of the sport in both nations. (Who in the United States, or in Cuba for that matter, cared much for Ping-Pong or saw that exotic game as a cultural lever?) That the ensuing decade-long effort in this direction met one obstacle after another and never ultimately panned out seems in retrospect to cry for more detailed analysis and explanation. What is uncovered by any such examination of events is rather clear evidence that most of the roadblocks sabotaging those vain efforts emanated directly from the American side. Fidel, for his part, seemed on the whole to be outspokenly receptive to such proposals and even quite desirous of exchanges of this type. When the Cubans did finally balk on several occasions, it was largely because of gross miscalculations by either Washington politicians or big-league club owners.

Such futile baseball diplomacy efforts seriously waned in the 1980s but were soon given an unexpected, if short-lived, boost in the final year of the twentieth century during the Clinton presidency, and then once again more than a decade later under the administration of African American president Barack Obama. First on deck were Clinton-sanctioned efforts launched by Baltimore Orioles owner Peter Angelos to stage a home-and-home exhibition series in early 1999, between his

American League club and the powerful Cuban national squad that had recently dominated the first two official Olympic baseball tournaments, staged in Barcelona and Atlanta. A handful of years later, in 2002, former president Jimmy Carter attempted to further advance mutual baseball interest during a brief goodwill mission to Havana by providing Fidel with an opportunity to put his national stars on display for the first sitting ex-president to visit during the four decades of Cuban Communist rule. Finally, in December 2014, Barack Obama announced the first serious full-scale effort to reestablish diplomatic ties and end long-standing embargo policies so distasteful to the Cubans. The Obama initiative resulted in little substantial change, despite some efforts to open doors to limited American business ventures, but it did produce a second arrival of a big-league team on the island; this time it was the Tampa Bay Rays who traveled to Havana during their March 2016 spring training schedule for a single heavily hyped exhibition match, with President Obama himself in tow.

Obama's personal excursion to meet face-to-face with the new Cuban leader, Raúl Castro, and also address the Cuban people would, in the end, completely overshadow the détente-oriented baseball exhibition. The baseball match, in fact, became something of a sideshow to the U.S. president's three-day whirlwind tour. Unlike the 1999 ESPN television broadcast of the Orioles–Cuba game, which exposed the surprising strength of the island squad, similar 2016 ESPN coverage took on a very different tone. The Cuban players were no longer a mystery after several years of high-profile defections. And, in reality, the Cuban squad playing the Tampa Bay big-leaguers was a much-diminished outfit.

Attention was paid almost exclusively to the American president, and his lengthy interview with ESPN announcers took center stage, blotting out several innings of actual play-by-play, including a game-deciding home run by Tampa Bay's James Loney.[3] The subtheme of the broadcast was an emotional return home by defector Dayron Varona, apparently added to Tampa's Havana roster primarily to emphasize how Cuban players were now abandoning the island. Baseball also no longer seemed the prime avenue to somewhat thawed U.S.–Cuba relations since in the months separating the December 2014 Obama policy announcement and the March 2016 ballgame little had changed regarding any willingness of Cuba to begin releasing its mother lode of star players for MLB service.

In sum, the various détente plans generated by government forces in Washington and the brain trust of MLB have amounted to little in the end. Oftentimes the efforts have actually stimulated more hostility than anything that might be seen as positive results. The Orioles–Cuba exhibitions (especially the May contest in Baltimore) offered unavoidable excuses for renewed efforts at anti-Castro demonstrations on the part of Miami Cuban American exiles. A short-lived exchange on the amateur level with USA Baseball, which saw top-flight Cuban squads visiting Millington, Tennessee, for matches with American collegiate all-stars were also sabotaged in the mid-1990s by a series of player defections orchestrated by Miami player-agent Joe Cubas. The earliest attempts under Nixon and Ford were doomed time and again by the continued Washington obsession with reported and often exaggerated efforts by Castro to export what were seen in Washington as Soviet-inspired communist-style revolutions in Africa and throughout Latin America.

That baseball détente efforts have been whistling in the wind should not be viewed with any degree of surprise. Reasons for such failures never reached far beyond the fact that the entire notion of shared baseball passions was repeatedly misapprehended and misconstrued by American commentators and politicians. The point missed time and again was that while Castro never abandoned, but instead exploited, the deep roots of the sport after the revolution, he did so with a radically new model of liberated socialist society in mind. The baseball Fidel fostered after 1961 was a sport entirely antithetical in nature and motive to the professional major-league brand, which was the heart and soul of a North American baseball culture. It was true that Cuba had enjoyed a close, if sometimes resentful, working relationship with Organized Baseball during a half-century of pre-1959 American cultural domination. But it was equally true that the roots of Cuban baseball were bound intimately to Cuban nationalism and the late nineteenth-century efforts to free the country from Spanish colonial rule. It was that same notion of employing baseball as a tool for fostering Cuba's long-overdue liberation from outside exploitation to which Castro would turn in the early 1960s. From the viewpoint of the Castro government, the national sport could easily be transformed from a painful illustration of distasteful American cultural control to a principle mechanism for beating the Yankees at their own game.

As mentioned at the outset of chapter 5, this was not at all a radical concept, but one with a long track record elsewhere throughout the world. Handed the game by the Americans, the Japanese reimagined it in their own image and were soon employing the sport to "Japanize" neighboring Asian countries on which they had imperialist designs. Korea and Taiwan, in turn, trace much of their strong baseball heritage to the years under Japanese occupation. Yet, the game also soon provided a double-edged sword and the perfect avenue for young Taiwanese and Korean athletes to "appease and challenge their colonizers."[4] Horsehide diplomacy—shorthand for politicizing the sport for service in spreading cultural hegemony or enhancing national image—was an idea Fidel had borrowed directly from the Americans themselves.

Détente has always been impossible through baseball channels for the simple reason that the two governments and the two baseball administrations that they house hold drastically different and contrasting visions of their respective national sports. Fidel Castro had not killed baseball in Cuba with his revolutionary upheaval at the end of the 1950s and his shift toward communist antiimperialism at the outset of the 1960s. He had only transformed it into a uniquely Cuban enterprise that was totally incompatible with North American conceptions and uses for the sport. Cuba's baseball was built upon the same anticapitalist foundations as the rest of the new Cuban society. At its heart was the notion that athletes shunned material rewards and played only for regional and national honors, and the pride of participation itself. There were no corporate club ownerships. There were no individually negotiated player contracts, no higher financial gains for the upper echelon of star ballplayers. At first, there were not even any ticket sales and thus no revenues for individual ballclub management. Players were servants of the state, and they were never servants of individual ballclub owners, who frequently traded them or sold their contracts.

Baseball in North America in the twentieth century had evolved into a capitalist-inspired entertainment business enterprise. Team owners always operated primarily from a profit motive. While players for more than a half-century were indentured property of the teams that originally signed them, player free agency in the 1960s revolutionized the game and at the same time brought increased labor strife to the sport. Athletes' salaries soared, but owners also saw profits skyrocket through various emerging forms of commercialization. Television took over the game in the late 1950s, and an immediate result was the reduction of minor-league operations and the narrowing of the professional sport's focus to a single major-league operation. The game was always about money, but by the second half of the twentieth century profit by players and owners had become the overwhelming obsession. Exploding television revenues resulted in the electronic media taking over the way the sport was managed. Games increasingly were staged at night for prime-time viewing. The World Series games—the season's climactic highlight—were no longer daytime affairs. Soaring ticket prices and the relocation of stadiums outside of the inner cities meant loss of young fans, as well as loss of interest by the African American communities.

One result of the corporate business orientation of MLB was the way big-league owners and the commissioners they employed began viewing the inevitable internationalizing of the game. There had been a major increase in Latin American and Caribbean talent after mid-century racial integration, and that phenomenon meant viewing the Caribbean countries as virtual player plantations available for handpicking of cheap "foreign" talent. MLB, which never suffered competition well (since that meant rivals for potential revenue), aggressively shut down such competitors as Jorge Pasquel's 1940s Mexican League and orchestrated numerous talent raids on Asian, as well as Caribbean, countries. While there were few imports from Japan due to a notion that Asians were too small for the American game, the Dominican Republic and Venezuela became home to dozens of big-league training academies, which scooped up available local talent, quickly abandoned youngsters who didn't make the grade, and shipped off the more promising talents to often-arduous internships in the North American minor-league systems. By the late 1940s, the Cuban winter league had been taken over as a means of placing its players under control of MLB clubs (see chapter 4). Other winter circuits suffered equally when MLB abandoned them for a more convenient Arizona Fall League operation.

Increasingly, "globalizing the game" meant two things to MLB management. The first and most important was controlling the ever-expanding international player market. With decreasing interest for the sport in inner city areas of the United States, the presence of international talent—especially Latin American and Caribbean talent—was becoming ever more crucial to MLB's future successes. The second meant selling MLB-produced or licensed merchandize throughout the world and establishing markets for the exploding television enterprise. This would be most obviously on display with Japan, when first Hideo Nomo and later Ichiro Suzuki arrived on the scene with MLB West Coast ballclubs in Los Angeles and Seattle. It wasn't long before Japanese fans were snapping up millions of Dodgers and Mariners caps, jerseys, and t-shirts. And overnight, the Asian nation was more riveted by predawn telecasts of big-league games featuring the handful of native stars than they were in the once passionately followed domestic Central and Pacific Leagues.

If the new Cuban model would politicize baseball and subsequently exploit it for international propaganda purposes, that was hardly a change from the way the sport had always been employed by nations that adopted it as their own showcase for cultural identity. Whether it was American sailors carrying bats and balls to Asian shores in the late nineteenth century, Spalding touring the Middle East as baseball missionary during the same epoch, Cubans transporting their inherited game to other Caribbean ports during an 1870s upheaval at home caused by rebellion against Spanish overlords, or the Japanese employing their revamped version of the American game to "Japanize" their Asian neighbors in China, Korea, and Taiwan, it has always been the same frequently replayed scenario.

Baseball has long served as a tool for cultural imperialism and cultural hegemony, one nation after another employing their versions of the sport to impose sacred cultural values and demonstrate the perceived advantages of their own ingrained political, economic, or social systems. In *The Empire Strikes Out*, Robert Elias provides the most eloquent statement of precisely how baseball became a tool for American cultural imperialism, how it was used for expanding the American empire at home and abroad.[5] From the earliest decades of the past century, the Americans had used the sport for nation-building and spreading the American value system overseas. Spalding's 1888 World Tour and Bud Selig's 2006 World Baseball Classic were equally aimed at the globalization of America's national pastime in the service of spreading the American dream of unfettered capitalism and freewheeling democracy. The Asians, first the Japanese, followed by the Koreans and Taiwanese, had long done the same. The difference with Castro's postrevolution

Cuba was only to be found in the precise type of cultural values or the nature of the social system their baseball aimed to foster. The motive itself had more than ample precedent.

American baseball was thus not only a capitalist enterprise; as far as Fidel and his most avid supporters were concerned, it was the epitome of American imperialism. Efforts by Organized Baseball bosses at consuming Cuban baseball under major-league business operations are detailed in chapter 4 with treatment of the demise on the island of both the Sugar Kings franchise and the satellite Cuban Winter League. Hence, North American baseball, as represented by the Organized Baseball professional leagues, was the very essence of all that Fidel's new vision of the sport rejected. The Cuban and American people might have both been passionate about their national pastimes, but after the spring of 1962, they were watching and enjoying two very different games, with very different motives and based on very different philosophies.

Rejection of the major-league brand was therefore the ideal symbol of everything Fidel's revolution stood for. The purpose—if not clear to many of his countrymen in the first years of transition toward Cuban Communism—was to finally throw off the shackles of odious North American control. The idea was for Cubans finally (and actually for the first time ever) to fully possess their own domestic resources and not have their economy or their native industries designed exclusively for profiteering by outside investors from the behemoth to the north. The same was now true of baseball, not only a native "industry," but also a true symbol of the national culture—perhaps even more so since baseball was, in fact, a lynchpin of Cuban society.

The sport was now also a reflection of Fidel's dream for a culture governed not by a drive for material profit, but rather by a deep-seated social consciousness. Fidel's dream, radical as it may have been, was of a moneyless culture, and although that dream was far too idealistic to harbor much hope for long-range success, it indeed was strong enough to overthrow a corrupt state structured around free-enterprise capitalism. Baseball would serve as an ideal showpiece, one that could never be blended with a MLB enterprise based on an entirely separate set of values.

✻ ✻ ✻

In the last analysis, the evidence is quite clear on the matter. During the 1960s, any efforts at U.S.–Cuba rapprochement were sabotaged by Cold War tensions, which severed diplomatic, as well as athletic, links. Fidel's repeated anti-American rhetoric, including his frequent boasting of sports triumphs over America's professionals, muddied the waters, as did growing Washington concerns about the Havana–Moscow ties, which seemed to threaten dangerous Soviet incursions into the Western Hemisphere. When the landscape shifted by the early 1970s and renewed signs of cooperation between East and West emerged, the Nixon and Ford administrations still held tightly to strong reservations about relaxing sanctions on Cuba without demonstrable signs that Fidel would both relax his own hostile stance and also refrain from meddling in other African and Latin American nations. But windows finally appeared to open, however slowly, after 1975, with high profile visits to Havana by such figures as senators George McGovern and Jacob Javits, plus MLB commissioner Bowie Kuhn's repeated efforts to establish baseball exchanges with INDER officials. Yet, the fatal rub was the true motives lurking behind Kuhn's sudden Cuba interests, which aimed more toward the expansion of league profiteering than political détente. It was MLB and not Fidel that once again—as in the case of the 1960 pullout by Organized Baseball—threw in the towel and walked away from serious efforts at playing ball with the Cubans.

The differences in the American approach to the sport and the Castro version were clearly on display in the earliest détente efforts of the 1970s. Novice MLB commissioner Bowie Kuhn revealed this divergence of viewpoint in his earliest pronouncements about globalization, anticipating views that predated a similar position eventually reiterated by MLB's twenty-first-century commissioner four-plus decades later. MLB as an institution has never relinquished its unending thirst for future talent sources, a game plan that in simplest terms translates baseball diplomacy into a blatant form of North American baseball imperialism.

Kuhn's tenure was launched with MLB's first international expansion as the Montreal Expos joined the National League for the 1969 season. But the new commissioner had grander globalization schemes in mind for the sport and, in an early press interview, made it quite clear that those plans translated into extending the reach and control of the top American professional circuit.[6] With the advent of jet air travel, Kuhn envisioned big-league clubs spread well beyond Canada and into other nations where the game was entrenched and thus potential markets were ripe for plucking—Japan, Mexico, other Asian countries, Europe (where the game was slowly gaining a following), Caribbean hotbed countries, and even perhaps Cuba.

A brief history of the détente overtures of the 1970s reveals just how far U.S. efforts went in attempting to bridge the gap through baseball and what the true motivations were that underlay those efforts. There is little debate in hindsight that Washington policymakers and MLB bosses held very different, if sometimes overlapping, agendas for Cuba in the early 1960s. Those agendas had already been exposed with the demise of professional baseball in Havana during the summer of 1960 and late winter of 1961, as discussed in chapter 4 at considerable length. MLB worried about safety issues with its players, that is to say it fretted about protecting its financial interests and heavy investments in athletic talent. Washington, in turn, was driven mainly by a relentless and largely irrational fear of communism—the global spread of the "red menace," which threatened to bury free-enterprise capitalism and the American notion of two-party democracy. It was, first and foremost, quite obviously a fear founded upon the premise that the communist system was simply bad for U.S. business interests. When it comes to assessing U.S. foreign policy at any point in the nation's history it is always a good starting point to follow the money trail.

Washington, for the most part, had religiously stuck by ruthless dictator Fulgencio Batista because, despite his brutality, his administration was dedicated to protecting the free rein of U.S. corporate interests that dominated the island's rather healthy economy. Moreover, because Batista pushed the right buttons in Washington by advocating his strong opposition to the communists, while at the same time promulgating fears of communist tendencies among the rebels in the Sierra Maestra. The history of America's backing of other ruthless dictators, especially in Latin America—as long as they appeared to be bulwarks against the threat of communist disruption of American business interests—is a deep one. American support for the imperialist French presence in Indochina and consequent abandonment of Ho Chi Minh's populist drive for national independence, due merely to its reputed communist leanings, would soon bear equally disastrous results in the form of costly involvement on the wrong side of the Vietnam independence struggle. It was this misguided Washington policy position that long caused Cubans to view American promotion of democracy as something of a sham. And their own form of political corruption and rigged elections under puppet governments with open American backing—stretching from the end of U.S. military occupation in 1909 through the unsavory administrations of Gerardo Machado, Ramón Grau San Martin, Carlos Prio Socarrás, and Batista himself—had only increased the growing skepticism.

From Washington's perspective, baseball employed as a diplomatic tool might bring Cuba back closer to the American democratic model, or so it was believed. And for MLB bosses, it might open the door wide enough to provide access to a lost mother lode of Cuban talent that might again be made available to big-league clubs. Once the doors were slammed shut on Cuban baseball and the Cubans surprisingly began using the sport to dominate international amateur events the attractiveness of the Cuban talent became greater still.

Earlier chapters have already demonstrated that there was little beyond open hostility throughout most of the 1960s as Americans charged Fidel with using sports, and especially baseball, as a Cold War tool. Fidel would even claim Cuban origins for the game once the war of words heated up between the two adversaries. In *Baseball Diplomacy, Baseball Deployment*, Turner places Fidel's baseball origin claims in the specific context of efforts in 1961 to first promote soccer as a new national sport more in tune with his new Soviet leanings and inclinations toward a socialist/communist society.[7] Failing to generate any real soccer interest, Castro aimed at revising the history of the national game by claiming in 1962 that it was not a North American invention but one derived from a pre-Colombian game on the island called *batos* (the name eventually adopted for the country's sports equipment manufacturing industry). An editorial in the *Christian Science Monitor* at the time facetiously remarks that the ridiculous Fidel boast should be indication enough that the island had indeed earned its Communist credentials (a reference to similar claims by the Russians that they, in fact, had invented the earliest versions of the sport).[8]

Debate about rule-bending Cuban use of perceived professionals first arose during the 1963 Pan American Games in São Paulo (see chapter 6). The Cubans would dominate the Americans in that event and U.S. coaches would consequently protest that the Cubans were using players that looked like professionals given their age and sophisticated skill level. Of course, they were not professional players by big-league standards. But the Cubans did have the advantage of using more experienced athletes (ones that trained year-round in the new competitive national league) and pulling them from the full island-wide talent crop—not just schoolboy amateur squads. The Americans were so outraged at their losses in Brazil that they boycotted the ceremony rather than collect their silver medals.

The debate continued to rage for much of the decade, and the Americans did their utmost to sabotage growing Cuban baseball success and either limit or discount its impact in international events. The dispute concerning the definition of amateurism, which had marred the 1963 Brazilian event, would continue to boil. The Cubans were kept out of the 1965 IBAF-sponsored Amateur World Series in Colombia for political reasons alone and thus prevented from defending their 1961 title won in Costa Rica. The Colombian government had already broken off diplomatic ties with the Castro regime and refused to issue visas necessary for the Cuban delegation to travel to Cartagena. There was similar political tension and controversy surrounding the 1966 Central American Games in San Juan, this time with the Americans threatening denial of visas (the location being a U.S. territory). Cuba appealed to the IOC and its top official Avery Brundage, ruled in their favor, denouncing the attempts to taint athletics with politics and threatening to move the games out of San Juan. Although the Cubans did make it to San Juan and capture the baseball prize over runner-up Puerto Rico, they were nonetheless blocked from flying directly to the games from Havana. Thus, much of their delegation missed the opening ceremonies.

While themselves uninvolved in the 1966 San Juan Games, the Americans finally tasted baseball victory at Winnipeg in 1967, during the next Pan Am Games reunion, the first time they were able to steal some glory from the Cubans in a center-stage amateur event. Although the Cubans did edge the U.S. squad in their preliminary round shoot-out, the Americans grabbed two of three championship playoff matches (details can be found in chapter 6). The Cubans would nonetheless bounce back at the 1969 IBAF Amateur World Series, staged in Santo Domingo, by running through the field with a perfect 10-game slate.

Again, the Santo Domingo games—the last such meeting during the turbulent 1960s—were played under considerable political tension, this time due to strong anti-American feelings spawned by a U.S. invasion of the Dominican Republic four years earlier. By decade's end, the Cold War hostilities were still every bit as alive on the sporting front as they were in the political arena.

Those early efforts throughout the 1960s to keep an increasingly strong Cuban baseball squad out of international tournaments would, in the end, constitute what might only be viewed as an American "sports embargo" of Cuba that paralleled the ongoing economic embargo launched by the Eisenhower administration in 1960 and still in full swing a half-century later. Throughout the first decade of Castro's control of the Cuban government, baseball had established itself as a vital tool of political diplomacy. But up to this point it had been a tool used to drive the two adversary nations further apart, not bring them closer together.

A new decade would launch a new type of diplomacy under the American presidency of Richard M. Nixon. While Cold War tensions had escalated and eventually peaked in the 1960s with the Bay of Pigs adventure and an almost disastrous missile crisis during Kennedy's tenure, plus continued American "communist paranoia" during both the Johnson and Ford presidencies, and also the extensions of Cuba-aimed boycott policies into the sporting arena, the changing landscape of the early 1970s seemed to hold renewed promise for at least small avenues of cooperation between the United States and the Communist bloc nations. That shift in diplomacy was focused largely on China in the years immediately following the November 1968 Nixon election. And if Cuba policy was now open for reexamination as well, Cuba still seemed to present a more difficult issue due to well-known personal hostilities between the newly elected American president and the entrenched Cuban prime minister.

Nixon had personal reasons for begrudging Fidel and his government since twice the Cubans had gotten in the way of his own personal political ambitions. Kennedy's outspoken criticisms of communism and his actions during the missile crisis had cost Nixon two recent elections. And despite the optimisms about a new era of open relations expressed in Nixon's January 1969 inaugural address, the new president quickly proved something of a Cold War hawk in the mold of Eisenhower, whom he had served as vice president. The new president seemed fixed in his adamant opposition to communism and unwillingness to deal with a communist government only 90 miles from the U.S. shoreline; however, if Nixon seemed an unlikely proponent of relaxing hostility toward Communist Cuba, his January inaugural did signal a shift toward replacing confrontation with an "era of negotiation." And the Cold War hawk he had been in the mid- and late 1950s was now apparently slowly transforming into a voice advocating the necessary reassessment of earlier Cold War policies.

As noted earlier, Bowie Kuhn simultaneously took over the reins of MLB, ascending to the post only days after Nixon's own Washington inauguration. The new commissioner also seemed open to détente with Cuba and, in tandem, a new president and new baseball commissioner were both soon launched on a course that seemed to signal an environment attuned to possible efforts at baseball diplomacy. Kuhn was quick to express optimism about a Cuban presence for MLB, observing that if the political environment were only a bit different, Havana might already be sporting a big-league franchise. That had been the dream of Sugar Kings' owner Bobby Maduro before the revolution, and Kuhn seemed to believe Cold War tensions were all that stood in the way of turning the clock back a decade or two. This view, of course, ignored the radical changes in baseball's role under the new Cuban administration.

Echoing Martin Luther King's rhetoric and displaying his own naiveté about the history of U.S.–Cuba relations (at least as seen from the Cuban perspective), Kuhn spoke to viewers of the CBS news program *Face the Nation* of his own "dream" that baseball could not only build bridges between races at home, but also repair political relations between adversarial nations on the international front. He cited rumors of "tremendous listenership in Cuba to big-league radio broadcasts" (apparently those beamed from Miami) and wondered why that interest "can't in some way build a bridge between the United States and Cuba."

Fidel, for his part, in turn made early overtures to the newly installed American president. Sending a message to the White House through Swiss ambassador Alfred Fischli, Fidel signaled his willingness to hold direct discussions on a number of issues of contention, especially Cuba's exporting of revolution to other Latin American countries, as well as Washington-sponsored raids on Cuba and the Cuban refugees being housed in Guantanamo. The bottom line was Castro and his government seemed willing to work on improving relations with Washington. National security advisor Henry Kissinger recommended to the president that the best policy would be to at least test the seriousness of the Cuban overtures and formally inquire about Fidel's specific future plans. But Nixon was still quite hesitant, and although agreeing with Kissinger about the wisdom of listening to Havana, he urged a mostly cautious approach to anything involving Castro and Cuba.

If there was any room for specific peace overtures from either side, it seemed they would initially have to involve "peripheral issues" and not major policy positions. One issue of contention that offered perhaps the best avenue for compromise was the one involving the spate of American commercial airplanes hijacked to Cuba in the late 1960s. The earliest hijackings at the outset of the decade had mostly involved Cuban planes commandeered by fleeing exiles hoping to reach Miami, but the trend had reversed in recent years. The problem of planes being diverted to Cuba would eventually even touch baseball. In October 1969, three major-league players and a coach traveling to winter-league assignments in Venezuela were victims of just such an incident that left them with an unscheduled layover in Havana. The National Airlines DC-8 flight out of Miami was only briefly detained on the island, and Kansas City Royals catcher Dennis Paepke would later report that the Cuban officials treated American passengers well and even handed out samples of quality Cuban cigars.

Despite his earlier positive overtures, it would be Fidel who would soon again be muddying the waters with his continued denunciations of the United States and frequent public addresses, which struck a distasteful tone in Washington. It was one such attack in particular that more than likely was an overriding factor in dooming the first serious effort at some kind of overt baseball diplomacy paralleling the China ping-pong overtures unfolding that same month.

In April 1971, on the 10th anniversary of the Bay of Pigs invasion, Fidel blasted Washington for meddling in Latin America and also for continuing the inhumane embargo policies against his nation.[9] Then, three months later, at annual patriotic July 26 holiday festivities commemorating the Moncada attack and M-26-7 movement, the theme was continued, along with a pledge never to stop resisting U.S. imperialism and, perhaps worse still to American diplomatic ears, a promise to work toward liberating every enslaved Latin American nation.

These disruptions by Fidel of any perceived thawing of tensions would ironically overlap with an initial venture from the American side to use baseball as a potential goodwill gesture in dealing with the Cubans. The first specific efforts at détente were initiated by San Diego Padres manager Preston Gómez in May 1971. The Cuba native, who had managed the Sugar Kings during their championship run in 1959, had received permission from Havana to visit his ailing father a year earlier. Gómez had known Fidel in the late 1950s through a personal connection with Celia Sánchez (they had grown up as neighbors in the sugar mill town of Preston, from which Gómez derived his given name) and sought out the Cuban leader during his 1970 stopover to initiate some personal baseball diplomacy. He assessed the Cuban league and its talent for INDER officials, chatted with Fidel about the island's new baseball system, and staged a few clinics for local athletes. A mere month after the first ping-pong diplomacy effort in China, Gómez announced his own plans to take a team of MLB stars to Havana, planning for an exhibition game he claimed had the full backing of Commissioner Kuhn. Gómez was also optimistic Fidel would welcome the visit of the big-leaguers since he was obviously such an avid baseball fan.

But the Nixon State Department was not about to lend its cooperation to any such full-blown effort at baseball diplomacy. There had only recently been the threat to peace in the hemisphere engendered by a CIA-discovered Soviet plan to construct a submarine base near Cienfuegos, off Cuba's southern coast. While that issue had been handled quickly, quietly, and behind the scenes with the Russians, in an obvious effort to avoid another missile-crisis-type showdown, there were still the repeated verbal attacks on the United States by Fidel, which rankled leaders in Washington. Nixon administration officials were not about to enter into any détente efforts with an outspoken enemy that might prove difficult to rationalize to a wary American public.

While one effort at renewed diplomacy tied to baseball had met an immediate roadblock, there was soon another less-noted setback connected with the amateur version of the sport. During the dozen years following the revolution, Cuban and American teams had confronted one another on a number of occasions in international tournament events, even if the meetings were anything but friendly in tone. But it had been almost 30 years since the last time an American squad had journeyed to Cuba for such a face-off, the last occasion being the IBAF Amateur World Series, staged in Havana in October 1942. That event, played under wartime restrictions, witnessed an understaffed American team win only one of seven matches, then withdraw from the competition and lose its final four games by forfeit. Havana was again set to host the 1971 Amateur World Series, and from the moment IBAF officials had voted to award the games to the Cubans, the United States Amateur Baseball Federation affiliate had threated to boycott. While initially citing the tense political climate as reason enough for skipping the games, the Federation president, Jim Fehring, would eventually cite other reasons, most of them financial (e.g., the cost of shipping two amateur clubs overseas in the same year) and seeming to hold little water.

There had, in fact, been a more limited sports-related détente effort in the spring of 1971, when an American men's volleyball team traveled to Havana. But that visit largely flew under the radar in the United States, as volleyball was not a high-profile sport for the Americans. And whatever goodwill had been generated by the volleyball exchange was largely swamped by the hostilities generated during the Pan American Games in Cali, Colombia, a few weeks earlier. There, Cuba finished a surprising second in the overall medal count while easily sweeping to victory in baseball, running the field in eight games and winning the single match with the runner-up American squad. Again, the results spurred complaints from the American quarter about sham amateurism on the part of the Cubans. And the games stirred a further spike in ill will when Colombian crowds appeared to be heavily pro-Cuban, cheered the Cubans heartily at opening ceremonies, and booed U.S. athletes with jeers of "*Yanqui* go home!"

With the Americans on the sidelines, the Cuban team also ran the table at the November IBAF Amateur World Series, its third title in a row. Castro, for his part, continued to tout baseball wins and other sports triumphs as propaganda victories. Thus, his rhetoric further inflamed tensions. Following the triumphant Cali Pan American Games in August, he appeared at a huge public rally in Havana to celebrate the strong Cuban showing. He welcomed his proud team home and delivered a lengthy address (more than an hour), labeling the win over the Americans a sports-version replay of the Bay of Pigs victory at Playa

Girón. He also noted that in catching up to the Americans in the overall medal race, Cuban athletes were signaling the inevitable demise of hated imperialism. Those arguing that Fidel and the Cubans were using sport as a political platform found much in Fidel's speeches to support their point of view.

Fidel would especially use baseball victories—particularly those against the Americans—a point he emphasized only weeks later on a visit to Chile, where he again took up the theme, this time to boast that although the Americans may have invented baseball, his Cuban teams could beat the *Yanquis* at their own game simply by abolishing professionalism and counting on athletes motivated only by true revolutionary spirit.[10] He further seized an opportunity to suggest that the American boycott of the Amateur World Series, scheduled in Havana that same month, not only signaled Washington's continued efforts at political sabotage but also reflected the American fear of being beaten at their own national sport by the superior Cuban baseball squad.[11]

Against this backdrop of continued hostility, a smaller effort at baseball exchange occurred only a few months later with little attention from the North American media. At the behest of Philadelphia club management and MLB officials, then-Phillies manager Frank Lucchesi would quietly visit Havana without fanfare in a low-key effort to further explore the potential for some kind of larger official exchange. Briefed by Preston Gómez before his departure, Lucchesi would spend four days on the island, attend three Cuban league games, hold still another clinic with Cuban players, and answer a request from INDER officials to offer candid appraisals of Cuban talent levels. There was no meeting with Fidel, however, who at the time was on a trip to Poland. Upon his return, the Phillies manager spoke to reporters about the level of Cuban baseball, which he saw as being held back mainly by a shortage of quality equipment. He would also soon be interviewed by CIA officials concerning any observed Soviet military presence, a fact that might shed further light on precisely why his trip might have been approved by Washington in the first place.

Personal antagonism and Cold War tension persisted throughout the final years of the doomed Nixon administration, and the stifling post-Watergate atmosphere greeting the new Washington administration of Gerald Ford provided few, if any, signals of modification on the Cuba issue. By 1974, there were a few new equally abortive efforts with little to show in the end. In April of that year, Sean Downey Jr., later known as television talk show host Morton Downey Jr., announced plans to develop an ambitious international baseball circuit to be known as the World Baseball Association. His idea was to build a league comprised of major U.S. cities without MLB clubs and also include such potential baseball hotbed ports as Mexico, Japan, the Philippines, Venezuela, and Cuba. The notion of such a professional league being a potential bridge between different cultures was at least given some lip service. Nonetheless, the Downey proposal lacked necessary financial backing and never moved out of the planning stage.

But in September of the same year, a Portland attorney named Donald Walker floated a similar concept and wrote directly to President Ford to tout the political potential of his own venture in opening doors with Cuba. Walker's parallel plan quickly fell on deaf ears in the White House, which cited too many legal and diplomatic obstacles and pitfalls if a franchise were planned for Havana. An even more creative request that same year came from a Washington lawyer, Joseph Gebhardt, who floated the prospect of MLB granting Havana an American League franchise. The State Department again vetoed the formal request from Gebhardt, but—more important still—there was also no evidence that MLB as a private enterprise would ever be supportive of any such expansions.

Preston Gómez, with the continued backing of Bowie Kuhn, was also not ready to abandon his enthusiasm on the Cuba front and would soon be making a second effort in that direction by March 1975. Kuhn originally approached Kissinger at a December 1973 Washington dinner party and was told to keep the secretary abreast of any new plans for a visit of MLB All-Stars to Havana. Kuhn, with this renewed encouragement, wrote to Kissinger in January with news that Gómez had met with INDER director Jorge García Bango, and it appeared the Cubans had encouraged a plan for a possible March 1975 exhibition. Kuhn also revealed that Bango had invited him to meet in Mexico City for further negotiations the following week. The proposal initially appeared to have some backing when Kissinger raised the issue of baseball diplomacy with the assistant secretary of state for inter-American affairs, William D. Rogers.

Rogers seemed perhaps more supportive than his boss, Kissinger, had anticipated and, in mid-January, sent a memo to the secretary of state suggesting that a message approving the exchange be forwarded to the Cubans with Washington–Havana go-between Frank Mankiewicz. The proposal would only die a quick death on Kissinger's desk when the top policymaker instructed Rogers to delete his passage about a baseball exchange and "straighten out this whole Bowie Kuhn thing."[12] It appeared that Kissinger was open to possible baseball diplomacy at some point in the future but was not prepared to move in that direction without more conciliation and compromise on the part of the Castro government.

Undiscouraged, Kuhn went ahead with his plan to meet Bango in Mexico City in late January 1975, and the discussions with INDER officials apparently offered so much promise the commissioner again phoned Rogers directly upon his return to press his point. Rogers, in turn, sent yet another memo to Kissinger detailing his conversation with the MLB commissioner and outlining specific plans for an exhibition trip already tentatively set for March 28. A group of MLB stars would fly to Havana for the weekend, hold a Friday afternoon clinic, play a Saturday exhibition, and fly home Saturday night. Kuhn, for his part, had stressed to Rogers that such a venture would project a positive image of American culture; he also revealed a vaguely guarded hope that the game would fuel aspirations of Cuban players for someday playing in the American majors. The true intentions of MLB's commissioner and its club owners for raiding Cuban talent were never far from the surface.

Rogers strongly advocated Kuhn's plan and even suggested that President Ford be involved in formally announcing the planned MLB visit to Havana. The assistant secretary of state adopted a position as Kuhn's advocate with the State Department by hinting that such a baseball overture could revive memories of Kissinger's promotions of the China ping-pong efforts. But such implied involvement of politics in the mix proved to be a fatal error since Kissinger was still adamant that Washington should not support such a high-profile public event without first seeing at least some accompanying political gestures from Fidel on the Cuban end. In short, for the top officials in the Ford administration—like those before them in the Nixon White House—baseball diplomacy was not as much a step toward improved Cold War relations as it was a type of carrot to be used for coaxing compromise and concession from Fidel. The sincerity attached to Washington's hopes (i.e.,

Cuban compromise) seems, in retrospect, as hollow as MLB's thinly veiled desires for reestablishing Cuba as a cheap available source for boatloads of new island-bred MLB talent.

If détente overtures were stalled on the baseball front, they did, at the same time, seem to inch forward in broader diplomatic circles, especially on the congressional front. Senators Jacob Javits of New York and Claiborne Pell of Rhode Island—both advocates of ending trade restrictions—had visited the island in September 1974, enjoyed a cordial private session with Fidel, and upon their return urged the Ford administration to work toward improved ties. More attention-getting was a goodwill trip by South Dakota senator George McGovern the following spring. On his May 1975 sojourn to Havana, McGovern conducted a lengthy nine-hour interview with Fidel. U.S. press coverage of the meeting highlighted Fidel's expression of desire for greater friendship with the Americans but also his renewed calls for lifting of the odious trade embargo. Even baseball diplomacy seemed to get a proper push when McGovern suggested that baseball and basketball exchanges between the two countries might thaw the diplomatic freeze. Castro's response was so positive that shortly thereafter he approached Europe-based IBAF officials about formal permission for his amateur ballplayers to stage a match against a team of American big-leaguers.

Unfortunately, the McGovern visit, promising as it was, also had its share of negative impact in Washington and elsewhere Stateside. In the aftermath of his dialogue with the American senator, Castro had made three surprisingly positive conciliatory overtures, first announcing plans to cut back on support for guerrilla activities elsewhere in Latin America, then turning over several individuals accused of the 1971 hijackings of American planes, and also returning $2 million in ransom money confiscated during an additional 1972 skyjacking. Kissinger responded by complaining that although Castro had finally made a noteworthy concession in returning the hijacking ransom, he did it in a way that seemed to favor his Democratic friends in Congress rather than more appropriately dealing directly with the White House. And in addition to this specter of partisan politics, the possibility of any weakening of a Washington hard-line stance on Cuba spawned renewed protests from the Cuban exile community, sparked especially by reports that the Organization of American States was about to relax its Cuba sanctions.[13] Also adding to renewed negativity were additional revelations about past CIA attempts at assassinating Fidel, reports that were seemingly destined to further antagonize Castro and again muddy the détente picture. [14]

Fidel also seemed to again sour on his own overtures toward the Americans by the fall of 1975. There were renewed reports of Cuban agents meddling in a new communist-inspired revolution in Portugal and also efforts by the Cubans to extract North Atlantic Treaty Organization secrets from the Portuguese military. But the spike in renewed tensions arose in late 1975, concerning Cuba's role in an Angolan civil war. Washington was alarmed that Fidel was supplying military aid to the leftist MPLA (Popular Movement for the Liberation of Angola), while the Americans were clearly on the other side of the conflict. The entire Angola affair took on the guise of yet another U.S.–Soviet Cold War stand-off.

While the Washington anger regarding Cuban support for Angolan leftist rebel leader Agostinho Neto threatened to sabotage several years of behind-the-scenes dialogue aimed at normalization with the Americans, Fidel apparently believed maintaining a foothold in Africa and the support his Angola operation was gaining among other Third World leaders outstripped normalizing relations with the United States. [15] Receiving new details on Cuba's Angola activities in November, Kissinger cut off talks with Havana. Simultaneously, he again pulled the plug on any possibility of proposed baseball exhibitions with the Cubans tentatively set for March 1976. [16]

There was only one bright spot on the Cuban front by the midpoint of the 1970s, and that came with a feel-good personal story surrounding exiled Cuban big-league pitcher Luis Tiant Jr., at the time a star hurler for the pennant-bound Boston Red Sox. The Tiant family saga provided still another dimension of the Cuban American divide and painful Cuban diaspora. The younger Tiant's parents had remained in Cuba when the pitcher departed his homeland in 1961 (after a single season in the Cuban winter league during that circuit's final winter), and the younger Tiant had not seen his father—a former star left-hander in the Cuban winter leagues and North American Negro Leagues—in 15 years. Now a 14-year big-league veteran, Tiant Jr. had long harbored hopes that his aging parents might someday see him pitch in the big leagues and only recently had reached out to Massachusetts senator Edward Brooke for some assistance in fulfilling his personal dream. Brooke, in turn, had sent a formal request to the Cuban authorities via McGovern, who was soon headed to Havana on his May diplomatic missions. McGovern, perhaps somewhat surprisingly, managed to obtain Fidel's cooperation in the matter. It was a gesture that two decades later would be twice repeated in the similar cases of the Hernández half-brothers Liván and El Duque (see chapter 8). Considerable publicity surrounded the elder Tiant's several-month visit, which saw him throw out a ceremonial first ball before finally seeing his son play in Fenway Park for the first time.

The first real glimmer of hope for an eventual ending of the long-drawn-out Cold War hostilities between Havana and Washington would emerge with the January inauguration of Democratic president Jimmy Carter. Shortly after being sworn in as the sixth U.S. president to confront Fidel's government, Carter began supporting initiatives that seemed to point toward the long-awaited normalization of U.S.–Cuba relations. Americans seemed disenchanted with Vietnam-era foreign policy stances, and the new, more liberal president was poised to reverse course and distance the country from some of its more unsavory ties and outworn anti-Communist stances.

In February, the new secretary of state, Cyrus Vance, signaled a meeting with the Cubans to renew the lapsed 1973 accord governing airplane hijackings. Vance had been lobbying for changes in Cuba policy even before taking office and had recommended to Carter dropping of the embargo on at least food and medicine. A Cuban military presence in Angola still seemed a stumbling block, but the new American administration seemed willing to put aside demands for Cuban withdrawal from Africa as a prerequisite for any future negotiations.

Interest in Cuba exchanges aroused in MLB by mid-1970s movements toward a potential normalization of diplomatic relations now also stretched beyond the office of Commissioner Bowie Kuhn. Aware of Fidel's reported enthusiasms for the New York club and benefitting from the presence of Gabe Paul as its new team president, the New York Yankees were soon getting into the act. A year earlier, the American League club had hosted Cuba's United Nations delegation for a game in their temporary home at Shea Stadium (Yankee Stadium was being renovated). In December 1976, Paul wrote to INDER director Jorge García Bango proposing a visit by his club to Havana the following spring, an overture that received surprising immediate support when Fidel himself expressed enthusiasm during a televised interview. More importantly, the Carter administration, now warming to the idea of baseball diplomacy and larger efforts at détente as well, gave its guarded, if not full, backing to the venture. Secretary Vance voiced support at a March 4 press conference; a day later, in a radio interview with Walter Cronkite, Carter hinted at lifting travel restrictions and called the Yankee trip a definite "possibility."

The Yankee visit to Havana took shape quickly in the form of a proposed three-game set on tap for either late March or early April. Owner George Steinbrenner seized on press interviews to stress the goodwill aspects of the tour, hiding for the moment some ulterior motives that would only later become blatantly apparent. Several Yankee players took a much lighter tone in joking about the involvement of Fidel Castro. Graig Nettles joshed that if Fidel wanted to bat against the big-leaguers the team might have an extended stay when the comandante failed to get a base hit.[17]

But although much of the former Washington reticence had seemed to evaporate this time around, surprisingly enough, this most recent venture met unexpected resistance from the most unlikely source. It was former détente champion Bowie Kuhn who now stepped forward to scuttle the latest efforts. One could speculate that the baseball commissioner was less than enthusiastic for a plan not of his own making. But Kuhn's opposition appeared rather to stem from protests from other club owners (Dodgers boss Walter O'Malley in the forefront) fearing that the Yankees might gain an unfair advantage in the scouting of Cuban talent. Kuhn had previously lobbied for trips by all-star teams and not individual MLB clubs, and he now stood fast in that position. It was clear that with Cuban détente under Carter increasingly viewed with optimism, the club owners, if not the commissioner as well, were focused not on any easing of political tensions, but only their wishful thinking that a huge stockpile of Cuban talent might soon be available for raiding.

The Cubans—meaning Fidel, of course—had seemingly welcomed the Yankee visit and now had waning interest in the commissioner's alternative proposal of substituting an all-star squad. And several members of the Yankees were quite outspoken in pointing a collective finger at the commissioner as fully responsible for vetoing their plans. Gabe Paul harped on the goodwill gestures being sabotaged by Kuhn's uncooperative stance. Manager Billy Martin questioned any commissioner's authority to dictate an individual team's exhibition schedule and played an even heavier "political" card in challenging the decision and the lobbying of other owners: "Their stubbornness might even get us into a war."[18] The Yankee brass also stressed that Fidel had specifically invited them and not an all-star squad. In the face of Kuhn's delays and vetoes, Fidel grew impatient. With no compromise between Kuhn and the Yankees on the horizon, the Cubans, who were already planning to shut down their own season for the visit, rescinded their invitation in mid-March.

But neither the Yankees nor Kuhn were finished with their dreams for a Cuban détente adventure. In the spring of 1977, the Carter administration lifted the long-standing travel ban on Americans visiting Cuba. That announcement came just a few days after Secretary Vance had informed the baseball commissioner that the State Department had no objections to plans Kuhn was still pushing for sending a group of league all-stars to play in Cuba. Any immediate exhibition trip now seemed a logistical uncertainty for the near future since the MLB regular season was only weeks away. But one immediate result was a small wave of cultural exchanges that included several sports-related ventures. McGovern returned to Havana in April with a pair of South Dakota college basketball squads for an exhibition series (University of South Dakota and South Dakota State teams were both drubbed by a more experienced Cuban national team). The Cuban basketballers would also return the visit in November, playing not only the same South Dakota squads, but also NCAA champion Marquette in Milwaukee. And a collection of American amateur boxers would also visit Cuba in February 1978, although plans by boxing promoter Don King to stage a professional heavyweight bout in Havana fell through.

Seizing on the new openings and relaxed travel regulations, Yankees owner George Steinbrenner made a surprise two-day excursion to Havana in May 1977, with Gabe Paul and former star pitcher Whitey Ford in tow. The Yankees entourage watched a pair of games, toured some training facilities, and wrangled a direct meeting with Fidel. But the rather transparent motives of the Yankees owner were quickly revealed when he antagonized his INDER hosts with reported inquiries about the possibilities of buying up some top Cuban ballplayers. And Steinbrenner was not alone in his open courting of Cuban talent. Chicago White Sox owner Bill Veeck also made an unannounced swing through

Havana that spring and talked openly about player acquisitions. Frank Mankiewicz would report in the *Washington Post* that Veeck had apparently learned from Steinbrenner's ill-timed tactics and took a very different approach.[19] Veeck reportedly offered only to lease players and thus make sure their salaries went directly to the Cuban officials in order not to jeopardize the athletes' amateur status.

In the aftermath of the Yankees fiascos, Kuhn once more resumed his own relentless efforts to send an all-star team of big-leaguers to Havana for a high-profile exhibition game. During Senator McGovern's second visit to Havana in the spring of 1977, to accompany South Dakota University basketball squads, Fidel had again extended a formal invitation to the American politician for a MLB all-star club to come to Havana. Cuba's number-one baseball fan was apparently still warm to notions of such an exchange even if disappointed the visitors might not be the New York Yankees. With a newly aroused optimism now apparent in both Havana and the MLB commissioner's office, officials from both sides agreed to meet in Mexico City in December 1977, to again try and hammer out details for a coveted, if long-frustrated, exchange.

But any advances had been more wishful thinking than substantive plans, and logistical problems seemed yet again destined to doom this second round of Mexico City meetings. There were immediate disagreements concerning both the length of any exhibition series and whether the Cubans might reciprocate with a U.S. visit of their own. And there were also reports, without details or specific sources, that the true stumbling block came with the MLB commissioner's new demands for Cuban authorities to make their ballplayers available on the market for MLB clubs. Kuhn apparently cancelled the proposed exchange when INDER boss Jorge Bango flatly refused to release any players for big-league export. If that were not enough, both sides also still feared likely threats of violence from an exile Cuban American community unwilling to abide any efforts to "play ball with the hated Castro regime."[20]

This final ill-fated effort would reveal precisely why baseball détente could not work in any of the forms in which Americans—both Washington politicos and MLB officials—had conceived it from the start. The Washington politicos wanted Fidel to drop his adventures in Africa and other Third World countries and curtail further anti-American rhetoric, conditions that were not likely to be met. Fidel held out for an end of the U.S. economic embargo, an idea that decades later is still not looked upon with favor in Washington. But the biggest stumbling block was a barely hidden agenda dear to Kuhn and the big-league club owners, who were seemingly only touting international friendship as a cover for extending MLB economic interests lost at the time of Fidel's ascension to power.

Although high-profile efforts at baseball diplomacy may have ended with the rift between Kuhn and Bango in Mexico City, there was one more quiet exchange far off the radar before the decade ended. In late 1977, the Houston Astros sent a small delegation of players and coaches to Havana to hold unapproved clinics with Cuban players on an informal basis.[21] The group was headed by manager Bill Virdon and included several frontline players (Bob Watson, Ken Forsch, and Enos Cabell) and coaches (Deacon Jones and Bob Lillis). Since no formal games were played and there was no meeting with Fidel or other top INDER officials, the visit received no mainstream press coverage. Apparently, Houston GM Tal Smith did not inform Kuhn of the trip since he feared being turned down.

While the American professionals were now done with efforts to arrange Cuban visits, there would be one final historic exchange in October 1979, when a U.S. amateur squad with future big-leaguers Joe Carter and Terry Francona took part in the Havana-based Intercontinental Cup tournament. It was the first visit by an American baseball squad—amateur or professional—since the International League had pulled up stakes and relocated to Jersey City in midsummer 1960.

If the decade of the 1970s had been marred by repeatedly renewed hopes and repeatedly failed efforts at U.S.–Cuba baseball diplomacy, a spike in Cold War hostilities of the early 1980s would usher in three further decades of persistent stalemate. The largest factor in the renewed post-Carter administration hostilities between the two nations seemed to come with the Mariel Boatlift saga, which launched the new decade. Mariel events themselves contained a small baseball backstory since banished Cuban star Bárbaro Garbey was one of the ex-prisoners released by Fidel in his attempt to embarrass a Miami Cuban exile community with a flood of convicts and undesirables. Garbey would become the first refugee from the Cuban League to reach the majors.

A decade later, the first cracks would appear in Fidel's baseball empire with the earliest defectors from the Cuban national team.

Throughout the 1990s, the only American focus on the Cuban game was, in fact, one of encouraging the slowly growing defector phenomenon. A brief exchange with the Baltimore Orioles in 1999 seemed an aberration and, in the end, only ramped up tensions and hostilities between MLB and the Cuban Baseball Federation with its surrounding protests from exiles and efforts of American player agents to drum up hoped-for defections. The first decade of the new century was marked by the first serious on-field encounters between top Cuban stars and big-leaguers during the inaugural MLB World Baseball Classic. But even that event notably was marred by last-minute efforts in Washington to block Cuban participation. With increasing player defections in the second decade of the new century, the two sides remained further apart than ever on the baseball front, with MLB ballclubs now scooping up players encouraged to abandon their homeland and INDER authorities therefore more incensed by perceived American baseball imperialism than ever.

Ultimately, it was a distinct irony that once the political climate seemed to change for the better in Washington after the Carter administration began to ease hard-line Cold War policies of the Nixon and Ford presidencies, it was suddenly MLB and not Washington that threw major roadblocks in the path of a long-hoped-for baseball détente. Cuba's Angola activities had been the largest obstacle to breakthrough diplomacy under Secretary of State Kissinger, but Fidel had begun backing away from African involvement by the late 1970s. Bourne details Fidel's shift in this period away from his earlier role as protagonist in Third World conflicts to a new guise as elder statesman and mediator.[22] And there were other efforts at compromise emanating from Havana.

Mutual support from both Fidel and Carter officials for a visit by the Yankees in 1977 offered the greatest promise in two decades. But once the Angolan obstacle was removed and Fidel's anti-American rhetoric tamped down, it was MLB that stepped in and blocked further progress. This was not all that surprising in retrospect since MLB had a far different agenda than Washington. Big-league owners and management only wanted to get their hands on a mother lode of Cuban players to fill MLB rosters and coffers. Political rapprochement was, for Kuhn and the MLB club owners, only an opportunity for a renewed MLB imperialism to which Castro and his INDER spokesmen had always been most adamantly opposed.

* * *

In broader perspective, what finally brought on a long-inevitable collapse of Cuban baseball was not Fidel's revolution of 1959 and its radical social transformations, but rather its much slower and largely unavoidable failures to merge the Maximum Leader's personal dreams of power and a lasting historical legacy with the needs of his increasingly disadvantaged people. It came not in 1961 (the early period of world revolutionary spirit), but in the recent 2010s (the era of a new global economy). As Fidel faded from the scene—the victim of aging and his own isolation from his once-adoring masses—Cuba's long-maintained isolation from an outside world faded as well. Nowhere was the collapse more dramatic perhaps than in the realm of Cuban baseball. The very successes that exposed premier Cuban ballplayers to the outside world also turned their heads in another direction. When it came to the cherished national sport, at least, Fidel's model was ultimately the victim of its own successes.

Barack Obama's efforts at renewed accords with the Castro government almost a third of a century after the collapse of once-promising détente efforts in the late 1970s were the most ambitious of the lengthy Cold War saga and sought to finally orchestrate a major course correction in troublesome U.S.–Cuba relations. The immediate response to Obama's surprise announcement of late 2014 was an uncontrolled euphoria from the North American press, much of it misguided and ill-informed. And the optimism seemingly had to do with renewed business opportunities for North Americans and thus a potential windfall of dollars that seemed finally looming on the horizon. American newspapers, news broadcasts, and internet sites were full of stories oriented toward an expected flood of tourism that would presumably overwhelm and convert the communist island. There was little attention paid to the Cuban position on such promised change—either their willingness to fully embrace it, or even to understand how they might deal with a new shifting political and economic landscape.

With Fidel finally gone from the scene (as a controlling figure, if not yet as a physically living spirit) it also seemed that a major crack might be appearing in Cuban baseball's long effective "Sugar Cane Curtain." Forces in MLB reacted to the latest Cuban détente overtures with the same uncontrolled optimism as the rest of the American business community and again renewed never-well-concealed lust for island baseball resources. Not the least important of those opportunities involved a presumed windfall of talented ballplayers; others were marketing opportunities for the MLB brand to a nation addicted to the sport—television deals, player development academies, spring training exhibition games, sales of all manner of MLB-brand products in the marketplace. Appetites had already been whetted by recent defectors like Abreu, Céspedes, Puig, and especially Chapman. MLB commissioner Rob Manfred wasted no time in revealing the standard big-league position on Cuba's blossoming détente prospects in the immediate aftermath of Obama's historic announcement concerning potential Cuban policy changes.

> I can envision a situation, assuming that it is consistent with the government's policy on Cuba, where we could have ongoing exhibition game activity. . . . *Cuba is a great market for us* [my italics—PCB] in two ways. *It's obviously a great talent market.* We've seen enough of that during the offseason [clearly a reference here to the signing frenzy surrounding super prospect Yoan Moncada, talented Héctor Olivera, and other recent defectors—PCB]. It is a country where baseball is embedded in the culture. It is someplace *it would be feasible for us to do business in an ongoing basis.*[23]

The message was loud and clear, and it was one that likely set off considerable alarm bells in INDER's inner circles—Fidel or no Fidel in the driver's seat.

There had already been signals that the Cubans were shifting their position ever so slightly in an effort to stem the tide of ballplayer defections. In September 2013, there had been a major announcement about opening the doors for at least some top players to earn increased salaries while on loan overseas. The most significant change was that the ballplayers in these agreements would maintain 80 percent of their earnings, and the remaining 20 percent would go into INDER coffers for the supposed purpose of upgrading league infrastructure. In the past, 80 percent of the salaries of Cuban professionals on loan (e.g., doctors, coaches, teachers, health-care workers, or scientists) was directed to the Cuban government. Regarding the 2013 plan, some State-side cynics questioned me about why the Castro government should be entitled to 20 percent. What was overlooked in that question was that MLB players have a far larger percentage seized in federal and local income taxes, and this was the Cuban equivalent. According to the Cuban system, there are no domestic income taxes.

It was an announcement that was quickly and widely misinterpreted in the North American press since it was assumed at first to be the opening of doors to Cuban stars as free agents bound for MLB clubs. The Cuban plan was in truth only an effort to loan specific players to Mexico and Japan, while at the same time maintaining control of those players for wintertime service on the home front. The handful sent out (Cepeda was the only one at first, becoming Cuba's first million-dollar ballplayer) would receive additional experience at a higher level than domestic play by itself might offer.[24] The selectees were also a mere handful being handed rewards for longtime faithful service. There was the implication that such opportunities might keep wavering stars at home. But there was no plan to relinquish players as unrestricted free agents having freedom to negotiate their own individual contracts with big-league clubs.

INDER's first effort was to exploit a Mexican connection, initially through a direct exchange with the Veracruz Red Eagles of the AAA-equivalent summer Mexican League. Victor Mesa managed briefly in Veracruz in 2010, but that exchange did not turn out well since he was promptly recalled by INDER, along with coach Agustín Marquetti, when the club management signed 2008 Cuban defector and 2006 World Baseball Classic hero Yadel Marti to shore up its pitching staff. A second managerial exchange, this time involving once highly successful national team manager Jorge Fuentes, ended in a far worse scandal in 2014. Skipper of the 1996 Atlanta Olympic champions and longtime Pinar del Río bench boss, Fuentes headed to the Campeche Pirates, the team that had hosted Cuban slugging star Alfredo Despaigne the previous summer. Fuentes lasted little more than a month before being sacked in the wake of a breaking sexual abuse scandal involving a teenage victim and several Pirates players.

The most important Mexican League venture involved superstar slugger Alfredo Despaigne. Despaigne has long been coveted by MLB scouts and player agents but had steadfastly remained loyal; therefore, he was rewarded with a INDER-initiated summer contact in Campeche, where he enjoyed a successful 2013 campaign, two months ahead of the historic INDER announcement. One highlight of the first summer in Mexico for the Cuban slugger came when he equaled a 1936 batting feat of Cuba's first Cooperstown Hall of Famer, Martin Dihigo, by collecting six hits in as many at-bats during a mid-July contest with Saltillo. But the exchange was eventually sabotaged by forces in Organized Baseball when Despaigne headed back to Mexico the following summer.

Mexican League officials were promptly informed that because their circuit fell under Organized Baseball's umbrella, the U.S. embargo rules applied to players such as Despaigne, who had to acquire third-country residence to receive salaries headed back to Cuba. The extraordinary events that followed were first reported by ESPN Dominican writer Enrique Rojas.[25] Despaigne turned up with a Dominican passport apparently forged by the Campeche club. INDER officials immediately denied any involvement in the trickery, but Despaigne was finished in Mexico and so was the entire plan for Mexican League exchanges. The highly valued slugger was quickly shipped off to Japan for a summer assignment in Lotte, as the full effort then shifted toward a Japanese league unaffiliated with MLB management and therefore free of possible politically motivated American interference.

The Japanese efforts have proven something of a buffer for the Cubans but have hardly been an overwhelming success. Frederich Cepeda proved a failure in Japan, just as Omar Linares had a decade earlier, and largely for the same reasons—the ravages of age and the difficulties of adjustment to an exotic Japanese baseball culture. Now in his 30s, Cepeda's best seasons were well behind him. He was a one-dimensional player, strictly a DH with little remaining mobility for outfield play. The placement of Yulieski Gurriel ended in a thick plot of international intrigue that mirrored the case of Despaigne in Mexico. Yulieski enjoyed a single successful season in Yokohama, but when he was held back on the eve of his second scheduled assignment due to mysterious circumstances—was it a legitimate injury, as claimed by INDER, or a hatching plot to peddle him to a MLB club as rumored on Havana street corners?—a rupture with Yokohama team officials took place that almost ended the Cuban enterprise in Japan.

There was, of course, considerable optimism in the immediate aftermath of the December 2014 Obama administration overtures. The American press was quick to envision a windfall of American business opportunities and a floodtide of American tourism soon bound for the island. Some business openings did slowly occur. American cell phone service is now operating, and commercial flights have been relaunched. Nonetheless, there were a handful of outspoken skeptics among longtime Cuba watchers. My own writing cast a note of caution and a warning against overoptimism, especially on the baseball front.[26] I could detect no signals that Cuban authorities were about to throw in the towel on protecting their uniquely structured, if uniquely challenged, baseball enterprise. And on the commercial and political fronts, there have been major reversals under a Trump administration that has seemingly harkened back to the darker days of all-out Cold War policies. That reversal has been highlighted by threats to close down the newly opened Havana Embassy in the wake of so-far unproven charges that Cuban operatives were responsible for mysterious "sonic attacks" damaging the health of American diplomatic personnel. Neither the legitimacy of such a charge or any possible Cuban involvement has so far been proven.

Other exchanges by INDER with Europe and Canada have done nothing to solve the island's sagging fortunes. In the summers of 2016 and 2017, a handful of players were shipped to the Can Am independent league up north, where they played for minuscule salaries (the Cam Am circuit was more akin to industrial-league baseball) that were barely above their Cuban earnings. The competition at that level also did little to hone the talents of such players as shortstop Yordan Mandulay (30 years old), catcher Yulexis La Rosa (36), or DH–first baseman Alexander Malleta (37). The players shipped out were also veterans performing near career's end and not young prospects in need of seasoning but also more likely to jump ship. Similarly, in recent years, a handful of veterans performed in lower-level circuits in Italy and France. Pitchers such as Ciro Silvino Licea and Norberto González would return to Cuba, but as coaches, and no longer as active league ballplayers. A pair of sluggers bound for Italy, Yosvani Pereza and Joan Carlos Pedroso, had already seen their careers at home end largely on sour notes (rumored defection attempts). Thus, the Europe exchanges were not any kind of pipeline for further training of future Cuban stars.

Growing weakness of the once-stable Cuban League was best revealed with the 2017 World Baseball Classic, in which the 2006 finalist and serious 2009 and 2013 challenger now barely limped into the second round before being embarrassed by newcomer Israel and powerhouse The Netherlands. In the first major tournament event after Fidel's death, his former showcase team was seemingly just as much on life support as the full society back home. Cuba was able to escape the opening round in Tokyo and advance to the second round for the fourth-straight time. But that occurred only thanks to one fortuitous swing of the bat (a grand slam homer by Alfredo Despaigne, providing a 4–3 win) in a showdown contest with Australia.

This was a huge contrast to 2013, on the same field in Tokyo, where although the Cubans bowed out in the same second-round matches, on paper they seemingly had the best team in the entire field and lost only due to some questionable late-inning managerial gaffs by flamboyant Victor Mesa (they were well on the way to the final round in San Francisco before a two-run lead over the Dutch melted in the final two frames). Seven players in the 2013 Cuban lineup would soon be in the major leagues, and those stalwarts included Abreu, Erisbel Arruebarruena, Odrisamer Despaigne, Guillermo Heredia, Raisel Iglesias, and eventually Yulieski Gurriel. Four years later, the island squad had no frontline pitching and but one genuine big-league prospect in Alfredo Despaigne, who was already starring in Japan with first Lotte and then Fukuoka. There was now growing speculation that Cuba would appear more like also-rans Brazil and Italy, or perhaps Nicaragua and Panama, by the time the 2021 Classic rolled around.

What then is the future for Cuban baseball? No easy answers appear, but what is clear is that it will never again be what it once was. An isolated baseball universe is no longer possible in a world that is as globalized on the sporting front as it is in the economic realm. All that Cuba might now hope for is holding on to some form of viable domestic league competition and thus avoiding the fate that much earlier befell the Dominican Republic, Puerto Rico, and Venezuela—now satellites of MLB's operations and little more than sources of its talent harvest.

Earlier in this book, I proposed one hopeful scenario on the defectors phenomenon, a system of player postings in which local stars serve an initial contract period at home and then become free agents available for bidding from MLB clubs that pay handsome negotiation fees to the original club or league. Such a scenario might not only have blocked defections, but also brought Cuba a new revenue source; however, it has not been played out that way. The Cubans have proven even more unprepared to embrace change than I earlier expected. Obama's overtures seemed to paralyze the Cuban government and caused more retrenchment than steps toward inevitable progress.

A major stumbling block was that the Cubans didn't understand how the world of North American and Asian professional baseball operated. They functioned at home without player contracts of the type known in free-market societies (viewing all athletes as automatically under obligation to the system that trained them) and had little understanding of what such contractual arrangements entailed. While several significant voices on the island, for example, INDER and IBAF official Tony Castro and national team manager Victor Mesa, spoke hopefully of a world in which their players would be free to move to MLB, they never seemed to quite understand what that actually meant.

In the end, perhaps the greatest irony was that Fidel's innovations, the ones that had built the league, which were a springboard to a half-century of on-field successes, also contained the seeds for eventual destruction. The stumbling block was always MLB's desire to harvest Cuban talent for its own uses. The Cubans wanted to maintain complete ownership of their players and thus have them return for winter duty even if they might be freed to earn big-league paychecks during the Caribbean offseason. But MLB's own player-control policies always made this impossible. Independent winter leagues were now a thing of the past for both MLB owners and players—with their exquisite long-term contracts players no longer needed the money brought by extra barnstorming; general managers and agents were not willing to risk injury or exhaustion with their valued property. And the U.S. Helms–Burton embargo policies still made it impossible for Cuban ballplayers to bring salaries back to their homelands as players from other Caribbean nations could do. It was an impossible impasse.

The new structure for revolutionary baseball in Cuba began with Fidel's pie-in-the-sky visions of an idyllic, nonmaterial society. Baseball was built on the same notions that were to control his more grandiose new communist realm—the goal was to sacrifice personal freedoms and personal desires for the well-being of the masses and thus put national pride and the shared satisfactions of a socialist utopia ahead of any material rewards and personal comforts. But constant threats to the regime's survival and the nation's economic stability—mainly decades of U.S. economic embargo, the disappearance of a support system from a shrinking Eastern European Communist bloc, and eventually the collapse of the Soviet Union, the one reliable external force that had kept the country afloat—would cause repeated demands for further sacrifice by citizens and repeated further losses of individual freedom. Of course, it was something of an idle dream from the onset. By the 1980s, after three decades in power, Fidel was already facing unsurmountable challenges to maintaining his visions for a utopian society. Biographer Bourne, in the mid-1980s, already had noted this looming challenge as constituting perhaps the greatest threat to Fidel's remaining tenure, which Bourne, with surprising foresight, projected might last as long as another 20 years.

Bourne, in fact, in his conclusion to what might be the most insightful of the many Castro biographies, writes perhaps the best epitaph on Fidel's entire half-century career. Had he only been more willing to relinquish some of his obsessive need for total dictatorial power over his fellow citizens and modify his all-consuming lust for the greatest possible historical stature for himself, he might not have continued to ignore the growing desires of his citizens for even a small upturn in their own sagging economic struggles. Fidel's revolution might have continued to prosper far longer than it did had his tunnel vision surrounding personal power not ultimately gotten in the way. Bourne suggests that what Fidel always failed to acknowledge was that in the end, his citizens en masse would most likely have been willing to trade at least some of the international prestige that the revolution had brought them for even a rather modest improvement in their long-sagging standard of living.

It should be noted that Bourne penned his insights into the ultimate shortcomings of the Cuban social experiment and Fidel's role in those failures on the eve of the collapse of the Soviet Union and the disastrous "Special Period" that would follow. At the close of the 1980s, Cuba's economy tumbled onto "life support," and it was a testimony to Fidel's hold on his people and powers of persuasion that his government and his nation didn't collapse completely. Thanks mainly to a shift toward dependence on a growing tourist industry, the country survived and rebounded ever so slightly during the next two decades—including Fidel's final 15 years in power—but the revolutionary dream was largely on life support. The country had evolved into one in which seemingly everyone had to cheat the system, steal from the workplace, hustle good-natured tourists, and abandon earlier idealism just to survive.

The same fate would await Cuban baseball, it just took a bit longer. There had always been cracks in the system, and by the early 1990s, there were already telling signs of growing player dissatisfaction. Early defectors like René Aroche and Liván Hernández complained of harsh control by INDER officials and even harsher conditions under which their families were forced to survive as motivations in their decisions to abandon team and homeland during overseas junkets. Author Steve Fainaru, in *The Duke of Havana*, repeats a story that Liván's disillusionment with the system resulted after repeated failures to obtain a replacement picture tube for the broken family television set from local party officials.[27] But Liván himself spoke even more poignantly during a 2014 documentary filming session for ESPN's *30 for 30* of mounting dissatisfactions resulting from overzealous team security agents confiscating such petty items as hotel soap and towels traveling players were attempting to bring home to desperate family members on the island. While the country sagged in the late 1980s and early 1990s, the island's international baseball fortunes nonetheless continued to thrive on the world stage. Perhaps a final collapse was temporarily forestalled by one surprising last great triumph in the inaugural 2006 World Baseball Classic. But that first triumphant exposure to vastly improved head-to-head competition with big-league stars in San Juan and San Diego was also the source of an inevitable death knell.

Just as Cuba's domestic economic crisis was, in no small part, caused by external world developments, most well out of Havana's control, the looming collapse in Cuban baseball would have a similar history. If the Cubans continued to produce enough top talent to offset what was initially a slow defection trickle, they simply couldn't keep pace once the face of international baseball altered. In the last year before the new millennium, international tournaments saw the introduction of top professional players, seasoned big-leaguers, and promising minor-league prospects. The opposition was no longer the same, and rivals were no longer much younger collegians just polishing their trade or industrial-league pretenders. The Cubans remained remarkably competitive but no longer dominated events in which, for decades, they had rarely lost a tournament or even a single international game. Spoiled fans on the island never appreciated the change, however, and once the national squad began failing in the biggest games—for instance, the Olympic finals in Sydney and again in Beijing—full disillusionment rapidly set in. One setback led to another; as fans lost interest, players had less motivation to remain at home. At the same time, the increased exposure in such events as the World Baseball Classic showed top Cuban stars what they were missing. Nonpareils like Abreu, Céspedes, Chapman, Martin, and Contreras, as well as dozens more, discovered that they could indeed compete at the highest level; it was inevitable that some at least would chose the path of any top athlete, the desire to prove oneself at the highest level. And that ingrained motive was only further spiked by the realization of the lifestyle and comforts they easily might earn for their families in the process.

This perfect storm caused a snowballing of successful defections, especially once Fidel—the number-one cheerleader—was no longer on the scene. More ballplayer abandonments from the system meant a weakened league, less impressive competition at home, and thus even further fan disaffection. Local fans who had once swelled with pride about the successes of the Cuban juggernaut now sought out a new contingent of heroes to which they could attach their Cuban pride. They found them among those renegades who became overnight stars in the big time on major-league diamonds. If government hard-liners still branded those who escaped traitors, for the fans at daily central park street corner baseball chat sessions, the Chapmans, Abreus, and Puigs were a true measure of just how great their island baseball was. It was a perfect domino scenario.

Had Fidel earlier opened up opportunities for players to move on after a short term of indenture at home, many likely would have stayed home voluntarily for a spell at least and enjoyed the pride of national victories. If there was a time to open the door for Cuban players to seek success off the island, especially if it could be done with some guarantees for survival of the domestic league, that opportunity had likely passed by the time power transferred from Fidel's hands. Some kind of posting system mirroring the Japanese model might have worked earlier, when there was still enough talent on the island to bring a windfall of dollars through bidding from big-league clubs.

The efforts made via the exchanges with Mexico and Japan announced in September 2013 were much too little and much too late. If a handpicked few like Cepeda, Gurriel, and Despaigne might be offered brief overseas tenures, which meant cash windfalls as reward for long-term INDER service, most younger Cuban prospects saw no hope for being included; at the same time, national team players were still suffering from severe discipline, which was universally resented. It was perhaps understandable why Cuban officials wanted to block defections, but with the old, worn-out ideologies now sagging, the methods no longer seemed effective. In the end, if they did anything by reverting to parroting themes of loyalty to the revolutionary dream they only ramped up the desires of many potential young stars and veteran mainstays to get off the sinking ship. With the league failing and the true heroes being the ones who had left, that dream was largely dead.

# NOTES

## ACKNOWLEDGMENTS

1. Lee Lockwood, *Castro's Cuba, Cuba's Fidel: An American Journalist's Inside Look at Today's Cuba—in Text and Pictures* (New York: Random House [Vintage Books], 1969), 325.

## PROLOGUE: A RATIONALE

1. Roberto González Echevarría, *The Pride of Havana: A History of Cuban Baseball* (New York: Oxford University Press, 1999), 352.
2. González Echevarría, *The Pride of Havana*, 352.
3. González Echevarría, *The Pride of Havana*, 352–53.
4. González Echevarría, *The Pride of Havana*, 352.
5. Thomas G. Paterson, *Contesting Castro: The United States and the Triumph of the Cuban Revolution* (New York: Oxford University Press, 1994), 50–51.
6. Robert E. Quirk, "Review: *Contesting Castro: The United States and the Triumph of the Castro Revolution* by Thomas G. Paterson," *Journal of American History* 82, no. 1 (June 1995): 357.
7. "Fidel Castro has stamped his seal on Cuba and it can never be erased. His influence on hemispheric affairs is still uncertain, although it is obviously great. He is the first man in the history of Latin America to achieve worldwide stature and fame during his lifetime." (Herbert L. Matthews, *Fidel Castro* [New York: Simon and Schuster, 1969], 16.)

8. Geyer (referring to the 30th anniversary of the Cuban Rrevolution on January 1, 1989) continues, "From Mexico to Moscow to Managua, and from the Universities of Minnesota, Mainz, and Minsk, Fidel Castro remained the single modern revolutionary of epicentral consequence." (Georgie Anne Geyer, *Guerrilla Prince: The Untold Story of Fidel Castro* [Boston: Little, Brown and Company, 1991], 3.)

9. "No one has written or can claim to write about Fidel Castro and the Cuban Revolution with objectivity, impartiality, balance, lack of bias, or whatever attitude may be considered devoid of emotion." (Herbert L. Matthews, *Revolution in Cuba: An Essay in Understanding* [New York: Charles Scribner's Sons, 1975], 2.)

10. Numerous sources document the various unsuccessful attempts on Castro's life, many of them bungled, harebrained schemes of cartoonish quality (at least one involved an exploding baseball), and many orchestrated by the CIA. At the time of Fidel's death in November 2016, one online story cited the former head of Cuban intelligence, Fabian Escalante, telling a British documentary crew that the CIA made more than 600 attempts during a span of four decades to eliminate Castro (Escalante's list of attempts per administration is as follows: Eisenhower 38, Kennedy 42, Johnson 72, Nixon 184, Carter 64, Reagan 197, Bush Sr. 16, Clinton 21). Escalante may have exaggerated, but recently declassified CIA reports indicate there were indeed numerous such efforts. ("How Castro Survived 638 Very Cunning Assassination Attempts," *ABC.net*, November 28, 2016, http://www.abc.net.au/triplej/programs/hack/how-castro-survived-638-assassination-attempts/8064788.)

11. Bourne suggests that Washington operatives believed the Mob would be highly motivated to see Fidel eliminated so they could reestablish lucrative gambling and prostitution operations in the Cuban capital city. (Peter G. Bourne, *Fidel: A Biography of Fidel Castro* [New York: Dodd, Mead and Company, 1986], 212–14.) A full and enlightening history of anti-Castro counterrevolutionary activities on the island (sponsored, in large part, by Washington and the Miami Cuban exile community) is provided by Jesús Arboleya, *The Cuban Counterrevolution*, trans. Damián Donéstevez (Havana: Editorial José Marti, 2002).

12. When Raúl Castro retired from office in April 2018, and was succeeded by Miguel Díaz-Canel as the country's 19th president, North American media widely and inaccurately reported that Cuba was finally without a president or leader named Castro for the first time since 1959. It was another blatant example of shallow American press attention to the facts of Cuban political history. Between 1959 and 1976, Fidel was the country's prime minister and not its president until the two offices were finally merged. Furthermore, the

true political leader of Cuba is not the president, but rather the first secretary of the Communist Party, a position Raúl still retains.

13. Peter C. Bjarkman, *Cuba's Baseball Defectors: The Inside Story* (Lanham, MD: Rowman & Littlefield, 2016), xv.

14. "No one can deny that Fidel Castro and his revolution have brought tragedy to thousands of Cuban families. Revolutions can no more be made without bringing suffering to many people than wars can be fought without sacrificing lives." (Matthews, *Fidel Castro*, 345.)

15. César Brioso, "How Fidel Castro's Revolution Ended Professional Baseball in Cuba," *USA Today*, November 27, 2016, https://www.usatoday.com/story/sports/2016/11/27/fidel-castro-cuba-baseball-sugar-kings-cuban-league/94517414/. Brioso presents the identical argument in his earlier book *Havana Hardball* (2015), especially in his epilogue.

16. González Echevarría, *The Pride of Havana*, 132–33.

17. Robert Elias, *The Empire Strikes Out: How Baseball Sold U.S. Foreign Policy and Promoted the American Way Abroad* (New York and London: New Press, 2010).

18. Matthews, *Fidel Castro*, 37.

19. Lee Lockwood, *Castro's Cuba, Cuba's Fidel: An American Journalist's Inside Look at Today's Cuba—in Text and Picture* (New York: Random House [Vintage Books], 1969), 336.

20. On April 10, 2012, the colorful and often outspoken Ozzie Guillen (a Venezuelan) was suspended five games by Marlins management for what were deemed inappropriate comments regarding the Cuban leader. Interviewed by *Time* magazine, Guillen is quoted as saying, "I love Castro. I respect Castro. You know why? A lot of people have wanted to kill Fidel Castro for the last 50 years, but that 'mofo' is still here." (Nick Carbone, "Ozzie Guillen Suspended by Marlins Following Castro Comment," *Time*, April 10, 2012, http://keepingscore.blogs.time.com/2012/04/10/ozzie-guillen-marlins-suspended-fidel-castro/.) Marlins management was, of course, sensitive to opinions in the greater Miami community and fearful of public reprisal. The Marlins would fire Guillen at the end of the season, citing as at least part of the reason the fact that stadium attendance flatlined and never recovered after the *Time* remarks.

21. Titles for such pieces are also quite often clues to their slant on the subject. To cite a small sample: "Castro Opens Season with a Delayed Pitch," *New York Times*, October 17, 1960; "Baseball Can Bring Castro to His Knees," *Washington Post*, April 25, 1982; "Señor Comrade Doubleday," *Christian Science Monitor*, March 22, 1962.

22. Patrick Symmes, *The Boys from Dolores: Fidel Castro's Classmates from Revolution to Exile* (New York: Pantheon, 2007), 266–71.

23. Personal correspondence, September 25, 1998.

24. Lockwood, *Castro's Cuba, Cuba's Fidel*, xix.

## 1. "HISTORY WILL ABSOLVE ME"

1. Theodore Draper, *Castro's Revolution: Myths and Realities* (New York: Frederick A. Praeger, 1962), 4–5.

2. According to Matthews, Franqui, in his *Book of the Twelve*, attributes that line as being spoken by Celia Sánchez to Haydeé Santamaría. Celia's full statement (as translated by Matthews) was, "Because you see Moncada as we see it—as the commencement of the struggle. Moncada—it was the mother of the revolution." (Herbert L. Matthews, *Fidel Castro* [New York: Simon and Schuster, 1969], 63.)

3. Eric Williams, *From Columbus to Castro: The History of the Caribbean, 1492–1969* (New York: Random House [Vintage Books], 1970), 481.

4. Georgie Anne Geyer, *Guerrilla Prince: The Untold Story of Fidel Castro* (Boston: Little, Brown and Company, 1991), 131, in particular, points out one specific passage in the later published version of Fidel's oratory that appears to be largely a direct (but uncredited) translation of Adolf Hitler's words spoken at the conclusion of his own 1924 Rathaus Putsch trial.

5. Matthews, *Fidel Castro*, 72.

6. Peter G. Bourne, *Fidel: A Biography of Fidel Castro* (New York: Dodd, Mead and Company, 1986), 98–99.

7. Marta Rojas would later be appointed editor of the Communist Party newspaper *Granma*. It was also Rojas who, in the immediate aftermath of the Moncada attack, smuggled photos of the tortured bodies of several slain attackers back to Havana, where they were immediately published as evidence of the atrocities committed by Batista's military. (Tad Szulc, *Fidel: A Critical Portrait* [New York: William Morrow and Company, 1986], 274.)

8. Draper, *Castro's Revolution*, 16–17, summarizes Fidel's early promises—ones usually pointed to by those who advocate that he abandoned the original revolution (simply because he abandoned such early promises)—by lumping the program expounded in the "History Will Absolve Me" document with other statements and documents that followed through late 1958. These included a letter to Cuban exiles in December 1957; an article published in *Coronet* magazine in February 1958; a May 1958 interview with his early biographer, Jules Dubois; and his July 1958 unity manifesto.

9. Bourne, *Fidel*, 100.

10. Matthews, *Fidel Castro*, 72.

11. Matthews, *Fidel Castro*, 72.

12. Matthews, *Fidel Castro*, 73.

13. Fidel, in this passage, was specifically responding to Matthews's questions about abuses in agrarian reform policies, which stripped many landowners of their properties, but as Fidel admits here, the problems brought by inexperienced leadership were endemic to the entire revolutionary program. (Matthews, *Fidel Castro*, 144.)

14. Williams, *From Columbus to Castro*, 487–88.

15. Williams, *From Columbus to Castro*, 496, without citing any specific source, quotes Matthews as follows: "It does not follow that the Cuban Revolution has been a failure; at least not yet. It will fail in the long run if the Cuban economy is not put on a healthy, viable basis, which among other things, means plentiful and unrationed food supplies. Cuba is still far from that in 1968."

16. Lee Lockwood, *Castro's Cuba, Cuba's Fidel: An American Journalist's Inside Look at Today's Cuba—in Text and Pictures* (New York: Random House [Vintage Books], 1969), 164.

17. Nowhere is Fidel's strong anti-Americanism and its rationale more concisely and revealingly stated than in his July 12, 1968, address to the International Cultural Congress in Havana (Matthews, *Fidel Castro*, 313). Here he would state, "There exists an enemy who can be called universal, and if there ever was in the history of humanity an enemy who was truly universal, an enemy whose acts and moves trouble the entire world, threaten the entire world, attack the entire world in one way or another, that real and really universal enemy is precisely Yankee imperialism."

18. Williams, *From Columbus to Castro*, 481.

19. Robert E. Quirk, *Fidel Castro* (New York: W. W. Norton, 1995), xi. Originally printed in 1993.

20. Matthews, *Fidel Castro*; Herbert L. Matthews, *Revolution in Cuba: An Essay in Understanding* (New York: Charles Scribner's Sons, 1975); Draper, *Castro's Revolution*; Theodore Draper, *Castroism: Theory and Practice* (New York: Frederick A. Praeger, 1965).

21. Geyer, *Guerrilla Prince*, 3.

22. Geyer, *Guerrilla Prince*, 391.

23. Draper, *Castro's Revolution*, 91.

24. Draper, *Castro's Revolution*, 57.

25. Matthews, *Fidel Castro*, 132.

26. Draper, *Castro's Revolution*, 51.

27. Matthews, *Fidel Castro*, 165.

28. Matthews, *Fidel Castro*, 188.

29. Matthews, *Fidel Castro*, 189.

30. Geyer, *Guerrilla Prince*, 244.

31. Bourne, *Fidel*, 230; Lockwood, *Castro's Cuba, Cuba's Fidel*, 294.

32. Draper, *Castro's Revolution*, 31.

33. Matthews, *Fidel Castro*, 358.

34. Louis Pérez Jr., *On Becoming Cuban: Identity, Nationality, and Culture* (Chapel Hill and London: University of North Carolina Press, 1999).

35. Margaret Randall, *To Change the World: My Years in Cuba* (New Brunswick, NJ, and London: Rutgers University Press, 2009), passim.

## 2. BASEBALL'S MOST OUTRAGEOUS MYTH

1. John Thorn, *Baseball in the Garden of Eden: The Secret History of the Early Game* (New York: Simon & Schuster, 2012), ix.

2. Earlier versions of much of the material in this chapter have appeared in my SABR Biography Project essay "Fidel Castro and Baseball" (online), as well as in my earlier *A History of Cuban Baseball, 1864–2006* (chapter 9) and journal articles for *Elysian Fields Quarterly* 17:1 (Summer 1999) and *National Pastime* 18 (1998). See the reference section at book's end for specific source details.

3. Tim Wendel, *Castro's Curveball* (New York: Ballantine, 2000). Originally printed in 1999.

4. J. David Truby, "Castro's Curveball," *Harper's Magazine*, May 1989, 32, 34. Originally appeared in "Great Moments," *Sports History*, March 1989.

5. Don Hoak, with Myron Cope, "The Day I Batted against Castro," in *The Armchair Book of Baseball*, ed. John Thorn, 161–64 (New York: Charles Scribner's Sons, 1985). Originally appeared in *Sport*, June 1964.

6. In September 1998, I wrote a personal note to NBC broadcaster Bob Costas questioning his on-air repetitions of the Fidel "prospect legend" during that fall's postseason broadcasts. Costas's intriguing response to my note is quoted at the end of the prologue.

7. This claim is fully supported in chapter 5 of this volume. A more detailed collection of evidence is also found in my earlier book, *A History of Cuban Baseball, 1864–2006* (especially chapter 8), and the more recent *Cuba's Baseball Defectors: The Inside Story* (2016).

8. Hoak, with Cope, "The Day I Batted against Castro," 164.

9. Everardo J. Santamarina, "The Hoak Hoax," *National Pastime* 14 (1994): 29.

10. Roberto González Echevarría, *The Pride of Havana: A History of Cuban Baseball* (New York: Oxford University Press, 1999), 325–26.

11. John Thorn, *The Armchair Book of Baseball* (New York: Charles Scribner's Sons, 1985), 161.

12. Tom Jozwik, "A Worthy Successor to the *Firesides*," *SABR Review of Books* 1 (1986): 67–68. It is also worth noting here the irony reflected in John

Thorn's willingness to reprint the tale without any signs of skepticism, especially when one considers the Thorn dictum quoted at the beginning of this chapter.

13. Kevin Kerrane, *Dollar Sign on the Muscle: The World of Baseball Scouting* (New York and Toronto: Beaufort Books, 1984), 268.

14. Kerrane, *Dollar Sign on the Muscle*, 268.

15. Michael M. Oleksak and Mary Adams Oleksak, *Béisbol: Latin Americans and the Grand Old Game* (Grand Rapids, MI: Masters Press, 1991), 34.

16. Oleksak and Oleksak, *Béisbol*, 34.

17. John Thorn and John Holway, *The Pitcher: The Ultimate Compendium of Pitching Lore* (New York: Prentice Hall, 1987), 212, includes their comments on the Fidel legend in a sidebar to a section devoted to little-known postrevolution Cuban League aces. While seeming to discount the fiction with Figueredo's comment, they also play it safe by injecting the Monte Irvin observation quoted at the end of this chapter.

18. Truby, "Castro's Curveball," 34.

19. Eugene J. McCarthy, "Diamond Diplomacy (The View from Left Field)," *Elysian Fields Quarterly* 14:2 (1995): 12–15.

20. Robert E. Quirk, *Fidel Castro* (New York: W. W. Norton, 1995), 4. Originally printed in 1993.

21. Tad Szulc, *Fidel: A Critical Portrait* (New York: William Morrow and Company, 1986), 109.

22. Quirk, *Fidel Castro*, 18.

23. Quirk, *Fidel Castro*, 19.

24. Peter G. Bourne, *Fidel: A Biography of Fidel Castro* (New York: Dodd, Mead and Company, 1986), 28.

25. Bourne, *Fidel*, 28.

26. Bourne, *Fidel*, 28.

27. Peter C. Bjarkman, *A History of Cuban Baseball, 1864–2006* (Jefferson, NC, and London: McFarland, 2014), 313–14. Originally printed in 2007. The full box score is reproduced there.

28. Hansen supplied this information in an e-mail correspondence with the author in late 2015. While the two Havana games are linked to the intramural campus tournament when Fidel played with the Law School squad, the nature of the October 1946 game remains mysterious. The teams were amateur squads apparently representing local municipalities. The date suggests the game would have been played just before Fidel returned to Havana for his second year of university studies. That Fidel would have been at home with his family at the Las Manacas estate in Birán during the late summer (and perhaps early fall) of 1946 is suggested by Quirk's comment that Fidel, only one month

later, began to break with his family and "in the summer of 1947, for the first time, he did not go home to Las Manacas." (Quirk, *Fidel Castro*, 23)

29. Lee Lockwood, *Castro's Cuba, Cuba's Fidel: An American Journalist's Inside Look at Today's Cuba—in Text and Pictures* (New York: Random House [Vintage Books], 1969), 188–91.

30. Lockwood, *Castro's Cuba, Cuba's Fidel*, 289.

31. Szulc, *Fidel*, 87.

32. Alex Q. Arbuckle, "Castro Plays Basketball: Fidel Castro Felt Basketball Was Perfect Training for Guerilla Warfare," *Mashable Retronaut*, October 16, 2016, https://mashable.com/2016/10/16/fidel-castro-basketball/.

33. Szulc, *Fidel*.

34. The words attributed to Monte Irvin here come from Thorn and Holway (*The Pitcher*, 212); the authors report Irvin as claiming that "young Castro, a great fan, used to hang around the stadium where the teams worked out." But no source is given for the quotation. Another noteworthy Irvin observation appears on the website AZ Quotes, where the octogenarian Hall of Famer is quoted as follows: "I played for Almendares in Cuba. Guess who was trying out for the team? Castro. Fidel Castro, as a pitcher. He could throw pretty hard, but he was wild. He didn't have any control." Again, there is no source given for Irvin's statement. We seem to have here yet another example of the dangers of placing much weight on the memories of aged ballplayers when they take to reminiscing about their early years as star athletes.

35. McCarthy, "Diamond Diplomacy," 12.


## 3. THE INFAMOUS "BARBUDOS" GAME

1. This popular quip attributed to the one-time State Department official is frequently cited and can be found in a dozen or more locations, but always without specific source for the original quotation. It appears prominently as an epigraph in the front matter of Tim Wendel's novel *Castro's Curveball* (my own source for the popular quotation).

2. Herbert L. Matthews, *Fidel Castro* (New York: Simon and Schuster, 1969), 15.

3. Peter G. Bourne, *Fidel: A Biography of Fidel Castro* (New York: Dodd, Mead and Company, 1986).

4. Quirk suggests that Fidel had planned to install Miró Cardona, his predecessor as prime minister, but that Raúl and other advisors convinced him that Cardona was too conservative and too pro-American. (Robert E. Quirk, *Fidel Castro* [New York: W. W. Norton, 1995], 251. Originally printed in 1993.)

5. The political events surrounding Urrutia's ouster are detailed succinctly by Bourne (*Fidel*, 182–83) and Georgie Anne Geyer (*Guerrilla Prince: The Untold Story of Fidel Castro* [Boston: Little, Brown and Company, 1991], 244–45), and in more detail in the massive biographies of Quirk (*Fidel Castro*, 250–53) and Tad Szulc (*Fidel: A Critical Portrait* [New York: William Morrow and Company, 1986], 504–5). Quirk briefly includes mention of the events at the ballpark but restricts them to Saturday night and thus has the Barbudos exhibition occurring on the wrong evening; he does correctly refer to Fidel pitching for a single inning. Quirk also fails to grasp the symbolic linkage between the political theater and the sporting event. He gives no mention to events at the ballpark that weekend, nor do Bourne and Geyer.

6. The Camilo quotation has become legendary but unfortunately has no documented sources and may possibly be apocryphal. It also appears in various similar versions and paraphrases, and there is no known Spanish version directly quoted as spoken. One recent version is, "I won't be against Fidel, in life or baseball," and it appears in the useful online article by Callum Hughson ("Los Barbudos: The 'Bearded Ones,'" *Mop-Up Duty, Cleaning Up the Mess Other Sites Leave Behind*, February 17, 2010, https://mopupduty.com/los-barbudos-the-bearded-ones/). The Hughson internet piece is especially valuable for its inclusion of more than a dozen photos of the July 24 exhibition event drawn from INDER archives and most not seen elsewhere. Hughson also discusses the makeup of the Barbudos team, as well as Fidel's support that same summer for the struggling Sugar Kings franchise. Regarding Fidel's team that night, it was managed by Eduardo Castellano and included Raúl Catala, Laudelio Reyes, Alfredo Carvajal, Ilcibiades Santos, Ruben Tamayo, Ronaldo Sánchez, Amador Torres, Ramiro Rodríguez, Sergio García, Bernardo Hechevarría (a later professional player), and future sports minister Felipe Guerra Matos (who was supposed to catch until Camilo demanded to take over that assignment with Fidel on the mound).

7. Quirk, *Fidel Castro*, 252–53.

8. Ellis F. ("Cot") Deal, *Fifty Years in Baseball—or, "Cot" in the Act* (Oklahoma City, OK: Self-published, 1992), 47.

9. Justin W. R. Turner, *Baseball Diplomacy, Baseball Deployment: The National Pastime in U.S.–Cuba Relations*, doctoral dissertation, University of Alabama, Tuscaloosa, 2012, 58.

10. Fidel's early support for the franchise has been frequently reported, although not always with the greatest accuracy. Hughson (see note 6) reports that one of Fidel's first acts as president (*sic*, he was prime minister) was to pledge to underwrite the team's debt and vow that the team would continue in Havana "even if I have to pitch." But the Hughson account is riddled with errors, for example, the claim that this statement was made with the team

perched atop the International League standings (they never were in first place that or any other year). He also claims that only five days after seizing power, Fidel's guerrilla army was invited to attend a Sugar Kings game free of charge and that when Carlos Paula slugged a homer, "one of the Barbudos jumped onto the field and embraced him." If that ever happened, it certainly was not in early January, as claimed, since the AAA club played in the summer months of April to September.

11.  Peter C. Bjarkman, *A History of Cuban Baseball, 1864–2006* (Jefferson, NC, and London: McFarland, 2014), 102–3. Originally printed in 2007.

12.  Roberto González Echevarría, *The Pride of Havana: A History of Cuban Baseball* (New York: Oxford University Press, 1999), 339.

13.  Turner, *Baseball Diplomacy*, 59.

14.  Stew Thornley, "Minneapolis Millers versus Havana Sugar Kings," in *The Inter-National Pastime*, ed. Peter C. Bjarkman (Cleveland, OH: Society for American Baseball Research, 1992), 44.

15.  In his introductory chapter to *Con Las Bases Llenas*, Havana baseball historian Félix Julio Alfonso López notes that Camilo Cienfuegos was Fidel's designated catcher for the ceremonial April 14 toss, opening the International League season in Havana, just as he would be for the Barbudos exhibition in July. (Félix Julio Alfonso López, ed., *Con Las Bases Llenas—Béisbol, Historia y Revolución* [Havana: Editorial Científico-Téchnica, 2008].)

16.  Thornley, "Minneapolis Millers versus Havana Sugar Kings," 42.

17.  Carl Yastrzemski and Gerald Eskenazi, *Yaz: Baseball, the Wall, and Me* (New York: Grand Central Publishing, 1991), 51. Yastrzemski provides a detailed description of the series in Havana from the standpoint of the visitors. He also repeats the popular Fidel myth in describing his short meeting with Fidel after his homer in the Havana opener: "Castro knew the game. He had pitched semipro."

18.  Thornley, "Minneapolis Millers versus Havana Sugar Kings," 42.

19.  Reig Romero's comments appear in an essay entitled "The First Inning of Revolutionary Baseball" (Alfonso López, *Con Las Bases Llenas*, 4). That book's title ("With the Bases Full") also carries symbolic weight.

20.  David Trifunov, "Hugo Chávez Baseball Career Gave Way to Politics," *Public Radio International*, March 6, 2013, https://www.pri.org/stories/2013-03-06/hugo-chavez-baseball-career-gave-way-politics.

21.  Quotations here come from a BBC World News online account filed the same evening (November 19, 1999).

22.  Steve Nidetz, "Castro Interview Worth Waiting For," *Chicago Tribune*, July 22, 1991, h ttp://articles.chicagotribune.com/1991-07-22/sports/9103210953_1_jim-mckay-fidel-castro-jesuits.

23.  Turner, *Baseball Diplomacy*, 104.

24. Quirk, *Fidel Castro*, 201

25. Turner, *Baseball Diplomacy*, 67.

26. Martin's reply to Williams's inquiry was both loyal and coy: "I think if Fidel had signed for the major leagues, as he has triumphed in everything else, he would have triumphed in that too." (Richard Williams, "Baseball: Diamond Passion of Castro's Cuba," *Independent Sport*, January 2, 1999, https://www.independent.co.uk/sport/baseball-diamond-passion-of-castros-cuba-1044537.html.)

## 4. SUGAR BARONS AND SUGAR KINGS, AND THE DEATH OF CUBA'S PROFESSIONAL BASEBALL

1. César Brioso, *Havana Hardball: Spring Training, Jackie Robinson, and the Cuban League* (Gainesville: University Press of Florida, 2015), 247.

2. Roberto González Echevarría, *The Pride of Havana: A History of Cuban Baseball* (New York: Oxford University Press, 1999), 364.

3. I capitalize Organized Baseball throughout this book, as it represents a formal organization comprised of Major League Baseball (the American and National Leagues) and its affiliated minor-league system under the management of the National Association of Professional Baseball Leagues.

4. Even César Brioso, flag waver for the theme that Fidel was the author of baseball's demise in Cuba in 1962, opens his recent book (*Havana Hardball*, 1) with the observations that, "From the start Cuba's fight for independence and its interest in baseball were inextricably linked."

5. Frank Mankiewicz and Kirby Jones, *With Fidel: A Portrait of Castro and Cuba* (Chicago: Playboy Press, 1975), 63.

6. American corporations heavily invested in Cuban sugar production before 1959 included the United Fruit Company, North American Sugar Industries, Inc., the American Sugar Company, and the Hershey Company, among others.

7. César Brioso, "How Fidel Castro's Revolution Ended Professional Baseball in Cuba," *USA Today*, November 27, 2016, https://www.usatoday.com/story/sports/2016/11/27/fidel-castro-cuba-baseball-sugar-kings-cuban-league/94517414/.

8. Herbert L. Matthews, *Fidel Castro* (New York: Simon and Schuster, 1969).

9. Matthews, *Fidel Castro*, 183.

10. Mankiewicz and Jones, *With Fidel*, 63.

11. Mankiewicz and Jones, *With Fidel*, 63.

12. Thomas Boswell, *How Life Imitates the World Series* (New York: Doubleday, 1987); Ron Fimrite, "In Cuba It's Viva El Grand Old Game," *Sports Illustrated*, June 6, 1977, 68–80.

13. Fidel's personal appearance at the 1959 opener created a festive atmosphere and seemed to signal optimism that the revolutionary upheaval of the past couple years had passed. There were fireworks and a ceremonial pregame pigeon release, and 20,000 spectators packed the ballpark and stood to cheer when he took the mound alongside the Canadian and American ambassadors to toss the ceremonial first ball. (Justin W. R. Turner, *Baseball Diplomacy, Baseball Deployment: The National Pastime in U.S.–Cuba Relations*, doctoral dissertation, University of Alabama, Tuscaloosa, 2012, 67.)

14. Herbert L. Matthews, *Fidel Castro* (New York: Simon and Schuster, 1969), 184.

15. Nicholas Dawidoff, "The Struggles of Sandy A," *Sports Illustrated*, July 10, 1989, 80.

16. Peter C. Bjarkman, *Cuba's Baseball Defectors: The Inside Story* (Lanham, MD: Rowman & Littlefield, 2016), passim; Peter C. Bjarkman, *Diamonds around the Globe: The Encyclopedia of International Baseball* (Westport, CT: Greenwood Press, 2005), passim.

17. Robert Elias, *The Empire Strikes Out: How Baseball Sold U.S. Foreign Policy and Promoted the American Way Abroad* (New York and London: New Press, 2010); Joseph A. Reaves, *Taking in a Game: A History of Baseball in Asia* (Lincoln and London: University of Nebraska Press, 2002).

18. The best available history of pre-Castro amateur leagues is Marino Martinez Peraza's Spanish-language *Por Amor de la Pelota—Historia del Béisbol Amateur Cubano* (Miami, FL: Ediciones Universal, 2008), valuable for its year-by-year statistical summaries and team standings and rosters, but unfortunately rather skimpy on explanatory text and analysis.

19. John Virtue, *South of the Color Barrier: How Jorge Pasquel and the Mexican League Pushed Baseball toward Racial Integration* (Jefferson, NC, and London: McFarland, 2008), passim.

20. Virtue, *South of the Color Barrier*, 132–33.

21. Brioso, *Havana Hardball*, 243.

22. Turner, *Baseball Diplomacy*, 60.

23. Turner (*Baseball Diplomacy*, 60) cites an unspecified *Washington Post* article of April 7, 1958 (entitled "Havana Will Play April 16") as the source for this Shaughnessy quote.

24. Turner, *Baseball Diplomacy*, 63–64.

25. Turner (*Baseball Diplomacy*, 81) again cites a *Washington Post* article ("Orioles Shun Havana, Cuba Writer Protest") along with several additional

*New York Times* and *Christian Science Monitor* stories appearing the same week as his main sources of information.

26. González Echavarría, *The Pride of Havana*, 345.

27. Turner, *Baseball Diplomacy*, 79.

28. Turner, *Baseball Diplomacy*, 88. Also "Havana Will Lose Its Baseball Club: Decision Due Today on Shift by International League—Jersey City Seeks Team," *New York Times*, July 8, 1960, 24.

29. Turner, *Baseball Diplomacy*, 88. Also "Havana Team Shift Called 'Big Mistake': Cubans Set to Quit," *Washington Post*, July 9, 1960, A13.

30. Howard Senzel, *Baseball and the Cold War: Being a Soliloquy on the Necessity of Baseball in the Life of a Serious Student of Marx and Hegel from Rochester, New York* (New York and London: Harcourt Brace Jovanovich, 1977), 123.

31. Turner, *Baseball Diplomacy*, 85.

32. Turner, *Baseball Diplomacy*, 86.

33. Félix Julio Alfonso López, *La Letra en el diamante* (Santa Clara, Cuba: Editorial Caprio, 2005), 81.

34. Fernando Ortíz, *Contrapunto Cubano del Tabaco y el Azúcar* (Caracas, Venezuela: Biblioteca Ayacucho, 1978).

35. Matthews, *Fidel Castro*, 52.

36. James Terzian, *The Kid from Cuba: Zoilo Versalles* (New York: Doubleday, 1967), chapter 6.

37. González Echavarría, *The Pride of Havana*, 351.

38. Fidel's reported 1963 contention that baseball was not North American in origin but evolved from the pre-Colombian game of *batos* might have little enough merit, but a most telling feature of American press accounts of Castro's claim was a choice to humorously title the *Christian Science Monitor* article "Señor Comrade Doubleday," which had the effect of simultaneously mocking traditional American claims about the sport's origins. (Turner, *Baseball Diplomacy*, 102–3.)

39. Paula J. Pettavino and Geralyn Pye, *Sport in Cuba: A Diamond in the Rough* (Pittsburgh, PA: University of Pittsburgh Press, 1994).

## 5. THE GRAND SOCIALIST BASEBALL EXPERIMENT

1. Eugene J. McCarthy, "Diamond Diplomacy (The View from Left Field)," *Elysian Fields Quarterly* 14:2 (1995), 15.

2. McCarthy, "Diamond Diplomacy."

3. Turner, *Baseball Diplomacy, Baseball Deployment: The National Pastime in U.S.–Cuba Relations*, doctoral dissertation, University of Alabama, Tuscaloosa, 2012, 104.

4. Robert Elias, *The Empire Strikes Out: How Baseball Sold U.S. Foreign Policy and Promoted the American Way Abroad* (New York and London: New Press, 2010), passim.

5. Joseph A. Reaves, *Taking in a Game: A History of Baseball in Asia* (Lincoln and London: University of Nebraska Press, 2002), passim.

6. The revamping of Cuban sport was one of the earliest formal projects of the new government, with Fidel naming Felipe Guerra Matos (one of his M-26-7 rebel captains) as chief of the new DGD (General Sports Direction, or Sports Ministry) a mere five days after taking over government control in Havana. Law 72 of February 13 (exactly a month later) officially replaced the old sports ministry with the new one, which would soon give way to INDER. Reig Romero's chapter ("Primer inning del béisbol revolucionario") in the 2008 book *Con Las Bases Llenas—Béisbol Historia y Revolución* (Havana: Editorial Cientifico-Técnica, 2008), celebrating the 50th anniversary of revolutionary baseball, details these early efforts at transitioning to a new structure for Cuban baseball. Additional attention to this evolution of the national sport is provided in the previous chapter.

7. Baseball games remained free of charge until the late 1980s, but eventually the economic toll of the "Special Period" forced a change. In the early 1990s, Cuban fans were charged one peso, and there was never any reserved seating except for special sections allocated for INDER officials, players' families, and local dignitaries or the local official sports society (*Peña Deportivas*, which existed in almost every city and town). Today the fee is 3 pesos (about 75 cents [U.S. dollars]), with foreigners being charged 3 dollars or Euro-equivalent CUCs (the tourist currency). How INDER subsequently funded operations, eventually including ballplayers' salaries, is discussed at length by Paula J. Pettavino and Geralyn Pye, *Sport in Cuba: A Diamond in the Rough* (Pittsburgh, PA: University of Pittsburgh Press, 1994) and is not relevant here.

8. The entire text of this famous speech is available online in the Castro Speech Database of the Latin American Network Information Center (http://lanic.utexas.edu/project/castro/db/1961/19610630.html).

9. Herbert L. Matthews, *Fidel Castro* (New York: Simon and Schuster, 1969), 34–35.

10. Herbert L. Matthews, *Revolution in Cuba: An Essay in Understanding* (New York: Charles Scribner's Sons, 1975), 448.

11. Peter G. Bourne, *Fidel: A Biography of Fidel Castro* (New York: Dodd, Mead and Company, 1986), 305.

12. Pettavino and Pye, *Sport in Cuba*, chapter 6.

13. Georgie Anne Geyer, *Guerrilla Prince: The Untold Story of Fidel Castro* (Boston: Little, Brown and Company, 1991), 237.

14. "Castro May Pitch for Sugar Kings," *Christian Science Monitor*, April 23, 1959, 14; Turner, *Baseball Diplomacy*, 68. See also "Havana Team to Stay: Sugar Kings Will Remain in Cuba, Says Club President," *New York Times*, April 24, 1959, 33.

15. Dagoberto Miguel Toledo Menéndez, *Béisbol Revolucionario Cubano, Las Más Grande Hazaña—Aquino Abreu* (Havana: Editorial Deportes, 2006), 32.

16. A popular legend still circulated in Havana claims that the heavily supported Industriales club—Cuba's New York Yankees—was founded by Che Guevara, a claim with no more substance than the mythology about big-league offers made to Fidel. Industriales actually began play in the fall of 1961, during the inaugural year of revolutionary baseball, but trailed Habana in the Western Zone regional tournament and thus was eliminated before the four-team finals designated as the National Series. The club's first manager was the popular Ramón Carneado.

17. The *INDER Official Baseball Guide* appeared most years in the 1960s, once in 1988, and then annually since the early 1990s. The 1963 guide is the first attempted, and like the others to follow, it contains a full summary of 1962–1963 Cuban baseball and therefore actually appeared at the outset of the following season. It is one of the most detailed and polished in design, including numerous photos, complete coverage of that year's Pan American Games baseball event in Brazil, and an appendix offering the entire league rule book (which takes up almost a third of the publication).

18. *Béisbol 1963: Guia Oficial* (Havana, Seminario Deportivo y INDER). This initial INDER guidebook to Cuban baseball carried no page numbers except for the official league rule book which comprises the second half of the publication. An initial ten-page section at the front ("… un triunfo de la pelota libre sobre la pelota esclava …" by Fidel Castro) contains the text of Fidel's opening day comments, which are quoted here as translated by the author.

19. Roberto González Echevarría, *The Pride of Havana: A History of Cuban Baseball* (New York: Oxford University Press, 1999), 364.

20. That the national team focus was an early priority—rather than the quality of or the fan support for league play—is emphasized in the *INDER Official Baseball Guide* for the 1968 season. There, INDER's goal is clearly stated: "Our highest sports organization has never taken into account attendance or the parity of a tournament, because its interest has always been the development of athletes, and there is no doubt that this expansion [the doubling of league size from six to 12 teams that year—PCB] would work in favor

of the more rapid development of players, as was the case." (*INDER Official Baseball Guide*, front matter explanatory notes)

21. Provincial realignment eliminated Habana Province and introduced Mayabeque and Artemisa for the 2011–2012 league season. The Havana Metropolitanos team was disbanded at the end of that same campaign. The Isla de la Juventud ballclub was known as the Pine Cutters until recent campaigns and Holguín recently switched its name from Perros (Dogs) to Cachorros (Puppies, or Cubs). Las Tunas was earlier known as the Magos, or Magicians.

22. This long-standing tradition came to an end in part with the advent of split-season play in recent campaigns. With eight provincial teams eliminated at the conclusion of the first 45-game round, star players from those squads are placed in a draft selection as "reinforcement" players. In what was initially six but now eight rounds of drafting (featured on national television), managers of the clubs entering the championship second round choose players to supplement their rosters from the reinforcements pool. Thus, several dozen players now play for two separate teams each season.

## 6. THE OTHER BIG RED MACHINE AND CUBA'S DOMINANCE OF INTERNATIONAL BASEBALL

1. Justin W. R. Turner, *Baseball Diplomacy, Baseball Deployment: The National Pastime in U.S.–Cuba Relations*, doctoral dissertation, University of Alabama, Tuscaloosa, 2012, 106.

2. Paula J. Pettavino and Geralyn Pye, *Sport in Cuba: A Diamond in the Rough* (Pittsburgh, PA: University of Pittsburgh Press, 1994), chapter 2.

3. Wenceslao Gálvez y Delmonte, *El Base-ball en Cuba—Historia del Base-ball en la Isla de Cuba, Sin Retratos de los Principales Jugadores y Personas más Caracterizadas en el Juego Citado, ni de Ninguna Otra* (Havana: Imprenta Mercantile, 1889).

4. Roberto González Echevarría, *The Pride of Havana: A History of Cuban Baseball* (New York: Oxford University Press, 1999), 76.

5. Turner, *Baseball Diplomacy*, 104–5.

6. Doubts surrounding the Cooperstown credentials of both Méndez and Torriente are voiced in my biographical essays on those two figures found in Peter C. Bjarkman and Bill Nowlin, eds., *Cuban Baseball Legends: Baseball's Alternative Universe* (Phoenix, AZ: Society for American Baseball Research, 2016).

7. González Echevarría, *The Pride of Havana*, 133.

8. González Echevarría, *The Pride of Havana*, 206.

9. "Cubans Get Asylum," *Washington Post*, April 26, 1961, C2.

10. Turner, *Baseball Diplomacy*, 107.

11. Turner, *Baseball Diplomacy*, 108.

12. Fidel's charges of American complicity in the IOC snafu were reported by the *New York Times* ("Castro Charges U.S. Schemes to Keep Cubans Out of Games," April 16, 1963); a second report in the same paper several days later added to the political overtones surrounding the games by stating that at the Opening Ceremonies, the American athletes received a warmer welcome and louder cheers than the Cubans ("Colorful Ceremonies Open Fourth Pan American Games," April 21, 1963).

13. Turner, *Baseball Diplomacy*, 110.

14. Betancourt's departure was immediately played up in the American press, which claimed he was a team pitching coach. That was not the case, although he had been working for INDER as a youth instructor back home, a service that led to his inclusion on the Baltimore trip. The former pitcher would later suffer great disillusionment related to his defection when he failed to obtain a hoped-for coaching position in the American professional ranks and was left in poor financial straits in Miami. Betancourt's saga is told both in my book, *Cuba's Baseball Defectors: The Inside Story* (Lanham, MD: Rowman & Littlefield, 2016), 309, note 25, and in a *Miami New Times* story written by Lissette Corsa ("The Cuban Coach," August 31, 2001), www.miaminewtimeas.com/news/the-cuban-coach-6353963.

15. The 1988 Amateur World Series in Parma, Italy, the last such event of the two decades, marked the official name change to "IBAF Baseball World Cup." It can also be noted that during the same two-decade stretch, the Cubans captured five of the six IBAF Intercontinental Cup tournaments they entered. The Cubans did not compete in the first three Intercontinental Cup events and lost the 1981 tournament in Edmonton, where they were shocked by the Americans in the finals.

16. Peter C. Bjarkman, *A History of Cuban Baseball, 1864–2006* (Jefferson, NC, and London: McFarland, 2014). Originally printed in 2007.

17. Ron Fimrite, "In Cuba It's Viva El Grand Old Game," *Sports Illustrated*, June 6, 1977, 68–80.

18. Thomas Boswell, *How Life Imitates the World Series* (New York: Doubleday, 1987), 81.

19. While Baez never emerged as a star in Cuba due to his early departure, he would become a notable big-league closer with Cleveland and Tampa Bay during the course of the next decade.

20. At a press conference opening the 2005 Baseball World Cup in Rotterdam, IBAF president Aldo Notari (Italy) explained the earlier legal moves by his organization to safeguard the World Cup label, first used to replace an IBAF "Amateur World Series" in 1988, and also voiced his hopes to maintain

the IBAF version as a true world series for international baseball. The former happened, the latter did not.

21. In discussing MLB plans for a World Baseball Classic and the underlying motivations for MLB "globalization," Robert Elias (*The Empire Strikes Out: How Baseball Sold U.S. Foreign Policy and Promoted the American Way Abroad* [New York and London: New Press, 2010], 289) notes, "The real form baseball 'globalization' has taken is not its export from the U.S. to foreign countries but the migration of baseball labor to the U.S."

22. Three prominent reasons for the George W. Bush administration relenting on their efforts to keep the Cubans on the sidelines for the MLB event were (in ascending order of importance): 1) the IBAF's threatened withdrawal of its announced endorsement for the games, 2) Puerto Rico's threat to withdraw as a host venue, and 3) threats from the International Olympic Committee that any blockage of Cuban participation could jeopardize the U.S. ability to host future summer or winter Olympic Games (cf. Gmelch and Nathan, *Baseball Beyond Our Borders*, 429).

23. Fidel's rapid "fall" from power took place in three closely approximated stages. On October 20, 2004, he fell during a speech in Santa Clara (suffering a broken knee and arm fractures) and effectively was placed on the "disabled list." On July 26, 2006, he publicly announced he had undergone complicated intestinal surgery and was delegating governmental control to Raúl. And on February 19, 2008, he finally and formally retired from public office.

24. Fidel's essay was published on an official government website devoted exclusively to carrying the weekly reflections of the retired leader on all manner of political and cultural topics. These essays appeared weekly and sometimes daily, and constituted his only remaining contact with his adoring masses and his only remaining active contribution to the ongoing revolution, now officially led by his brother (http://www.cuba.cu/gobierno/reflexiones/2009/ing/f190309i.html, March 19, 2009).

25. Of the regular starting lineup presented by the Cubans in Tokyo, the following players defected to MLB in the coming months: José Abreu (first base), José Miguel Fernández (second base), Erisbel Arruebarruena (shortstop), Yulieski Gourriel (third base), Guillermo Heredia (center field), Yasmani Tomás (right field and DH), and pitchers Raisel Iglesias and Odrisamer Despaigne. Abreu specifically claimed that the event in Tokyo convinced him he had the talent to play in the big time.

26. Pettavino and Pye, *Sport in Cuba*, 3.

27. Pettavino and Pye, *Sport in Cuba*, 3.

## 7. THE FICTIONAL PERSONAS OF FIDEL CASTRO

1. John Krich, *A Totally Free Man: The Unauthorized Autobiography of Fidel Castro (a Novel)* (New York and London: Simon and Schuster, 1988), 173. Originally printed in 1981.

2. J. David Truby, "Castro's Curveball," *Harper's Magazine*, May 1989, 32, 34. Originally appeared in "Great Moments," *Sports History*, March 1989.

3. Milton Jamail, *Full Count: Inside Cuban Baseball* (Carbondale and Edwardsville: Southern Illinois University Press, 2000).

4. Jamail, *Full Count*, 26–27.

5. Peter G. Bourne, *Fidel: A Biography of Fidel Castro* (New York: Dodd, Mead and Company, 1986).

6. Robert E. Quirk, *Fidel Castro* (New York: W. W. Norton, 1995). Originally printed in 1993.

7. Roberto González Echevarría, *The Pride of Havana: A History of Cuban Baseball* (New York: Oxford University Press, 1999).

8. Fidel Castro, *Fidel Sobre el Deporte* [Fidel on Sports], rev. ed. (Havana: INDER, 1980).

9. The emphasis on equal weight for all recreation and sports activity has long been reflected in the country's top news daily, the Communist organ *Granma*, an eight-page publication whose one-page sports section offers only a small corner section on daily baseball results during the National Series season.

10. Lee Lockwood, *Castro's Cuba, Cuba's Fidel: An American Journalist's Inside Look at Today's Cuba—in Text and Pictures* (New York: Random House [Vintage Books], 1969), 188.

11. Howard Senzel, *Baseball and the Cold War: Being a Soliloquy on the Necessity of Baseball in the Life of a Serious Student of Marx and Hegel from Rochester, New York* (New York and London: Harcourt Brace Jovanovich, 1977).

12. Richard C. Crepeau, "Book Review of *Baseball and the Cold War* by Howard Senzel," *Journal of Sports History* 6:3 (Winter 1979): 60–62.

13. Crepeau, "Book Review of *Baseball and the Cold War*," 60–62.

14. Crepeau, "Book Review of *Baseball and the Cold War*."

15. In his acknowledgments, Krich cites Lockwood's *Castro's Cuba, Cuba's Fidel* as a "major source of inspiration" and draws details of his subject's life from the Castro–Lockwood interviews. He also cites a half-dozen additional sources that suggest he had at least combed the Castro literature available in the late 1970s.

16. *Review of A Totally Free Man: An Unauthorized Autobiography of Fidel Castro* by John Krich. Anonymous review. *Kirkus Reviews* online (December 15, 1981), www.kirkusreviews.com.

17. Krich, *A Totally Free Man*, 22.

18. Fidel Castro and Ignacio Ramonet, *Fidel Castro: My Life—A Spoken Autobiography*, trans. Andrew Hurley (New York: Scribner, 2006). The Ramonet book does contain a photo of Fidel "playing baseball with former U.S. president Jimmy Carter" (it is actually an image of the two on the pitcher's mound before Carter launched a ceremonial first pitch in Latin American Stadium), but in the section devoted to Carter's May 2002 Havana visit there is no mention of the subject.

19. Norberto Fuentes, *The Autobiography of Fidel Castro*, trans. Anna Kushner (New York: W. W. Norton, 2010). Originally printed in 2004.

20. John Krich, *El Béisbol: Travels through the Pan American Pastime* (New York: Atlantic Monthly Press, 1989).

21. Review of *El Béisbol: Travels Through the Pan American Pastime* by John Krich. Anonymous review. *Kirkus Reviews* online (May 20, 2010), www.kirkusreviews.com.

22. Krich, *El Béisbol*, 269.

23. Michiko Kakutani, "Fiction Trying for Truth in Novel's View of Dictator," *New York Times*, December 14, 2009, https://www.nytimes.com/2009/12/15/books/15book.html.

24. Kakutani, "Fiction Trying for Truth in Novel's View of Dictator."

25. Kakutani, "Fiction Trying for Truth in Novel's View of Dictator."

26. Kakutani, "Fiction Trying for Truth in Novel's View of Dictator."

27. Randy Wayne White (writing as Randy Striker), *Cuban Death-Lift* (New York: Signet Books [New American Library]), 1981.

28. Randy Wayne White, *North of Havana*. A Doc Ford Novel. (New York: Berkley Prime Crime Press, 1997), 218.

29. Tim Wendel, *Castro's Curveball* (New York: Ballantine, 2000). Originally printed in 1999.

30. Tim Wendel, "Fidel Castro, Ballplayer," *Society for American Baseball Research*, November 8, 2016, https://sabr.org/latest/wendel-fidel-castro-ballplayer.

## 8. THE CUBAN BASEBALL DEFECTORS PHENOMENON

1. S. L. Price, *Pitching around Fidel: A Journey into the Heart of Cuban Sports* (New York: Ecco Press [HarperCollins]), 2000, 7.

2. Louis A. Pérez Jr., *Cuba: Between Reform and Revolution* (New York: Oxford University Press, 1988), 337.

3. Price, *Pitching around Fidel*, 6–7.

4. The EIR schools (Schools of Revolutionary Instruction) were a project Fidel had launched in 1960. These mysterious schools, largely hidden from public view, offered courses to handpicked budding revolutionary leaders that stressed the centralized planning toward which Castro's government mechanism was trending. Emphasis was placed on what Fidel would later refer to as the materials of Scientific Communism, the needs of the ideological fight against capitalist imperialism and the construction of a proper communist party, but Fidel would also later reportedly say that such schools were designed to offer "a master's degree in Communism." (Georgie Anne Geyer, *Guerrilla Prince: The Untold Story of Fidel Castro* [Boston: Little, Brown and Company, 1991], 286.)

5. Geyer, *Guerrilla Prince*, 285.

6. Paula J. Pettavino and Geralyn Pye, *Sport in Cuba: A Diamond in the Rough* (Pittsburgh, PA: University of Pittsburgh Press, 1994), passim.

7. Geyer, *Guerrilla Prince*, 287.

8. Pettavino and Pye, *Sport in Cuba*, 126.

9. Robert Whiting, *The Meaning of Ichiro: The New Wave from Japan and the Transformation of Our National Pastime* (New York: Grand Central Publishing, 2009), 96.

10. Also implicated in Cuba's worst ballpark scandal was promising stellar infielder Rey Anglada. But Anglada's story took a very different turn. He would remain at home, undergo a lengthy rehabilitation period that lasted more than two decades, and eventually reemerge as manager of both the Industriales (where his club won back-to-back titles in 2002 and 2003) and the Cuban national team at the 2006 Central American Games (gold medal), 2007 World Cup (silver medal), and 2007 Pan American Games (gold medal).

11. Peter C. Bjarkman, *Cuba's Baseball Defectors: The Inside Story* (Lanham, MD: Rowman & Littlefield, 2016), 110–11.

12. The Office of Foreign Assets Control embargo regulations required Cuban players to have an established third-country residence before signing a contract with Organized Baseball clubs since Helms–Burton legislation (an extension of the original Eisenhower embargo policy signed into law by President Clinton in 1997) outlawed any money paid directly to Cuban citizens. As I suggest in *Cuba's Baseball Defectors*, one could only imagine the public outcry in the United States if under similar reasoning European soccer teams or basketball teams required American players to renounce U.S. citizenship to play in those countries. It was this same law that led to the flap concerning Alfredo Despaigne playing in the Organized Baseball–affiliated Mexican League without first renouncing his homeland.

13. The early defections of several players at the 1972 Jamaica tournament also had brought a similar charge, but those earlier players were not recog-

nized heroes of a well-established national team, and their losses had been easily dismissed as hardly worthy of public notice. Such earlier defections came at a time of less public disillusionment and were deemed less of a threat to the revolutionary system.

14. Steve Fainaru and Ray Sánchez, *The Duke of Havana: Baseball, Cuba, and the Search for the American Dream* (New York: Villard, 2001), 52–53.

15. Fainaru and Sánchez, *The Duke of Havana*, 52.

16. Moncada's story is treated at some length in chapter 7 of *Cuba's Baseball Defectors*. He would "retire" as a 20-year-old hot prospect coveted by big-league scouts. But because of the changing environment in Havana by 2013, and because Moncada agreed he would not embarrass authorities and the league with a defection attempt, a plan was worked that allowed him to leave the country by a legal, if long-drawn-out and circuitous, route.

17. Prieto would later serve as a minor-league pitching coach in the Oakland system and, after 2012, for a short term as a translator and handler for prized Cuban defector Yoenis Céspedes. Most recently, he has occupied a similar role with the Arizona Diamondbacks and their Cuban outfielder, Yasmany Tomás.

18. Fainaru and Sánchez, *The Duke of Havana*, 109.

19. L. Jon Wertheim and Don Yaeger, "Fantastic Voyage: Three Fellow Refugees Say the Tale of Yankees Ace Orlando (El Duque) Hernández's Escape from Cuba Doesn't Hold Water," *Sports Illustrated*, November 30, 1998, 60–63.

20. Fainaru and Sánchez, *The Duke of Havana*, 308.

21. The entire tale is retold in detail by Fainaru and Sánchez (*The Duke of Havana*, 285–88), and also recounted in *Cuba's Baseball Defectors* (chapter 5, 127). A key player was City College of New York international relations professor Pamela Falk, who arranged the cooperation of the archbishop and also smoothed out the family's speedy U.S. entrance with Washington officials. Fainaru reports that when Cardinal O'Connor's envoy, Mario Paredes, entered to plead the case, Fidel was alone in his office watching the final game of the World Series on a color television when the messenger arrived. Agreeing to the request, Fidel (perhaps somewhat regretful of the earlier harsh INDER sanctions) had only the highest praise for Hernández as an individual and ballplayer (*The Duke of Havana*, 290–91).

22. Bjarkman, *Cuba's Baseball Defectors*, 90–91.

23. Bjarkman, *Cuba's Baseball Defectors*, 26–28.

24. The details of Chapman and Puig's possible roles as informers falsely fingering alleged smugglers to buy their own reprieves in Cuba is told in some detail in *Cuba's Baseball Defectors* (15–17 and 90–91). Further details can be found in Stacy St. Clair, "How Cuba's Aroldis Chapman Helped the Castro

Regime before Cuban Defection," *Chicago Tribune*, October 6, 2016, http://www.chicagotribune.com/news/ct-cubs-aroldis-chapman-cuba-20161005-story.html, and Scott Eden, "No One Walks Off the Island," *ESPN the Magazine*, April 17, 2014, http://www.espn.com/espn/feature/story/_/id/19678696/mlb-prospects-cuba-trapped-dream. There is also evidence that Diamondbacks outfielder Yasmany Tómas bought favor and reinstatement on the eve of the 2013 World Baseball Classic by turning over names of those who orchestrated his earlier failed defection attempt (he claimed he had been kidnapped and was not actually desiring to leave); one of those fingered was a cousin and another was a longtime friend (*Cuba's Baseball Defectors*, 168–69).

25. Michael E. Miller, "Who Is José Abreu? After Defecting from Cuba the Sox Slugger Had One of the Best Rookie Seasons Ever. Yet His Story Has Remained Largely a Mystery. Until Now," *Chicago*, April 2015, http://www.chicagomag.com/Chicago-Magazine/April-2015/Jose-Abreu-Chicago-White-Sox/.

26. Curt Anderson, "Cuban Players Paid Smugglers $15 Million, Prosecutors Say," *Miami Sun-Sentinel*, April 27, 2016, http://www.sun-sentinel.com/sports/sfl-cuban-players-paid-smugglers-15-million-prosecutors-say-20160427-story.html.

27. Peter C. Bjarkman, "MLB's Next Headache: Cartels, Gangsters, and Their Cuban Superstars," *Daily Beast*, April 18, 2014, https://www.thedailybeast.com/mlbs-next-headache-cartels-gangsters-and-their-cuban-superstars.

28. I have often been questioned about why INDER should extract 20 percent and had to point out that U.S. income taxes on the salaries of MLB players extract a far higher cut.

29. Almost a dozen Cubans played in the lower echelon Canadian circuit in 2016 and 2017, including star Villa Clara catcher Yulexis La Rosa, and Granma ace pitcher Lázaro Blanco. Others, like pitchers Norberto González and Ciro Silvino Licea, catcher Frank Camilo Morejón, and slugger Joan Carlos Pedroso, have been farmed out during the past half-dozen years for summer service in pro leagues in France and Italy.

30. Bjarkman, *Cuba's Baseball Defectors*, 243–44.

31. The nature of Yulieski's injuries were never clear, although he might have been fatigued from a lengthy double season. Yunito, however, suffered a severe wrist bruise when hit by a pitch near season's end in a game at Matanzas, which I actually witnessed.

32. Bjarkman, *Cuba's Baseball Defectors*, 220.

33. Scott Eden, "The Lost Prospects of Cuba," *ESPN the Magazine*, June 26, 2017, http://www.espn.com/espn/feature/story/_/id/19678696/mlb-prospects-cuba-trapped-dream.

34. Geyer, *Guerrilla Prince*, 391.

## 9. THE ULTIMATE COLLAPSE OF CUBAN BASEBALL

1. Nixon was inaugurated on January 20, 1969, and Kuhn was installed in office only two weeks later, on February 4.

2. A delegation of U.S. table tennis players made a 10-day visit to Communist China in April 1971. It was the first friendly act between the two Cold War adversaries in decades and paved the way for President Nixon's own historic visit to China the following year. Nixon had vowed to make improved relations with the Chinese government a top priority of his new administration when he took office in January 1969.

3. In his interview with ESPN broadcasters Karl Ravich, Eduardo Perez, and Doug Glanville, Obama stressed how business from the United States would help give the United States better leverage in Cuba. This itself was a clear signal that the game and telecast were about much more than baseball. See Richard Sandomir, "In Havana, Rapprochement through the Lens of ESPN," *New York Times*, March 23, 2016, https://www.nytimes.com/2016/03/23/sports/baseball/cuba-tampa-bay-rays-espn.html.

4. Joseph A. Reaves, *Taking in a Game: A History of Baseball in Asia* (Lincoln and London: University of Nebraska Press, 2002), 139.

5. Robert Elias, *The Empire Strikes Out: How Baseball Sold U.S. Foreign Policy and Promoted the American Way Abroad* (New York and London: New Press, 2010).

6. Ed Rumill, "Kuhn Sights Global Baseball: High-Speed Air Travel, Careful Promotion Needed, 'America Loves the Underdog,'" *Christian Science Monitor*, July 31, 1969, 10.

7. Justin W. R. Turner, *Baseball Diplomacy, Baseball Deployment: The National Pastime in U.S.–Cuba Relations*, doctoral dissertation, University of Alabama, Tuscaloosa, 2012, 102.

8. "Señor Comrade Doubleday," *Christian Science Monitor*, March 22, 1962, 16.

9. "Castro's Bay of Pigs Anniversary Speech," *Castro Speech Data Base*, April 20, 1971, http://lanic.utexas.edu/project/castro/db/1971/19710420.html.

10. "Castro's Bay of Pigs Anniversary Speech."

11. Martin Schram, "Castro Chides U.S. over Triumphs by Cuban Sports Team," *Washington Post*, August 17, 1971, A13.

12. Turner, *Baseball Diplomacy*, 148–49.

13. Turner, *Baseball Diplomacy*, 159.

14. Revelations came in the form of the Church Committee (the Senate Select Committee to Study Governmental Operations with Respect to Intelligence Activities), which uncovered CIA contributions to political assassinations of Rafael Trujillo in the Dominican Republic and Patrice Lumumba in the Congo Republic. Also revealed were at least eight assassination attempts aimed at Castro, including a most recent effort involving overtures to mafia bosses John Roselli and Sam Giancana to complete the task. (Turner, *Baseball Diplomacy*, 159.)

15. Peter G. Bourne, *Fidel: A Biography of Fidel Castro* (New York: Dodd, Mead and Company, 1986), 281.

16. "Politics Squelch Cuba Trip," *Washington Post*, December 3, 1975, D3. Turner, *Baseball Diplomacy*, 162–63, reviews these developments in detail.

17. Turner, *Baseball Diplomacy*, 171.

18. Murray Chass, "Yanks Upset as Kuhn Vetoes Their Trip," March 9, 1977, A17.

19. Frank Mankiewicz, "Waiting for Rain: Out-Batting the Batista of Baseball," *Washington Post*, July 31, 1977, 262.

20. Turner, *Baseball Diplomacy*, 178.

21. Milton Jamail, *Full Count: Inside Cuban Baseball* (Carbondale and Edwardsville: Southern Illinois University Press, 2000), 126–27.

22. Bourne, *Fidel*, 293–95.

23. Commissioner Rob Manfred's comments were made at a March 9, 2015, spring training tour press conference in Jupiter, Florida, then widely circulated in an online Associated Press news release.

24. Mary Murray and Orlando Matos, "Cuban National Signs First Million-Dollar Baseball Contract: Cuban Outfielder Frederich Cepeda Has Scored One for the History Books," *NBC News*, April 23, 2014, http://www.nbcnews.com/news/world/cuban-national-signs-first-million-dollar-baseball-contract-n87526.

25. Enrique Rojas, "Despaigne juege como Dominicano," *ESPN*, May 13, 2014. https://espn.com/noticias/nota?s=bei&id=2086820&type=story.

26. Peter C. Bjarkman, "U.S.–Cuba Thaw Is Not So Hot for MLB," *Daily Beast*, February 19, 2015, https://www.thedailybeast.com/us-cuba-thaw-is-not-so-hot-for-mlb.

27. Steve Fainaru and Ray Sánchez, *The Duke of Havana: Baseball, Cuba, and the Search for the American Dream* (New York: Villard, 2001).

# SOURCES CITED AND SUGGESTED FURTHER READINGS

## FIDEL CASTRO BIOGRAPHIES AND PORTRAITS

Bourne, Peter G. *Fidel: A Biography of Fidel Castro*. New York: Dodd, Mead and Company, 1986.

Castro, Fidel. *Fidel: My Early Years*. Ed. Deborah Shnookal and Pedro Alvarez Tabío. Melbourne and New York: Ocean Press, 1998.

———. *Fidel en la memoria del joven que es*. Havana: Casa Editora Abril, 1998.

Castro, Fidel, and Ignacio Ramonet. *Fidel Castro: My Life—A Spoken Autobiography*. Trans. Andrew Hurley. New York: Scribner, 2006.

Conte Agüero, Luis. *Cartas del Presidio*. Havana: Editorial Lex, 1959.

———. *Fidel Castro: Vida y Obra*. Havana: Editorial Lex, 1959.

Dubois, Jules. *Fidel Castro: Rebel-Liberator or Dictator?* Indianapolis, IN, and New York: Bobbs-Merrill, 1959.

Elliott, Jeffery M., and Mervyn Dymally. *Fidel Castro: Nothing Can Stop the Course of History* (an Interview). New York and London: Pathfinder Press, 1986.

Geyer, Georgie Anne. *Guerrilla Prince: The Untold Story of Fidel Castro*. Boston: Little, Brown and Company, 1991.

Halperin, Maurice. *The Rise and Decline of Fidel Castro: An Essay in Contemporary History*. Berkeley and London: University of California Press, 1972.

Lockwood, Lee. *Castro's Cuba, Cuba's Fidel: An American Journalist's Inside Look at Today's Cuba—in Text and Pictures*. New York: Random House (Vintage Books), 1969.

Matthews, Herbert L. *Fidel Castro*. New York: Simon and Schuster, 1969.

Meneses, Enrique. *Fidel Castro*. New York: Taplinger, 1968.

Morejón, Gerardo Rodríguez. *Fidel Castro: Biografía*. Havana: P. Fernández and Company, 1959.

Quirk, Robert E. *Fidel Castro*. New York: W. W. Norton, 1995. Originally printed in 1993.

Szulc, Tad. *Fidel: A Critical Portrait*. New York: William Morrow and Company, 1986.

# THE FICTIONAL PERSONAS OF FIDEL CASTRO

## Books

Fuentes, Norberto. *The Autobiography of Fidel Castro*. Trans. Anna Kushner. New York: W. W. Norton, 2010. Originally printed in 2004.

Krich, John. *A Totally Free Man: The Unauthorized Autobiography of Fidel Castro (a Novel)*. New York and London: Simon and Schuster, 1988. Originally printed in 1981.

Wendel, Tim. *Castro's Curveball*. New York: Ballantine, 2000. Originally printed in 1999.

White, Randy Wayne. *Cuba Straits*. A Doc Ford Novel. New York: G. P. Putnam's Sons, 2015.

———. *North of Havana*. A Doc Ford Novel . New York: Berkley Prime Crime Press, 1997.

——— (writing as Randy Striker). *Cuban Death-Lift*. New York: Signet Books (New American Library), 1981.

## Print Articles and Online Sources

Carbone, Nick. "Ozzie Guillen Suspended by Marlins Following Castro Comment." *Time*, April 10, 2012, http://keepingscore.blogs.time.com/2012/04/10/ozzie-guillen-marlins-suspended-fidel-castro/.

Hoak, Don, with Myron Cope. "The Day I Batted against Castro." In *The Armchair Book of Baseball*, ed. John Thorn, 161–64. New York: Charles Scribner's Sons, 1985. Originally appeared in *Sport*, June 1964.

"How Castro Survived 638 Very Cunning Assassination Attempts." *ABC.net*, November 28, 2016, http://www.abc.net.au/triplej/programs/hack/how-castro-survived-638-assassination-attempts/8064788.

Truby, J. David. "Castro's Curveball." *Harper's Magazine*, May 1989, 32, 34. Originally appeared in "Great Moments," *Sports History*, March 1989.

Wendel, Tim. "Fidel Castro—Ballplayer." *The National Pastime Museum*, November 8, 2016, www.thenationalpastimemuseum.com/article/fidel-castro-ballplayer.

# FIDEL CASTRO AND THE CUBAN REVOLUTION

Ali, Tariq. *Pirates of the Caribbean: Axis of Hope—Evo Morales, Fidel Castro, and Hugo Chávez*. London and New York: Verso, 2006.

Arboleya, Jesús. *The Cuban Counterrevolution*. Trans. Damián Donéstevez. Havana: Editorial José Marti, 2002.

Bonsal, Philip W. *Cuba, Castro, and the United States*. Pittsburgh, PA: University of Pittsburgh Press, 1971.

Brenner, Philip, et al. *The Cuba Reader: The Making of a Revolutionary Society*. New York: Grove Press, 1989.

Cardenal, Ernesto. *In Cuba*. Trans. Donald D. Walsh. New York: New Directions Books, 1974.

Castro, Fidel. *History Will Absolve Me*. Havana: Editorial Ciencias Sociales, 1975.

Casuso, Teresa. *Cuba and Castro*. Trans. Elmer Grossberg. New York: Random House, 1961.

Domínguez, Jorge I. *Cuba: Order and Revolution*. Cambridge, MA: Harvard University Press, 1978.

Draper, Theodore. *Castroism: Theory and Practice*. New York: Frederick A. Praeger, 1965.

———. *Castro's Revolution: Myths and Realities*. New York: Frederick A. Praeger, 1962.

Eckstein, Susan Eva. *Back from the Future: Cuba under Castro*. Princeton, NJ: Princeton University Press, 1994.

Farber, Samuel. *The Origins of the Cuban Revolution Reconsidered*. Chapel Hill: University of North Carolina Press, 2006.

Franqui, Carlos. *Diary of the Cuban Revolution*. New York: Viking, 1976.

Goldenberg, Boris. *The Cuban Revolution and Latin America*. New York: Frederick A. Praeger, 1965.

Mankiewicz, Frank, and Kirby Jones. *With Fidel: A Portrait of Castro and Cuba*. Chicago: Playboy Press, 1975.

Matthews, Herbert L. *Cuba*. New York: Macmillan, 1964.

———. *The Cuban Story*. New York: George Braziller, 1961.

———. *Revolution in Cuba: An Essay in Understanding*. New York: Charles Scribner's Sons, 1975.

Oppenheimer, Andrés. *Castro's Final Hour: The Secret Story behind the Coming Downfall of Communist Cuba*. New York: Simon and Schuster, 1992.

Paterson, Thomas G. *Contesting Castro: The United States and the Triumph of the Cuban Revolution*. New York: Oxford University Press, 1994.

Pérez, Louis A., Jr. *Cuba: Between Reform and Revolution*. New York: Oxford University Press, 1988.

———. *On Becoming Cuban: Identity, Nationality, and Culture*. Chapel Hill and London: University of North Carolina Press, 1999.

Randall, Margaret. *To Change the World: My Years in Cuba*. New Brunswick, NJ, and London: Rutgers University Press, 2009.

Rosenthal, Mona. *Inside the Revolution: Everyday Life in Socialist Cuba*. Ithaca, NY, and London: Cornell University Press, 1997.

Selser, Gregorio. *La Revolución Cubana*. Buenos Aires: Editorial Palestra, 1966.

Smith, Earl E. T. *The Fourth Floor: An Account of the Castro Communist Revolution*. New York: Random House, 1962.

Smith, Robert Freeman. *The United States and Cuba: Business and Diplomacy, 1917–1960*. New York: Bookman Associates, 1960.

Suárez, Andrés. *Cuba: Castroism and Communism, 1959–1966*. Cambridge, MA: MIT Press, 1967.

Suchlicki, Jaime. *Cuba: From Columbus to Castro*, 3rd ed. Washington, DC, and New York: Brassey's, 1990.

Symmes, Patrick. *The Boys from Dolores: Fidel Castro's Classmates from Revolution to Exile*. New York: Pantheon, 2007.

Thomas, Hugh. *Cuba: The Pursuit of Freedom*. New York: Harper and Row, 1971.

Wyden, Peter. *Bay of Pigs: The Untold Story*. New York: Simon and Schuster, 1979.

## Articles

Anderson, Jon Lee. "Castro's Last Battle: Can the Revolution Outlive Its Leader?" *New Yorker*, July 31, 2006, https://www.newyorker.com/magazine/2006/07/31/castros-last-battle.

———. "Havana Journal: The Plague Years." *New Yorker*, January 26, 1998, 62–68.

Cartier-Bresson, Henri. "Inside Castro's Cuba: This Is Castro's Cuba Seen Face-to-Face." *Life*, March 15, 1963, 28–41.

Matthews, Herbert. "Cuban Rebel Is Visited in Hideout." *New York Times*, February 24, 1957, 1.

Mead, Walter Russell. "Castro's Successor?" *New Yorker*, January 26, 1998, 42–49.

Walsh, Bryan. "The Castro Era's Long Goodbye." *Inside the New Cuba*, a *Time* magazine Special Issue, September 2015, 82–87.

# CUBAN BASEBALL HISTORY
# (FIDEL CASTRO AND BASEBALL)

## Books

Alfonso López, Félix Julio, ed. *Con Las Bases Llenas—Béisbol, Historia y Revolución*. Habana: Editorial Científico-Téchnica, 2008.

———. *La Esfera y El Tiempo*. Habana: Editorial Unicornio, 2007.

Bjarkman, Peter C. *Cuba's Baseball Defectors: The Inside Story*. Lanham, MD: Rowman & Littlefield, 2016.

———. *A History of Cuban Baseball, 1864–2006*. Jefferson, NC, and London: McFarland, 2014. Originally printed in 2007.

Bjarkman, Peter C., and Bill Nowlin, eds. *Cuban Baseball Legends: Baseball's Alternative Universe*. Phoenix, AZ: Society for American Baseball Research, 2016.

———. *Leyendas del Béisbol Cubano: El Universo Alternativo del Béisbol*. Trans. Reynaldo Cruz. Phoenix, AZ: Society for American Baseball Research.

Boswell, Thomas. *How Life Imitates the World Series*. New York: Doubleday, 1987.

Brioso, César. *Havana Hardball: Spring Training, Jackie Robinson, and the Cuban League*. Gainesville: University Press of Florida, 2015.

Cases, Edel, Jorge Alfonso, and Alberto Pentana. *Viva y en juego*. Havana: Editorial Científico Técnica, 1986.

Codina, Norberto. *Cajón de Bateo—Algunas Claves dentre Béisbol y Cultura*. Matanzas: Ediciones Matanzas, 2012.

Deal, Ellis F. ("Cot"). *Fifty Years in Baseball—or, "Cot" in the Act*. Oklahoma City, OK: Self-published, 1992.

Fainaru, Steve, and Ray Sánchez. *The Duke of Havana: Baseball, Cuba, and the Search for the American Dream*. New York: Villard, 2001.

Figueredo, Jorge S. *Béisbol Cubano: A un Paso de las Grandes Ligas, 1878–1961*. Jefferson, NC, and London: McFarland, 2005.

———. *Cuban Baseball: A Statistical History, 1878–1961*. Jefferson, NC, and London: McFarland, 2003.

Gálvez y Delmonte, Wenceslao. *El Base-ball en Cuba—Historia del Base-ball en la Isla de Cuba, Sin Retratos de los Principales Jugadores y Personas más Caracterizadas en el Juego Citado, ni de Ninguna Otra*. Havana: Imprenta Mercantile, 1889.

Garay, Osvaldo Rojas. *Fidel nunca se poncha*. Santa Clara: Ediciones Capiro, 2016.

González Echevarría, Roberto. *La Gloria de Cuba: Historia del béisbol en la isla*. Madrid: Editorial Colibrí, 2000. (Spanish-language version of *The Pride of Havana*.)

———. *The Pride of Havana: A History of Cuban Baseball*. New York: Oxford University Press, 1999.

*Guia Oficial del Béisbol Cubano*. Havana: Editorial Deportes, various years. (An annual Cuban baseball statistical guide published irregularly from the 1960s through the 1970s and regularly since 1998.)

Jamail, Milton. *Full Count: Inside Cuban Baseball*. Carbondale and Edwardsville: Southern Illinois University Press, 2000.

Martínez de Osaba y Goenaga, Juan A. *El Niño Linares*. Havana: Casa Editorial Abril, 2002.

Peraza, Marino Martinez. *Por Amor de la Pelota—Historia del Béisbol Amateur Cubano*. Miami, FL: Ediciones Universal, 2008.

Rucker, Mark, and Peter C. Bjarkman. *Smoke: The Romance and Lore of Cuban Baseball*. New York: Total Sports Illustrated, 1999.

Thorn, John. *The Armchair Book of Baseball*. New York: Charles Scribner's Sons, 1985.

Toledo Menéndez, Dagoberto Miguel. *Béisbol Revolucionario Cubano, La Más Grande Hazaña—Aquino Abreu*. Havana: Editorial Deportes, 2006.

## Chapters, Print Articles, and Online Sources

Anderson, Curt. "Cuban Players Paid Smugglers $15 Million, Prosecutors Say." *Miami Sun-Sentinel*, April 27, 2016, http://www.sun-sentinel.com/sports/sfl-cuban-players-paid-smugglers-15-million-prosecutors-say-20160427-story.html.

Bjarkman, Peter C. "Aquino Abreu: Baseball's Other Double No-Hit Pitcher." *Baseball Research Journal* 43:1 (Spring 2014): 68–76.

———. "Baseball and Fidel Castro." *National Pastime: A Review of Baseball History* 18 (1998): 64–68.

———. "Cristóbal Torriente." In *Cuban Baseball Legends: Baseball's Alternative Universe*, ed. Peter C. Bjarkman and Bill Nowlin, 400–408. Phoenix, AZ: Society for American Baseball Research, 2016.

———. "The Cuban League." *SABR Baseball Biography Project*, February 2011, revised June 2016, https://sabr.org/bioproj/topic/cuban-league.

———. "The Cuban League (Post 1962)." In *Cuban Baseball Legends: Baseball's Alternative Universe*, ed. Peter C. Bjarkman and Bill Nowlin, 13–29. Phoenix, AZ: Society for American Baseball Research, 2016.

———. "Fidel Castro and Baseball." In *Cuban Baseball Legends: Baseball's Alternative Universe*, ed. Peter C. Bjarkman and Bill Nowlin, 30–47. Phoenix, AZ: Society for American Baseball Research, 2016.

———. "Fidel Castro and Baseball." *SABR Baseball Biography Project*, August 2013, revised June 2016, https://sabr.org/bioproj/topic/fidel-castro-and-baseball.

———. "Fidel Castro y el Béisbol." In *Leyendas del Béisbol Cubano: El Universo Alternativo del Béisbol*, ed. Peter C. Bjarkman and Bill Nowlin, 31–49. Trans. Reynaldo Cruz. Phoenix, AZ: Society for American Baseball Research, 2016.

———. "Fidel Castro y el Béisbol." Trans. Reynaldo Cruz. *Universo Béisbol* 7:74 (December 2016): 32–43.

———. "José de la Caridad Méndez." In *Cuban Baseball Legends: Baseball's Alternative Universe*, ed. Peter C. Bjarkman and Bill Nowlin, 271–82. Phoenix, AZ: Society for American Baseball Research, 2016.

———. "La Liga Cubana Después de 1962." In *Leyendas del Béisbol Cubano: El Universo Alternativo del Béisbol*, ed. Peter C. Bjarkman and Bill Nowlin, 13–30. Trans. Reynaldo Cruz. Phoenix, AZ: Society for American Baseball Research, 2016.

———. "MLB's Next Headache: Cartels, Gangsters, and Their Cuban Superstars." *Daily Beast*, April 18, 2014, https://www.thedailybeast.com/mlbs-next-headache-cartels-gangsters-and-their-cuban-superstars.

———. "Omar Linares." In *Cuban Baseball Legends: Baseball's Alternative Universe*, ed. Peter C. Bjarkman and Bill Nowlin, 121–21. Phoenix, AZ: Society for American Baseball Research, 2016.

———. "Orlando (El Duque Hernández) and Liván Hernández." In *Cuban Baseball Legends: Baseball's Alternative Universe*, ed. Peter C. Bjarkman and Bill Nowlin, 191–202. Phoenix, AZ: Society for American Baseball Research, 2016.

———. "Zoilo Versalles." In *Cuban Baseball Legends: Baseball's Alternative Universe*, ed. Peter C. Bjarkman and Bill Nowlin, 409–18. Phoenix, AZ: Society for American Baseball Research, 2016.

Brioso, César. "How Fidel Castro's Revolution Ended Professional Baseball in Cuba." *USA Today*, November 27, 2016, https://www.usatoday.com/story/sports/2016/11/27/fidel-castro-cuba-baseball-sugar-kings-cuban-league/94517414/.

Corsa, Lissette. "The Cuban Coach." *Miami New Times*, August 30, 2011. www.miaminewtimeas.com/news/the-cuban-coach-6353963.

Costello, Rory. "Bobby Maduro." In *Cuban Baseball Legends: Baseball's Alternative Universe*, ed. Peter C. Bjarkman and Bill Nowlin, 232–45. Phoenix, AZ: Society for American Baseball Research, 2016.

———. "Sandy Amoros." In *Cuban Baseball Legends: Baseball's Alternative Universe*, ed. Peter C. Bjarkman and Bill Nowlin, 70–76. Phoenix, AZ: Society for American Baseball Research, 2016.

Cruz, Reynaldo. "Los jugadores Cubanos de la ultima década: los mejores de la historia." *La Calle del Medio* 82 (February 2015): 12–13 (interview with Peter C. Bjarkman).

Eden, Scott. "The Lost Prospects of Cuba." *ESPN the Magazine*, June 26, 2017, http://www.espn.com/espn/feature/story/_/id/19678696/mlb-prospects-cuba-trapped-dream.

———. "No One Walks Off the Island." *ESPN the Magazine*, April 17, 2014, http://www.espn.com/espn/feature/story/_/id/10781144/no-one-walks-island-los-angeles-dodgers-yasiel-puig-journey-cuba.

Fimrite, Ron. "In Cuba It's Viva El Grand Old Game." *Sports Illustrated*, June 6, 1977, 68–80.

Hopkins, Jared S. "José Abreu's Mysterious Journey." *Chicago Tribune*, November 7, 2014, http://www.chicagotribune.com/sports/baseball/whitesox/ct-abreu-chicago-cuba-spt-1102-20141107-story.html.

Hughson, Callum. "Los Barbudos: The 'Bearded Ones.'" *Mop-Up Duty, Cleaning Up the Mess Other Sites Leave Behind*, February 17, 2010, https://mopupduty.com/los-barbudos-the-bearded-ones/.

Jozwik, Tom. "A Worthy Successor to the *Firesides*." *SABR Review of Books* 1 (1986): 67–68.

Katz, Jesse. "Escape from Cuba: Yasiel Puig's Untold Journey to the Dodgers." *Los Angeles*, April 13, 2014, http://www.lamag.com/escape-from-cuba-yasiel-puigs-untold-journey-to-the-dodgers/.

Madden, Bill. "Steinbrenner: The Last Lion of Baseball." *New York Daily News*, May 10, 2010, http://www.nydailynews.com/sports/baseball/yankees/steinbrenner-lion-baseball-explores-boss-relationship-barbara-walters-article-1.445363.

McCarthy, Eugene J. "Diamond Diplomacy (The View from Left Field)." *Elysian Fields Quarterly* 14:2 (1995): 12–15.

———. "Why Not Fidel for Baseball Commish?" *USA Today*, March 14, 1994, 13A.

Reig Romero, Carlos E. "Primer Inning del béisbol revolutionario." In *Con Las Bases Llenas—Béisbol Historia y Revolución*, ed. Félix Julio Alfonso López, 1–13 (Havana: Editorial Cientifico-Técnica, 2008).

Robertson, Linda. "What Will Become of Baseball's Decline in Cuba? The Field Might Open Further in U.S." *Miami Herald*, December 28, 2014, https://www.miamiherald.com/news/local/community/miami-dade/article5078058.html.

Rojas, Enrique. "Despaigne juege como Dominicano." *ESPN*, May 13, 2014, https://espn.com/noticias/nota?s=bei&id=2086820&type=story.

Santamarina, Everardo J. "The Hoak Hoax." *National Pastime* 14 (1994): 29–30.

Saslow, Eli. "A World of His Own: Since He Lit Up Baseball with his 105 M.P.H. Fastball, Reds Closer Aroldis Chapman Has Lived the American Dream." *ESPN the Magazine*, February 17, 2014, 60–64, 66.

Shouler, Kenneth. "El Duque's Excellent Adventure: How Cuba's Ace Pitcher Escaped Political Oppression to Become Part of a Great American Success Story." *Cigar Aficionado*, March–April 1999, 78–99.

Siegel, Robert, and Eyder Peralta. "The Big League Next Door." *Inside the New Cuba*, a *Time* magazine Special Issue, September 2015, 62–67.

Wertheim, L. Jon, and Don Yaeger. "Fantastic Voyage: Three Fellow Refugees Say the Tale of Yankees Ace Orlando (El Duque) Hernández's Escape from Cuba Doesn't Hold Water." *Sports Illustrated*, November 30, 1998, 60–63.

Williams, Richard. "Baseball: Diamond Passion of Castro's Cuba." *Independent Sport*, January 2, 1999, https://www.independent.co.uk/sport/baseball-diamond-passion-of-castros-cuba-1044537.html.

# ANALYSES OF CUBA–U.S. RELATIONS

## Books and Academic Theses

Elliston, Jon. *Psywar on Cuba: The Declassified History of U.S. Anti-Castro Propaganda.* Melbourne and New York: Ocean Press, 1999.

Erikson, Daniel P. *The Cuba Wars: Fidel Castro, the United States, and the Next Revolution.* New York: Bloomsbury Press, 2008.

Franklin, Jane. *Cuba and the United States: A Chronological History.* Melbourne and New York: Ocean Press, 1997.

Leogrande, William M., and Peter Kornbluh. *Back Channel to Cuba: The Hidden Story of Negotiations between Washington and Havana.* Chapel Hill and London: University of North Carolina Press, 2014.

Leonard, Thomas M. *Encyclopedia of Cuba–United States Relations.* Jefferson, NC, and London: McFarland, 2004.

Schwab, Peter. *Cuba: Confronting the U.S. Embargo.* New York: St. Martin's, 1999.

Senzel, Howard. *Baseball and the Cold War—Being a Soliloquy on the Necessity of Baseball in the Life of a Serious Student of Marx and Hegel from Rochester, New York.* New York and London: Harcourt Brace Jovanovich, 1977.

Sweig, Julia E. *Inside the Cuban Revolution.* Cambridge, MA, and London: Harvard University Press, 2002.

Turner, Justin W. R. *Baseball Diplomacy, Baseball Deployment: The National Pastime in U.S.–Cuba Relations.* Doctoral dissertation, University of Alabama, Tuscaloosa, 2012.

## Articles

Bjarkman, Peter C. "Stalled U.S.–Cuba Détente and the Uncertain Future of Cuba's National Pastime." *Public Diplomacy: Adversarial States* 17 (Winter/Spring 2017): 37–43.

———. "U.S.–Cuba Thaw Is Not So Hot for MLB." *Daily Beast,* February 19, 2015, https://www.thedailybeast.com/us-cuba-thaw-is-not-so-hot-for-mlb.

Sweig, Julia E., and Michael J. Bustamante. "Cuba after Communism: The Economic Reforms That Are Transforming the Island." *Foreign Affairs* 92:4 (July–August 2013): 101–14.

# ADDITIONAL MISCELLANEOUS SOURCES

## Books

Alfonso López, Félix Julio. *La Letra y el diamante.* Santa Clara, Cuba: Editorial Caprio, 2005.

Bjarkman, Peter C. *Diamonds around the Globe: The Encyclopedia of International Baseball.* Westport, CT, and London: Greenwood Press, 2005.

Brân, Zöe. *Enduring Cuba.* Melbourne and London: Lonely Planet Publications, 2008. Originally printed in 2002.

Carter, Thomas F. *The Quality of Home Runs: The Passion, Politics, and Language of Cuban Baseball.* Durham, NC, and London: Duke University Press, 2008.

Castro, Fidel. *Fidel Sobre el Deporte.* Havana: INDER, 1975.

———. *Fidel Sobre el Deporte,* rev. ed. Havana: INDER, 1980.

Elias, Robert. *The Empire Strikes Out: How Baseball Sold U.S. Foreign Policy and Promoted the American Way Abroad.* New York and London: New Press, 2010.

Gmelch, George, and Daniel A. Nathan, eds. *Baseball Beyond Our Borders: An International Pastime.* Lincoln and London: University of Nebraska Press, 2017.

Kerrane, Kevin. *Dollar Sign on the Muscle: The World of Baseball Scouting.* New York and Toronto: Beaufort Books, 1984.

Krich, John. *El Béisbol: Travels through the Pan American Pastime.* New York: Atlantic Monthly Press, 1989.

Merle, Robert. *Moncada, Premier Combate de Fidel Castro.* Paris: Robert Laffont, 1965.

Oleksak, Michael M., and Mary Adams Oleksak. *Béisbol: Latin Americans and the Grand Old Game.* Grand Rapids, MI: Masters Press, 1991.

Ortíz, Fernando. *Contrapunto Cubano del Tabaco y el Azúcar.* Caracas, Venezuela: Biblioteca Ayacucho, 1978.

Pettavino, Paula J., and Geralyn Pye. *Sport in Cuba: A Diamond in the Rough.* Pittsburgh, PA: University of Pittsburgh Press, 1994.

Price, S. L. *Pitching around Fidel: A Journey into the Heart of Cuban Sports.* New York: Ecco Press (HarperCollins), 2000.

Reaves, Joseph A. *Taking in a Game: A History of Baseball in Asia.* Lincoln and London: University of Nebraska Press, 2002.

Rodríguez Cruz, Juan Carlos, et al. *Cuba: The Untold History.* Trans. Karen McCartney. Havana: Editorial Capitán San Luis, 2003.

Terzian, James. *The Kid from Cuba: Zoilo Versalles.* New York: Doubleday, 1967.

Thorn, John, and John Holway. *The Pitcher: The Ultimate Compendium of Pitching Lore.* New York: Prentice Hall, 1987.

Virtue, John. *South of the Color Barrier: How Jorge Pasquel and the Mexican League Pushed Baseball toward Racial Integration.* Jefferson, NC, and London: McFarland, 2008.

Ward, Fred. *Inside Cuba Today.* New York: Crown, 1957.

Whiting, Robert. *The Meaning of Ichiro: The New Wave from Japan and the Transformation of Our National Pastime.* New York: Grand Central Publishing, 2009.

Williams, Eric. *From Columbus to Castro: The History of the Caribbean, 1492–1969.* New York: Vintage Books (Random House), 1970.

Yastrzemski, Carl, and Gerald Eskenazi. *Yaz: Baseball, the Wall, and Me.* New York: Grand Central Publishing, 1991.

## Print Articles and Online Sources

"Admite Cuba que existio pasaporte falso de Despaigne." *Zona de Strike*, May 23, 2014, https://zonadestrike.wordpress.com/2014/05/23/admite-cuba-que-existio-pasaporte-falso-de-despaigne/.

Arangure, Jorge, Jr. "What Happens to the Cuban Ballplayers Who Never Make It." *Vice Sports*, October 1, 2014, https://sports.vice.com/en_us/article/z4d5mx/what-happens-to-the-cuban-baseball-players-who-never-make-it.

Arbuckle, Alex Q. "Castro Plays Basketball: Fidel Castro Felt Basketball Was Perfect Training for Guerrilla Warfare." *Mashable Retronaut*, October 16, 2016, https://mashable.com/2016/10/16/fidel-castro-basketball/.

Bangert, Dave. "Lafayette Author Recalls Castro's Call to the Dugout." *Lafayette Journal and Courier*, November 29, 2016, 1A, 4A.

"BayStars Void Gourriel's Contract." *Japan Times*, April 2, 2015, https://www.japantimes.co.jp/sports/2015/04/02/baseball/japanese-baseball/baystars-void-gurriels-contract/#.WzojN7gnbIU.

Beaton, Andrew, and John W. Miller. "How an Open Door to Cuba Could Benefit Baseball: Thawing of U.S.–Cuba Relations May Lead to Great Cuban Presence in Majors." *Wall Street Journal*, December 17, 2014, https://www.wsj.com/articles/how-an-open-door-to-cuba-could-benefit-baseball-1418861933.

Berkow, Ira. "Joe Cubas Helps Cuban Ballplayers Defect." *New York Times*, August 15, 1996, https://www.nytimes.com/1996/08/15/sports/joe-cubas-helps-cuban-ballplayers-defect.html.

Bjarkman, Peter C. "American Baseball Imperialism, Clashing National Cultures, and the Future of Samurai *Besuboru*." *Studies on Asia Series III*, Special Issue: Baseball and *Besuboru* in Japan and the U.S. 3:2 (Fall 2006): 123–40.

"Castro Charges U.S. Schemes to Keep Cubans Out of Games." *New York Times*, April 16, 1963, 41.

"Castro May Pitch for Sugar Kings." *Christian Science Monitor*, April 23, 1959, 14.

"Castro's Bay of Pigs Anniversary Speech." *Castro Speech Data Base*, April 20, 1971, http://lanic.utexas.edu/project/castro/db/1971/19710420.html.

Chass, Murray. "Yanks Upset as Kuhn Vetoes Their Trip." *New York Times*, March 9, 1977, A17.

"Colorful Ceremonies Open Fourth Pan American Games." *New York Times*, April 21, 1963, S1.

Crepeau, Richard C. "Book Review of *Baseball and the Cold War* by Howard Senzel." *Journal of Sports History* 6:3 (Winter 1979): 60–62.

"Cubans Get Asylum." *Washington Post*, April 26, 1961, C2.

Dawidoff, Nicholas. "The Struggles of Sandy A." *Sports Illustrated*, July 10, 1989, 79–81.

Eden, Scott. "Feds Interviewing Cubans in U.S." *ESPN*, September 16, 2014, http://www.espn.com/mlb/story/_/id/11539728/feds-interviewing-cuban-players-us-part-investigation-smuggling.

"Havana Team to Stay: Sugar Kings Will Remain in Cuba, Says Club President." *New York Times*, April 24, 1959, 33.

Kakutani, Michiko. "Fiction Trying for Truth in Novel's View of Dictator." *New York Times*, December 14, 2009, https://www.nytimes.com/2009/12/15/books/15book.html.

Lavigne, Paula. "Cuba Has to Budge: Antonio Castro—Son of Fidel—Believes the Future of Cuban Baseball Relies on Severing Ties with the Country's Political Past." *ESPN the Magazine*, February 17, 2014, 57–59.

Mankiewicz, Frank. "Waiting for Rain: Out-Batting the Batista of Baseball." *Washington Post*, July 31, 1977, 262.

Miller, Michael E. "Who Is José Abreu? After Defecting from Cuba the Sox Slugger Had One of the Best Rookie Seasons Ever. Yet His Story Has Remained Largely a Mystery. Until Now." *Chicago*, April 2015, http://www.chicagomag.com/Chicago-Magazine/April-2015/Jose-Abreu-Chicago-White-Sox/.

Murray, Mary, and Orlando Matos. "Cuban National Signs First Million-Dollar Baseball Contract: Cuban Outfielder Frederich Cepeda Has Scored One for the History Books." *NBC News*, April 23, 2014, http://www.nbcnews.com/news/world/cuban-national-signs-first-million-dollar-baseball-contract-n87526.

Nidetz, Steve. "Castro Interview Worth Waiting For." *Chicago Tribune*, July 22, 1991, http://articles.chicagotribune.com/1991-07-22/sports/9103210953_1_jim-mckay-fidel-castro-jesuits.

Noyes, Rich. "Fidel's Flatterers: The U.S. Media's Decades of Cheering Castro's Communism." *Media Research Center*, February 7, 2007, http://archive.mrc.org/specialreports/2007/castro/welcome.asp.

"Politics Squelch Cuba Trip." *Washington Post*, December 3, 1975, D3.

Quirk, Robert E. "Review: *Contesting Castro: The United States and the Triumph of the Castro Revolution* by Thomas G. Paterson." *Journal of American History* 82:1 (June 1995): 357.

Rhoads, Christopher. "This Yanqui Is Welcome in Cuba's Locker Room." *Wall Street Journal*, November 9, 2009, A1, A16.

Richmond, Peter. "Cuban Star Fixed Games to Support His Family: Refugee from Mariel Still May Reach Majors." *Miami Herald*, May 22, 1983, 1A.

Rumill, Ed. "Kuhn Sights Global Baseball: High-Speed Air Travel, Careful Promotion Needed, 'America Loves the Underdog.'" *Christian Science Monitor*, July 31, 1969, 10.

Sandomir, Richard. "In Havana, Rapprochement through the Lens of ESPN." *New York Times*, March 23, 2016, https://www.nytimes.com/2016/03/23/sports/baseball/cuba-tampa-bay-rays-espn.html.

Schram, Martin. "Castro Chides U.S. over Triumphs by Cuban Sports Team." *Washington Post*, August 17, 1971, A13.

"Señor Comrade Doubleday." *Christian Science Monitor*, March 22, 1962, 16.

St. Clair, Stacy. "How Cuba's Aroldis Chapman Helped the Castro Regime before Cuban Defection." *Chicago Tribune*, October 6, 2016, http://www.chicagotribune.com/news/ct-cubs-aroldis-chapman-cuba-20161005-story.html.

Thornley, Stew. "Minneapolis Millers versus Havana Sugar Kings." In *The Inter-National Pastime*, ed. Peter C. Bjarkman, 42–44. Cleveland, OH: Society for American Baseball Research, 1992.

Trifunov, David. "Hugo Chávez Baseball Career Gave Way to Politics." *Public Radio International*, March 6, 2013, https://www.pri.org/stories/2013-03-06/hugo-chavez-baseball-career-gave-way-politics.

# INDEX

Abreu, Aquino, 161, 184, 187
Abreu, José, 141, 162, 163, 167, 257, 259, 266
Agrarian Reform Law, 60, 91
airplane hijackings to and from Cuba, 293, 299, 301
Alfonso López, Félix Julio, 120
Almeida, Rafael, 174
aluminum bats in Cuba, 163
Amateurism in Cuban baseball, xxiv, 95, 96–97, 152, 185
Ameijeiros, Gustavo, 6
American baseball imperialism, 107, 108, 125, 135
American Cuba policy, xxviii; Cold War hostilities and, xvi, xxi, 92
American politicization of baseball, xxv, 107
American Seasons in Cuba, xxv, 104, 173–174, 175
American Sugar Barons, 91
Amaro, Ruben, 41–42
amateur baseball in Cuba, 105
Amateur World Series, 95, 136
Amoros, Edmundo (Sandy), 15, 102–103, 123
Angola War, 300, 301
Anglada, Rey, 158
Angelos, Peter, 80, 280
Arbuckle, Alex, 53
Arocha, René, 165; defection by, 248

Arrojo, Rolando, 80, 96; defection by, 250
Arroyo, Luis (Tite), 74
Athens Olympic Games (2004), 195
Atlanta Olympic Games (1996), 81, 189, 190, 250

Babe Ruth in Cuba, xxv, 31
Baltimore Orioles, 99, 116; exhibition versus Team Cuba, 80, 149, 187, 305; visit to Cuba by, 80, 154, 280–281
Bango, Jorge García, 297, 298, 301, 304, 305
"Barbudos" pitching exhibition, xxvii, xxxi, 44, 61, 62–65, 65, 73, 79
Barros, Sigfredo, 83
baseball as political tool, 104
baseball détente efforts, 80, 215, 216, 282, 291–305
baseball diplomacy, 278, 287, 293–295, 299
baseball imperialism, 283, 285, 287
Batista, Fulgencio, xxii, xxx, xxxi, 4, 7, 17, 21, 22, 37, 39, 40, 41, 58, 75, 93, 114, 176, 289
Bay of Pigs invasion, xx–xxi, 14, 71, 123, 145, 169, 181, 183, 240, 279, 293
Beahon, George, 64, 65, 216
Beijing Olympic Games (2008), 200
Belén (secondary school), 46, 47–48, 180, 210, 212
Bell, Alexei, 142, 158, 159

Betancourt, Rigoberto, 187, 335n14
Birán, 46
Blue Marlin Corporation, 44
*Bohemia* (magazine), 7
*Bolsa Negra* (Black Bag) smuggling
    operation, 247
Borges, Sergio, 164, 193, 194
Boswell, Thomas, 95, 189
Bourne, Peter, xxi, 6, 8, 12, 24, 28–29, 48,
    49, 60–61, 136, 306, 313–314
Bowsfield, Ted, 77–78
Brioso, César, xxiii, 93, 94, 96, 111, 122,
    256
"Brothers in Exile" ESPN 30 for 30
    documentary film, 253, 315
Brundage, Avery, 186, 290
Buffalo Bisons, 73

Cambria, "Papa" Joe, 33, 36, 41, 43, 45,
    47, 48, 84, 106, 112
Canónico, Daniel, 178
Cárdenas, Leo, 65, 69, 74
Cardona, Miró, 59
Caribbean Series, 123, 151–152, 167
Carneado, Ramón, 164
Carter administration, 301, 303, 306
Carter, Jimmy, 83–84, 280, 301
Castaño, Tony (Antonio), 79, 103, 117,
    146, 265–266
Castro, Angel (father), 46, 50
Castro, Antonio (Tony) (son), 265–266,
    313
Castro (Díaz-Balart), Mirta (wife), 9
Castro, Fidel: anti-Americanism of, 17;
    anti-American rhetoric by, 293, 294,
    295; anti-materialism of, 239, 286; as
    athlete, 46, 47–48, 49, 51; as baseball
    fan, xv, 53, 72, 76, 81, 85, 129, 212,
    294; as basketball player, 46, 51,
    52–53; as destroyer of Cuban baseball,
    xxii, xxiii, xxiv, xxxii, 16, 30, 307, 315,
    316; as fictional character, xxxi,
    218–222, 224–235; as Havana
    University law student, 49, 50; as
    Marxist-Leninist, 22, 23, 23–24, 101,
    134, 240; as military tactician, 10; as
    pitching prospect, xvi–xvii, xxvii, xxxi,
    33, 41–44, 45, 48; as political hero, xix,
    xxx, 29; as prime minister, 59, 60, 66;
    as secret communist, xxii, 19–20, 22,
    30; assassination attempts on, xx, 279,
    299; banning of professional baseball
    by, 14, 16, 101, 103, 135; betrayal of
    revolution by, xxii, 18, 19, 20–21, 30;
    biographies of, xvi, 47; ceremonial
    inauguration of Cuban National Series
    by, 145–146; ceremonial pitching
    performances by, 76, 80, 130, 138,
    150; claims that Cuba invented
    baseball by, 125, 289; contempt for
    money by, 134–135, 137, 138;
    comments about 1958 World Series
    by, 85; comments about MLB World
    Baseball Classic by, 201; Cuban press
    reports on baseball skill of, 85; denials
    of baseball prowess by, 84, 211;
    détente efforts by, 292–294; Don
    Hoak story and, xxxiii, 37–39, 41, 57;
    EIR schools created by, 240; efforts to
    save Sugar Kings franchise by, xxiii, 15,
    72, 98, 137–138; founding of Cuban
    National Series by, 103, 139, 145;
    Hitler comparisons to, 6; Isle of Pines
    incarceration of, 6–7;
    micromanagement of Cuban baseball
    team by, 191–192; Moncada trial
    speech ("History Will Absolve Me")
    by, 4, 6–7, 8, 9; myths about, xvi, xxx,
    xxxiii, 4, 18–19, 22, 30, 57; on
    basketball as revolutionary training,
    52–53; politicization of baseball by,
    xxv–xxvi, 53, 104, 130, 136, 169, 285;
    relationship with Soviet Union, xx, 21,
    22, 120; revolutionary baseball
    philosophy of, 146–149; role in killing
    Cuban baseball, 256, 307, 313, 314,
    316; views on amateurism of, 93, 130,
    134–135, 137
Castro, Lidia (sister), 6
Castro, Raúl (brother), xxviii, 137–138,
    183, 281
Central American Games, 177–178, 179,
    182–183, 186–187
Cepeda, Frederich (Freddie), 163, 166,
    167, 196, 263, 268, 309, 310
Cerro Stadium. *See* Latin American
    Stadium
Céspedes, Yoenis, 162, 258

Chandler, A. B. (Happy), 110
Changa Mederos Stadium (Havana), 153–154
Chapman, Aroldis, 141, 162, 165, 257, 259, 261, 274; defection by, 247
Chávez, Hugo, 81–82
Chávez, Pedro, 181, 184
Che. *See* Guevara, Ernesto
Cienfuegos, Camilo, 63, 64, 65, 77; famous quotation of opposing Fidel by, 327n6
Cincinnati Reds, 34, 73, 99, 116, 119, 174
Clinton administration, 280
collapse of Cuban baseball, 307, 315–316
Constitution of 1940, 8, 59
Contreras, José Ariel, 83, 165, 192, 193, 194
Conte Agüero, Luis, 9
Cope, Myron, 34, 37, 38, 207
Costas, Bob, 34
Crepeau, Richard, 214, 217
Cronin, Tom, 250
Cuba as *béisbol paradiso*, 105, 180
Cuban baseball defectors phenomenon, xxi, xxxii, 96, 162, 168, 182–183, 193, 242, 255, 305
Cuban baseball amateurism, 289–290, 295
Cuban baseball player human trafficking, 247, 258–259, 260, 270
Cuban baseball player smuggling, 245
Cuban baseball stadiums, 153
Cuban Communist Party (PSP), 10, 13, 20, 22, 24, 25, 29, 60
Cuban Independence War and baseball (1895–1898), 171–172
Cuban League Selective Series, 108, 142
Cuban League National Series, 80, 84, 96, 107, 142; founding of, xxiv, 133, 145; inaugural game of (1962), 145; professionalism in, 89, 96; structure of, xxiv, 141, 144, 150–151, 152
Cuban National Federation League, 110
Cuban player loans to Canada and Europe, 311
Cuban player loans to Japan, 267–268, 268, 310
Cuban player loans to Mexico, 268, 309–310

Cubans as apostles of baseball, 107
Cuban Sugar Kings, xxiii–xxiv, 53, 58, 62, 67–71, 72–79, 90, 92, 98–100, 112, 113–115, 137, 153, 180; relocation of, xxii, 14, 99–100, 117–121; Washington politicians' role in relocation of, 99, 118–120
Cuban Super League, 142, 143
Cuban Winter League, 110–111, 116; closing of, 14, 92, 121–125; MLB control of, 110–112, 116, 121
*Cuba's Baseball Defectors* (Peter C. Bjarkman), xxi, xxxii, 162, 247, 269
Cubas, Joe, 193, 229, 245–246, 249, 250–251, 253, 282
Cuba–USA "Friendly" Series, 189, 247, 250, 282
Cuevas, Miguel, 184, 187

Dawidoff, Nicolas, 102
Deal, Ellis (Cot), 67–71
De la Cruz, Tomás, 105, 106, 110
Despaigne, Alfredo, 159, 163, 166, 167, 203, 257, 268, 309–310
*Diario de la Marina* newspaper, 63–64
Díaz, Enrique, 167
Díaz Lanz, Pedro, 60, 117
Díaz-Canel, Miguel, 320n12
Dorticós, Osvaldo, 61, 77
DGD (*Dirección General de Deportes*), 126, 132–133, 176; *Campeonato de Béisbol Amateur* of, 133
Draper, Theodore, xxx, 8, 13, 18, 19, 20–22, 23, 25, 30

Echevarria, José Antonio, 40
Einstein, Charles, 41
Eisenhower administration, 13, 60, 117, 120, 124
El Cerro Stadium shooting incident, 65–71
Elias, Robert, xxvi, 104, 107, 108, 119, 197, 285
ESPN, 44, 281
Estalella, Roberto, 105, 106

Fainaru, Steve, 248, 251, 253, 254, 315
Fernández, Osvaldo (Ozzie), 249
*Fidelismo*, 13

Fidelito (Fidel Castro Jr.), 64, 226
Figueredo, Jorge, 42
Fimrite, Ron, 95, 189
Fleitas, Andres, 93, 256
Florida International League, 112
Ford administration, 296, 298
Formental, Pedro, 37, 38, 39, 110
Franco, Francisco, xv
Franqui, Carlos, 134
French Revolution, 3
Frick, Ford, 14, 34, 95, 99, 100, 112, 116,
    118, 120, 121, 123–124
Fuentes, Jorge, 164, 309
Fuentes, Norberto, 221, 223–224

Gálvez y Delmonte, Wenceslao, 172
game fixing scandals in Cuban baseball,
    158, 243
Garbey, Bárbaro, 158, 242, 305
Geyer, Georgie Anne, xix, 6, 19, 24, 240,
    276
Gómez, Preston, 67, 74, 294, 296, 297
Gonder, Jesse, 68
González Echevarría, Roberto, xv–xvi,
    xxiii, xxv, xxxi, 40, 73, 89, 93, 96, 104,
    124, 150, 172, 175, 212, 277
González, Elian, 254
González, Tony, 74, 76
Gourriel Sr., Lourdes, 189, 242, 264
Gourriel Jr., Lourdes. See Gurriel Jr.,
    Lourdes (Yunito)
Gourriel, Yulieski. See Gurriel, Yulieski
Governors' Cup, 72, 99
Gran Stadium (del Cerro). See Latin
    American Stadium
Greenberg, Hank, xvii–xviii, 109
Griffith, Clark, 33, 41, 42, 44, 48, 113, 116
Guerra, Mike (Fermín), 38, 103, 146
Guerra Matos, Felipe, 70, 126, 132
Guevara, Ernesto (Che), 10, 12, 19, 59,
    77, 123, 134, 137, 138
Guillen, Ozzie, xxvii; quotes on Fidel
    Castro by, 321n20
Gurriel Jr., Lourdes (Yunito), 264
Gurriel, Yulieski, 156, 163, 167, 189, 196,
    200, 310; defection of, 264, 272;
    Japanese contract of, 271–272
Guzetta, Frank, 68–69

Haak, Howie, xviii, 43, 45, 52, 207–208
Hansen, Jonathan, 50, 210
Havana Cubans, 106, 112–114, 153, 177,
    179, 180
Havana Sugar Kings. See Cuban Sugar
    Kings
Helms-Burton embargo policies, 313
Hernández, Alberto, 249
Hernandez, Bart, 259
Hernández, Liván, 34, 96, 141, 165, 246,
    250, 251–252; reasons for defection by,
    251
Hernández, Manuel Enríque, 183
Hernández, Melba, 6, 9
Hernández, Orlando (El Duque), 34, 96,
    141, 156, 165, 210, 245, 246, 315;
    defection by, 252–254
Hernández Nodar, Juan Ignacio, 246,
    249, 252
Herter, Christian, 119, 120
Hitler, Adolf, 6
Hoak, Don, xviii, xxxi, 34, 36–37, 38–39,
    57, 63, 207, 208
Hotel Nacional (Havana), 70
Houston Astros, 305
Huelga, José Antonio, 80, 95, 153, 188,
    213

IBAF (International Amateur Baseball
    Federation), 133, 186
IBAF Amateur World Series, xxiv, 133,
    158, 176–178, 180, 181, 185, 187, 188,
    195, 196–197, 200, 202
IBAF Baseball World Cup, 158, 166, 197,
    256
IBAF Intercontinental Cup, 190
ICAIC (Cuban Institute of Cinematic Art
    and Industry), 134
INDER baseball guide books, 146,
    333n17, 333n20
INDER (National Institute of Sports,
    Physical Education, and Recreation),
    xxiv, xxviii, 14, 16, 80, 93, 101, 102,
    103, 126, 130, 143, 239, 241; loans of
    Cuban players by, 308–309
INDER Law 546, 133
INDER Law 936, xxxi, 94, 126, 132, 184
Industriales Blue Lions, 141, 151, 156,
    158; founding of, 146

International League, xxiii, 14, 34, 70, 73, 76, 79, 93, 113, 118
International Olympic Committee (IOC), 183, 185, 186
Irvin, Monte, 54
Isle of Pines, 39, 51

Jamail, Milton, xxiii, 119, 210–211, 231
Japanese baseball defections, 241
Japanese baseball imperialism, 107
Japanese baseball posting system, 269, 312, 316
Japanese politicization of baseball, xxvi
Jersey City Sugar Kings, 73, 75–79, 132
Jones, Kirby, 91, 95
Joe Cubas ballplayer defection scheme, 245, 246, 247
July 26th Movement (M-26-7), xx, xxxi, 6, 9, 10, 13, 19, 21, 22, 25, 40
Junior World Series (1959), 15, 71–72, 74, 77, 79, 98, 100, 114

Keegan, Bob, 67
Kerrane, Kevin, 41–42
Kindelán, Orestes, 142, 151, 161, 162–163, 189, 190, 192–193, 195
Kissinger, Henry, 292, 297–298, 299, 300
Krich, John, 218, 218–224
Kuhn, Bowie, 280, 287, 292, 294, 297–298, 301, 302–303, 304, 305; baseball globalization schemes of, 287; Cuban player recruitment motives of, 298

Lasorda, Tommy, 194
Latin American Stadium, xxix, 62, 65, 81, 83, 113, 145, 153–154
Lavigne, Paula, 265–266
Lazo, Pedro Luis, 82, 162–163, 192–193, 194
Linares, Omar, 82, 142, 151, 161, 162–163, 166, 189, 190, 193, 195, 244
Lincoln, Abraham, 21
Lockwood, Lee, xxvii, xxxiii, 13, 24, 51–52, 208, 213
Lucchesi, Frank, 296
Luque, Adolfo, 112, 141, 174

M-26-7. *See* July 26th Movement

Machado, Gerardo, 178
MacPhail, Lee, 99, 116
Maduro, Roberto (Bobby), 14, 16, 72, 73, 74, 91–92, 98, 113, 115–117, 119–120, 120, 137, 292
Maestri, Amado, 38, 63, 64
Manfred, Rob, 307–308
Mankiewicz, Frank, 91, 95, 297, 303
Mann, Leslie, 176–177
Mariel Boatlift (1980), 158, 224, 242–243, 305
Mariné, Colonel Jaime, 176, 177
Marrero, Conrado, 47, 54, 106, 110, 113, 114, 178
Martin, Eddy, 85
Marsans, Armando, 174
Martí, José, 8
Martin, Leonys, 258
Matthews, Herbert, xix, xxii, xxvii, xxx, 3, 9, 9–10, 11, 12, 18, 19, 21, 22–23, 23–24, 25, 30, 57, 94–95, 102, 134, 135
Mauch, Gene, 75–76, 77
Maya, Yunieski, 165
Méndez, José de la Caridad, xxv, 173–175
Mesa, Germán, 82, 245, 246, 251
Mesa, Victor, 165, 202, 248, 265–266, 309, 313
Metropolitanos Warriors, 141, 154
Mexican League, 91, 108, 110
Minneapolis Millers, 72, 75–76
Miñoso, Orestes (Minnie), 105, 110, 112, 122, 123, 141
MLB (Major League Baseball), xxiv, xxxi; Baseball globalization and, 284; closing of Cuban winter league by, 94, 112, 121; concerns for player safety in Cuba by, 116–117, 118, 121; détente efforts with Cuba by, 168, 282; hypocrisy on gambling by, 243–244; internationalization of baseball by, 284; ownership of Cuban winter league by, 110–111, 121; wars on competitors by, 108
MLB World Baseball Classic, xxiv, 97, 149, 151, 157–158, 164, 166, 193, 197, 315
Molina, Tinti, 124
Moncada garrison assault, 3, 45
Moncada, Yoan, 141, 249, 266, 308

Monroe Doctrine, 17
Montreal Royals, 73, 115
Morales, Kendrys, 83, 141, 156, 166, 196
Morejón, Daniel, 75, 76
Moreno, Julio (Jiqui), 106, 113
McCarthy, Eugene (Senator), xxvii, 33, 44, 54, 129
McGovern, George (Senator), 299, 300, 303
McKay, Jim, 84, 211

New York Giants, 33, 44
New York Yankees, 33, 42, 301, 303
Nixon administration, 278, 280, 291, 292, 294, 296
Nixon, Richard, 60; personal reasons for hostility toward Fidel Castro by, 291
no-hit games in Cuba, 160
Notari, Aldo, 335n20

Obama administration, xxi, xxviii, 168, 269, 280, 281, 307; impact of détente efforts by, 307
Ochoa, Arnaldo, 223, 228
Oleksak, Michael and Mary, 42
Olivera, Héctor, 142, 200, 308
Olympic Games as Cold War battlefields, 182, 185, 197
Organized Baseball, 26, 79, 81, 99, 104, 110–111, 112, 113, 256, 282; closing of Cuban Winter League by, xxii, 15, 90, 92, 93; vested interest in Cuba of, xxiii, xxxi, 91
Ortiz, Fernando, 120

Pacheco, Tony, 73
Padrón, Ian, 156
Pan American Games, 84, 96; Chicago Games (1959), 179, 201; Indianapolis Games (1987), 190; São Paulo Games (1963), 183–184, 185, 289; Winnipeg Games (1999), 82, 187, 191–193
Pasquel, Jorge, 38, 91, 108–110, 111, 284
Paterson, Thomas, xvii–xviii
Paul, Gabe, 34, 119, 301, 302, 303
Pedro Betancourt League, 105, 132
Pérez Jimenez, Marcos, xv
Pérez Jr., Louis A., 27, 237
Perón, Juan, xv

Pettavino, Paula and Geralyn Pye, 126, 136, 170, 203, 240, 241
Philadelphia Phillies, 37
ping-pong diplomacy with China, 278, 280, 293
Pittsburgh Pirates, 33, 42
Platt Amendment, 17, 28, 173
Pompez, Alex, 43, 52, 207–208
Price, S. L., 237–239
Prieto, Ariel, 249
PSP (Popular Socialist Party). See Cuban Communist Party
Puig, Yasiel, 141, 162, 258, 274; defection by, 247

Quirk, Robert, xviii, 18, 46–48, 49, 66, 208, 212
Quivicán League, 105, 132

racial segregation in Cuban amateur baseball, 105, 180
Ramírez, Alexei, 257
Ramonet, Ignacio, 221
Randall, Margaret, 324n35
Rawlings Sporting Goods Corporation 124
Reaves, Joseph A., xxvi, 104
Reig Romero, Carlos, 78, 132–133
Reyes, Napoleon, 73, 117
Richmond Vees, 72
Rickey, Branch, 108
Rochester Democrat and Chronicle, 63, 64, 216
Rochester Red Wings, 58, 62, 67–71, 215–216
Rodríguez, Carlitos, 192
Rodríguez, Maels, 83–84, 143, 160, 193, 194
Rodríguez, Oscar, 112
Rogers, William D., 297–298
Rojas, Enríque, 310
Rojas, Marta, 7

Sabourín, Emilio, 171, 172
Sánchez, Celia, 59, 220, 294
Sánchez, Raúl, 73, 74, 76
Santamaría, Haydeé, 6
Santamarina, Everardo, 39
Santín, Jorge, 145–146

Selig, Bud, 80
Sené, Ismael, 78
Senzel, Howard, 118–120, 214–218
Shaughnessy, Frank, 34, 70, 73, 93, 95, 99, 100, 115, 117, 118–119, 120, 121
Sheets, Ben, 194
Sierra Maestra campaign, 6
Sisler Jr., George, 70, 70–71, 216
Smith, Earl E. T., 115
Solzhenitsyn, Alexander, 219
Somoza, Anastasio, xv
sonic attacks on Havana U.S. Embassy, xxi, 311
Soviet sports system, 136, 170, 240–241
Spalding, Albert, 285
Spanish–American War (1898), 27, 173
Special Period in the Time of Peace, xx, 29, 239, 242, 249, 251, 255
Steinbrenner, George, 302, 303
Stiglmeier, John C., 115
Stoneham, Horace, 33, 43–44, 52, 207–208
sugar mill leagues, 107, 108
sugar production and baseball, 108, 118, 120, 120–121, 126
Sydney Olympic Games (2000), 191, 193–195
Symmes, Patrick, xxix
Szulc, Tad, 52–53, 208

Tampa Bay Rays Havana exhibition, 280–281
Ten Million Tons Harvest, 11, 142
Thorn, John, 41, 42
Thornley, Stu, 75, 77
Tiant Jr., Luis, 216–217, 252, 300
Tiant Sr., Luis, 252, 300
tobacco industry versus sugar industry in Cuba, 120
Topps Chewing Gum Company, 45
Torriente, Cristóbal, xxv, 173
Tropical Stadium, 110, 112, 177

Truby, J. David, xviii, 33, 43–44, 52, 207–208
Trump administration, xxi, 311
Turner, Justin, xxvii, 72, 85, 98, 100, 104, 119, 120, 129–130, 136, 169–170, 172, 289

Umphlett, Tommy, 75, 76, 77
Urrutia, Manuel, 59, 60–61
Urrutia, Osmani, 159
USA–Cuba "Friendly" Series. See Cuba–USA "Friendly" Series

Vance, Cyrus, 301
Veeck, Bill, 303
Vélez, Higinio, 97, 143, 164, 195, 198–199, 201, 239
Verdi, Frank, 65, 69, 215
Verdura, Modesto, 145, 184
Versalles, Zoilo, 123
Virdon, Bill, 305
Virtue, John, 109

Walters, Barbara, 29, 84, 211, 277
Washington Senators, 31, 33, 41–42, 44, 47, 48, 84, 106, 112, 116
Wendel, Tim, 31, 34, 211, 218, 227, 229, 230–235
White, Randy Wayne, 218, 224–230
Whiting, Robert, 241–242
Wiend, Ted, 74–75
Williams, Eric, 6, 12, 17
World Baseball Classic I (2006), 197–199, 239, 305
World Baseball Classic II (2009), 200
World Baseball Classic III (2013), 202, 257
World Baseball Classic IV (2017), 312

Yastrzemski, Carl, 72, 75, 78
Yanes, Carlos, 163
Year of Planning (1962), 133, 135, 239

# ABOUT THE AUTHOR

**Peter Bjarkman** is the recognized authority on Cuba's post-1961 revolutionary-era baseball. Best known for his recent book, *Cuba's Baseball Defectors: The Inside Story* (2016), he is also author of the seminal *A History of Cuban Baseball, 1864–2006* (2014, 2007) and coauthor (with Mark Rucker) of *Smoke: The Romance and Lore of Cuban Baseball* (1999). Bjarkman has witnessed domestic league Cuban baseball firsthand during more than 50 visits to the communist country since 1997, and has also followed the Cuban national team to international events in Latin America, Europe, Canada, and Asia since 1999. A former linguistics professor, he is featured as celebrity chef Anthony Bourdain's Havana guide on the 2011 Travel Channel episode of *Anthony Bourdain's No Reservations* featuring Cuba (season 7). A regular consultant on Cuban baseball for the North American media, his many television appearances include a featured role in the 2014 ESPN *30 for 30* documentary film "Brothers in Exile" (the story of Cuban pitchers Orlando "El Duque" and Liván Hernández). He is a 2017 winner of the prestigious SABR Henry Chadwick Award, offered by the Society for American Baseball Research to honor baseball's greatest historians and researchers.

Author Peter Bjarkman (left) with Mark Rucker (right) and Cuban mentor Ismael Sené (center) during an early Cuban ballpark visit in 1999. *From the author's collection*